CROSSCURRENTS OF CRITICISM

Crosscurrents of Criticism

Horn Book Essays 1968 - 1977

selected and edited by Paul Heins

THE HORN BOOK, INCORPORATED · BOSTON

Printed in the United States of America

Library of Congress Cataloging in Publication Data

Main entry under title:

Crosscurrents of Criticism: Horn Book Essays 1968-1977
    Includes index.

    1. Children's literature — History and criticism — Addresses, essays, lectures. I. Heins, Paul. II. The Horn Book Magazine.
PN 1009. AlC697   809'.8982   77-2456
ISBN 0-87675-034-X

To the present editor of The Horn Book
Ethel L. Heins

Preface

L IKE its predecessors, *A Horn Book Sampler* and *Horn Book Reflections*, the present volume is a collection of *Horn Book* articles drawn from the contributions of a stated period; and again, like its predecessors, the present volume groups the articles in sections. In the earlier books the various sections were given such titles as "How the Story Happened," "What Fairy Tales Mean to a Child," or "Inspiration — How It Comes"; they obviously served as magnets to attract essays which seemed to belong in a specific category. In the present volume the various subdivisions themselves are interrelated; and although the individual articles were never written to expound or illustrate a critical theory, they are grouped where they seem to belong together — as contributions in the consideration of various problems, attitudes, and possibilities faced by critics of children's literature.

No specific theory or authoritarian set of standards is set up to account for the choice of essays, but rather the separate areas have been laid out to accommodate the invariable questions that beset the criticism of children's books: the classification, defense, and evaluation of children's literature. Moreover, the link passages introducing each division are ultimately related to each other and to many of the ideas originally presented in "Out on a Limb with the Critics: Some Random Thoughts on the Present State of the Criticism of Children's Literature" and "Coming to Terms with Criticism." These two essays are not only crystallizations of the thought of the former editor of the *Horn Book* regarding the criticism of children's literature but an indication of the principles which led to his choice of most of the articles in the present volume.

Since an attempt has been made to present as unhackneyed a selection as possible, very few of the articles chosen have appeared in other anthologies. Some critical topics have not been touched upon because they could not be fitted into the plan of the book or — more important — because they did not contribute to the ongoing dialogue of the essays. There are no articles on illustration because that subject will — in the near future — be presented in a separate book to be published by The Horn Book, Incorporated.

I wish to thank all of the contributors, who have so kindly given permission to reprint their articles. Special thanks is also due to all members of the *Horn Book* staff who have assisted in the preparation of this book but, above all, to Karen Klockner.

P.H.

Table of Contents

Acknowledgements

are made to the following publishers, authors, and agents for their kind permission to quote copyrighted material. Every effort has been made to trace ownership of such; the publisher regrets any acknowledgement which may have been omitted, and would appreciate being informed of it.

AMERICAN MERCURY (Box 1306, Torrance, CA 90505): "High John de Conquer" by Zora Neale Hurston. Published in *The American Mercury*; reprinted in *Book of Negro Folklore*, edited by Langston Hughes and Arna Bontemps (Dodd, 1958).

R. R. BOWKER COMPANY: *The Rise of Children's Book Reviewing in America, 1865-1881* by Richard Darling. Copyright © 1968 by R. R. Bowker Company.

CHILDREN'S BOOK CENTRE LTD.: "The Irrelevance of Children to the Children's Book Reviewer" by Brian Alderson. *Children's Book News*, January-February 1969.

WILLIAM COLLINS & WORLD PUBLISHING COMPANY: *In Spite of All Terror* by Hester Burton. Copyright © 1968 by Hester Burton. Permission also granted by OXFORD UNIVERSITY PRESS.

COWARD, MC CANN & GEOGHEGAN, INC.: *The Three Owls, Third Book: Contemporary Criticism of Children's Books 1927-1930*, by Anne Carroll Moore. Copyright 1931 by Coward-McCann, Inc.; renewed 1959 by Anne Carroll Moore.

DOUBLEDAY & COMPANY, INC.: *Bless the Beasts and Children* by Glendon Swarthout. Copyright © 1970 by Glendon Swarthout. Permission also granted by A. WATKINS, INC. *The Girl on the Floor Will Help You* by Lavinia Russ. Copyright © 1969 by Lavinia Russ. *Yellow Back Radio Broke-Down* by Ishmael Reed. Copyright © 1969 by Ishmael Reed.

WILLIAM PÈNE DU BOIS: Remarks from a letter to Jane Langton.

E. P. DUTTON & COMPANY, INC.: *Earthfasts* by William Mayne. Copyright © 1966 by William Mayne. Permission also granted by HAROLD OBER ASSOCIATES, INC. and DAVID HIGHAM ASSOCIATES LTD. Published in England by HAMISH HAMILTON LTD. *The House in Norham Gardens* by Penelope Lively. Copyright © 1974 by Penelope Lively. Permission also granted by WILLIAM HEINEMANN LTD.

FARRAR, STRAUS & GIROUX, INC.: *Mystery and Manners* by Flannery O'Connor. Permission also granted by MC INTOSH, MC KEE & DODDS.

GALE RESEARCH COMPANY: *The Life and Letters of Lewis Carroll* by Stuart Dodgson Collingwood. Reprint, 1967 by Gale Research Company; originally published by THE CENTURY COMPANY, 1898.

iv

Introduction
Criticism Comes of Age

I T is not surprising that in an era when real children's books were few and far between, the true criticism — the literary criticism — of children's books was not even dreamed of. In the United States, children's literature as we know it was given great impetus in the 1860's by the publication of *Hans Brinker; or The Silver Skates, Little Women,* and *The Story of a Bad Boy,* but in the eighteenth century there were only books adopted by children and a few books published for them rather than a body of children's literature. It is interesting to consider the possibilities open to young readers of the time, although one can assume that children, then as now, tended to read what they were capable of reading and what attracted them.

A Library of Congress pamphlet — *Children's Reading in America, 1776* — lists some of the primers, stories, rhymes, and other reading matter available to American children at the opening of the Revolution and includes items published on both sides of the Atlantic. The Bible in various paraphrases; James Janeway's *A Token for Children, Being an Exact Account of the Conversion, Holy and Exemplary Lives and Joyful Deaths of Several Young Children;* and Isaac Watts's *The First Set of Catechisms and Prayers: or The Religion of Little Children Under Seven or Eight Years of Age* — these surely represented the kind of reading sponsored and encouraged by the conventions of adult eighteenth-century society. Less overtly didactic were the books which attempted to combine entertainment with instruction: *The Renowned History of Giles Gingerbread,* which tells how Giles learned his alphabet from gingerbread letters; *Tom Thumb's Play-Book: To Teach Children Their Letters As Soon As They Can Speak. Being a New and Pleasant Method to Allure Little Ones in the First Principles of Learning,* and Isaac Watts's *Divine Songs Attempted in Easy Language for the Use of Children.*

But most interesting of all, from a critical point of view, are the stories and narratives available to children of the Revolutionary era. Already they had adopted Charles Perrault's *Fairy Tales, or Histories of Past Times* and such traditional English material as *Guy of Warwick, Jack the Giant-killer,* and *Whittington and His Cat;* and, as we all know, three significant works of seventeenth- and eighteenth-century adult literature had become staples of children's reading: *Pilgrim's Progress, Robinson Crusoe,* and *Gulliver's Travels.*

The role of the publisher was also evident in the books being sold for children in 1776. John Newbery's *A Little Pretty Pocket-Book* was available in New England as well as in old England, and the catalog of the printer Isaiah Thomas of Worcester, Massachusetts, contained an enterprising announcement: "A very large Assortment of BOOKS, bound and gilt, with Cuts, suitable for CHILDREN of all Ages, among a Variety of others are the following, which will be sold by Wholesale or Retail; great Allowance to those who buy to sell again." One wonders how much of the original text or meaning of such eighteenth-century novels as *Tom Jones* or *Clarissa* was left intact in the advertised abridgments for children. On the other hand, Thomas's catalog contained a familiar-sounding list of reading available to children in the fourth quarter of the eighteenth century: the Holy Bible, *Robinson Crusoe, Margery Two Shoes, Capt. Gulliver's Travels, Mother Goose's Melody,* and *A Little Pretty Pocket-Book.*

In 1776, then, few books were produced specifically for children, but since — as I have suggested before — literary criticism needs a body of works to come to terms with, whether favorably or unfavorably, there was at the time neither opportunity nor need for critical essays on children's literature or even for discussions of the most recent trends in books for children.

But the end of the eighteenth century saw the development of a definite point of view towards children's books, especially in England; and the rise of a didactic, moralistic school of writing for children in both England and America gave impetus to some very definite expressions of opinion. The solemn utterances of Mrs. Barbauld aroused the ire of Charles Lamb, who with his sister Mary left one of the few literary legacies for children's reading from the early part of the nineteenth century: *Tales from Shakespeare.* On one occasion Lamb wrote in strong terms to his friend the poet Coleridge about Mrs. Barbauld:

"Goody Two Shoes" is almost out of print. Mrs. Barbauld's stuff has banished all the old classics of the nursery; and the shopman at Newbery's hardly deigned to reach them off an old exploded corner of a shelf, when Mary asked for them. Mrs. B.'s and Mrs. Trimmer's nonsense lay in piles about. Knowledge insignificant and vapid as Mrs. B.'s books convey, it seems, must come to a child in the *shape* of *knowledge,* and his empty noddle must be turned with conceit of his own powers when he has learnt that a Horse is an animal, and Billy is better than a Horse, and such like. . . .

Damn them! — I mean the cursed Barbauld Crew, those Blights and Blasts of all that is Human in man and child.

Mrs. Trimmer, the other worthy lady mentioned by Lamb, made statements about traditional children's reading that now seem outrageously amusing. In a review of a new edition of Perrault's fairy tales she wrote the following:

> These Tales are announced to the public as *new translations,* but in what respect this term applies we are at a loss to say, for, on the perusal of them we recognized the identical *Mother Goose's Tales,* with all their *vulgarities of expression,* which were in circulation when those who are now grandmothers, were themselves children. . . . A moment's consideration will surely be sufficient to convince people of the least reflection, of the danger, as well as the impropriety, of putting such books as these into the hands of little children, whose minds are susceptible of every impression; and who from the liveliness of their imaginations are apt to convert into realities whatever forcibly strikes their fancy.

On the other hand, one must acknowledge that Mrs. Trimmer had an honorable respect for the power of a child's imagination.

During the second quarter of the nineteenth century in the United States, Samuel Goodrich (1793-1860), author of the original Peter Parley tales, echoed Mrs. Trimmer in such statements as "children's books were either full of nonsense, like 'hie diddle diddle' in *Mother Goose,* or full of something very like lies, and those very shocking to the mind, like *Little Red Riding Hood.*" Incidentally, Goodrich was the inventor of the Mother Goose parody "Higglety, Pigglety, Pop!" which — as we all know — became the text for one of Maurice Sendak's most remarkable books. In a sense, Sarah Trimmer and Samuel Goodrich created the critical climate for the battle of the fairy tale; but, coincidentally, the age of didacticism also saw the publication of the Grimm Brothers' tales and of Hans Christian Andersen's stories as well as of Hawthorne's *A Wonder Book* and *Tanglewood Tales.*

One of the signs that critical studies of children's literature have now come of age was the publication in 1975 of Anne Scott MacLeod's *A Moral Tale: Children's Fiction and American Culture 1820-1860.* In it she states that most of the books published during the first half of the nineteenth century were "narrow, stilted, and wholly given over to didacticism,"[1] and she develops the thesis that these didactic books "came into being, not to entertain children, but to prepare them for their momen-

1. Anne Scott MacLeod, *A Moral Tale: Children's Fiction and American Culture 1820-1860* (Hamden, Connecticut, Archon, 1975), p. 10.

tous role in the preservation of the Republic."[2] Here is an excellent summarizing paragraph from her book:[3]

Not art, but outlook shaped these tales. The distortions, the omissions, the characteristic imbalance between inner and outer experience, were all products of the authors' angle of vision. Writers included in their juvenile books those aspects of life they believed children must know and understand, both for their own protection and for the sake of American society. From their point of view, what they told children *was* realistic, and would serve to prepare them for their encounter with the world. If the world they pictured in fiction was dangerous, it was because they believed that the real world was indeed dangerous for the unprepared. If the accounts of physical and social reality were vague, it was because most of these authors saw significant experience in moral rather than physical or social terms. The single most vivid element in every tale was the moral lesson, for the very good reason that morality seemed at once the quality most necessary to the survival of the Republic and most threatened by the competitive, shifting realities of American life.

Three crucial concepts in this paragraph are worth stressing. First of all, the author realizes that these tales were not intended to be artistic creations. Secondly, she stresses the realistic aspect of these stories, which, thirdly, was subordinated to the moralistic. And going beyond these analytical concepts, she places the narratives in the context of American life of the time. It is noteworthy that she describes mid-nineteenth-century American life by such terms as *competitive* and *shifting*, terms that are still all too familiar to us.

Published in 1968, Richard L. Darling's *The Rise of Children's Book Reviewing in America, 1865-1881* (Bowker) refutes some of the statements made by Anne Carroll Moore, Superintendent of Work with Children, The New York Public Library, and the imperial mentor of children's literature in America during much of the first half of the twentieth century. In 1918 Miss Moore broke a lance for the proper criticism of children's books.

For many more years than any of us like to recall children's books, if read at all when written about, were read for ulterior ends. They were considered en masse rather than individually, both in the educational field and in the publishing field. They were tagged for moralistic trends, for a physical age limit, for collateral reading, for anything and everything save appraisal of them as books in relation to books in general.

Standards of appraisal consistently applied to the consideration of children's books as holding a place in contemporary criticism were unknown in 1918 when I was invited to contribute a general article

2. *Ibid.*, p. 40.
3. *Ibid.*, pp. 67, 68.

on the children's books of the year to the *Bookman*. I had long felt the need for such recognition of children's books but I had looked for a seasoned critic to appear and carry forth such leads as Horace E. Scudder . . . had given while editing the *Riverside Magazine*.*

More important, however, than Dr. Darling's marshaling of material to show that magazines and literary journals in the third quarter of the nineteenth century were reviewing children's books are some of the specific details and quotations he uses in pursuing his thesis. For example, he quotes a very important statement made by Horace Scudder in the *Riverside Magazine*, January 1867.

A literature is forming which is destined to act powerfully on general letters; hitherto it had been little disturbed by critics, but the time must soon come, if it has not already come, when students of literature must consider the character and tendency of *Children's Letters*; when all who have at heart the best interest of the Kingdom of Letters must look sharply to this Principality.

This statement was not only prophetic; it also recognized children's literature as an autonomous realm. In its quiet way it was a declaration of independence from both eighteenth-century critical indifference and nineteenth-century moralism.

Dr. Darling also devotes a chapter of his book to a discussion of the numerous reviews of the best-remembered children's books of the era: *Hans Brinker, Alice's Adventures in Wonderland, Little Women, The Story of a Bad Boy, The Adventures of Tom Sawyer*, and *The Prince and the Pauper*. It was especially interesting during 1976, the year of the centenary of the publication of *Tom Sawyer*, to read what Dr. Darling had to say about an unusual review of one of Mark Twain's best-known books.

The one review that did appear was full of praise for the book, and, indeed, was written by one of the most distinguished American literary critics of the time, William Dean Howells. Howells probably had a copy of the book for reviewing largely because he was a close friend of the author, and because he had served as his literary adviser. The review ran to about 1,200 or 1,500 words, analyzing the book carefully from a literary point of view. Howells compared the book with Aldrich's [*The Story of a Bad Boy*], finding them similar in many ways; Clemens having dealt with the natural boy in a Western setting in a manner not unlike that with which Aldrich dealt with the same kind of boy in New England. He described the quality of characterization, particularly the skillful development of Tom's personality, showing that Tom was actually a realistic boy, mischievous but not bad, and related various incidents that added to the appeal of

*Anne Carroll Moore, *The Three Owls, Third Book: Contemporary Criticism of Children's Books 1927-1930* (New York, Coward-McCann, 1931), p. 2.

the book. He concluded that Tom Sawyer was at least the equal of Tom Brown and Tom Bailey, high praise indeed from the reviewer who had pronounced *The Story of a Bad Boy* a true innovation in American literature.*

Dr. Darling did not go beyond the year 1881 in his discussion of the critical reviewing of children's books in the latter part of the nineteenth century. It was in 1882, however, that Caroline M. Hewins, the librarian of the Hartford (Connecticut) Public Library, published her *Books for the Young, A Guide for Parents and Children*, which Elizabeth Nesbitt in *A Critical History of Children's Literature* (Macmillan) termed one of the first authoritative book lists for children. Miss Hewins, who was interested in promoting what she considered excellence in children's reading, suggested to parents rules on "How to Teach the Right Use of Books." For example, "Do not let . . . [the children] read anything you have not read yourself. . . . Remember . . . to give children something that they are growing up to, not away from, and keep down their stock of children's books to the very best." These precepts, of course, pointed the way to the development of the idealistic standards of such crusaders for children's literature as Anne Carroll Moore and Bertha Mahony Miller.

As time went on, Bertha Mahony Miller also became aware of the importance of criticism, and as the editor of a journal whose chief purpose was to signalize the publication of good books, she frequently wrote about the need for a method of judging children's books. As far back as 1933 she stated:

> The basis of criticism is an understanding and an appreciation of real creative ability and a recognition of the fact that the critic is less important than the artist. It is the latter who gives the critic his reason for being. But the artist wants and needs the resistance of the intelligent, appreciative, but honest and salty judge of his work. Commendation without this resistance of critical judgment pats an author's work softly and puts it to sleep. Genuine criticism helps to keep it alive indefinitely.**

In many ways the subsequent history of the *Horn Book* has been based on the concept of selection aided and abetted by critical judgment.

If criticism presupposes creation, the last half-century, not only in America but all over the world, ought certainly to have been favorable to the development of critical writing about children's books. Although prize-winning books should not be the sole exemplars, it is very convenient to pick titles at random

*Richard L. Darling, *The Rise of Children's Book Reviewing in America, 1865-1881* (New York, Bowker, 1968), p. 247.
**The Horn Book, February 1933, p. 1.

from such lists as those of Newbery and Carnegie Medal winners and Boston Globe-Horn Book awards to demonstrate how children's literature has increased and multiplied. *Johnny Tremain* (Houghton), *Island of the Blue Dolphins* (Houghton), *From the Mixed-up Files of Mrs. Basil E. Frankweiler* (Atheneum), *The High King* (Holt), *Sounder* (Harper), *The Slave Dancer* (Bradbury), *M.C.Higgins, the Great* (Macmillan), *The Grey King* (Atheneum/Margaret K. McElderry), *The Borrowers* (Harcourt), *Tom's Midnight Garden* (Lippincott), *A Stranger at Green Knowe* (Harcourt), *The Owl Service* (Walck), *Josh* (Macmillan), *Watership Down* (Macmillan), *The Wizard of Earthsea* (Parnassus), *The Intruder* (Lippincott) are ample evidence of the range and quality of twentieth-century writing for children. Such books give much to talk about and write about; much to evaluate, to judge and — best of all — to appreciate.

Finally it must be remembered that children's literature is not national but international; and as far back as the nineteenth century and the early twentieth century, children had at their disposal not only books originally written in English, but the stories of Perrault, the Grimm Brothers, and Andersen; *Pinocchio, Heidi, The Swiss Family Robinson,* and *The Wonderful Adventures of Nils.* Similarly, in the twentieth century the criticism of children's literature has matured in the perceptions of men and women from many countries. Although most of the *Horn Book* essays in the ensuing volume owe their origin to the English-speaking world, they are touched at many points by critical eddies coming from a larger community.

PAUL HEINS

I

STATUS

From time to time the very existence of a noteworthy body of children's books is called into question; and even if the devil's advocate avoids the puerility and the vulgarity of the term "kiddy lit," he is apt to flaunt such an expression as "so-called children's literature." Or those who take children's literature seriously often take it too seriously and fall into the trap of didacticism. For authors, editors, or critics whose lives are devoted to the creation and understanding of children's books, a comfortingly happy method of defense or apology often assumes the form of humor, not to say of satire.

In the three articles which follow, one should not be misled by the appeal to absurdity, for the mask of the jester only hides great seriousness of purpose. When Betty Jean Lifton has the Mother of her imaginary symposium ask Edward Lear, "Or did you graduate to writing for adults?" she touches upon a much irritated sore spot that many children's writers suffer from. Astrid Lindgren's statement "Nobody can teach you how to write a good book for children" is resonant with the simplicity of truth. And Aidan Chambers speaks from the heart as well as from the mind in his dictim "[L]iterature's primary pupose . . . is . . . to re-create the texture of life, to explore and seek for meanings in human experience."

A SHORT TALK WITH A PROSPECTIVE CHILDREN'S WRITER*

By Astrid Lindgren

SO, YOU'RE GOING to write a children's book? You're not the only one. Plenty of people who can hold a pen — and more than a few who can't — get it into their heads every now and again that now is the time to set about writing something for children. What could be easier? All you have to do is make a start, and the rest follows automatically — all that childish stuff that the silly little things get so much fun out of. Let's see now, what would be a good beginning? "Once upon a time there was an old kitchen boiler who went out walking with Great Aunt Euphemia Cauliflower" — why, that's just right. Just tie them up together, and keep them at it page after page, and that's it.

Is that what you thought? No, of course not. Your standards are higher than that, so high, in fact, that before you even put pen to paper you keep asking yourself: What should a good children's book be like? If you were to ask me, then — no matter how hard I might rack my brains — I would only be able to say: It ought to be good. I assure you that I have given the matter some thought for a considerable length of time, but still I can only say: It ought to be good.

What makes a good anthology of poetry? What makes a good novel? Why has nobody ever asked either of those questions? Is it because there is no recipe for a good poem or a good novel, so that it is confidently left to the poet and the novelist to extract their creations from the innermost recesses of their souls without any guidance from outside?

Yes, of course; but you may object when it's just a case of a short book for children, hoping the while for a miracle-working recipe. Oh, but, of course, there are recipes.

Take a bunch of jolly urchins, mix with a few villains, add a stupid policeman, and a nagging mother; carefully stir in an uncomprehending father; spice well with quarrelsome dialogues

*First published in Barn och kultur (1970/6). Translated from the Swedish by Roger G. Tanner.

and a spot of rough stuff; and then, hey ho, for the publisher's table!

Or again, whisk together Cyril the Squirrel, wise old Mother Owl, and Little Boy Blue, a touch of zany and umpteen jolly little quips; and there you are again. Serve cool. Of course, you could try a hash-up of the loveliest, liveliest little whirlie-curlies on the world's loveliest horses, sitting in the world's surest saddles, and bounding over the world's highest and most formidable obstacles. Oh, yes, there are plenty of recipes. But since you are about to embark on your career as a writer in this year of grace 1970, it may have come to your notice that all this business of recipes, heaven be praised, is completely and utterly washed-up. The hashes and puddings of today are made up of completely different ingredients.

Take one divorced mother — plumber if possible, otherwise an atomic physicist will do quite nicely — the main thing being that she does not fall into the slough of domesticity and maternal devotion; add two parts effluent and two parts air pollution, a few pinches of global starvation, parental repression and teacher terror; carefully insert two dumplings of racial problems, two more of sexual discrimination, and a soupçon of Vietnam; sprinkle generously with copulation and drugs; and you have a good and durable concoction which serves any purpose.

All right, I'm being unfair. You didn't want that kind of recipe. No sensible person expects to produce a good children's book simply by following a recipe, and no doubt you fully realize that what goes for poetry also applies to children's books — if there is to be any point in them — and to any other kind of literature.

Seriously, then, you wanted to know how to be a good children's writer — didn't you? Nobody can teach you how to write a good book for children. For heaven's sake, don't go thinking that I am sitting here glorying in my own books and posing as your guide, philosopher, and friend simply because of them. Far from it, but I have spent almost a quarter of a century as a children's publisher, watching manuscripts of all kinds floating through, so that, one way and another, I think I have learned a few lessons which could be useful to you as well. Just a few basic rules — the rest is up to you and your innate creativity.

4

First, language. I think this is perhaps the most important thing — for the language and content of a book to harmonize. If you write about Cyril the Squirrel (but you won't, will you?), in other words if you're writing for five-year-olds as being the age group most susceptible to squirrels, then you must not use words and expressions that cannot be comprehended by anyone under ten.

Now I've made you cross. Fancy having the nerve to sit here feeding you such platitudes! Fair enough. But tell me, why does one come across so many children's books that have to be translated into simpler language before they can be understood by the children their subjects are intended for? Not long ago I read a book for linguistically advanced five-year-olds. It was an infantile thing about little trolls, so it can hardly have been meant for older children. I read it straight off, without translating anything, just stopping every now and then to ask my five-year-old listener: What does *rectify abuses* mean? What does *good council* mean? What does *abide together* mean? And every time the five-year-old answered, "How should I know?"

One very good author I know put it this way: "I have found that the best way of writing is to practice a style which even a child could understand." And yet, he was writing for intellectual adults. It is even more vital for people actually writing for children to write so that children can understand them. There is no shame in writing lucidly even above the five-year-old level; simplicity need not necessarily imply banality and emptiness. Often a poet will speak of life, death, and love, and all the most profound aspects of human existence in such simple words that even a child can understand: Have you ever stopped to think of that?

On the other hand, some writers take umbrage if you criticize their language and ask whether they realize that they are writing for children. One should never underestimate children, they say, never talk down to them, for they understand far more than we imagine. Granted. In my view one can and should talk to children about most things. But there still remains the question of *how* to talk to them, if they are to understand what is being said to them; nor can one altogether disregard the limitations of their frame of reference. If, to take one example, a children's book is made to include an extremely funny skit on the minutes of a board meeting — and this in fact has been done — then, as I see it, the writer's efforts have been in vain. To appreciate a parody you have to be *au fait* with the thing that is being mocked, and I know very few children who have ever read the minutes of a board meeting. This, then, is one rule worth bearing in mind when you start writing. By all means, write things that *only* children will find amusing; and by all means, write things that both children *and* adults will find amusing; but never include in your children's book anything which your own common sense ought to tell you can *only* be amusing to adults. You are not writing in order for the critics to eulogize your ready wit and your neat turn of a phrase — and don't you forget it! Many people ostensibly writing for children are prone to sly winks over the children's heads at an imaginary adult reader, so that the children are left out of their own book. Please don't do anything of the kind.

The best of luck, then. And enjoy yourself. Believe me, writing for children is fun. At least, I hope you think so; otherwise you might as well give up before you start. And I hope you will not be unduly oppressed by that business about "What makes a good children's book?" — today, tomorrow, and thereafter. Don't bother about it too much. Write freely and write as you please. I wish you and all other children's writers freedom, the self-evident freedom of an adult writer to write as he pleases about what he pleases. If you want to write a disturbing book for children about how difficult and impossible it is to be human in the world today, then you are perfectly entitled to do so. If you want to write about racial discrimination, then again you are perfectly within your right. And if you want to write about a verdant islet in a coral sea, then you are perfectly entitled to do that as well. Yes, even in this year of grace 1970, you are still entitled to write about a verdant isle without necessarily having to stop and think: What rhymes with *sewage* and *oil slick*? In a word: Liberty! For without liberty the flower of poetry withers and dies, no matter where it may grow.

From *The Horn Book* for June 1973

ON CHILDREN'S LITERATURE: A RUNCIBLE SYMPOSIUM

By Betty Jean Lifton

The following is a transcript of a symposium held recently in the basement of the Timballo Tavern. The subject of the panel was "Should Children's Books Enter the Mainstream of Literature or Remain in the Stagnant Ponds They Now Inhabit?"

Summoned specially for the occasion was that eminent purveyor of nonsense, Edward Lear. Also participating were a concerned mother, a children's librarian, the editor of that prominent adult journal, *The New Haven Review*, a local bookseller, and a pragmatic publisher. A child was invited to give his views, but unfortunately he came down with the mumps at the last moment and could not appear.

MODERATOR: Before we begin our symposium on children's literature, would any of our panelists like to ask a question?

MOTHER: I have one for Mr. Lear. Since he lived a hundred years ago, could he refresh our memories on some of his titles? There are so many children's books around, one can't keep track of them all.

MODERATOR: Well, perhaps, since he's come such a long way, Mr. Lear wouldn't mind telling us something about himself and his work.

LEAR: *How pleasant to know Mr. Lear!*
  Who has written such volumes of stuff!
Some think him ill-tempered and queer,
  But a few think him pleasant enough.

MOTHER: Oh, don't stop there. Tell us more. Did you mind writing books mainly for kiddies? Or did you graduate to writing for adults?

LEAR: *His mind is concrete and fastidious,*
  His nose is remarkably big;
His visage is more or less hideous,
  His beard it resembles a wig.

  He has ears, and two eyes, and ten fingers,
    Leastways if you reckon two thumbs;
  Long ago he was one of the singers,
    But now he is one of the dumbs.

7

MOTHER: I'm so happy to know about you, Mr. Lear. I'll be sure to ask for your books when I do my Christmas shopping. I never take a chance on all those new writers. It's safer to stick with the old classics if you want real value, don't you think?

LEAR: *There was a young mother of Kew,*
Who was terrified of the new;
So she stuck out her chins, and bought The Bobbsey Twins —
For the price of one she got two.

BOOKSELLER: Now, Mr. Lear, I'm sure you don't mean to knock the old-timers. We still have a good run on *Black Beauty, The Bobbsey Twins, Dr. Dolittle* — and good sales, too. That's where it counts. We stock only the big sellers, but we try the new ones, too. Of the three thousand books for children published each year, we carry at least three. No room for more in our store, what with the run on *Portnoy's Complaint* this season. Do you know that book, Mr. Lear?

LEAR: *There was a bookseller of Tainte,*
Who stocked up on Portnoy's Complaint;
When a youngster said, "Oy, are there no books
for a boy?"
He replied, "You are right, there ain't."

MOTHER: They should make abridgments of books like *Portnoy's Complaint* for children then. Or advertise children's books next to the Beatles or Norman Mailer — so we'd be sure to notice them.

PUBLISHER: Madam, why should we spend our good money advertising children's books, good or bad, when eighty percent of our sales are to the school and public libraries? We put ads in their journals and in the *The Horn Book*.

MOTHER: But I never see library journals and I've never heard of *The Horn Book*. The only reviews I come across are on a special page in some book section. And as soon as I start reading one, it's over. Why must they be so short? And why aren't they ever signed by someone I've heard of — like Jacqueline Susann?

EDITOR: Because there's no money or prestige in children's reviewing. And furthermore it has never been settled who should review the books: the child, the librarian, the adult, or the children's book writer. Until it is treated as a literary problem, reviewing will remain in this primitive state.

MODERATOR: Which brings us to one of the topics of our discussion. Tell us, Mr. Lear, who do you think should review children's books?

LEAR: *There was an old man of Saybrooks,*
Who reviewed only children's books.
But they said — "It's absurd to encourage this bird!"
So they burnt him along with the books.

LIBRARIAN: I think librarians should review children's books. Who could be more qualified, surrounded as we are by books and children all day?

MODERATOR: What do you think of that, Mr. Lear?

LEAR: *There was a librarian of Pooles,*
Who would always set her own rules;
The birds, bees, and elves were banned from her shelves,
That umbrageous librarian of Pooles.

LIBRARIAN: That's not fair, Mr. Lear. I'll have you know that since your day there have been some very inspiring children's librarians. The best in juvenile literature owes much of its encouragement to distinguished figures like Anne Carroll Moore, Frances Clarke Sayers, and Ruth Hill Viguers. They have held up the standards which good writers could measure themselves by.

EDITOR: But keeping children's books confined to the libraries all these years made them conform to the dimensions of the catalogue card. And the conduct of proper ladies. No drinking or swearing here, please.

9

PUBLISHER: Now wait a minute. That shows how much you know. The lid's been lifted in the children's field. The taboos are gone. Writers are now free to write about real things — like rape and incest and drugs.

LIBRARIAN: That's right. I recently ordered a book about two boys who — well, you know what — with each other. And another about a girl who had an illegitimate baby. If you can imagine such a thing.

PUBLISHER: The field is really coming into its own as a result of all this. Why there was even a slot made for it in the National Book Awards this year. The public is going to learn that children's writers aren't all little old women — that they can be quite ordinary people like everyone else. I, myself, recently met a young one who was extremely attractive. And quite opinionated, too. You have to be careful of them, Mr. Lear.

LEAR: *There was a young children's writer,*
               With the left hook of a prize fighter.
               When they said, "Watch your prose," she
               punched them in the nose!
               That attractive young children's book writer.

MODERATOR: I'd like to get us back to the question of children's reviewing, which we haven't quite solved.

MOTHER: I'd like to also. I personally think mothers should review children's books. Who could possibly know children the way we do? Certainly not a librarian. Why, most of them aren't even married.

LIBRARIAN: I'm married. For the third time, too.

MOTHER: Well, I'm sure there are some exceptions. But most mothers would find reviewing children's books a good way to use their college degrees. There's not much else we can do with them. They're not even soft enough to make good diapers.

PUBLISHER: It's something to consider. Mothers wouldn't need much remuneration. And doing things for

10

children should be an idealistic pursuit anyway. One shouldn't think of money. In fact, everything connected with those little dears should be little. Little books, little reviews, little ads, and above all, little paychecks. Don't you agree, Mr. Lear?

LEAR: *There was a reviewer of Le Havre,*
Who was practically ready to starve.
His ears grew so thin they almost fell in
The book he reviewed in Le Havre.

EDITOR: As a literary man, I think that neither librarians nor mothers should review children's books. Librarians are trained in technical work, not in literature. Mothers can criticize their children, but that doesn't make them critics. I think children's writers should do the reviewing. Just as novelists and poets review each other's work.

PUBLISHER: That's a radical idea.

EDITOR: We've never concerned ourselves with children's books in *The New Haven Review* because, frankly, they don't bring in ads and, therefore, are not relevant. But I'll make a deal with you, Mr. Lear. I'll give a page in my magazine to children's books, if you'll write your reviews in those famous limericks of yours. You probably know we produce the finest literary review in the country — maybe in the world. Everyone who's anyone reads it. It will guarantee the success of any book you praise, destroy any book you damn — and we only damn the best. We'll give you an office of your own, an editorial assistant to answer your phone. What do you think, Mr. Lear? Can you picture it all?

LEAR: *He sits in a beautiful parlour,*
    With hundreds of books on the wall;
He drinks a great deal of Marsala,
    But never gets tipsy at all.

EDITOR: Of course, we'll have to ask a child to go over your reviews, for we want to be sure your taste will appeal to the kiddies. The younger set might have been satisfied with Owls and Pussycats, Pobbles, Jumblies, and Yonghy-Bonghy-Bo's on that estate of the Earl of Derby, but they're a different breed of cat now. They live in an age of TV, spaceships, computers, and nuclear weapons. Do you think they can dig you?

LEAR: *When he walks in a waterproof white,*
The children run after him so!
Calling out, "He's come out in his night-
Gown, that crazy old Englishman, oh!"

PUBLISHER: Well, it's an advantage to be a little bit crazy. I don't know how it was in your day, Mr. Lear, but you'll find there is condescension toward anyone in children's books. Writers are looked upon as failed novelists, and reviewers as working their way up to adult reviewing. Not that it can't change, mind you, but like all things — like the race problem, the poverty program, the war in Vietnam — it takes time.

EDITOR: I sometimes wonder if there *should* be separate books for the young. In the old days there was no separation between children and adults. Children worked right at the grownup's side and chose what they wanted from the adult world. Books like *Gulliver's Travels, Don Quixote,* and *Huckleberry Finn* weren't written for them — they just took them over.

MOTHER: When did all that change?

EDITOR: When we began to recognize children as having needs of their own, we protected them with humane laws guarding their rights and their health. We gave them prolonged youth and delayed responsibilities. But we also segregated them. The toys they play with, the books they read, have nothing to do with the adult world now.

LIBRARIAN: Then you are saying in effect that we librarians have not usurped the field of children's books. It

12

was handed over to us. Adults who would never ask us to choose and review *their* books, have turned their children over to us completely.

MOTHER: When you put it that way, I can't help feeling guilty. I've made no effort to guide my children's reading. I've just relied on our school lists each year without question. Oh, I could weep when I think how foolish I've been.

LEAR: *He weeps by the side of the ocean,*
He weeps on the top of the hill;
He purchases pancakes and lotion,
And chocolate shrimps from the mill.

MOTHER: But to defend myself, chocolate shrimps are probably much cheaper than the fantastic prices for children's books. Why can't they cost less?

PUBLISHER: Because printer's prices have gone up. It is expensive to reproduce color illustrations. And we feel children like color — it sells. Then there's the bindings. We pride ourselves in America on our bindings. Children can rip and tear and pull and stamp on our library bindings without affecting them at all.

MOTHER: That's all right for the libraries. But I'd settle for some inexpensive paperbacks. Why, you could distribute them at the supermarket. I could pick up a few with the breakfast cereal. Don't you agree, Mr. Lear?

LEAR: *There was a mother of Barket,*
Who bought all her books at the market,
She said, "These will do, just fine for my stew,
They're cheaper than meat here in Barket."

MODERATOR: I see our time is running short. We've talked about who should review children's books, let's discuss who should write them. Mr. Lear, you and Lewis Carroll wrote some of the greatest classics. Yet you never married or had children. I wonder if there are any rules as to who is best suited to write for children.

13

MOTHER: I think parents are. We tell them the most wonderful bedtime stories. Frankly, Mr. Lear, I've often thought of writing mine down. It's just that I don't have the time.

LEAR: *There was a bold parent of Wales*
Who made up her own bedtime tales;
But her sweet little dear developed a tin ear,
Which no doctor could cure in all Wales.

PUBLISHER: Are you implying that only a writer should write children's books, Mr. Lear? As far as I'm concerned, children's writers are a difficult bunch. They're always complaining about something — lack of ads in adult journals, lack of intelligent reviews, lack of big advances, lack of large royalties. Some of them even think they should have literary cocktail parties! And after all we do for them! Why, we arrange speaking engagements at library conferences all over the country! We even advertise our lists in *The New York Times* special section for children's books twice a year! And do they appreciate this? No!

EDITOR: I can understand their wanting individual ads instead of being grouped in seasonal lists — like four and twenty blackbirds baked in a pie.

MODERATOR: I hate to end this challenging symposium, but our time is up. We may not have been able to solve who should write and review children's books, but we still know who should read them. The children, of course! Thank you for being with us. And our special thanks to you, Mr. Lear, for making this unusual pilgrimage to our panel. Would you like to make one last statement before our time vanishes completely?

LEAR: *He reads, but he cannot speak, Spanish,*
He cannot abide ginger beer:
Ere the days of his pilgrimage vanish,
*How pleasant to know Mr. Lear!**

*In the article, the verses with the indented lines are drawn from Edward Lear's "How Pleasant to Know Mr. Lear."

From *The Horn Book* for June 1970

REVIEWERS' RAILMENTS:
A GAME FOR
CHILDREN'S BOOK PEOPLE

By Aidan Chambers

REVIEWERS' RAILMENTS is a pretty old game. Authors have played it in one form or another ever since children's books first got noticed in the press. All you need is a collection of children's book reviews, and you can settle down to enjoy yourself for hours, either on your own or with any number of others. You don't need to know the books themselves; every railment is easy to diagnose just from reading the reviews.

I took up the game when my first book for young people was mentioned in a national woman's magazine — the kind that mixes recipes with romance, and tips about being feminine with bits about women's lib. My reviewer started off with one of those fillets of flattery that publishers love to quote in their ads. "Hard hitting," she said, "with emotions cut to the minimum." Great! I thought, preparing to be famous. (I was raw to the business of being a writer then.) My book was about a boy athlete who suffered a nasty accident and had to learn how to come to terms with his catastrophe. At least, that's what I thought it was about. Being the author, I couldn't be certain, of course. And I was wrong, it seemed. Because the reviewer went on to say that my story "shed a good deal of light on the potentials of a nursing career." Since then, I've played the Railment Game regularly.

Newcomers to this fascinating pastime will need to know that there are many different railments. Each time you discover one contaminating a review, you give yourself appropriate points out of ten. The winner is the person with the highest score. (Skilled players very quickly learn which journals and which reviewers yield the best crop of railments and know just where to turn to collect a high score.) Naturally, you only win your points if you can name the railment and can diagnose its cause.

Take, for example, one of the easiest to come by: *English Teacher's Elbow*. This crippling affliction nudges a reviewer into appreciating a book not for any literary merit it may have, but for the nice way it teaches the kiddies about language. Everyone knows, of course, except the reviewer, that literature isn't a language laboratory, a teaching machine that grinds away, turning us all into skilled manipulators of standard English (or American). You can see the *Elbow* poking sharply through this extract from a notice of one of William Mayne's slighter works, *The Yellow Aeroplane:*

Easily understood sentences vary and offer patterns worth assimilating. Repetition of difficult words helps readers stretch their vocabularies.

(Perhaps I should say here that none of my examples are invented. Not by me, anyway. They are all culled from my collection of railment gems. For the sake of the poor, stricken reviewers, I have omitted by-lines and the names of the unfortunate journals which printed the notices.) Such a choice railment is worth at least eight points in anyone's game. Provided, as I say, you can go on to point out that the source of this sickness is *Barbauld Poisoning,* a fatal disease named for dear Mrs. Barbauld, who first exhibited it in *Evenings at Home,* her "budget of instruction and entertainment" for children, published in 1792. *Barbauld Poisoning* stunts the mind, allowing you to find in literature nothing more than a sugar-coated pill by which dull and often unnecessary lessons can be taught to children while they are distracted by the author's entertaining way with a story.

A number of other railments are associated with the *Elbow. Historian's Blight,* for example. This railment is common, because so many children's books have historical settings. Even when the pedagogic value is tenuous, reviewers afflicted with the *Blight* make as much of it as they can. One of them did with John Grant's *Littlenose,* a book for very young children that few would label "historical fiction" by any credible definition. *Littlenose* was, the reviewer said,

about a Stone Age boy and his pet mammoth. Fanciful, certainly, but behind the friendly humour are sturdy facts about nomadic people and their life.

Apart from being withered by the *Blight* (worth about five points in this case), one cannot help commenting on how poorly written the review is: the commonplace misuse of "Fanciful"; the "sturdy facts," which could mean anything or nothing. But then poor-quality writing seems to go along with all the railments. Look again at my example of *English Teacher's Elbow* — the cacophonous concoction of awkward phrases and misconceived ideas ("offer patterns worth assimilating"; "helps readers stretch their vocabularies"). Sadly there are no extra points given for spotting deficiencies of this kind; they merely provide depressed authors with a sour amusement.

The *Blight*, like *Geographer's Grump* and *Scientist's Sclerosis*, sends reviewers obsessively burrowing into literary texts for information considered good for children (those "sturdy facts," maybe?). These sicknesses all follow from the idea that literary writing is no more than a self-indulgent form of encyclopedia compilation. Of course, literature does often tell us about historical events or unfamiliar settings, or even involve scientific principles. But it is not literature's primary purpose to do so. It is, rather, to re-create the texture of life, to explore and seek for meanings in human experience.

The *Blight* and the *Grump* often attack a reviewer simultaneously (becoming a compound railment — the *Blump*, perhaps?), as in a review of Fay Goldie's *River of Gold*.

This book should prove popular with young adults (12 up) who will gain a good knowledge of some of the history of South Africa, as well as a memorable impression of its beauty and the generosity of its people.

Apart from having the *Blumps*, the notice also has that irritating rash, *Reviewer's Tosh*. South Africa may be beautiful, but to suggest that a book gives a memorable impression of South African generosity is to use that word fuzzily and nonsensically. (After all, the elite group in South Africa that keeps the majority of the people under its totalitarian heel can scarcely be called generous.) A knowledge of the book reveals the fault to be the reviewer's. *Books for Children: Homelands of Immigrants to Britain*, an excellent annotated list edited by Janet Hill, notes that *River of Gold* "highlights the enmity between the people of the impoverished rural republic and the fortune-seeking diggers which was to erupt, years later, in the Boer War."

One of the least pleasant railments is the terrible scourge of *Jargon Diarrhea*, to which there seems no antidote just now, for it is spreading with alarming rapidity. Books fall victim to the infected reviewers week after week. A. Rutgers Van der Loeff's *Flight from the Polar Night* was one.

Because he treats a single theme simply, with a kind of dry passion the author makes Peer a convincing hero whose adjustment problem is a real one.

Worth seven points at least. I cannot help proposing that a bonus point be awarded to any player noting the bathetic phrase "a kind of dry passion," which sets the jargonistic "adjustment problem" trembling with unfathomable but nevertheless suggestive meaning.

Of late, however, top marks for samples of the jargon railment must go to those who clipped the reviews of Maurice Sendak's *In the Night Kitchen*, which included such terms as "masturbation phantasy." My favorite among these came from a bouncy professor of education, who wrote with a condescension only a third-rate mind would be capable of: "as to Freudian sex symbols, there are so many that it is a romp to identify and discuss them."

Jargon Diarrhea is more an American weakness than a British. To square the account, the British succumb to *Raised Nose*, something that brings down any reviewer who is so eaten up with snobbery that he entertains a feeling of literary superiority both to children's books in general and to certain kinds in particular. Usually, in Britain it is books for adolescents that come in for the most attention by reviewers who hold themselves in such an uncomfortable position.

The problems inherent in the situation are frankly faced and if they are resolved a little facilely, well, perhaps no more is really to be expected of a book designed for readers in their lower teens.

This snooty nonsense was offered in judgment of *The Lord Mayor's Show* by Vian Smith, and one might be excused for asking meekly why no more than the facile is to be expected of a book for the early teens. Observers of the way railment reviewers mangle the language will, I expect, be fascinated by the pejorative use of "facile," as against the invariably complimentary employment of "facility." And "frankly faced" will not be allowed to slip by those who play that other amusing review game, *Hunt the Cliché*.

I guess that by now uninitiated readers will have latched on to the idea. The Railment Game is really very simple to play, and because reviewers supply so many examples, you can go on for hours quite happily — provided you have a tough stomach or plenty of Alka Seltzer handy. I haven't, of course, catalogued all the railments. There are many, many more. But no definitive work has ever been written on the game for fear the reviewers wouldn't know what to say about it. So, newcomers are best advised to make up their own filing system. Some infirmities not so far mentioned ought to be included in everyone's list. *Racist's Slip*, for example, an indisposition that causes a reviewer unknowingly to reveal his cultural and tribal prejudices. *Technician's Cataract*, too, a blinding malady that concentrates a reviewer's attention on technique to the exclusion of content. Then there's that high school girl's problem, *Plotster's Paradise*, that impels reviewers to recount every detail of what happens in a story and leaves them unable to offer a more critical comment than something like "A beautiful and well-written book." At the other extreme from *Paradise* is *Adult's Paralysis*. Many reviewers nowadays suffer from it; they all want to be highly academic critics and think that children's books are not for children at all but are for the gratification of adults only.

Before I finish, I really must give a couple of choice pickings from *Reviewer's Last Will and Testament*. Rather than a sickness, this is a signing of one's death warrant as a reviewer — a death warrant wrapped in fatuous judgments blown about on the hot air of opinionated dogmatism.

It is a very distinguished novel, and, I think, cannot fail to be popular with young readers.

. . . no child with imagination will want to put this book down, or indeed be satisfied with only one reading of it.

If, like myself, you are a reviewer and want to add a touch of spice to the game, take out your own notices and add them to the pile. The experience is excruciating but salutary.

Luckily, children do not read reviews. Left to their own devices, they choose the books they want to read by a secret formula they manage to keep from adults. In the end, that's why Reviewers' Railments is only a game and not something serious and worrying. Or is it. . . ?

From *The Horn Book* for April 1972

II

CLASSIFICATION

The development and the proliferation of children's books during the past century have created a peculiar problem in the criticism of these books. "What is a children's book?" or "Is this book really a children's book?" are besetting questions that often pop up in discussions. Compounding these dilemmas is the observable fact that children have for a long time chosen certain adult books for their own, and adults have similarly adopted some children's books for themselves. A further complication arises when classification reflects publishing expediency and adds further confusion to an already confused subject. It may be said that of classification there is no end, but as long as its purpose is to make valid distinctions, it can promote the interests of clarification.

As in the other sections of this collection of critical essays, various perspectives are opened up. For instance, there is a considerable shift in point of view from John Tunis's article to that of Isabelle Holland's. If Janet McNeill points out the literary transition between childhood and youth and Isabelle Holland makes us aware of the historical changes in our concept of childhood, John Rowe Townsend tackles the problem on literary as well as on organizational grounds and has a word to say about the significance of young adult literature.

Milton Meltzer's plea for the literary integrity of nonfiction for young readers may not seem too closely related to the previous materials under discussion, but it actually represents an important facet in the critical aspect of the classification and evaluation of children's literature.

WHAT IS A JUVENILE BOOK?

By JOHN R. TUNIS

IT MUST HAVE BEEN back about 1934 or 1935. In between doing three columns a week for the New York *Evening Post* and a weekly sports piece for *The New Yorker*, plus an occasional magazine article, I worked evenings and weekends on a novel. It was the story of a Middle-Western boy from a small high school who comes East and gets lost in the big world of Harvard. Ever a believer in going to the top, I sent the book, with a note, to Mr. Alfred Harcourt, the genius and president of Harcourt, Brace and Company. Ten days later he repaid my brashness by asking me to come to New York and see him. Next Thursday at eleven fifteen.

But instead of holding the conference I had anticipated and perhaps asking for changes, he went directly to the point, stating he had read the book (I doubt whether he ever did) and would like to publish it as a juvenile. This offer was before the term juvenile delinquency had been invented; certainly I had never before heard the word juvenile used in publishing. At any rate, he led me, confused and bewildered, out of his office. With the book in his hand, he took me firmly by the arm and walked me briskly down the hall to a tiny cubicle where sat an alert, brown-eyed woman. He introduced her as Mrs. Hamilton, dropped the book on her desk, and fled. These events all took less than two minutes.

Tactfully smiling and ignoring my frown of dismay, she explained that she was head of the Juvenile Department (another new term to me) and would indeed like to publish my novel. While I sat speechless with annoyance, she explained that there was a real market for such a book and that she felt it would sell. (Her judgment was entirely correct; it has sold seventy thousand copies in hard cover, and brings me in a comfortable annuity of several thousand a year.) At the time, I was torn between inviting her to chuck the book out on 45th Street and signing the contract on her desk. Fortunately I settled on the latter course.

It must have been just before this, or perhaps a year earlier, that Mrs. Munro Leaf, then working in a bookshop, suggested it would be helpful to everybody if publishers listed in their catalogues and promotional matter the age group for which each book was intended. Although at that time only about two hundred books for children were published each year, the number was growing and many publishers had spring and fall lists. As a consequence, bookstore clerks did not have enough time to read these books. The trade-book salesmen liked the idea immediately. To have a book with the age of the intended reader specified was a gimmick with which to sell the bookseller or buyer.

All this was more than thirty years ago. Today the business has grown to such an extent that each children's book is carefully assigned to a certain age group. To classify, list, bracket, and define every product from soup to soap, from wearing apparel to educational institutions, is one of the great American passions. Everything is catalogued, ticketed, and listed for the Consumer Market.

Take cars, for instance. The big manufacturers — and today there is no other kind making automobiles — produce many models of many cars. You can have a "specialty car" or a "personal car." You may buy a two-door hardtop, a four-door sedan, a family wagon, or a convertible; a Charger, a Firebird, a Marlin, a Mustang, a Barracuda, a Cougar, an Impala, a Fury, or a Polara. Are you interested in automatic transmission? Do you prefer one of the four kinds of V-8 engines, a 6 or a 4? A heavy-duty suspension, power brakes, disk brakes, or no brakes? The airlines have classified their services too. There are a dozen different kinds of trips — a 17-day excursion, a 21-day excursion, a monthly round trip, a low rate for you and your family of six, or a journey with your wife, who goes at half fare except when the moon is full.

In recent years this frenzy for classification has penetrated writing and publishing. Writers are tagged, taped, coded, branded. A detective-story writer is not supposed to write a life of Benvenuto Cellini. Books are also ranked and pigeonholed. Since the forties, especially, when publishing began to go on to higher, nobler things by combining with radio chains or becoming appendages of Time, Inc., books for children have become big business for businessmen. This is not precisely news. But the fact is that the zeal for classifying books has intensified. Each book is a piece of merchandise, dropped into its slot, graded according to its market.

This book, for instance, is for children ages 3-6. This one is for ages 5-8. Or ages 7-9. The next is for children 12 and up. Up to where is not specified.

This book is a Junior book. This is a Juvenile. (As distinct from a Senile book, presumably.) This book here is for — you should pardon the expression — Young Adults.

Who says so? Who determines what kind of a book is best for ages 5-7, or 7-9? What is a Young Adult? When does he or she become an Adult? Can you imagine a mother saying to a friend, "I want you to meet my son Henry, a Young Adult"!

The arbitrary listing by publishers' standards probably started, then, in the thirties. Certainly the term juvenile was seldom if ever heard in publishing circles before the middle twenties. There were few if any children's book departments at the time; they were to come later. One of the first was presided over by Mrs. Ellen Harcourt at Harcourt, Brace and Company in the twenties. Her assistant was Mrs. Hamilton, fresh from library work in New Jersey, who took over from Mrs. Harcourt in the early thirties.

One thing is sure. Back in the nineteenth century books were just books: some you liked, some your ten-year-old grandson liked, some were read by adults, while many writers such as Dickens were also enjoyed by children. There were also a number of books specially produced for a young audience. The popular novels of Captain Mayne Reid — *The Boy Hunters, The Desert Home, The Young Voyagers*, and others — were published by Routledge, Warne and Routledge, both in London and New York. Their general presentation was the same as that of other kinds of books in the sixties and seventies. Similarly produced were the Henty books, which came along later, also published in New York and London, by A. L. Burt. We were a backward nation in that distant era, before we had invented computers, supersonic aircraft, napalm, and other advantages of the Great Society. Books were just books, with no designation or coding.

Ruth Hill Viguers, formerly editor of *The Horn Book*, agrees that the classification of children's books was generally adopted after the development of children's book departments in publishing firms. The trend was accelerated in the thirties. In the fifties and sixties it became a landslide. "Because so many children's books were dull stuff," says Mrs. Viguers, "booksellers seldom read them and needed clues to sell them — therefore the grading and classifying."

Last year a collection of the famous Lawrenceville stories by the late Owen Johnson was reprinted by Simon and Schuster. These stories, written around 1910, depicted life in the Lawrenceville School in New Jersey, and the boys and masters who composed it. At the time, Booth Tarkington, then a leading novelist, said of one story, "*The Varmint* is serious writing. It is worth thousands of the fancy, pretentious things lately prevalent; it's infinitely rarer and harder to do." Today these stories would have been thrust into a juvenile category, and as a consequence thousands of delighted adults would have missed them.

Were the Lawrenceville stories juvenile in the accepted meaning of the term today? Of course not. They were for everyone. As Cleveland Amory in his witty introduction to the new edition points out: not only were they serialized in *The Saturday Evening Post*, but "they were read by millions of men of twelve and boys of eighty."

That odious term juvenile is, therefore, the product of a merchandising age. Like the new taxes that rain upon us each year, the term is here to stay. Although publishers combine, expand, grow larger and more successful, education is growing and changing even faster. The joy of exploration, of discovery, by young, eager minds — a joy which exists as it always has — is not likely to be increased by a classification that limits readers to ages 7-9. Just as important is the fact that writers, too, need to explore. But many of them are tabbed and classified like motor cars and cheese. Those authors who keep turning out more of the same kind of book year after year, end up by becoming hacks. To develop, an author must tackle different and harder tasks. Such development is extremely difficult if he is assigned to a category or an age group and expected to produce for that group alone.

Books that twenty, or even ten, years ago were suitable for a certain age group no longer fit that group. Today, with the "individualized" methods of teaching reading and other subjects, a child reads at his capacity. The book which once enchanted the fifth-grader may now be too young. Therefore, it comes down to this: Is the classification of books for children to be made by trained librarians and specialists in the field who work with children, or by executives in publishing who use grading as a marketing device? Or should the whole method of grading and classification be scrapped in favor of Pamela Travers' comments, which have also given rise to other kinds of controversy? "For me, all books are for children. There is no such thing as a children's book. There are books of many kinds and some of them children read."

From *The Horn Book* for June 1968

THE WALLS OF CHILDHOOD

By Isabelle Holland

W HEN PEOPLE OUTSIDE the publishing world ask
me what kind of books I write, I sometimes say —
especially if I'm in a hurry — "children's books."
"Oh!" is the reply. A vague look comes over the face of the
questioner who is trying to be polite and show interest. Then
he or she brightens. "You mean picture books?" "No, I don't
mean picture books — books for teenagers." Sometimes I simply
describe them as books for elderly children. The subject grows
more complicated when one of my own books, *The Man Without a Face* (at least in Lippincott's paperback edition), is found
more often in the regular paperback sections of bookstores than
in the children's. People who mean well but don't know any
better have said, "But that's really an adult book."

This is the kind of remark that sends most children's book
editors — certainly all I have known — straight up the wall.
Because, however well meant, such a remark illustrates a commonly held belief that children's books (other than the picture-
book variety for the very young reader) are simply lesser adult
books and that the writers of children's books are adult-book
writers *manqué*: They couldn't quite make it up to the adult-
book level. This attitude is fortunately becoming less prevalent.
But when people say such and such a book really should have
been an adult book (and they have said it about books other
than mine), they mean that adults can enjoy it and that, therefore, it should have been upgraded.

Now, what this really indicates is a misunderstanding on the
part of the general public as to what children's books, more
especially the young adult or teenage books, are all about.
Brought to an even deeper level, the question really means:
What is childhood? Or adolescence? Where are its boundaries?
And it is in the differing and rapidly changing ways we view
this question that we find the limitations and possibilities of
young adult literature.

John Rowe Townsend, in the upcoming revision of his book,
Written for Children (Lippincott), quotes a modern writer as
saying that in 1693 John Locke, the English philosopher, "published his *Thoughts Concerning Education* and invented the

27

child." And though, as Mr. Townsend says, the statement is an exaggeration, there's a lot of truth in it.

Childhood, until relatively modern times, didn't exist for the vast majority of children. Beginning in England with the Tudor era, the children of upper-class families had a few brief years of instruction before the boys were ready to go to court and the girls to marry. By the Victorian age this period was expanded, and it is in the late Victorian era that the tale for children, the school story, the adventure story — as opposed to the sophisticated novel for grownups — flourished. But what cannot be forgotten in any study or chronology of how the child and childhood are viewed is that education, and along with it the schools and school stories, was for the upper classes; for the majority, childhood was still more or less nonexistent. Children worked in factories, were apprenticed to craftsmen and tradesmen, and were sent out for domestic service. They were miniature people. They were not children.

And at fourteen they were adults. Before that, the only way in which they were considered to be different from adults was in their smaller physical stature. Also, they could be — and were — bullied, whipped, and otherwise mistreated, frequently by people who were not especially monsters, but who thought, as did the rest of their generation, that this was the way to instruct.

Childhood, then, really expanded in the length of its tenure and came to include other classes of society in the very late nineteenth, and in the twentieth century. It was during this time that books for children and books for adults were most sharply defined and widely divided.

Since I am not an expert on children's literature, I can only tell you about the books that I personally enjoyed and read right up through my adolescence (and sometimes, sneakily, later). Since I grew up in England, the ones I read were English rather than American: hundreds and hundreds of school stories. Other than these and such delights as the William books by Richmal Crompton, which I don't think ever crossed the Atlantic, I read and loved the Anne of Green Gables and the Pollyanna series, and all the Alcott books. By the way, I agree with Mr. Townsend that though the traditional school story is now rather looked down upon as representing a limited and snobbish view of life (they were all about boarding schools that only the upper classes could attend), in many ways those stories enjoyed a marvelous advantage. The school world was isolated; in effect, a sort of desert island. Being isolated, though, it was a world in miniature, and the children were encountering and dealing with problems — interpersonal, ethical, and moral — that would not exist for them in quite the same intensity outside a boarding school. At school, they were full citizens of their world, while at home they played a lesser and more amorphous part in their parents' world.

I also read books written originally for adults, but read by children and now considered children's classics: *Oliver Twist*, *A Christmas Carol*, *Gulliver's Travels*, *Robinson Crusoe*, and *Pilgrim's Progress*. At school we read such adult classics as *Jane Eyre* and *David Copperfield* up to the point where the central characters leave childhood: That is, *Jane Eyre* ended for us with the death of Helen Burns; and *David Copperfield*, when David was adopted by Betsy Trotwood.

I am going into detail because I grew up at a time when the custodial concept of childhood as a world deliberately walled off was at its peak. That world, as far as reading was concerned, went from six years to sixteen or seventeen. This segregation was a result not only of Victorian morality and moralism, nor even of the Victorian reformers who salvaged childhood for many by forcing through laws forbidding the terrible abuses of child labor, it also reflected a metaphysical difference, a shift from the Christian concept of human nature as fallen from birth to the viewpoint that became popular in the late eighteenth century under the general terms of the Romantic Movement. To the orthodox Christian, the child, however lovable, was a fallen creature out of whom must be trained and disciplined the works of the devil. The Romantics, on the other hand, believed with Wordsworth that the child came trailing clouds of glory. So far from needing to have fallen nature whipped out of him, Wordsworth stated, "Heaven lies about us in our infancy. Shades of the prison-house begin to close upon the growing boy." The custodial view of childhood was a monument to that belief, and the wall built around childhood was designed to keep out adult vices and follies.

Of course, this was a situation possible to maintain for a variety of other reasons: It's hard to decide which of these is the first or most important, because when that isolated world of childhood went, all the buttresses that supported it collapsed as well. But before the collapse, the authority of the parent and of the teacher was still pretty much unchallenged. Curiously and ironically, the wall sheltering the young and supposedly innocent from the vices and follies of the adult world also protected the adults. Maintaining their distance, they could also maintain their moral authority. This created a society that was vertical, rather than horizontal.

I doubt if anyone today in his or her late teens or early twenties could appreciate how utterly staggering I find the independence of the young. I don't like to give the impression that I am a hundred and two. But my life, psychologically, has spanned a longer time than my age would actually warrant. Two factors contributed to this: One was that both my parents were forty-three when I was born. They were Americans who grew to their adulthood in the 1890's, the last years of the Victorian era, and they lived those years in a small, conservative Southern town. But my father went into the foreign service and during my growing years was posted in northern England. Thus, in addition to having middle-aged parents, I grew up in the rather strictly defined childhood of the England of that day. The authority of my parents and of the school was total. My rebelliousness remained an inner turmoil until my mid-twenties. When young people today hear that I finally got my courage together and ran away from home when I was twenty-four, they roll on the floor. But if I had run away before that time, I would have had nowhere to run to. Today, there is a whole society of young people that did not exist when I was young. Whether for good or for ill, children from their early teens up simply leave home and find, at the end of a bus route, whole areas where they can lose themselves among other youngsters. There are, according to statistics, hundreds of thousands of them. They have a society of their own, relating to one another at a common social level rather than primarily and vertically to the adults of their own circle — their parents and teachers. And this has had an enormous effect upon those young people who do not leave home. There is that world out there waiting. They know it. Their parents know it. And simply knowing it gives the youngster the power that the adult once had. In other words, the pecking order of the parent-child world has reversed itself.

If one aspect of the crumbling of the wall around childhood has been the erosion of adult authority, the demolition was hastened by two other very powerful factors: television and the paperback. Television, which has been credited, at least in part, with arousing the awareness of minority groups to their civil rights, also brought history into the family living room. War, riots, marches, bombings, violence of all kinds have paraded across the screen night after night for more than a decade. After that steady, relentless exposure, isolation for the young was no longer possible.

And at about the same time the paperback soared into prominence. In my young days I read (after I was in New York and away from home, I need hardly say) an unexpurgated copy of *Lady Chatterley's Lover* in expensive hardcover, published in France, smuggled into the States, and passed from hand to hand. I read it with the greatest curiosity in the world, since "pornography" was hard to come by. And books that hovered on the border were also sold at a price far beyond anything young people could afford or were in locked-away sections of public libraries. Some years ago, when I was working on a magazine, I was told to go to the New York Public Library to look up a reference in a book called *The Romantic Passion*. Feeling bored, I went. My boredom vanished when I handed in my slip and was told I had to see one of the librarians. When I reached him, he asked me — courteously, but firmly — if I were over twenty-one. I assured him I was, told him where I worked, and was finally given permission to see the book. By this time, my excitement and anticipation knew no bounds. (That's one thing, by the way, to be said for an innocent childhood — I somehow doubt if today anybody over the age of ten would experience that delicious titillation at the thought of reading a forbidden book.) Anyway, I was led into a sort of wired-off cage, and the book was brought to me. It turned out to be a serious study of the romantic passion in European literature. All the passages that had caused it to be put in the reserved section were either in German or in Latin. I was never so frustrated in my life. What is interesting and hardly credible is that such a different approach to erotic writing could have occurred within twenty-odd years. Today, far more sensational eroticism can be found on any paperback rack in any stationery store, newsstand, or drugstore, and can be bought for under two dollars.

The teenager of today would not put up with and would not read books damned beyond remedy by being called "suitable." And anyway, what is suitable? Is there any subject which is not openly discussed on television, in school, or among the children themselves? The teenagers' world has become pervaded with sex, pregnancy, abortion, venereal disease, drugs, crime, divorce, and homosexuality. These have always existed, to some degree, among adolescents, but they were hidden away. Such things did not happen to "nice" boys and girls. The sufferer, or culprit, as he or she was certainly looked upon, was shipped away in disgrace and not mentioned. And teenage literature occupied itself with suitable adventures and who took whom to the junior prom.

But, as we all know, that has changed, and what is preoccupying the authors of young adult literature has, of necessity, changed with it. All of these subjects — drugs, sex, pregnancy, abortion, homosexuality, parental divorce, dropping out, and crime — have entered the novels of Jeannette Eyerly, John Donovan, Barbara Wersba, Paul Zindel, and my own two young adult books, *The Man Without a Face* and *Heads You Win, Tails I Lose* (Lippincott), to mention only a few. The custodial walls have fallen.

So, in a sense, we have come full circle, back to the time before the English philosopher John Locke invented childhood. Because, as far as subject matter is concerned, we have almost uninvented it.

But, along with this, there is another interesting phenomenon. Adult fiction has grown more — for want of a better word — sophisticated. It is true the old-fashioned "little English novel" dear to female readers of light fiction is enjoying a brand-new life in paperback. Lady authors, whose books were dropped with a patronizing smile from hardcover publishing lists and whose world view has been the subject of much satiric amusement among trendy editors, have come into their own again. Authors now dead and once considered buried are suddenly appearing in paperback reprint. There are many readers for those innocent novels of manners where nothing too much happens, where the people are likable, and where the love scenes are fully clothed and end this side of the bedroom door.

But this is not considered serious fiction. And serious fiction presents more and more a viewpoint that has been called decadent, cynical, and nihilistic. One result of this has washed into the reading of young adults. Books that today are considered classics in young adult reading, and for this reason are still in print and going strong, were published as adult books when adult readers were, perhaps, less liberated in certain areas, but were also allowed a wider range of taste. Such books include, for example, *To Kill a Mockingbird* — by today's standards most definitely a children's book. Then there is the prototype of the modern novel, *Catcher in the Rye*. Golding's *Lord of the Flies*, Kipling's *Kim*, Tolkien's *Lord of the Rings*, Mary O'Hara's *My Friend Flicka*, as well as the previously mentioned classics — *Robinson Crusoe*, *Gulliver's Travels*, and *Pilgrim's Progress* — all now considered children's masterpieces, were written for adults. My first book, *Cecily*, was published by Lippincott's adult department. It was reviewed rather sniffily by some of the major adult review media. It was reviewed (to my everlasting gratitude) enthusiastically as a young adult book by the young adult media. That was seven years ago. I am almost certain that today it would not be taken as an adult book. And it was *Cecily* that made Jean Vestal, then children's book editor at Lippincott, say, "Isabelle, I think you could write children's books." At first I was (God help me!) slightly offended. Then I lost my job, got broke, and became, suddenly, much more interested. Out of that came *Amanda's Choice* (Lippincott), *The Man Without a Face*, and *Heads You Win, Tails I Lose*.

Winston Churchill, a noted Conservative and Tory, started his political career as a Liberal, English style. He always maintained that he remained the same: It was the Liberal party that moved away from him. In a sense, this is true of books. Many classics, such as those mentioned above, remain classics. It is the adult readership and criteria that have moved.

So we come back to the original question with which I started: If no subject is taboo, if the young adult book must deal with reality as it is known by today's young adult, then where does the demarcation between juvenile and adult books lie?

I would say the difference lies in two areas. The first is technical: a book for teenagers stays with one viewpoint much more steadily than does its adult counterpart dealing with the same subject — for example, teenage abortion, as in Jeannette

Eyerly's *Bonnie Jo, Go Home* (Lippincott), or homosexuality, as in John Donovan's *I'll Get There. It Better Be Worth the Trip* (Harper), and *The Man Without a Face*.

The second difference is in attitude. I spoke of the cynicism and nihilism that provide the underlying attitude of much of serious fiction today. I'd like to quote Mr. Townsend again. In speaking of the rather old-fashioned story with its continuing moral crises of cribbing and cheating, he grants its remoteness from today's children. Yet he states, "I believe myself that children *want* to act rightly and bravely and *want* things to matter."

It is in that *wanting* things to matter, the underlying assumption that to the central character they *do* matter, that I see strong and successful and truly moral books for teenagers. The crises being dealt with may be drugs or sex or divorce or crime or abortion. The realities of the adult and children's worlds have flowed together. The walls of childhood are down. In fact, we're back to square one: In subject matter there is no childhood. But in its attitude towards these subjects — in the sense that what one does about them *matters* — lies the strength and the reality of the young adult book.

From *The Horn Book* for April 1974

WHEN THE MAGIC HAS TO STOP

By JANET McNEILL

THERE COMES A DAY when conversations with play-things and domestic animals fail to satisfy, and the magic in the storybook is discovered to have been nothing more than a conjurer's box of tricks. The child reader who has romped elbow deep in fantasy now rebels against the demands that are being made on his credulity. He may do all this the more vigor-ously because he feels that a kind of deception has been practiced on him. He was happy enough to be deceived for a time — even to collaborate in the deception — but now he has grown too old for it. He applies the brakes to his imagination all the harder be-cause his imagination has been allowed to have such a free rein. He may come back to the world of fantasy in later life and realize its value — it is like the world of the old photograph album in which reality and unreality, past and present, compete with each other to establish truth, and we can return to it again and again, and still experience the same fascination and renewal. But in the meantime, for the child reader, the magic has to stop.

There is no specific age at which the animals hold their tongues and enchantment pales and becomes silly. Each child makes the discovery in his own time, sometimes indignantly, sometimes with sorrow. There are children to whom animals never spoke and for whom no spell ever worked. But the child who has en-joyed these things and who now discovers that the pleasure is over makes the discovery because he is living less and less within the four walls of his own identity. He is stretching out with crit-ical curiosity towards the other people in his world. He is devel-oping a sense of society and of his own position within it. Liking and disliking other people has become important and interesting. The growing child is forming relationships with his fellow chil-dren and has probably learned to weather some personal criticism within the family circle and in the junior cloakroom. He reacts most strongly to his contemporaries; adults still fall into defined categories — Parents, Aunts and Uncles and Grandparents, Peo-ple in the Shops, Teachers, Policemen — all firmly typecast by their nature and function.

What sort of reading can a child look for when he has come to this stage? A critic of children's books recently wrote that once magic and talking animals had been discredited there was little of sufficient dramatic content in a child's daily life to make good material for a realistic story. Is this, I wonder, why so often the plastic characters of the highly colored adventure-story take over from the cardboard fairies? Sometimes the characters in such stories are children, but children neatly stripped of adults, operating within the scope of their own age group. More often, the characters may appear to be adult, but they are, in fact, no more than manikins, without any depth of character; they are just targets for the custard pie, victims for the lurking banana skin. "Ouch!" and "Wow!" make up most of their conversation. This isn't surprising; how could they find breath to say anything else? For in writing of this kind, something is always happening: Cliff top succeeds cliff top, one catastrophe breeds another, and chase follows chase. Provided Goodies and Baddies are instantly distinguishable, there is sufficient entertainment at least to keep the pages turning and the child's mind ticking over, in the same way chewing gum engages his jaws.

Surely this isn't enough. Can't writers do better than this for the child reader who has laid down his fairy story? Science fiction has certainly tried to do more. Its enormous popularity is due partly to the brave army of very skillful and ingenious writers that it attracts and partly to the fact that its mechanics, behind the dead-pan presentation, demand a degree of the "willing suspension of disbelief," which a child recently weaned from fantasy may still be eager to offer.

Perhaps the idiom of the science-fiction story is about to supersede completely the idiom of the fairy story. Perhaps flying saucers are the logical descendants of fairies, and death rays only an extension of the magic that once bristled from the tips of the witch's fingers. Perhaps the future will vindicate the most improbable flights of science fiction by demonstrating that it has all come true. We can only speculate. But meanwhile, can't we offer the child reader a book which will be of more interest and value to him as he grows up? Can't we present in more depth a picture of the world he knows? Involvement and identification are of great importance to the reading child, and in the sensational adventure story and in science fiction these can only be of a limited and unrewarding kind. He will discover nothing about himself in such reading, nothing about the nature of his immediate society and his relationship to it.

The child is now on the edge of the adult world, and he is naturally curious about it, though he may not admit this fact to himself. Not every child likes to consider adults as real people, and he may develop his own defense against any attempt to make him do so. He often succeeds in this through his natural genius for caricature, for the candid eye of a child makes him a ready and able caricaturist. He can always discover in an adult's appearance, speech, attitudes, mannerisms, enough to make an adult odd, exceptional, "funny"; and if he can do this, the child is absolved from taking the comical adult seriously. How many schoolboys enjoy the light-hearted cruelty they inflict on the master they call by the nickname they have given him, the nickname which excuses them from considering that any of their conduct would hurt him? "Piano Toes" has a funny face and a collection of affectations, some of them highly entertaining and pleasantly easy to imitate. There is no need to think that he may have feelings.

This defense against identification with adults is really a last-ditch Peter Pan attitude, a way of preserving the Us-Them classification for just as long as possible. If he can do this, the child is exempt from feeling pity or any other inconvenient response which might be forced on him, or from realizing that some day he too will grow up.

I was brought up in an Edwardian nursery, in a society where "God made them high or lowly, And ordered their estate." The function of adults, the distinction between adults and children was strongly emphasized. Being a child was a valid and recognized occupation. We came downstairs step by step from the nursery and put up our hair when we were ready to enter the drawing room. Today's child grows up more quickly and in much closer contact with his parents; he shares the occasions of daily life with them. Today's houses are seldom large enough to contain nurseries; the toys must be spread out round the legs of the grownups. Surely it would be of value to the growing child to learn from the books he reads that adults are human beings — that they are, in fact, an extension of himself.

It may be argued that today's child also shares his living quarters with the television set and so learns much more about adult life and its strains and tensions than a nursery-reared child ever knew. Certainly, there has been a great deal of discussion about the suitability of many adult television programs for the child-viewer. From much of what is offered by the small screen, a visitor to this planet from outer space might deduce that crime was our motivation and violence our only form of action. Many television programs for children are undoubtedly excellent, but it must be admitted that children often have an opportunity to see a great deal that is unsuitable simply because it was never intended for them. This may confuse and mislead them. Characterization in dramatic writing is often raised to an unnatural pitch of emphasis, and the child who shares with his parents a story of adult life need not expect to understand those parents any better for having done so.

The adults in my childhood were established figures, possessing an infallibility and a reliability which were by turns irritating and consoling. "Because I say so" and "Because God made it" were the two standard replies to my persistent questions. I was reasonably content to let it go at that. The arrangement had the advantage of absolving me of all responsibility if things became awkward. Why worry? The Almighty or a Parent was in charge. Living as we were at a little distance from each other, we found these attitudes easy to maintain. The generation gap was accepted as one of the necessary facts of life. I remember the shock, the indignation with which I realized as I grew older that parents could be wrong, could be unhappy, could experience uncertainty. I felt they had no right to these weaknesses, they were my property, my grounds for excuse.

Today's children are encouraged to grow up earlier than we were, but the generation gap, instead of shrinking, has widened, has become a source of grievance from both shores. The parents complain that they can't retain the children's confidence as they had hoped to; the children are distressed because the old gods have fallen and now have little relevance although they still command some kind of affection and loyalty.

This is why today's child reader urgently needs a book in which adults and children act and react with each other. He needs a sympathetic picture of a society made up of more than one age group. He needs to learn that adults are people.

When I was writing *The Battle of St. George Without* (Little), I was handling a society where children and adults were packed closely into the flats and apartments and bed-sitting rooms which crammed the decrepit old houses of Dove Square from attic to basement. The children's lives and the lives of the adults were unavoidably tangled with each other, but the children were just

38

young enough to insist on maintaining the Them-Us distinction, even when they were living at such close quarters. As a result, some of my adult characters are caricatures: Dan-Boy, for instance, is never anything more than the standard Baddy; Ma Flint is the female Battle-ax; Shaky Frick is the eccentric old soldier type; Cousin Maudie's loud-mouthed dottiness is as easily identified as her richly dyed hair. But when I was dealing with Matt's Mother, with Miss Harrison, and in the last chapter perhaps even with the Bishop, I encouraged the children in my story to recognize the picture of a wholly rounded person. They understand and respond readily to Miss Harrison's loyalty to the broken-down church and her memories of its past glory. Matt is critical of his mother's anxiety about giving cause for offense to her neighbors, and dimly senses that this springs from her widowed loneliness. When in the last sentence the Bishop reaches to pull the bell rope, the hands of the children prickle in sympathy, and adults and children of Dove Square together share in the celebration of St. George's Day.

But when I came back to these children in the next book, *Goodbye, Dove Square* (Little), they were older. Matt, in his conflict between the loyalty he feels to Shaky Frick and his need to protect Madge and her mother from the Sinister Salesman, learns that responsibility can be painful and that sometimes there are two correct answers to one question. He learns that adults are fallible beings who engage his sympathy and perhaps his reluctant admiration. He can't laugh at Madge's dotty Cousin Maudie the way he used to laugh because he now knows her history and is forced unwillingly to see her as faintly heroic. When he goes with his mother to lay the Christmas wreath on the grave of his father, he has become mature enough to resent the way in which she has protected him from the experience of grief: She should have taught him how to mourn.

When I was writing *The Other People* (Little), I had for my chief character Kate, who was detached from people she knows — her only link being with the aunt who proves so different from the smart Hotel Manageress of Kate's imagination. The hotel is a tatty boarding house, the "other people" in it, with whom she becomes involved, teach her the importance of involvement. Contrasted with them is the lonely figure in the blind house whose unhappiness has excluded him from human contacts. Kate sees the Mad Hatter both as a figure of fun and as an adult who is inadequate to the demands life has made on him. The elderly couple, Mr. and Mrs. Tweedle, are comical and yet their close dependence on each other gives her some insight into the glory of love lasting into old age. And I hope that when the holiday was over and Kate went home to learn to live with her new stepfather, she was able to give him a readier welcome, because of her experiences at Sunny Bay.

There are, of course, many aspects of adult life for which a child is not ready. We must avoid forcing these on him; they would be half-digested and misunderstood, and our stories would be spoiled. But we can suggest to the child who has outgrown talking animals and magic that adults are people with the same mental and emotional equipment as his own, people who differ from him mainly because they have had to use that equipment for a longer time. If we do this, his involvement with the story will be richer, and he may find that he can now talk more readily to the adults whom he meets in his daily life.

We shall break his faith in the omniscience, the omnipotence, the invulnerability of grownups, but in his new understanding of them he may be steered to look for a faith, a source of strength that will be much more enduring than any of his lost magic.

From *The Horn Book* for August 1972

AN ELUSIVE BORDER

By John Rowe Townsend

IN 1924, as everyone knows who knows the *Horn Book*, Miss Mahony announced her intention "to blow the horn for fine books for boys and girls." In December 1973, Paul Heins, the present editor, asked: "Should one any longer speak of children's books, or should they be regarded as a somewhat late Victorian invention that is fast becoming superannuated?"

Mr. Heins, who was discussing Alan Garner's recent novel *Red Shift* (Macmillan), did not stay to answer his own question. Perhaps it was asked with tongue in cheek and did not require an answer. If there were a serious possibility that the reply might be, "No, one should no longer speak of children's books; yes, they are a late Victorian invention that is fast becoming superannuated," then the next question obviously would be: "Has not then the *Horn Book* outlived its reason for existence?" And it is clear, if only from the fact that it enters its second half-century in vigorous health and in strong demand, that the *Horn Book* is no mere empty survival. As long as there are children who read, and homes and schools and libraries where books are introduced to them, there must in some sense be children's books, regardless of whether they exist as a separate literary form or publishing category; and there must be a need for discussion of such books and guidance in their selection. It is, however, often difficult today, especially with fiction, to understand what a particular book is doing on the children's list.

Interestingly, the early numbers of the *Horn Book* do not contain, so far as I can see, any examination of what constitutes a book for children. This is not a serious omission. Sensible and busy people do not spend their time on questions of classification that are not actually giving them any trouble. Presumably to Miss Mahony and her colleagues in the early days, there was no great problem in distinguishing between children's and adult books; you could tell by looking at them. The question now heard so often — "Yes, but is it *really* a book for children?" — cannot have been a frequent one in 1924.

If Mr. Heins had had room in the two brief pages of his article to discuss his own question, I imagine that he would have distinguished between the literary and the organizational aspects of children's books. It can be argued that in literary terms there never has been any real distinction between imaginative literature for children and for adults; there is just imaginative literature. Critics are often inclined to take this view and to dismiss the organizational issues as not being their concern. And in a field where pragmatism reigns and standards are — to say the least — confused, there certainly is a place for literary purism. But the fact that children's books do form a separate category and have their own corner in the worlds of publishing, reviewing, and librarianship creates problems in itself, both literary and practical.

The most obvious and recurrent practical problem is that of drawing lines in individual cases. Should *Red Shift* (or *Jonathan Livingston Seagull* [Macmillan] or *Watership Down* [Macmillan]) be published on a children's list, reviewed among children's books, and bought by children's libraries? Are they children's or general fiction? Or both? Border skirmishes are inevitable where frontiers have to be drawn through a vague and shifting landscape. Admittedly, such disputes are not necessarily of much long-term importance. A first-rank book will find its place in the end, whatever that place may be.

But there are many good books of the second and third rank, and these are important; they form the plateau of achievement from which one hopes the highest peaks will rise. The existence of such children's books (and, latterly, of young adult books) raises other and more difficult questions. Do these books miss critical notice, or fail to reach their proper audience, by being confined in a pen labeled *children's* or *young adult*? Are authors impelled to write books which they should not really be writing or to write them in ways in which they should not really be written, because there is a publishing slot which they are expected to fill? Are there indeed authors who are refugees from the adult novel, taking advantage of the curious structure of the children's book world to get books published which, in fact, are of no great interest or value to children? Can reading children be detained too long in a literary world designed specially for them or adolescents be encouraged to encapsulate themselves in a self-absorbed preoccupation with current problems of adolescence rather than getting out into a wider world of literature where people of all ages and all times rub shoulders together?

These questions are unanswerable; they are not even all the same kind of question. But it is possible that by surveying that elusive border between children's and adult books one may find not answers, but vantage points from which possible answers may be glimpsed.

*

The late Victorian invention was not, I suspect, children's books but rather children's literature — the specialized concern of a number of adults in related professions. By that time, there had been children's books of one kind and another for centuries past, and there had been children's fiction for at least a hundred years. The instructive stories of the late-eighteenth and early-nineteenth centuries, the huge output that poured from tract societies and the like, the boys' adventure stories in endless series-of-six by Oliver Optic and lesser contemporaries, the disapproved material such as dime novels in America and penny dreadfuls in England add up to a great expenditure of paper and print on young people's behalf. And highly reputable authors had written or were writing consciously for children. The Alice books, *Tom Sawyer*, *Little Women*, and *Treasure Island* were produced by people who knew perfectly well that their potential audience was a young one. Borderline problems had already arisen: Mark Twain said in the preface to *Tom Sawyer* that "[a]lthough my book is intended mainly for the entertainment of boys and girls, I hope it will not be shunned by men and women on that account." *Huckleberry Finn* can be considered as a children's book, or it can be considered as the great American novel. *The Wide, Wide World*, the Elsie Dinsmore books, and Charlotte Yonge's *The Heir of Redclyffe* appealed to girls and women alike, and the heyday of the adventure novel for both boys and grownup boys was in the years before World War I.

But the children's book world, the children's literature industry, surely was the creation not of writers or publishers but of the band of American ladies in the late-nineteenth and early-twentieth centuries who built up library work with children and started a mission that was to extend itself into the educational and publishing fields: Miss Hewins, Miss Moore, Miss Jordan, and many other distinguished women. There were also the magazine editors, especially Mrs. Dodge of *St. Nicholas*, the early reviewers, and eventually the pioneer children's book editors —

Louise Seaman, Helen Dean Fish, May Massee. Miss Mahony's Bookshop for Boys and Girls and *The Horn Book Magazine* itself were part of this movement.

I share the respect with which these ladies are regarded. They saw things that needed to be done, and did them. I have said before, and firmly believe, that on balance the children's library has been a blessing to authors and publishers as well as to children and has made possible the writing and publication of many excellent books which otherwise could never have appeared. But it has undoubtedly resulted in an excessive degree of literary stratification. It has also resulted in the setting up of a machine that has to be fed and of an apparatus which has removed or at least distorted the usual workings of the law of supply and demand. For many years it has been possible for books to do well on the children's list which are not strikingly popular with children and which are ploddingly worthy rather than vital or perceptive.

For authors who can please editors, reviewers, and librarians, there has been a reasonable living — with an occasional bonanza (such as Title II) thrown in. Some have been attracted by the supposed ease or lucrativeness of writing for children; some have had the innocuous aim of doing a little good and earning an honest dollar at the same time. Not much need be said about either of these groups. But many highly-gifted authors have also been drawn, for a variety of reasons, into children's writing. Curiously, one of the most frequent reasons seems to be accident; somehow or other, without intending it or knowing exactly how it happened, the author finds himself or herself figuring in the children's list and obtaining creative satisfaction from writing children's books. When I was working on my collection of essays, *A Sense of Story*, I had contact with nineteen leading children's writers; and more than half of them told me, either in comments supplied for publication or in private correspondence, that they wrote primarily for themselves rather than for children. Their remarks were often illuminating. Paula Fox said:

I never think I'm writing for children, when I work. A story does not start *for* anyone, nor an idea, nor a feeling of an idea; but starts more for oneself. . . . What applies to good writing is, I think, absolute, whether for children or grown-ups, or the blind or the deaf or the thin or the fat. . . . I am just starting another children's book and another novel — and I hope I shall remember which is which.

44

Madeleine L'Engle:

I write because I am stuck with being a writer. This is what I am. It is the premise on which my whole life is built.

Scott O'Dell:

Books of mine which are classified officially as books for children were not written *for* children [but] . . . were written consistently in the emotional area that children share with adults.
This area is much wider and much deeper than commonly it is supposed to be.*

These three, and many other leading English-language children's writers, have written adult books as well; and I know of none who regards children's books as a soft option, or who would be content with a lower standard when writing for children than when writing for adults. Indeed, I can think of several whose books for children are undoubtedly their best.

Clearly, to writers of this caliber the distinction between children's and adult books is of no great importance. The difference, perhaps, is that when writing for the children's list the author will attempt to make his books accessible to children; whereas in books for adults, he will not be confined by the child's limited experience of life and of other literature. There may well be a tendency among such writers, and even more so among able writers who for one reason or another do not figure in an adult list, to stretch the conventional bounds of the children's book quite unconsciously in the normal course of stretching their own imagination.

Editors, who do not wish to cramp their writers and, indeed, do not like to be cramped in their own creative role of editorship, are inclined, I think, to abet this tendency. Together, authors and editors give meaning to Mr. Heins's comment that "the dividing lines between children's books and adult books have grown more and more faint." It could be said that the movement for quality in children's books is the victim, or the beneficiary (according to taste), of its own success: It has encouraged creative writing for the children's list, but the creative writers have followed the irresistible urge of the creative person to go his own way, wherever it takes him.

Yet, although the dividing lines grow fainter, they still exist

*Quotes from *A Sense of Story* by John Rowe Townsend. Copyright © 1971 by John Rowe Townsend. Reprinted by permission of J. B. Lippincott Company.

and give rise to problems and anomalies. Some books which should appeal to the general reader remain little known because they appeared on the children's list. Russell Hoban's fantasy, *The Mouse and His Child* (Harper), about the pair of linked toys in search of love, security, and "self-winding," seems to me and to many other commentators to have the qualities of a classic. But although there is plenty in it to appeal to children at their own level, it needs an adult reader to appreciate much of its pathos and satire; and the book is not well-known among adults. Leon Garfield's novels, surely, are general fiction; he has said himself that he tries to write "that old-fashioned thing the family novel, accessible to the twelve-year-old and readable by his elders." Perhaps now that his latest book, *The Sound of Coaches* (Viking), has become a Literary Guild alternative choice, he will become known to a broader adult public.

Alan Garner's case is less straightforward. Garner has followed his own line of development, which appears to have taken him steadily away from children's books and into forms of the novel which are difficult for readers of any age. Yet his work has remained on the children's lists. Discussing *The Owl Service* (Walck), Eleanor Cameron suggested that in tailoring his work to a teenage audience and determining the members of his eternal triangle to be immature teenagers, Garner had "debilitated" his material. This is a serious charge, involving the integrity of the book. I am not at all sure that it is justified; but, moving from the particular to the general, I see the charge as indicating the clear possibility that a writer could invalidate his work (perhaps unconsciously) by distorting it to fit the needs of the list he was writing for. Garner's newest book, *Red Shift*, does not make any concessions to a young readership; and his British publishers said frankly that they had published it on the children's list mainly because it was through his other books on this list that Garner's reputation and power as a novelist had grown. The decision is understandable; nevertheless, Garner's position on the children's list seems an uneasy one.

William Mayne, writer of many undoubted children's books, caused qualms with his psycho-fantasy *A Game of Dark* (Dutton). Here again the knowledge and experience required for an adequate reading are more than can reasonably be expected of children. The book is valid in its own terms, and, indeed, is a remarkable one; but it appears to be misplaced; and its inclusion

46

on the children's list may have caused it to miss most of its proper (adult) readership.

Appearance on a children's list has not, of course, always prevented books from achieving a wider audience. Among recent examples, Ursula Le Guin's Earthsea books have been extraordinarily successful with adults, both in America and Britain. But then, any book that has, in addition to substantial merit, the mysterious literary equivalent of "star quality" or the potentiality for becoming a cult will rise to fame — as Richard Adams' *Watership Down* has demonstrated.

An illustration of the twists and turns of the elusive border with which I am concerned is provided by the American publication of *Red Shift* and *Watership Down* by Macmillan. *Watership Down*, which to my knowledge has been enjoyed by a great many children, appears on the general trade list; *Red Shift*, with little or nothing in it for children and for most teenagers, is on the children's list. At first sight, a reversal of this position would seem more reasonable. But Susan Hirschman, the head of Macmillan's children's book department, has explained to me:

This department published Alan Garner's RED SHIFT and so it was published on a children's list. We sent review copies to adult reviewers and, because this country's librarians are so stratified, we sent the book to young adult collections for review rather than to straight children divisions. The book was not reviewed in the New York Times or Publishers Weekly as a children's book but was reviewed on the regular adult pages. Nonetheless, the sponsoring department was this one.

In the case of WATERSHIP DOWN, the book was, as you know, bought by me with every expectation of publishing on this list. In September, however, the president of an adult paperback reprint house saw it, read it, and made a substantial offer for it. The book assumed "bestseller" potential and it seemed only fair to the author and everyone else concerned to have it published on the general trade list where it could be given the broadest possible exposure.

I suppose in both these cases what we had was a *book*, not a children's book and not an adult book but simply a book. Or in this instance, two books. The sponsoring department in each case was the one who, in our opinion, would do the most for the book and help it to achieve its fullest potential. Really, the fact of one department being a children's book department and other being an adult department was almost incidental.

47

This is sound common sense; but it indicates the difficulty of dealing with work that does not fit into the conventional pigeonholes.

In Britain, as in America, some publications reviewed *Red Shift* on the adult pages by conscious decision; but, in at least one recent case, a children's book has been reviewed among adult novels by sheer accident. This was Penelope Farmer's *A Castle of Bone* (Atheneum), published in England with a somewhat adult-looking jacket and sent by the (ex-Manchester) *Guardian* to a reviewer of novels, who took it, as it came, along with adult books. It was well able to hold its own in this company — as, indeed, I would expect a good modern children's book to do.

The books referred to in the present article have been mostly borderline cases because of complexity, emotional subtlety, or requirements of knowledge and experience which make it doubtful whether children can appreciate them sufficiently. But a far greater number of books are well within the bounds of children's literature, in that they are undoubtedly readable by children; yet they make the border seem a regrettable irrelevancy. They are good books by any standard; they would be enjoyed by grownups, if grownups knew about them. And the more ground that can be shared by adults and children, the better.

I do not know of any simple solution to the problem of the books that are unduly confined by their inclusion in the children's list. But perhaps some answers are beginning to emerge of their own accord. It is evident in Britain just now that many parents and teachers are discovering with surprise that there are children's books which are worthy of their own attention; and news about books tends to get around. Increasingly, there are signs in both countries that publishers and librarians are heading towards a liberal and highly desirable policy: If there's something in a book for adults as well as for children, why not offer it to both? In England, the same paperback publisher issued *The God Beneath the Sea* (Pantheon), by Leon Garfield and Edward Blishen, on its children's and adult lists at the same time — with covers that differed only in color. In America it is not uncommon for children's books (especially, I think, fantasy and science fiction) to appear on general sale in soft covers. This is excellent. It would help if suitable new books could not only be published on both lists but reviewed among children's and adult books in the same media; but that would amount to preferential treatment and is rather a lot to expect when review space is so limited.

*

The most obvious, but not the most interesting, border question arises at the meeting ground of the adult and young adult novel. The growth of young adult lists supports, I think, my belief that the creation of a category will be followed by the production of material to fill it. In England, which has been slower than America to accept a further subdivision of humanity, there have been hardly any young adult novels until very recently. Authors and publishers appeared to believe that people suddenly grew overnight from children to adults somewhere around their fourteenth birthday. There was little effort to deal with themes that are of perennial interest to teenagers: striking out new kinds of relationship, discovering who you are and what you might become. On the other hand, in America it was perhaps too readily accepted that "teenagers today want to read about teenagers today."* At one time, there was a rush of writers whom I described as "aunts in miniskirts," eager to write about sex, drugs, mental illness, strife with parents, unmarried motherhood, abortion, and other such matters as were considered up-to-date and relevant. (I remember thinking how refreshing it would be to read a book about young people who enjoyed life, did well in school, had happy relationships with their parents, and neither became nor made anybody pregnant. But fictionally, I suppose, that would be a dull life).

It seems to me that the border here remains clear, because most young adult books don't really cross any frontiers. They would not qualify for publication on the general list; they simply are not very interesting to anyone who is not actually passing through the phases they describe. There is no reason, of course, why they shouldn't be interesting. Some of the books by such writers as Paul Zindel, Barbara Wersba, John Donovan, and Isabelle Holland could well be regarded as general fiction: not because they are controversial or daring, but because they deal sensitively with enduring truths of human nature. They pass the tests that would be valid for distinguishing good fiction of any kind anywhere.

*S. E. Hinton "Teen-Agers Are for Real," *The New York Times Book Review*, August 27, 1967.

On the whole, however, this is very much a field of the concocted book, designed to exploit a market and/or to force home some basically trite message or assertion of values. A useful test for the routine young adult book, as for the routine children's book, is whether it lends itself to the easy extraction of some "developmental value." If you can assign it a simple function in helping a young person achieve adaptability, consideration for others, democratic understanding, devotion to a cause, adjustment to parental divorce or remarriage, concern for the environment, the surmounting of personal handicaps, improvement of intercultural relationships, or any of 57 other desiderata, then you are almost certainly finding the book to be didactic in aim and essentially a children's book, nowhere near general literature. All right, so the author can use four-letter words and describe goings-on that would have surprised (but not daunted) the pioneers of library work with children; but the old beaten instructional path is still being followed; and when the immediate relevancy has faded, the book will die. And when that time comes, Charlotte and Wilbur, Winnie the Pooh, Mole and Rat and Toad will still be wandering happily across all borders; they are infinitely more a part of general literature than a disturbed, bisexual, smack-shooting dropout in a taboo-busting, young adult novel.

From *The Horn Book* for October 1974

WHERE DO ALL THE PRIZES GO?
The Case for Nonfiction

By MILTON MELTZER

EVERY YEAR SINCE 1922 the Newbery Medal has been awarded to an author for "the most distinguished contribution to American literature for children." Of the fifty-three Newbery winners to date, how many have been nonfiction? Only five: Hendrik Van Loon's *Story of Mankind* (Liveright), the very first, in 1922; Cornelia Meigs' *Invincible Louisa* (Little), 1934; James Daugherty's *Daniel Boone* (Viking), 1940; Elizabeth Yates' *Amos Fortune, Free Man* (Dutton), 1951; and Jean Latham's *Carry On, Mr. Bowditch* (Houghton), 1956.

What about the Boston Globe-Horn Book Awards or the National Book Award for children's literature? Is the picture different? No. Nor is it different for most of the other children's book prizes designed to honor the best literary work. The laurels crown the storytellers. Librarians, teachers, reviewers — the three groups who usually administer the awards or serve as judges — seem confident that only fiction can be considered literature. But what is Henry David Thoreau's *Walden*? What is James Boswell's *Life of Samuel Johnson*? What is Tom Paine's *Common Sense*? Not one of them literature? All merely nonfiction?

Let's go to the dictionary. "Literature," says the one at my elbow, "is writing in which expression or form, in connection with ideas of permanent and universal interest, are characteristic or essential features — such as poetry, fiction, history, biography, essay." What about art? Can such works as those I have named be considered artistic? To the dictionary again: it defines art as "the quality, production or expression of what is beautiful, appealing, or of more than ordinary significance." Does Thoreau's *Walden* satisfy that? Literary art has, I think, two related aspects: the subject and the means the writer uses to convey his ideas — the craft. The craft is the making, shaping, forming, selecting. And what the reader gets from the exercise of the writer's craft upon a subject is an experience. If the subject is significant, and the artist is up to it, then the book can enlarge, it can deepen, it can intensify the reader's experience of life.

Imagination, invention, selection, language, form — these are just as important to the making of a good book of biography, history, or science as to the making of a piece of fiction. Yet in Sheila Egoff's collection of pieces on children's literature, *Only Connect* (Oxford), there is barely a reference to nonfiction. Nor, using that catchall definition of literature as "the best that has been thought and written," does Egoff herself ever mention nonfiction in her book. Of the contributors, only two refer to nonfiction, each mentioning but one example they consider to be of literary value. John Rowe Townsend, the British critic, ignores nonfiction entirely in his piece. Perhaps the fact that he writes children's novels explains his bias.

I looked again at Isabelle Jan's recent book, *On Children's Literature* (Schocken). She deals primarily with French and English literature but talks, too, about the writers of many countries. And again, nothing about nonfiction. Yet at the very end of her closing chapter, she has this to say:

Why indeed should a certain form of artistic expression be judged superior to another, considered to be the only one worthy of being called "literature," and established as the norm, when all that really counts is that human expression should have the widest possible range, no matter from where it springs or what form it adopts? What is important is man's ability to create.

I agree. Then why, I wonder, did she exclude nonfiction from her own book?

Lillian Smith in *The Unreluctant Years* (ALA) devotes one chapter of the book to nonfiction, but I find I disagree with her argument. She says the difference between a book of knowledge and a story book is one of intention. In the former, the writer tries to impart knowledge; in the latter, he has a story to tell. And this is where I think she goes wrong: "In the telling of a story the author's whole mind and heart are necessarily engaged and his preoccupation is with the art of literature. This can only be a secondary consideration with the writer of an informational book. His interest must center in the special field of knowledge he is to present." She concludes that informational books are for this reason "infrequently literature and seldom do they survive the generation for which they are written." But I say that the best writers of nonfiction put their hearts and minds into their work. Their concern is not only with what they have to say but with how they say it. Lillian Smith, like so many others, is guilty of bearing in mind only the finest writers of fiction when she discusses children's literature and thinking only of run-of-the-mill writers when she discusses information books. She compares the rare few — the best — in fiction with the hacks in nonfiction. But there are as many stories as there are works of nonfiction which deserve to be promptly forgotten. In both cases no art is exercised, nor does the writer put his whole heart and mind into the book. Or if he does, it is a second-rate mind and an unfeeling heart.

Even more lamely, Lillian Smith goes on to say that there are three ways of writing informational books for children. One way is to present facts; a second is to present facts and interpret them; and a third is to do both and create literature at the same time. I can hardly accept this separation, as though literary quality were applied like a coat of paint.

Nonfiction — the very name, as Aidan Chambers points out, is so "curiously negative and off-putting." While it has not been completely ignored, he goes on, nonfiction "does get brushed off and pushed to the back . . . as though information books were socially inferior to the upper-crust stuff we call literature." The doyens of children's literature, he complains, have narrowed its meaning to encompass only stories, poems, and plays — "the holy three" he calls them. "We'd do better by children, and ourselves if we revised its accepted definition to include all that is published . . . . every book, no matter what its content and purpose, deserves and demands the respect and treatment — the skill and care — of art."

But I can think of only a few critics who have given serious attention to nonfiction. One is England's Margery Fisher. In her own review journal, *Growing Point*, she has always discussed both nonfiction and fiction with the same care and acuteness of vision. Three years ago she published a five-hundred-page evaluation of nonfiction called *Matters of Fact* (Crowell). As writer and occasional reviewer, I find it as useful and stimulating as her monthly magazine. What I like especially about Fisher is that she does not treat each new book — whether it be science fiction, a life of Lincoln, or a study of cowboys — as though nothing had ever been written on the subject before. She constantly compares and evaluates, drawing upon her knowledge of the whole body of children's literature. Often Fisher summons up works long past to inform us that something better is available. I treasure her critical essays on books grouped by theme or genre not only for the specific assessment of each title but for the general principles to be deduced from the comparative analysis. In her introduction to *Matters of Fact*, the author points out that "the writers of non-fiction for children are not universally thought of as writers in the same way as authors of junior novels. . . . Because of an unexpressed feeling that information books are not 'creative,' they are far more often reviewed for their content than for their total literary value."

Happily, Zena Sutherland is not that kind of reviewer. Like Margery Fisher, she does all the reviewing for the magazine she edits, the *Bulletin of the Center for Children's Books*. She believes, she says, that some nonfiction books *"are* read for pleasure and *do* teach without drudgery." In her essay Sutherland insists that "[g]ood literary style, often erroneously attributed only to works of fiction, can and does exist in nonfiction." She praises some books for "the flow and cadence of language, the distinctive way in which an author uses words and phrases. Such grace may be more often found in fiction, but no reader who has savored the lyric prose of Victor Scheffer in *Little Calf* (Scribner's, 1970) or the dry humor of Edwin Tunis in *Chipmunks on the Doorstep* (Crowell, 1971) can deny that an informational book can be enjoyed for its style. No reader who has enjoyed the lucidity and vigor of Issac Asimov's science books or Alfred Duggan's rare combination of erudtion and wit can deny that nonfiction can be creative."

Reader, yes, but reviewer? Rarely. I have heard the children's book editor of *The New York Times Book Review* dismiss works of nonfiction categorically as "non-books." Perhaps he was irritated by the assembly-line information books some publishers have unloaded on schools and libraries. Such mass-produced books are often perfunctory, tasteless, and unreadable, although as a feeble defense it is said they fill an educational need. The book review editor cannot conceive of such books making any contribution to literature. But in his distaste he has gone to the extreme of rarely opening his pages to the discussion of nonfiction for children, although he does take picture books and novels quite seriously.

The *Saturday Review* for the past two years has been limiting itself to two seasonal roundups of children's books, choosing only a small, favored fraction of the total number published.

William Cole's spring and fall pieces touch lightly on books for the three-to-eight and the eight-to-eleven age groups, omitting books for the older child. Nonfiction is included, but like everything else in his grab-bag, individual titles are lucky to get more than a sentence.

In the specialized children's review media there is a better balance between space given to fiction and nonfiction. The *Horn Book* issues I have tested show a two-to-one ratio — that is, picture books and fiction taken together receive twice the space of nonfiction. But often more than twenty novels are reviewed while only one biography or one history book is singled out for attention. Science books are treated in intelligent roundups, with helpful comparisons drawn. If space is at a premium, why not try this method sometimes with history or biography?

In all media, the reviewer of nonfiction most of the time limits himself to asking how much information the book contains. And how accurate or up-to-date it is. Infrequently a reviewer will compare the book with others on the same subject, but only as to factual content. Rarely will he ask what more there is to the book than the mere facts. I would want to ask how well it is organized. What principle of selection animated the writer; what is the writer's point of view; does the writer acknowledge other opinions of value? And then, beyond all this, what literary distinction, if any, does the book have? And here I do not mean the striking choice of word or image but the personal style revealed. I ask whether the writer's personal voice is heard in the book. In the writer who cares, there is a pressure of feeling which emerges in the rhythm of the sentences, in the choice of details, in the color of the language. Style in this sense is not a trick of rhetoric or a decorative daub; it is a quality of vision. It cannot be separated from the author's character because the tone of voice in which the book is written expresses how a human being thinks and feels. If the writer is indifferent, bored, stupid, or mechanical, it will show in the work. The kind of man or woman the writer is — this is what counts. Style in any art is both form and content; they are woven together. The historian Peter Gay, who cares enough about this question to give a whole book to style in history, shows how in all the classic historians — Gibbon, Burckhardt, Macaulay, Ranke — "style shapes, and in turn is shaped by substance."

To go back to one of my prize examples, Thoreau. What

literary work is more crammed with factual substance than his? His interest in the particular and the minute informs many of his best pages. But there was something more than facts which he wished to set down:

> Facts should only be as the frame to my pictures; they should be material to the mythology which I am writing; not facts to assist men to make money, farmers to farm profitably, in any common sense; facts to tell who I am, and where I have been or what I have thought: as now the bell rings for evening meeting, and its volumes of sound, like smoke which rises from where a cannon is fired, make the tent in which I dwell. My facts shall be falsehoods to the common sense. I would so state facts that they shall be significant, shall be myths or mythologic. Facts which the mind perceived, thoughts which the body thought, — with these I deal.

Please don't misunderstand me; I make no claim that every piece of nonfiction written for children — or adults, for that matter — has literary merit. Only a few. A great many books are only mediocre, and a number of them should never have been published. But the same is true of novels. Who will remember ninety percent of them five years later? One year? Tomorrow? Still, to go back to the Newbery Awards, I would guess that some of the novels given the prize in the past might easily have been matched or surpassed in literary quality by works of nonfiction, if only the judges had not swallowed the nonsense that fiction alone can be literature.

If one goes by the outcome of the work done each year by the Newbery Award committees, one can only conclude that fiction is everything to them. Nonfiction must be given short shrift in their discussions. What can one do to help them realize that nonfiction can have more literary value than a Sears Roebuck catalog or the telephone directory?

But I have found one judge who has the courage to publish her opinions and confess to her prejudices. It is the children's novelist, Jane Langton, who told all in *Publishers Weekly*. Langton once served as one of the two judges for the Book World Children's Spring Book Festival Awards. Her three-page article deals honestly with the problems of the judge drowned in scores of entries. She was dead certain she could tell a good novel from a bad novel without any academic set of standards to go by. One sniff, and she knew. But she was all at sea in judging the nonfiction entries. Finally, after much rummaging through the stacks of books and thinking about her responses, some standards emerged for the nonfiction. To be in the running a book had to "exude some kind of passion or love or caring." If the author didn't care, why should the judge? The book had to have literary quality. She, the judge, had to like it; and she had to feel that the book could make a mark on the young person reading it, change him or her in some way. Which meant, as well, that the young reader, too, had to like it.

Good! Those standards appeal to me. But what happened when it came time to apply them? Langton and the other judge conferred feverishly by mail and phone in order to arrive at the final list of five. In the last moment over the phone, Langton said, "Now don't you think we've got to have at least *one* nonfiction book? What about . . ." and she named one title. "Yes," said the other judge, "I think that's the best one." So that's how winners are made.

Was it fair? Langton asked that herself. No, she answered; they chose only one book of nonfiction among the five winners out of "sheer naked prejudice and personal bias in favor of fiction." Recognizing that bias, that prejudice, which I have tried to demonstrate is almost universal, Langton urges that fiction and nonfiction should be given separate awards and judged by separate judges. What do you think?

From *The Horn Book* for February 1976

III

STANDARDS

It will have become obvious by now that the various sections of this book are not locked into topics. Unavoidably, there is a certain amount of overlapping; and in discussions about standards one is apt to meet statements about subjects already dealt with, such as status or classification. Similarly, themes appearing later in the book will also have been anticipated or touched upon in earlier sections. This kind of overlapping or — even better — interweaving is both natural and good, because it indicates the necessity for the recognition and the correlation of the elements constantly cropping up in any consideration of children's literature.

Standards may be approached from many points of view. Ivan Southall deals with the subject personally — one might say ethically and emotionally — and emphasizes the sources of an author's integrity and growth. John Rowe Townsend makes the point that "children's books need to be appraised with coolness and detachment, simple enthusiasm being little better than simple unawareness." Paul Heins's two essays explore the diverse facets of the criticism of children's literature and will, it is hoped, supply an overall pattern for many of the topics considered in this book. Ethel Heins's "Literature Bedeviled" is an example of the application of critical standards to the methods used in adapting children's literature to audiovisual forms.

DEPTH AND DIRECTION

By IVAN SOUTHALL

IT IS NOT the "done thing" for authors to write critical appreciations of their own work — perhaps in barren times a point to be mourned! But one person only can trace with ultimate insight the evolution of a particular writer's work, and that is the writer himself. Such an exercise may clarify a few of his own thoughts and may be of interest to others.

The capacity for detached self-examination comes early to some. To me it came late, perhaps not in relation to actual years lived, but I started writing at the age of twelve and paused scarcely ever afterward. A significant self-appraisal at an earlier date might have been profitable.

From way back, my nonfiction books for adults had never lacked critical attention, but my annual imaginative offerings for children, once the critics became *seriously* aware of them, were equated I used to feel with cyanide — calamitous in small doses and fatal in bulk.

I was moved by this criticism to periods of pained bewilderment. My books were wholesome, swashbuckling adventure stories, firmly in the tradition of the Sunday-school prizes I had admired most as a boy. One or two loyal critics, affectionately intentioned, grouped me with respected names of the past and from this I took comfort (rereading the operative clauses a hundred times), until the significance began slowly to sink in. My books were not advancing; they were consolidating a type of world that modern man had to outgrow. No critic told me this, except inversely; I had to discover it and believe it for myself. A few things more I had to discover and believe: that writing for children was not a second string to the bow, not a rest between more important matters, not a release from the responsibility for truth, not an excuse for mediocrity however honest, but an exhausting, if exhilarating, demand upon heart, talent, and self.

American children met me for the first time with the New York edition of *Hills End* in 1963. Australian children had known me since *Meet Simon Black* in 1950.

Meet Simon Black I wrote as a schoolboy of fourteen back in 1935, then waited fifteen years to see a much-revised version in

60

print. I have not been brave enough to open it for a very long time, and I regard it, even firmly shut, with dismay.

In that first book about my superhero — and in the eight that followed it — probability was the victim. Onto Simon were grafted all the best things of my wartime service in the Royal Australian Air Force and a few of the lesser things I was not perceptive enough to discern. I suppose he was a form of propaganda, ingenuously committed, dedicated to the proposition that decorated former officers, particularly of the R.A.A.F., were the hope of the world.

Simon possessed in incredible measure virtue, honor, righteous anger, courage, and inventiveness. Every incredible difficulty he cheerfully overcame with dignity, grandeur, and a very stiff upper lip. To each book I gave my conscientious best, but collectively these books were limiting the development not only of the reader, but of the writer. Their artificial morality was in fact touching everything else I wrote, and I have sometimes wondered whether their denouement came with the forgetful chairman who introduced me to an audience as Squadron Leader Simon Black.

I woke up one morning in 1960, thirty-nine years of age, determined never to write another book for children. The dear little darlings could go jump in the lake. The thought of producing one more word about my superhero was more than I could stomach. The sense of relief, of escape, of freedom was bliss indeed.

At the time, I was considering a theme for a novel. I had never written a novel and had never pretended to be a creative writer in the strictest sense, but I was faced with a time delay before I could start in earnest my next documentary, which was to take me to the Woomera Rocket Range; and Woomera was not ready to receive me. As doubtfully endowed as I felt my talent for literary experiment to be, the theme for the novel began to look seriously like a vehicle of the most ordinary kind for children. But, I had, after all, sworn off children's books and with my Simon Black mentality had never peopled any book with flesh-and-blood average folk, adults *or* children. For children, I had produced superheroes; for adults, giants, all larger than life. If a subject had failed to attain heroic proportions he had failed also to hold my professional interest.

Now, for the first time, I found myself looking at my own children and their friends growing up round about me. In their lives interacting one upon the other at an unknown depth, I began to suspect with genuine astonishment that here lay an unlimited source of raw material far more exciting than the theme itself. This there came a positive moment of decision for me.

Hills End, one of the most exciting adventures of my life, physical or mental, poured out from first word to last in six weeks, a fraction of the time I had devoted to anything else. Six to twelve months was the usual run. *Hills End* did not stick to plan and veered far from the predetermined plot; the characters dominated and directed its course. It surprised my fondly respected Australian publishers, not favorably at first. I had to defend it with spirit, and for various reasons publication was delayed for two years. This interminable time convinced me they were printing it only to please me, and discouragement sent me off in other directions. Not until June, 1964, was I free to look seriously at the surprising fact that *Hills End* possessed merit discernable to others and might indicate an area I should examine again.

Would it be possible to recapture a mood that lay four years astern? Chasing moods was a luxury for amateurs of private means; professionals had to live with creditors. Despite books that enjoyed success by the standards of Australia — a country of immense distances but few people — I remained solvent by less than a whisker and could not expend work time without certainty of income. But it was also a time of weary revolt against the complications of years of documentary writing. Truth had become a will-o'-the-wisp and worn me thin in its pursuit. Longing to be free of nervous people perpetually changing their minds, to be answerable to no one but myself, I made my decision.

It was a dour and disappointing period. The first book to come out of it the publishers called a disaster, and they were right. The second I abandoned halfway and I concluded, glumly, that it had cost me six valuable months to learn that *Hills End* had been an accident and was not to happen again. So it was back to nonfiction, and quickly, or we would be out on the street; but I had nothing planned except a half-baked conception of a possible documentation of the great bushfires of 1962 that had come close to wiping out my particular part of the world. I had witnessed that dreadful event, and the background material I lacked would be readily obtainable.

There was a touch of desperation in me, a feeling that through recklessness I had lost a frail security hard won from seventeen years as an independent writer. The decision to go ahead was a hurried one, and in the same hour I started thinking back to those days of fear as they had affected my own children. In a few tense moments of reflection something happened. It was not the birth of *Hamlet*, but for me it was a suspicion that destiny was only a paragraph away.

Ash Road came, as *Hills End* had come, clearly with elation, filled with the excitement of discovering the minds of children and of finding a degree of involvement worth every moment of the months of search. I felt that I had become a child again, that I was writing *out* of my own childhood, and that the standards of maturity were necessary only as a filter of the most superficial kind. *Ash Road* was a raising-up, not a writing-down. It was an appreciation of the vivid color of childhood, of its heightened reality, of the tensions, impressions, perceptions, toughness and anxieties that the adult forgets and dismisses as ultimately unimportant. Heaven forbid that I should imply that these qualities infuse the book, but they were *my* reward, *my* dividends.

There was also the discovery that truth is more purely expressed through the medium of fiction than it is in works allegedly of fact. A critical discovery, far from unique or profound, but something that each writer must learn from life for himself. Writing had always been a fulfillment, but never before, except with *Hills End*, in this particular way.

Hills End, I suppose, was a diversion; but *Ash Road* was the conscious if imperfect beginning of a different professional and private life.

Truth is not the how, but the why; not the deed, but the motive. Froth and bubble is the substance of so many children's books: plot without character, action without reason — meat for some children, starvation for others, but growth for none.

Truth, in relation to books for children, carries the writer past the point where stories usually stop. This vast territory full of thorns and pits I see as reality, and it is where I have come to find myself, not by intention, nor I suppose by chance, but by accepting from my own experience that the real adventures of childhood, as of maturity, are in the wonderland of the mind. My journey of discovery has scarcely begun. I am bound to make mistakes of depth and direction, but, pray God, not too many.

From *The Horn Book* for June 1968

IN LITERARY TERMS*

By John Rowe Townsend

SURVEYS OF CHILDREN'S BOOKS are numerous, and so are aids to book selection, but discussion at any length of the work of individual contemporary writers is scarce. Such discussion may be thought unnecessary. I know from conversations over a period of years that there are intelligent and even bookish people to whom children's literature, by definition, is a childish thing which adults have put away. Such people may have a personal or professional interest — it is useful to have some ideas on what books to give to their children or to read to a class — but they do not pretend to be interested on their own account, and regard such an interest as an oddity, an amiable weakness. It is not my intention to quarrel with them. We cannot all be interested in everything.

Yet, children are part of mankind and children's books are part of literature, and any line which is drawn to confine children or their books to their own special corner is an artificial one. Wherever the line is drawn, children and adults and books will all wander across it. Long ago *Robinson Crusoe* and *Gulliver's Travels* were adopted as children's stories. Adults have taken over *Huckleberry Finn,* argue about *Alice,* and probably enjoy *The Wind in the Willows* as much as their children do. Dickens and other Victorian novelists wrote books for the whole family; Stevenson and Rider Haggard and John Buchan and Anthony Hope wrote for boys and grown-up boys alike; and it can be offered as a pseudo-Euclidean proposition that any line drawn between books for adults and books for children must pass through the middle of Kipling.

Arbitrary though it is, the division has become sharper in the present century. The main reasons have been the expansion of school and public libraries for children, and corresponding changes in the book trade. On the whole, I believe that the children's library has been a blessing to authors and publishers as well as to children. The growth of a strong institutional market has eased some of the cruder commercial pressures and has made possible the writing and publication of many excellent

*Drawn from the Introduction to Mr. Townsend's book *A Sense of Story,* published by the Penguin Books, Ltd., in England, and by J. B. Lippincott Co. in the United States. Copyright © 1971 by John Rowe Townsend. Reprinted by permission of the publishers.

books which otherwise could never appear. But it has hardened the dividing line between children's books and adult books into a barrier, behind which separate development now takes place.

Although the distinction is administrative rather than literary, it must have some effect on the way books are written. Yet, authors are individualists, and still tend to write the book they want to write rather than one that will fit into a category. Arguments about whether such-and-such a book is "really for children" are always cropping up, and are usually pointless in any but organizational terms. The only practical definition of a children's book today — absurd as it sounds — is "a book which appears on the children's list of a publisher."

Books are, in fact, continually finding their way onto the children's lists which, in another age, would have been regarded as general fiction. Abetted by their editors, writers for children constantly push out the bounds of what is acceptable. Yet, because of the great division, these writers and their books are probably more shut off than ever from the general public. (And, from this point of view, the probable growth of "young adult" lists may raise still more fences and create new pens in which books can be trapped.) Such artificial barriers, however, give rise to a sense of dissatisfaction; a feeling that there are writers for children who deserve a wider public; a belief that many books which are good by any standard will now only be found by looking on the children's side of the line.

In fiction, at least, the balance of talent has shifted sharply between adult books and children's books in recent years. Brian Jackson,[1] director of the Advisory Centre for Education, in an essay on Philippa Pearce in *The Use of English* for Spring, 1970, declared that "ours is the golden age of children's literature" — a view with which I agree, although the figure of speech grows wearisome — and expressed surprise that "the great outburst of children's books this last thirty years" should come about when there is no longer a sturdy adult literature to support it.

Children's writing [he said] is a large and apparently self-contained genre, as it never was before. It is independent of the current adult novel. On the face of it, you wouldn't therefore expect its burgeoning richness. Could it be, ironically, that precisely because the adult novel is so weak in this country, some talents have been drawn into the children's field and flourished (as others have been drawn into scientific fiction and perished)?

The weakness of the current adult novel — which is not a solely British phenomenon, although it is more obvious here than in the United States — hardly needs to be demonstrated. Among much converging testimony, I draw almost at random from a few books and articles that come to hand. Anthony Burgess,[2] in *The Novel Now*, quotes Evelyn Waugh's view that "the originators, the exuberant men, are extinct, and in their place subsists and mostly flourishes a generation notable for elegance and variety of contrivance"; and Burgess, while questioning the "elegance" if not the "variety of contrivance," adds on his own account: "We cannot doubt that the twenty years since the Second World War have produced nothing to compare with the masterpieces of, say, the half-century before it." Storm Jameson,[3] in *Parthian World*, asks how many of us dip twice into "the endless flow of social trivia, on its level interesting, which pours from the pens or typewriters of contemporary novelists." The American novelist Isaac Bashevis Singer,[4] writing in *The New York Times Book Review* on November 9, 1969, expressed the belief that "while adult literature, especially fiction, is deteriorating, the literature for children is gaining in quality and stature." Explaining why he began to write for children in his late years, Singer declared that the child in our time

has become a consumer of a great growing literature — a reader who cannot be deluded by literary fads and barren experiments. No writer can bribe his way to the child's attention with false originality, literary puns and puzzles, arbitrary distortions of the order of things, or muddy streams of consciousness which often reveal nothing but the writer's boring and selfish personality. I came to the child because I see in him a last refuge from a literature gone berserk and ready for suicide.

I am not sure that despair over the state of adult fiction is a good reason for becoming a writer for children. But I believe that the general picture of an ailing adult literature in contrast with a thriving literature for children is broadly correct and would be accepted by most people with knowledge of both fields. I do not mean to say that children's books are "better" than adult books, or to claim for them an excessively large place in the scheme of things. And I admit that plenty of rubbish is published for children — as indeed it is for grown-ups. But I am sure there are people writing for children today who are every bit as talented as their opposite numbers among writers for adults.

The reasons for the strength of modern fiction for children are too many and complex to be dealt with in this short essay, but some of them can be hinted at. Adult fiction means, effectively, the novel. The novel is a recent form, and may be only a transitional one. Its heyday was the rapidly changing but preelectronic Victorian age. At present, the novel gives the impression of shrinking into a corner: narrow, withdrawn, self-preoccupied. But children's literature has wild blood in it; its ancestry lies partly in the long ages of storytelling which preceded the novel. Myth, legend, fairy tale are alive in their own right, endlessly reprinted, endlessly fertile in their influence. Modern children's fiction is permeated by a sense of story. Many writers, knowingly or unknowingly, return again and again to the old themes, often reworking them in modern or historical settings. And even where the children's novel runs parallel to its adult counterpart, there is often a freedom, speed, and spontaneity which the adult novel now seems to lack.

This, I believe, is the result of an odd but happy paradox. On the one hand, most modern writers for children insist that they write — with the blessing of their editors — the books they want to write for their own satisfaction. The classic statement of this position was made by Arthur Ransome[5] in a letter to the editor of *The Junior Bookshelf* as long ago as 1937:

You write not for children but for yourself, and if, by good fortune, children enjoy what you enjoy, why then, you are a writer of children's books. . . . No special credit to you, but simply thumping good luck.

C. S. Lewis[6] said that the only reason why he would ever write for children was "because a children's story is the best art-form for something you have to say . . ."; he[7] also remarked that "I am almost inclined to set it up as a canon that a children's story which is enjoyed only by children is a bad children's story." Yet anyone writing a book that will appear on a children's list must be aware of a potential readership of children. This is the fruitful contradiction from which the children's writer benefits. However much he is writing for himself he must, consciously or unconsciously, have a special sense of audience. As Arthur Ransome,[8] rightly unworried by any inconsistency, went on to say in the letter already quoted: "Every writer wants to have readers, and than children there are no better readers in the world."

An author can — as I have said elsewhere — expect from the reading child as much intelligence, as much imagination, as from the grown-up, and a good deal more readiness to enter into things and live the story. He can take up his theme afresh as if the world were new, rather than picking it up where the last practitioner let it drop and allowing for the weariness and satiety of his readers. He cannot expect children to put up with long-windedness or pomposity or emperor's clothes; but that is a discipline rather than a restriction. True, the child's range of experience is limited. There are still some kinds of books that are not likely to appear on the children's list: not because they will corrupt a child but because they will bore him. But, in general, children and their books are much less inhibited now than they were in Arthur Ransome's day. In my experience, children's writers do not feel much hampered; mostly they are able to do what they want to do. They are fortunate people. Their sense on the one hand of scope and freedom, on the other of a constantly renewed and responsive readership, freshens their work and makes this an exhilarating sector to be concerned with.

Nevertheless, children's books need to be appraised with coolness and detachment, simple enthusiasm being little better than simple unawareness. A critical approach is desirable not only for its own sake but also as a stimulus and discipline for author and publisher, and — in the long run — for the improvement of the breed. This indeed is the strongest reason for it. Donnarae MacCann, introducing a series of articles in the *Wilson Library Bulletin* for December, 1969, quoted from Henry S. Canby's *Definitions:*[9]

Unless there is somewhere an intelligent critical attitude against which a writer can measure himself . . . one of the chief requirements for good literature is wanting. . . . The author degenerates.

In the United States and Britain, the positions of writers for children in the league table are well known among specialists in the field; possibly too well known. But, as Donnarae MacCann[10] says, "There is no body of critical writing to turn to, even for those books which have been awarded the highest literary prizes in children's literature in Britain and America." Few children's authors have been the subject of any sustained critical appraisal. The children's writer, when his work begins to make any impression, can expect his new book to get a few reviews: some by specialists with much knowledge but little critical acumen, some by nonspecialists with — presumably — critical acumen but not much knowledge of children's books, some by people with no obvious qualifications at all. With luck the book may be reviewed in two or three places by critics who can place it in its context and can exercise some worthwhile judgment; but they are unlikely to have much space in which to work. And reviewing, even at its best, is a special and limited form of criticism: a rapid tasting rather than a leisurely consideration.

Mention of the criticism of children's books will usually lead to an argument about the relevance of various criteria. It seems to me that it is perfectly possible to judge books for children by nonliterary standards. It is legitimate to consider the social or moral or psychological or educational impact of a book; to consider how many children, and what kind of children, will like it. But it is dangerous to do this and call it criticism. Most disputes over standards are fruitless because the antagonists suppose their criteria to be mutually exclusive; if one is right the other is wrong. This is not necessarily so. Different kinds of assessment are valid for different purposes. The important thing is that everyone should understand what is being done.

The critic who is concerned with a book as literature cannot, however, carry his "standards" around with him like a set of tools ready for any job. He should, I believe, approach a book with an open mind and respond to it as freshly and honestly as he is able; then he should go away, let his thoughts and feelings about it mature, turn them over from time to time, consider the book in relation to others by the same author and by the author's predecessors and contemporaries. If the book is for children he should not let his mind be dominated by the fact; but neither, I think, should he attempt to ignore it. Myself — as one who remembers being a child, has children of his own, and has written for children — I could not, even if I wished, put children out of my mind when reading books intended for them. Just as the author must, I believe, write for himself yet with an awareness of an audience of children, so the critic must write for himself with an awareness that the books he discusses are books written for children.

But this awareness should not, I think, be too specific. Neither author nor critic should be continually asking himself questions such as "Will this be comprehensible to the average eleven-year-old?" We all know there is no average child. Children are individuals, and will read books if they like them and when they are ready for them. A suggestion that a book may appeal to a particular age group or type of child can be helpful, especially in reviews, but it should always be tentative and it should not affect one's assessment of merit. It has always seemed clear to me that a good book for children must be a good book in its own right. And a book can be good without being immensely popular and without solving its readers' problems or making them kinder to others.

SOURCES REFERRED TO IN THE TEXT

[1]Brian Jackson, "Philippa Pearce in the Golden Age of Children's Literature," *The Use of English*, Vol. 21, No. 3 (Spring 1970).

[2]Anthony Burgess, *The Novel Now* (New York, W. W. Norton & Company, 1967).

[3]Storm Jameson, *Parthian World or the Barrel Organ's Complaint* (New York, Harper & Row, Publishers, 1970).

[4]Isaac Bashevis Singer, " 'I See the Child as a Last Refuge,' " *The New York Times Book Review*, Section 7-Part II (November 9, 1969), p. 1.

[5]Arthur Ransome, "Letter to the Editor," *The Junior Bookshelf*, Vol. 1, No. 4 (1937).

[6]C. S. Lewis, "On Three Ways of Writing for Children," *Of Other Worlds: Essays and Stories* (New York, Harcourt Brace Jovanovich, Inc., 1966), p. 23.

[7]*Ibid.*, p. 24.

[8]Arthur Ransome, *op. cit.*

[9]Henry Seidel Canby, *Definitions; Second Series* (New York, Kennikat Press, Inc., 1967), p. 218.

[10]Donnarae MacCann, "A Valid Criticism for Children's Books," *Wilson Library Bulletin*, Vol. 44, Number 4 (December 1969), p. 395.

From *The Horn Book* for August 1971

OUT ON A LIMB WITH THE CRITICS:

Some Random Thoughts on the Present State of the Criticism of Children's Literature*

By Paul Heins

To BE A CRITIC — a literary critic — is almost, by definition, to be out on a limb. In addition to being in a precarious position, one never knows whether one will be top-heavy and crack the limb because of his weight or whether somebody will come along with a saw. Either way, the position is fraught with danger. Yet, since critics rush in where angels fear to tread, there must be some justification or explanation for their existence.

I do not think we have to be concerned about the criticism of what might be called adult literature. Aristotle started the business long ago, and it is enough to mention Coleridge and Goethe, Dr. Johnson and Matthew Arnold, I. A. Richards and Allen Tate, to show that whenever literature is produced, critics are sure to follow. What does concern us, however, is the criticism of children's literature — a formidable task, and much more difficult than the criticism of adult literature.

Children's literature — for good or for bad — is not the concern of children alone. Parents, teachers, and librarians as well as authors, illustrators, and publishers are potential judges of books for children. Questions of suitability and vocabulary jostle with personal likes and dislikes, and there is always the question of whether a particular book written for children will appeal to children. We have also been made painfully aware of the fact that we are dealing with a generation conditioned by television; and we are being told that children's literature should be realistic and should absorb, in some form or other, the social and psychological problems of the day.

Even a philosopher can say something — at times — that has a bearing on children's literature. In 1957, Suzanne K. Langer, in *Problems of Art: Ten Philosophical Lectures,* made a number of statements worth considering:

*Expanded from a talk entitled "Scratching the Surface, or Some Random Thoughts on the Reviewing and Criticism of Children's Books," first given on April 24, 1969, at a meeting of the Children's Book Guild, Washington, D.C. Delivered in its present form on June 18, 1969, at the Fifth Intermountain Conference on Children's Literature, the University of Utah, Salt Lake City, Utah.

Every generation has its styles of feeling. One age shudders and blushes and faints, another swaggers, still another is godlike in a universal indifference. These styles in actual emotion are not insincere. They are largely unconscious — determined by many social causes, but *shaped* by artists, usually popular artists of the screen, the juke-box, the shop window, and the picture magazine. (That, rather than incitement to crime, is my objection to the comics.)

Furthermore, she comes to a rather stringent conclusion about what she calls "art education"; and if we think about children's literature at all, it does not seem too farfetched to consider it in the category of the arts.

According to Mrs. Langer, "Art education is the education of the feeling, and a society that neglects it gives itself up to a formless emotion. Bad art is corruption of feeling." How many of us are willing to say that the moving-picture versions of *Mary Poppins* and *Dr. Dolittle* were bad art? Some of us will, because we believe that each picture version failed to capture the spirit of the book on which it was based. How many of us would go so far as to say these cinematic productions were not only bad art, but — because they were bad art — were corrupt in feeling? I, for one, am willing to say so.

Incidentally, critics of children's literature have frequently spoken up against shoddy methods and shoddy productions. Perhaps three of the most famous *Horn Book* articles represented this kind of frontal attack on mediocrity: "Walt Disney Accused" (Frances Clarke Sayers, *Horn Book*, December 1965), "Not Recommended" (Ruth Hill Viguers, *Horn Book*, February 1963), and "An Imaginary Correspondence" (Rumer Godden, *Horn Book*, August 1963), which delightfully accomplished its aim indirectly — by satire, humor, and irony. The chief value of this kind of criticism — of debased classics, of vocabularized texts — consists of clearing the decks for a more positive kind of criticism.

It has been said that people who insist that they have no philosophy or no religion will ultimately, in the course of conversation or discussion, reveal their explanation of the universe or of the beliefs which guide their lives. We are all critics whether we know it or not; and every time we pass judgment on a book or express enthusiasm for it, we are engaging in a critical act.

In her recent amusing book *The Girl on the Floor Will Help You*, Lavinia Russ speaks of "that crashing bore of a question which inevitably totters into any discussion of children's books,

73

'Are they written for children or for adults?' " Now, Mrs. Russ is naturally entitled to her opinion, not to say to her emotions; but she immediately follows up her condemnation by adding two statements: "She [E. Nesbit] didn't write for adults; she didn't write for children; she wrote for herself. Not her adult self, but to please and delight the child in herself — the child she remembered with fondness." In spite of her boredom, in spite of her initial outburst, Mrs. Russ was drawn into an act of criticism; and although she did not develop a point of view at length — as did Eleanor Cameron in her article "Why *Not* for Children?" (*Horn Book*, February 1966) — Mrs. Russ was actually delivering herself of an opinion on a topic which — as she herself states — unavoidably crops up in many discussions concerning children's literature. Mrs. Russ is a critic in spite of herself.

Children's books and authors, naturally, are not exempt from the random impressions and evaluations of readers. Perhaps the time has come for the criticism of children's literature to be more conscious than ever before of its existence — and better still of its function. It should learn to speak with precision and to qualify its enthusiasms. There is certainly available a large body of worthwhile children's books that invites critical consideration. As a matter of fact, because of the proliferation of good books for children during the last fifty years, the era has been termed a "golden age."

Incidentally, the term "golden age" is not without its difficulties. It can be a confusing term, for it seems that there are two golden ages. Both of them are mentioned in John Rowe Townsend's brief but excellent literary history *Written for Children: An outline of English children's literature.* In it we find an interesting summary of the last years of the first golden age:

In children's literature at least, the opening years of the century were the last of a golden age. . . . the shortest of short lists . . . must include nearly all of E. Nesbit's work and much of Kipling; the play of *Peter Pan; The Wind in the Willows; The Secret Garden;* and — Beatrix Potter's splendid little books for small children.
The Victorian-Edwardian era ended gloriously.

Elsewhere in Townsend's book, the two golden ages are brought into focus:

The half century before 1914 was the first golden age of children's literature. The second golden age is now.

In *A Critical History of Children's Literature*, Part Four is entitled The Golden Age 1920-1950.* In this book, the term is applied to children's literature in both the United States and England, and Ruth Hill Viguers naturally discusses both American and English books. In "The Book and the Person" (*Horn Book*, December 1968), Mrs. Viguers names more than two dozen men and women who during the twentieth century have written outstanding books that "give pleasure to children"; and in her list of "... Twentieth-century Children's Books Every Adult Should Know" she supplies titles by thirty authors. Although voices are occasionally raised deploring what the uninitiated call the inadequacy of children's literature, students of children's literature and people working with books and children know that there is almost an embarrassment of riches.

Along with the growth in the number of outstanding books for children, there has crystallized a feeling — to use Eleanor Cameron's words — that "children's literature does not exist in a narrow world of its own, but is enmeshed in a larger world of literature. . . ." Moreover, this perception of the locus of children's literature carries with it a further consequence. To quote again from Mrs. Cameron: "the highest standards of the one hold good for the other." And more than twenty years ago Bertha Mahony Miller wrote in a *Horn Book* editorial (May-June 1946):

Arts flourish where there is sound critical judgment to examine and appraise. The critic must, first of all, have a real point of view about his subject. The essential point of view grows out of acquaintance with the best children's books past and present, and also with the world's best literature for everyone.

This high standard for the criticism of children's literature may be seen exemplified in such works as *Books, Children and Men* and *The Unreluctant Years*. It continues with unabated significance in Mrs. Cameron's recent volume *The Green and Burning Tree*.

About the relationship between children's literature and literature in general, John Rowe Townsend also has made some clear and definite statements:

I believe that children's books must be judged by much the same standards as adult literature. A good children's book must not only be pleasing to children: it must be a good book in its own right.
Where the works of the past are concerned, I have much faith in the

*In the Revised Edition of *A Critical History of Children's Literature* (1969) this section is entitled Golden Years and Time of Tumult 1920-1967.

75

sifting process of time — 'time' being the shorthand for the collective wisdom of a great many people over a long period of time. . . . Survival is a good test of a book. . . . With present-day books, the sifting process is incomplete and judgments [Townsend is modestly referring to his own] are provisional.

But what of reviewing? Is reviewing criticism, or should it be criticism? Actually, criticism cannot be kept out of reviewing. Even the short capsulelike review cannot avoid making some critical comment, and a long review tends to become a critical essay.

What is the function of reviewing? I know of no better discussion of the subject than is found in a pamphlet published by the Hogarth Press in England in 1939. Entitled *Reviewing*, it was written by Virginia Woolf, some of whose previously unsigned reviews have recently been identified and republished in the London *Times Literary Supplement*. She states her observations in a definitive manner. When reviewing rose in importance at the beginning of the nineteenth century, "Its complex task was partly to inform the public, partly to criticize the book and partly to advertise its existence." During the present century, "The critic is separate from the reviewer; the function of the reviewer is partly to sort current literature; partly to advertise the author; partly to inform the public." Present-day authors will doubtless acquiesce in her opinion that "it is a matter of very great interest to a writer to know what an honest and intelligent reader thinks about his work." And when Virginia Woolf states that "It is impossible for the living to judge the works of the living," one recognizes the confession of an honest reviewer, who was also a critic in her own right.

Although a review serves the practical purpose of giving information and of advertising — using the word in its Woolfian sense — it cannot avoid making certain critical gestures. To consider only children's books: Of the thousands published yearly, how many of them is it physically possible to review? If a journal, like *The Horn Book Magazine*, reviews only books considered worthy of mention, the very task of selection is, by its very nature, a task of criticism — of judgment. Any form of literary classification, comparison, or evaluation must also be considered a form of criticism. Actual — one should even dare to say serious — criticism will occur only when judgments are being made in a context of literary knowledge and of literary standards. If a reviewer perceives clearly the intention of the author and states it, the author will surely appreciate the intelligence — that is, the critical acumen of the reviewer. If the reviewer tries to indicate how well the author has succeeded in accomplishing his intention, the reviewer — once again — assumes the role of the critic.

Reviewing, however, is only concerned with what is imminent in publishing, with what is being produced at the present time; and does its job well by selecting, classifying, and evaluating — evaluating for the time being. Criticism deals with literature in perspective and places a book in a larger context — be it historical, aesthetic, psychological, or what you will. I deliberately say "what you will" for there are — as we all well know — Marxian critics, Thomistic critics, and psychoanalytical critics, who concern themselves with evaluations which are not always purely literary.

As I have suggested before, the reviewing and criticism of children's literature is more complex and more fraught with misconceptions than any other kind of reviewing and criticism. If children's literature — at its best — is worthy of consideration with the rest of literature, if the understanding and appreciation of children's literature is to lead to the development of relevant and reliable criticism, one must never forget that the term *children's* remains a specifying term and, willy-nilly, must be respected.

It is certainly important and necessary at times to consider children's literature purely as literature. Questions of style, structure, and technical subtlety are as applicable to children's literature as to any of the other branches of literature. Julia Cunningham's *Dorp Dead* (Pantheon) may be considered as an exemplar of the Gothic novel; and one could learn much by comparing the structure of her story with that of *Jane Eyre*. Incidentally, a good reviewer's critical apparatus should obviously include a wide knowledge of universal literature. The reviewer of Scott O'Dell's *The Dark Canoe* (Houghton) who confessed to an ignorance of — that is, of having never read — *Moby Dick* could scarcely begin to do justice to Mr. O'Dell's book, whatever its ultimate literary significance or value may be.

However, even if children's literature should be considered as literature, it does not cease to be children's literature. But, unfortunately, there is no simple, or clear and easy way by which to determine the proper relationship between the term *children's* and the term *literature*. The most one can do is to consider a few varying points of view.

To ask a child invites defeat. Often his response is primitive or rudimentary; a child's enthusiasm for a book is a much better indication of what the book means to him and does for him than any direct answer to a question posed at him. Jean Karl, editor of children's books, Atheneum, has stated the child's case with great common sense:

No book is for every child and no book should be made to appeal to every child. A book is made to be loved and cherished by the child it is right for and rejected by those who prefer others.

Or one may consider the point of view of the literary purist, as in Brian Alderson's article "The Irrelevance of Children to the Children's Book Reviewer" (*Children's Book News*, London, January-February 1969). One may agree with Mr. Alderson that such remarks as "My Euphemia loved the tasteful blue and yellows" does not get one very far; but when he states that

It may be objected that to assess children's books without reference to children is to erect some absolute critical standard relating neither to the author's purpose or the reader's enjoyment. To do much less, however, is to follow a road that leads to a morass of contradictions and subjective responses, the most serious result of which will be the confusion of what we are trying to do in encouraging children to read.

I wonder whether Mr. Alderson has not sidetracked one of the chief problems in the consideration of children's literature — literary merit — by speaking of "encouraging children to read," which is a pedagogical point of view and therefore should also be irrelevant to the children's book reviewer.

Interestingly enough, John Rowe Townsend looks upon "acceptability to a child as a preliminary hurdle rather than a final test." Personally, I question whether Mr. Townsend has not put the cart before the horse. In discussions of recently published children's books, generally after a discussion of a book of rare value, one often hears the voice of the devil's advocate: "But, will children like it?" or more pessimistically, "What child will read it?" Surely the question of acceptability to a child is a question concerning book selection and not a fundamental critical question — not a question of literary criticism.

A conciliatory point of view is found in the editorial by Bertha Mahony Miller previously referred to. In it, she modified her statement about the criticism of children's literature by adding an important qualification. "This point of view — this measuring stick —" (by which she meant literary standards) "must also bear some relation to children themselves and their reaction to books today." The word "some" is significant. Mrs. Miller's chief accomplishment was to have considered the child and the book together, not in an intellectually critical way, but appreciatively — one may say, intuitively. Some of her intuitions still bear repeating:

Who can say what is the right book for the right child? That, thank God, is the child's own adventure (*Horn Book* editorial, November 1933).

... it is foolish to say 'we ought only to give the child conceptions it can understand.' His soul grows by wonder over things it cannot understand (*Horn Book* editorial, January 1934).

These statements may seem both inspirational and idealistic in form and utterance, but in essence they show a deep respect for the child as a person.

Except by taking polls and by compiling statistics, one could not determine the frequency of appeal of William Mayne's *Earthfasts* (Dutton) or Alan Garner's *The Owl Service* (Walck) among children. But popularity is only a descriptive, not a critical term. Among mature readers, how many are there who read *Paradise Lost* or *Finnegan's Wake* for the sheer pleasure of it? There are some, of course, who do; and if children's literature has so developed in richness and scope as to have produced a number of recondite masterpieces, these works should first be respected and treated as works of literature before one goes through the agony of deciding: To how many, to what kinds of children will these works appeal?

Finally, reviewers and critics are but readers; and if they function properly, should simply be better readers than most. Perhaps they should try to be humble rather than clever. Lewis Carroll once managed to be both in a letter that was disarmingly simple and devastatingly logical:

As to the meaning of the Snark (he wrote to a friend in America), I'm very much afraid that I didn't mean anything but nonsense. Still, you know, words mean more than we mean to express when we use them; so a whole book ought to mean a great deal more than the writer means. So whatever good meanings are in the book, I'm glad to accept as the meaning of the book. The best that I've seen is by a lady (she published it in a letter to a newspaper), that the book is an allegory on the search after happiness. I think this fits in beautifully in many ways

— particularly about the bathing machines:* when people get weary of life, and can't find happiness in towns or in books, then they rush off to the seaside to see what bathing machines will do for them.†

One of Carroll's statements — "whatever good meanings are in the book, I am glad to accept as the meaning of the book" — invites speculation. He does not consider a possible logical loophole — the possible bad meanings. I am sure that Freudian critics have already taken care of the loophole. As for the lady's idea that "the book is an allegory on the search after happiness," Carroll delightfully and logically destroys her interpretation by pursuing it to its absurd extreme. And yet, Maurice Sendak was to give creative vitality to a very similar bizarre situation in *Higglety-Pigglety Pop!* by transforming nonsense into allegory. During the past year, the editor of *The Horn Book Magazine* received a letter from a student of children's literature who was planning to investigate symbolism in Beatrix Potter. She was — unfortunately — unacquainted with Lewis Carroll's letter.

In *Notes Towards the Definition of Culture*, T. S. Eliot stated what he considered to be "the three permanent reasons for reading: the acquisition of wisdom, the enjoyment of art, and the pleasure of entertainment." It is certainly the third of these reasons which is the most nearly universal. Most children become aware of words at an early age and advance naturally to the more complicated pleasure of listening to stories. If conditions are favorable, children will discover that the world of books can still further augment their verbal pleasures. The prime function, then, of the reviewer and even of the critic of children's books is to signalize those books which appealing at present to children will seem even better when they are reread by those same children in their adulthood.

*Bathing machine — a small bathhouse on wheels, to be driven into the water, for bathers to undress, bathe, and dress in (*Webster's New International Dictionary of the English Language*, Second Edition, Unabridged, 1943).

†Quoted by Bertha Mahony Miller from *The Life and Letters of Lewis Carroll* by Stuart Dodgson Collingwood in a *Horn Book* editorial, February 1932.

BIBLIOGRAPHY

ALDERSON, BRIAN W., "The Irrelevance of Children to the Children's Book Reviewer." *Children's Book News* (Jan.-Feb. 1969), pp. 10-11.

ALLEN, ARTHUR T., "Literature for Children: An Engagement with Life." *The Horn Book Magazine*, Vol. XLIII (Dec. 1967), pp. 732-737.

CAMERON, ELEANOR, *The Green and Burning Tree: On the Writing and Enjoyment of Children's Books*. Boston, Little, Brown and Company, 1966.

————, "Why *Not* for Children?" *The Horn Book Magazine*, Vol. XLII (Feb. 1966), pp. 21-33.

COLLINGWOOD, STUART DODGSON, *The Life and Letters of Lewis Carroll*. Detroit, Gale Research Company, 1898.

ELIOT, T. S., *Notes towards the Definition of Culture*. New York, Harcourt, Brace and World, 1949.

GODDEN, RUMER, "An Imaginary Correspondence." *The Horn Book Magazine*, Vol. XXXIX (Aug. 1963), pp. 369-375.

KARL, JEAN, "The Real and the Unreal." *Wilson Library Bulletin* (Oct. 1966). Based on an address made at a meeting of The School and Children's Section, Michigan Library Association, Oct. 13, 1965.

LANGER, SUZANNE K., *Problems of Art: Ten Philosophical Lectures*. New York, Charles Scribner's Sons, 1957.

MARTIN, BILL, JR., "Helping Children Claim Language Through Literature." *Elementary English*, Vol. XLV (May 1968), pp. 583-591.

MEIGS, CORNELIA ET AL., *A Critical History of Children's Literature*. New York, Macmillan, 1953.

MILLER, BERTHA MAHONY, Editorials. *The Horn Book Magazine* (Feb. 1932); (Nov. 1933); (Jan. 1934); (May-June 1946).

RUSS, LAVINIA, *The Girl on the Floor Will Help You*. New York, Doubleday & Company, 1969.

SAYERS, FRANCES CLARKE, "Walt Disney Accused." *The Horn Book Magazine*, Vol. XLI (Dec. 1965), pp. 602-611.

TOWNSEND, JOHN ROWE, *Written for Children: An outline of English children's literature*. New York, Lothrop, Lee & Shepard Co., Inc., 1967.

TUNIS, JOHN R., "What Is a Juvenile Book?" *The Horn Book Magazine*, Vol. XLIV (June 1968), pp. 307-312.

VIGUERS, RUTH HILL, "Not Recommended." *The Horn Book Magazine*, Vol. XXXIX (Feb. 1963), pp. 76-78.

————, "The Book and the Person." *The Horn Book Magazine*, Vol. XLIV (Dec. 1968), pp. 657-665.

WOOLF, VIRGINIA, *Reviewing (With a Note by Leonard Woolf)*. Hogarth Sixpenny Pamphlets, No. 4, London, 1939.

From *The Horn Book* for June 1970

COMING TO TERMS
WITH CRITICISM*

By Paul Heins

I F WE ARE GOING TO COME TO TERMS with criticism, especially the criticism of children's literature, we should state the terms. Actually, "Out on a Limb with the Critics" (*Horn Book*, June 1970) was an attempt to suggest some of the critical problems worthy of exploration and, if possible, of clarification. Let us now spell out what these problems are, perhaps indicate certain areas of discussion, or — better still — list certain topics worthy of consideration.

1. Children's literature is a part of general literature; and even at the risk of overemphasizing the notion of branches, children's literature may be said to be a branch on the tree of literature. There have been authors like Stevenson, Mark Twain, and Kipling who in the past have written for both children and adults, as well as more recent writers like Thurber, C. S. Lewis, and E. B. White. And in pursuing the relationship further, one could discover that perhaps Long John Silver, despite his lovable traits, is a distant cousin of schizophrenic Dr. Jekyll; and that C. S. Lewis' Christianity is reflected in his Narnia stories.

It is obvious that the folk tales and hero tales of children's literature are descended from literary forms that were created to entertain whole strata of society and that the minstrels who sang and told of Odysseus and Beowulf would have been surprised to learn that their works would one day be recast for children. Contemporary children's books, also, often suggest analogies with books for adults. The proportions of the world of *The Borrowers* (Harcourt) or of *The Return of the Twelves* (Coward) suggest the relativity of big and small found in the first two voyages of *Gulliver's Travels*.

2. If children's literature is a part of all literature, then the criticism of children's literature becomes a part of the criticism of all literature. A children's book deserves to be probed as much as an adult book for general questions of diction, structure, significance of detail, literary integrity. Not for the purpose of what is often called "dry" analysis, but for the joy of discovering the skill of the author.

*Delivered on June 19, 1969, at the Fifth Intermountain Conference on Children's Literature, the University of Utah, Salt Lake City, Utah.

3. A much more difficult area to localize is found in the attempt to decide what distinguishes a children's book from an adult book. Thus far, discussions have led to a violent taking of sides — in such articles as John Tunis's "What Is a Juvenile Book?" (*Horn Book*, June 1968) or in Eleanor Cameron's, "Why Not for Children?" (*Horn Book*, February 1966). Perhaps it would be wise to distinguish, on the one hand, between books written for adults and books written for children, and to distinguish, on the other hand, between books read by adults and those read by children.

If children made *Robinson Crusoe* one of their own books long ago, adults have since adopted *Alice in Wonderland* for themselves. In the 1968 Commencement Address at Colby College (Waterville, State of Maine), the poet David McCord listed what he called "good" books, "wise" books — and included *Alice* along with *The Tempest, The Oregon Trail*, and *War and Peace*. The literary essays of Graham Greene include a discussion of the writings of Beatrix Potter — a discussion which the creator of Peter Rabbit and Jemima Puddleduck did not approve of, because she considered the critic's point of view to be unnecessarily Freudian. Even in serious philosophical criticism, a writer will occasionally draw from children's literature for examples. In *The Mind of the Maker* (Harcourt), Dorothy L. Sayers discusses, among other things, writers whose "work and every part of it can be referred to as a coherent and controlling unity of Idea." Along with Blake, Aquinas, and Euclid, she mentions Lewis Carroll and the Alice books.

4. The child as reader. Is what a child reads significant from the point of view of criticism? Spontaneous young readers may be devoted to one kind of book, may read indiscriminately, or may be inspired to read certain books as the result of the suggestions of teacher, librarian, or any other kind of miscellaneous adult. A knowledge of what they read, however, is essentially valuable for an understanding of their personal or intellectual development, and will naturally always be interesting to those of us concerned with children's books. But it is a subject only occasionally related to literary criticism.

Edward Fenton, in an article entitled "Mystery" which appeared in the June 1968 *Horn Book Magazine*, presented an author's point of view about one possible relationship:

Children's interests are as broad as the horizon. They are interested in practically everything — with the exception of sexual love, which bores them, being beyond their experience. They know that grownups fall in love and marry, but it is a convention they accept without caring about the details. As for all the other problems related to life (including death), it is impossible to overestimate the capacity of children to feel, suffer, understand, and share them all if properly presented. But they must be in terms of action and plot.

The proper presentation to children of these "problems related to life" does concern criticism, and Mr. Fenton does specifically emphasize the primacy of action and plot.

5. The child as critic. Generally it is not a child's reasoned opinion — after all, he is not ready for that — but his reactions that are significant. Ranging from the lukewarm tolerance of calling a book "all right" to positive dislike or enthusiasm, his reactions are generally worth considering for their emotional overtones, which — again — are only indirectly related to critical judgments. The statistical approach, also, is not particularly significant: I know of one community in which children do not care to read Lloyd Alexander's fantasies and of another in which the children were very anxious to purchase for themselves paperback copies of *The Book of Three* and *The High King* (both Holt/ Dell Yearling).

6. The apologetics of children's literature is a very important branch of criticism. Just as romantic poets and realistic novelists have had in the past to defend their positions, just as fiction itself and drama have had to withstand puritanical and other kinds of religious attacks and criticism, children's literature — especially the quality of present-day children's literature — needs constant defending. The June 1968 editorial of *The Horn Book Magazine* touched on the situation. "Recently, some voices have been raised — generally those of psychologists and educators — in protest against the inadequacies of children's books. Books for children are accused of being condescending, out of touch with the reality of a child's life, and superficially optimistic." Although other champions of children's books may have at times spoken more eloquently, the editorial proffered a simple suggestion: "Before carping about the quality of literature for children, the dissenters should become more familiar with it." If we are living in the midst of a golden age of literature for children, many people are not aware of the fact. The existence of the term "kiddy lit" shows that crusaders still have enough left to do.

7. A topic closely related to the defense of children's literature is concerned with the castigation of inferior literary productions intended for children. "Walt Disney Accused" (*Horn Book*, December 1965), "Not Recommended" (*Horn Book*, February 1963), and "An Imaginary Correspondence" (*Horn Book*, August 1963) are important examples of this kind of criticism.

8. The trends of the age. This very important topic, although historical in nature, is closely interlinked with critical problems. In recent years the subject matter of children's books has expanded considerably to include social problems, questions of prejudice, urban and academic situations, and psychological dilemmas; in addition, there has been a greater stress than ever before on realism of presentation; and the vocabulary of children's books is beginning to reflect the spirit of the times. Even though we have left far behind us what George Santayana once called the "genteel tradition" of American literature (and life), the problems of literary criticism remain constant. After we have absorbed new kinds of subject matter and new points of view, we still have to ask not only what a book tries to do, but how well it does it.

9. Although something has already been said about reviewing and criticism, at least one further comment is necessary. Reviewers do not sift for eternity; they are kept busy selecting the best or the most significant of the books available during a given period of time. Incidentally, a similar method is followed by judges of book awards; the Newbery Award, as we all know, considers the contributions to children's literature during a given year. But time alone is the ultimate judge of the value of a book. Age in a book is not necessarily a sign of decay; it may indicate what in the book has resisted decay. Even a review may — after the passing of time — emerge triumphant: During the 1920's *The New York Times Book Review* called Joyce's *Ulysses* "the most important contribution that has been made to fictional literature in the twentieth century."* A reviewer does not have to be a prophet, but merely a sensitive reader who is able to perceive the quality of a new book. If the reviewer is in tune with literature, he may often make an uncanny judgment that will be justified by time.

*From "The Story of *The New York Times Book Review*," an essay by Francis Brown, editor of *The New York Times Book Review*, appearing as the introduction to the bound volumes for the years 1896-1968.

10. In an era that has been made increasingly aware of the interrelationships of the various branches of knowledge, criticism can serve as a borderline service by stressing excellence. Teachers of history have long used historical novels and other forms of literature to vivify the background of their subject; and at the present time, the link between literature and the teaching of language is being stressed. I shall only mention in passing the excellent article "Helping Children Claim Language Through Literature" by Bill Martin, Jr.

I should like to quote, however, from Hester Burton's novel *In Spite of All Terror* (World):

Then, too, there was the problem of the way she talked.

Liz, like most of her friends at the Weavers Green Grammar School, was bilingual in two kinds of English. In Nile Street and in the school playground she spoke cockney. . . . One recited Shakespeare and read the New Testament lesson in Assembly in "posh," and one always addressed the teachers in this way. . . .

The trouble now, however, was that [her] quick ear told her that the vowel sounds of Weavers Green "educated" English differed in some respects somewhat embarrassingly from that of the Breretons.

The quotation casts an interesting sidelight on the relationship between language and literature, which is obviously a universal problem. But the critic's ultimate responsibility is to judge any book on its own — its literary — merit.

The listing of ten areas of possible discussion from the point of view of the criticism of children's literature, especially from that of the literary criticism of children's literature, was not intended to be exhaustive. The number is an arbitrary one; but the listing was intended to demonstrate the complexity of the problems of judging children's books: to show that there is a lot going on — at one and the same time.

"Out on a Limb with the Critics" attempted to give one an idea of the currents and crosscurrents, the jostling but dynamic contradictions, and the interplay of the various phases found in discussions of children's books. "Coming to Terms with Criticism" tries to isolate the various phases, and suggest the value or the importance of each. But these phases, in reality, are coexistent and react on one another, so that the whole subject of the criticism of children's books may be visualized as a huge mobile consisting of many parts delicately and effectively balanced.

Perhaps one should distinguish, in the long run, between the two different ways of approaching children's books: (1) the criticism of these books as they concern the different kinds of people who use and work with these books and (2) the literary criticism of children's literature. But I still feel that a conscious and enlightened literary criticism should direct and govern our whole approach to children's literature. Whether it rules as a constitutional monarch or as a duly elected president makes little difference.

From *The Horn Book* for August 1970

LITERATURE BEDEVILED:
A Searching Look at Filmstrips

By ETHEL L. HEINS

SEVENTEEN YEARS AGO, I innocently embarked on a project to explore the maze of current storytelling and dramatic recordings for children. Searching for something of value, I was almost immediately appalled at what I found — an overabundance of commercial discs which lacked any respect for the literature reproduced as well as for the children who were to listen. "[W]ith sentimentality substituting for emotional depth, and dreary silliness for real humor. . . . diluted retellings [and dramatizations] of well-loved tales . . . totally fail to keep the spirit of the originals."*

At that time, the multi-media approach to children's literature was still in its infancy; not until the next decade did Marshall McLuhan prophesy the doom of the printed word. In the sixties, educational technology became both an industry and a respected profession. Visual aids — in addition to aural — were hailed as an essential factor in motivating a new generation of children to learn to read and even to appreciate literature; and there was a great proliferation of the little rolls of transparencies known as filmstrips.

From the very beginning, Morton Schindel, founder of Weston Woods, wisely realized that much of the appeal of picture books lies in their illustrations and in the interdependence of artwork and text. The unique Weston Woods films and filmstrips, phenemonally successful in schools and libraries all over the world, have demonstrated the feasibility of producing book-based audio-visual materials scrupulously faithful to the originals. In this work, Morton Schindel clearly was the pioneer.

Other companies are now making filmstrips — usually accompanied by cassettes or records — with pictures accurately reproduced from books. Teaching Resources Films, for example, has issued filmstrips made from such favorites as the Amelia Bedelia stories, the Curious George books, and Virginia Lee Burton's *Maybelle the Cable Car* and *Katy and the Big Snow*. Viking Press has prepared an excellent group of filmstrips made from its own picture books; and Macmillan has

*Ethel L. Heins, "For Listening Children," *Horn Book* XXXIII (December 1957), p. 514.

moved similarly into the audio-visual field with Threshold Filmstrips, filmed from a dozen of their own titles. At this writing, another forthcoming group of picture-book filmstrips has just been announced as a joint venture of Scribner/Miller-Brody. Spoken Arts' *Treasury of Modern Tales* includes Edward Fenton's *The Big Yellow Balloon* and Don Freeman's *The Guard Mouse*; and McGraw-Hill Films has made filmstrips of eight Happy Lion stories.

Several sets of splendid filmstrips have been adapted by Lyceum Productions from Ann Atwood's handsome photographic books. *Teeka the Otter* and *Sammy the Crow*, both written by Elizabeth Baldwin Hazelton, are pleasing nature stories. Much more important are the filmstrips solely based on Ann Atwood's work. *The Wild Young Desert* — a successful combination of geology, ecology, and aesthetics — is straightforward yet poetic, factual yet lyrical. *Haiku: The Mood of Earth* series consists of beautiful, experimental filmstrips in which two pictures are used to express the haiku: first the long vew of a whole scene and then the closeup of a fragment. Thus, "it might be said that the words illustrate the photographs." *Haiku: The Hidden Glimmering*, based on Ann Atwood's recent book *My Own Rhythm: An Approach to Haiku*, discusses imagination, emotion, and insight in the work of three Japanese poets — Bashô, Issa, and Buson. The author's aim is to sharpen awarenes of and to quicken responses to the natural world; authentic Japanese music is used sparingly and discreetly. Such filmstrips are really photographic essays combining visual and verbal poetry; and in the melding of words and pictures, they demonstrate the peculiar characteristics and limitations of the medium used to the fullest advantage.

But popular McLuhanism, joyfully proclaiming the new media, has frequently ignored the study of the message. And the development, technology, and organization of the media center have often been of more urgent concern to some librarians than the significance of its materials. Not surprisingly, scores of filmstrips have been reiterating and compounding the sins of many of the old literature recordings of the 1950's.

We need not discuss the role of the filmstrip in general instruction. It is obvious that for any subject which can be clarified by photographs or diagrams, a good filmstrip can smooth the road to learning; indeed, a graphic representation of facts or abstractions is often essential to understanding.

But reading a literary work is not like studying science or history; nor is it the same as looking at a picture book. There is nothing wrong with the idea of translating a wholly verbal work into a pictorial composition; but the filmstrip — unlike the film, which has developed into a legitimate art form — is severely limited. Reducing a story to a collection of indifferent drawings, a filmstrip can only be — like the Emperor's nightingale — an impoverished imitation. Nowhere is the inevitable failure more obvious than in the filmstrips concocted from Newbery Medal books (Miller-Brody). Consider the *Horn Book* review of *Mrs. Frisby and the Rats of NIMH:* "a talking-beast tale which blends scientific probability and fantasy. . . . an intriguing adventure made plausible through vivid descriptive prose and meticulous selection of detail." And of *The High King:* "More than a series of exciting adventures, the book has the philosophical depth and overtones of great fantasy." Can the producer of these filmstrips — carefully researched and planned though they are — claim that the essence of the books is captured in a series of colored pictures? Where is the subtlety of characterization, the emotional power, the style? Where is true wit, and the virtuosity of great writing?

The timeworn defense of mediocrity — that the filmstrip will inspire an unenthusiastic child to read the complete book — is unsupported. Not only do most filmstrips present a warped idea of the story, they also remove some of the excitement of discovery by leaving a vague, false impression of familiarity. But listening to the story read aloud might well send the child to the book; no filmstrip can whet the appetite like oral reading articulated with conviction and zest by a teacher or a librarian. And the more reluctant or inept the reader, the more desperate is his need to be read to.

For we must preserve language, not dismiss it. "We have the most inarticulate generation of college students in history," said the poet Karl Shapiro; and Richard Peck, speaking of adolescent readers, wrote: "Many young people. . . . are patients in the remedial reading clinic. Some of them appear to be terminal cases. The permissive home and the watered-down school curriculum have betrayed them. The basic skills were not imposed, and attention spans were not stretched."*

As filmstrips, many books and stories long-treasured in the

*Richard Peck, "In the Country of Teenage Fiction," *American Libraries* IV (April 1973), p. 205.

public domain have been subjected to one indignity after another; many of them are no more than classic comics updated. Typical is a series called *Favorite Children's Books* (Coronet), in which *Peter Pan*, *Gulliver's Travels*, *A Little Princess*, *Robinson Crusoe*, *A Wizard of Oz*, *The Happy Prince*, and *A Dog of Flanders* are all reduced by an anonymous artist to their lowest common denominators.

One of the most ambitious productions consists of the thirty-six filmstrips in the McGraw-Hill Films *Children's Literature Series*. "In all cases our primary concern was to capture the flavor and nuances of the book, while creating an entertaining and exciting filmstrip. In some instances, there was not enough original artwork in the book or the pictures would not have adapted well to the filmstrip format, so new artwork was created. Color was added to drawings where appropriate." Hence, *Peter's Long Walk*, deprived of Barbara Cooney's crisp, fresh illustrations, moves into the tawdry filmstrip world where cats and rabbits so often look like greeting card kittens and bunnies. *The Limerick Trick*, drastically abridged, loses the individuality of its characters; while the flat, bare pictures fail even to approximate the lively fun of the book. *A Pair of Red Clogs* fortunately retains Kazue Mizumura's illustrations; but why should *Many Moons*, a Caldecott Medal winner, have been chosen for re-illustration? *Evan's Corner*, too, has been tossed into the blender; and now, without the sympathetic, warmly effective drawings, it has been reincarnated with garish pictures of expressionless children. As artistic units, the books have been destroyed. And surely, *Mr. Magoo's Literature Series* (also McGraw-Hill) — an incredible collection of classics such as *William Tell*, *King Arthur*, *Treasure Island*, and *The Three Musketeers* filtered through the mindless interpretations of the cartoon character "to join learning and laughter" — is a total travesty.

A flagrant example of contempt for both children and books in the pursuit of crass commercialism is the filmstrip world of the folk tale. Largely a universal plastic kingdom, it is populated with comic-book characters wearing regulation masks for horror, anger, innocence, or joy. One is reminded of the Mock Turtle's branches of arithmetic — "Ambition, Distraction, Uglification, and Derision." But just as folk tales can be made into beautiful picture books, so they could, conceivably, provide the texts for acceptable filmstrips — if first-rate illustrators were employed. However, after years of critical attention to picture books and to the art of illustration, a dismaying double standard still permits an audio-visual reviewer to criticize a filmstrip set of legends for having flat and lifeless pictures, and then to observe that the series would be useful for school curricula and story hours. Yet the American Library Association's 1969 *Standards for School Media Programs* specifically admonishes the professional staff to guide "students to develop desirable reading, viewing, and listening patterns, attitudes, and appreciations."

One experienced producer of many acceptable recordings (Spoken Arts) issues filmstrips abounding in coyness and sheer ugliness. Mother Goose, wearing sun glasses, resembles a senior citizen on a holiday. *The Happy Prince,* in a dreadful, watered-down version, only widens the gap between literature and its audio-visual transformations. In "Rapunzel" (Troll), the princess' tower room — like an illustration in a domestic magazine — is furnished with blue wall-to-wall carpeting and a tip-top table; the princess' father wears a stiff Victorian collar while the prince's costume is pure seventeenth-century baroque. Recalling Adrienne Adams' charming books, one shudders at the same producer's renderings of "Jorinda and Joringel" and "The Elves and the Shoemaker."

Other producers are even further from the mark. In a mockery of "The Three Billy Goats Gruff," the troll wears red breeches and a blue jacket; and in the simplified text printed directly on the film, the gamboling goats gently say: "I hope this bridge is safe. . . . I hope the old troll is fast asleep." Many traditional stories are distorted with didacticism. One "Little Red Riding Hood," hitting hard at filial obedience, ends with: "Now she was always going to remember to mind her mother"; while "Cinderella" turns into a moral tale as her sisters beg for forgiveness. In "The Boy Who Could Do Anything," gaudy coloring masquerades as Mexican atmosphere, while the sound-effects technicians, as meticulous as ever, imitate every twanging arrow, every chirping bird. *African Legends and Folktales* (CCM Films), a set of six filmstrips, conscientiously researched, is to be praised for its authentic folklore and for its effective storytelling by Moses Gunn. But the filmstrips are often commonplace and inelegant, and do not bear comparison with the brilliant Anansi interpretations of Gerald McDermott or Gail Haley.

American tall tales and legends — especially those about Paul Bunyan, Pecos Bill, John Henry, and Johnny Appleseed — have been thoroughly exploited. Paul is often pictured as a fat, rather voluptuous infant; Babe as excessively blue, with curly hair and long eyelashes. Undignified, sentimental, grossly unattractive, and inaccurately costumed, the figures, lacking the cleverness of true cartooning, show only the vapid, familiar faces of cheap comics. And on the recorded texts, sounding like television at its worst, are conventionalized folksy voices, speaking incongruous, tasteless, present-day slang and jargon. Perhaps no character has been so bowdlerized as Johnny Appleseed — piously bearing his Bible; wearing the inevitable saucepan on his head; surrounded by smiling rattlesnakes, bears looking like benign stuffed toys, and Indian stereotypes; and at the end of his life, walking away into the setting sun.

Classical mythology fares no better than other traditional literature. The few attempts at filmstrip presentation are oversimplified or ludicrously popularized. A set entitled *Mythology Is Alive and Well* (Guidance Associates) is a barbarous attempt to justify and prove the relevance of mythology to older young people. Pictures of mythological subjects alternate with photographs of present-day adolescents — all synchronized with a fatuous, yet pompous, text in dialogue form. To heighten audience appeal, a rock group intermittently sings popular music. A discussion of Pluto, for example, is followed by several photographs of a cemetery, highlighting a flower-bedecked coffin; and a sequence on Apollo includes a picture of the rocket — "which has at last soared to the moon, bringing Apollo to Artemis" — preceding a photograph of a modern bathing beach crowded with young sun-worshippers. At one point, one hears: "You can still see Hermes doing his thing for the flowers-by-wire services"; and from Aphrodite, we are told, comes the cry "that what the world needs now is 'love, sweet love.'"

Hans Christian Andersen, Kipling, and Washington Irving are all dealt cruel blows by producers eager to capitalize on well-loved stories. With grotesqueness and maudlin sentimentality replacing humor and subtlety, and with texts diluted almost beyond recognition, the Andersen tales look like outrageous caricatures of the originals. In "Five Peas in a Pod," the green peas have round, dimpled faces; the mother duck in "The Ugly Duckling" wears a kerchief around her head. "The Nightingale" appears again and again in many versions, all of them full of pseudo-Chinese clichés, the Emperor a figure of offensive vulgarity. *The Jungle Book* also has been abridged and debilitated. An elaborate offering (Spoken Arts) includes the usual added attractions: a collection of activity sheets for student participation and a guide for teachers. Unfortunately, whatever dramatic quality is preserved in the abbreviated story is wasted on the pallid, insipid pictures. In a *Just So Stories* series (Coronet), the Elephant's Child, thoroughly emasculated, looks like a blood brother of Dumbo; and there is no evidence of any attempt to preserve the tokens of Kipling's genius. Thus one looks in vain for the Bi-Coloured-Python-Rock-Snake, the Kolokolo Bird with his mournful cry, or the slushy-squshy mud-cap — as well as for the author's effervescent diction.

Not even poetry has been immune. Certainly, visual images can reinforce verbal ones, and pictorial analogy can be important in the study of poetry. One need only look at the photographs on the handsomely-designed pages of *Reflections on a Gift of Watermelon Pickle and Other Modern Verse* to perceive how a poem can be illuminated and its emotion intensified by parallel images. But mundane, literal interpretations stifle, rather than stimulate, the imagination. Two filmstrips, *Favorite Poems about Children's Adventures* and *Favorite Poems of Fun and Laughter* (Troll), offer dull, flat drawings, easily surpassed in creativity and spontaneity by the pictures which school children themselves often make in response to oral poetry.

Two other productions, both frankly educational tools aimed at the classroom, present an interesting contrast. A program called *What Is Poetry?* (Caedmon) consists of ten recordings, beautifully read by Claire Bloom and featuring also the voices of Carl Sandburg and Ogden Nash. The readings are matched by imaginative filmstrips, in which the pictures, speaking a visual language of their own, merely suggest and intimate, but never mimic. On the other hand, Lee Bennett Hopkins has made a set of six sound filmstrips, *Pick a Peck o' Poems* (Miller-Brody), to provide "a unique conceptual approach to learning through poetry." But while the texts are carefully selected and prepared, and the reading, for the most part, is acceptable, the filmstrips are weak and undistinguished. Once again, literal, commonplace pictures utterly fail as analogies to the figurative language of poetry; and the drab, realistic drawings merely show the objects mentioned in the poems rather than convey an idea of the moods and images created by them.

"Where are the enduring classics of the filmstrip? Who quotes them? Who remembers them?" So asked, somewhat plaintively, William R. Eshelman in *The New York Times Book Review.** Teachers, librarians, parents are all eager to inspire creativity in children; but literature in filmstrip form is too often a nonproductive short-cut, blandly entertaining, or at its worst, rendering only custodial service. For such filmstrips — with their predetermined, superimposed pictures — make no demands on the imagination; and literature, in this form, is shorn of its power to humanize, to stir, or to enliven the wasteland of indifference in which so many children are wandering. "It's not the book that suffers," says Lloyd Alexander. "Great literature is eminently durable; it survives all sorts of bedevilments." But the children "come out a little poorer, a little smaller than [they] might have been."†

*William R. Eshelman, "Audio-Visual Aids: Fallout From the McLuhan Galaxy," *The New York Times Book Review* (May 6, 1973), p. 32.

†From a speech given on July 31, 1973, at the 6th International Summer Seminar on Children's Literature, Towson State College, Towson, Maryland.

From *The Horn Book* for June 1974

IV

AT CRITICAL CROSS-PURPOSES

A S WAS TO BE expected, the controversy between Roald Dahl and Eleanor Cameron regarding *Charlie and the Chocolate Factory*, along with the editorial in the February issue of *The Horn Book Magazine*, has stirred up a buzz of controversy. At present, it appears that the intensely felt responses from *Horn Book* readers — both pro and con — will provide subject matter for the Letters to the Editor page for the next issue or two.

What is needed now, however, is an attempt to clarify the situation — to sort out the different kinds of premises on which the various arguments are based. Most of them seem to reflect three entirely different kinds of consideration. (1) How should *Charlie and the Chocolate Factory* be regarded as a work of literature? (2) Are children to be the final arbiters of children's books — or of any books — they read? (At this juncture, nobody is suggesting that children do not know what they like or should not read what they like.) (3) How important in the literary judgment of a book is the fact that it helps to improve reading skill or even to attract potential readers?

Much of the controversy, then, has been conducted at cross-purposes. A criticism of *Charlie and the Chocolate Factory* on literary grounds (which any adult has a right to make) is often met with a statement regarding the popularity of the book; or its defense is made in terms of purely utilitarian principles. Interested adult readers of children's books would do well to avoid confusing the nonliterary with the literary merits of books. Devoted and serious critics have long been engaged in a struggle to secure respect for a body of literature which is often sneeringly classified as "kiddy lit." Is it too much to expect that those who proffer books to children know something of the various ways of looking at the characteristics and the meaning of these books?

Editorial: *The Horn Book* for April 1973   PAUL HEINS

McLUHAN, YOUTH, AND LITERATURE

By Eleanor Cameron

IN AN AGE of television watching, I am probably, like most of you, a reading animal. It might even be that this hunger for reading, which seems to increase with age, is being sharpened by my aversion to those attitudes and practices which have called forth the ideas of Marshall McLuhan. I think that a good many persons, mostly nonreaders (and McLuhan is not one of these), feel that bookish people allow reading to take the place of experience, that we are afraid of or want something to substitute for life. But I have always found that, far from substituting for it, my reading enlarges life, intensifies the flavor of it, intensifies my seeing, that it deepens each experience by giving me echoes and reverberations and bridges, compelling me always to obey E. M. Forster's precept, "Connect — only connect!"

For many years I have found it a pleasure to mingle the reading of children's books with those written for adults, so that I am actually enmeshing children's literature in the net of all literature as I believe it is enmeshed in spirit. Sheila Egoff, in a *Horn Book* article (April, 1970) on a Canadian's view of current American fiction for children, speaks of two ways of reading children's books: as children do, purely for enjoyment; and as librarians do, who seek generalizations, interrelationships, and trends of a social nature. She doesn't mention specifically the third way — the librarian's seeking for excellence in the conception and the writing of these books; but she indicates this concern when she says that most of America's current children's books will not last.

I believe that she is right, but I believe also that this must hold true for any country and not just for the United States. And I would ask as well, in reply to her statement: When in any age of the world's history has much of any art lasted? Out of the thousands upon thousands of works constantly being produced, most sink away and are forgotten. Only a very few are powerful enough — for elusive, perhaps unexplainable reasons — to be remembered and kept alive because of a continuing spiritual and aesthetic need for them. Sappho of Lesbos speaks to us, miraculously enough, out of the beginnings of the sixth century B.C. After 2,570 years, those who read her in the original still take delight in her admirable choice of words, still feel her passion, her direct and forceful simplicity, her intensity. Who of those writing in our time will be remembered 2,570 years from now — should there be any alive to put down words with passion and intensity and simplicity?

As for those books children go on reading decade after decade, we recall that *Robinson Crusoe* was published in 1719, *Gulliver's Travels* in 1726, *Alice's Adventures in Wonderland* in 1865, *Little Women* in 1868, and *Pinocchio* in 1883. Will any one of the children's books written in the past thirty years be alive and beloved one hundred years from now? It is a profoundly unsettling question for those who write with seriousness and not wholly for money. And when I have finished reading what I believe to be a really fine book for children — the kind I buy and put on the bookshelf in my study — I say to myself, "Surely this will last — surely!" And yet, who knows? Only the future — if Marshall McLuhan should, by some blessed chance, be wrong in his firm belief that the importance of the written word is over and done with, and remains only to be buried with a hurried phrase or two over the casket.

By heaven, it is not over and done with yet! But I did catch a tooth of McLuhan's wind from the graveyard when I read the words of a reviewer of one of Eudora Welty's novels entitled, prophetically enough, *Losing Battles*. The reviewer said, "Reading this book is both an exhilarating and saddening experience. Exhilarating because you are in the hands of a master, and saddening because that kind of mastery is rapidly disappearing from the world, from culture, from consciousness itself. Miss Welty's eighth book and fourth novel finds her in such ripe maturity as a sensibility and a craftsman that she seems like a creature from another world, which indeed she is." And the tooth of that wind was felt even more keenly when the reviewer said at the close of his review that she is one of the last of the writers who is truly a storyteller, and that her book exemplifies his belief that "the art of the storyteller is reaching its end because the epic side of truth, wisdom is dying out." I can only say: One for whom the appreciation of writing is a precious part of life, for whom stories written with truth and wisdom are treasurable, could weep at those words, "is dying out."

In view of McLuhan's world and the increasingly desperate

battle with nonreaders in all levels of schooling, it is hard to imagine what can be saved of literature in the years to come. The poet Karl Shapiro has spoken of the contempt and the staggering illiteracy of youth: "We have the most inarticulate generation of college students in history."* Therefore, it would seem to me that more consciously and devotedly than ever, writers for children, librarians, and particularly parents and elementary school teachers *must* involve the child with literature from the moment he can be read to. I should like to say to all parents: Your small child *must* be read and sung the Mother Goose rhymes at the earliest age, *must* be read the Beatrix Potter stories and the finest of the picture books. (Go to the library and find out what they are!) He can scarcely be too young to be given his first taste of the English language in nursery rhymes and fables and stories. Remember that the poet Dylan Thomas' father read him Shakespeare when he was four; and of this experience Thomas' biographer Constantine FitzGibbon has said, "The effect upon the little boy, in his sickbed or before sleep, was profound and lasting. The greatest poetry in the English language, perhaps in any language, flooded into an open, receptive and above all fresh mind, for the little boy knew nothing else."†

I should like to travel up and down the country going to elementary schools and saying to all the teachers: Find out about the good children's books. Believe me, it is of the most pressing importance that you leave half an hour, fifteen minutes even, to read what is best to the children in your charge, and I mean year after year from kindergarten through the eighth grade — even beyond. And the lower the ability of your group, the more you must read to them. For textbooks alone, unless they include selections of what is enduring in children's literature, can never give, aesthetically or spiritually, the sense of what is precious in literature. We must not *let* stories written with truth and wisdom die out. Elementary school teachers must know what is good. They must find out what is good and read these books to their children. If they do not, it may very well be that the children will never find them, because a children's librarian cannot do everything. In fact, what she can do is depressingly nullified by what parents and teachers do not do — by indifference or apathy or

*In a speech given at a pre-conference session of the California Library Association in San Francisco. Excerpts appeared in *Human Events*, July 11, 1970, pp. 9-10.
†Constantine FitzGibbon, *The Life of Dylan Thomas*. Boston: Atlantic-Little, Brown, 1965, p. 33.

ignorance. Obviously, the future devolves upon all of us who are concerned with children's minds and imaginations. How else can one look at the matter?

Which brings me directly back to Marshall McLuhan, who places all emphasis upon electronic media rather than upon content. Indeed, he is not in the least interested in content as being of any importance whatever: The medium itself is the message. The *massage*, as he puts it, for he is all out for the ear and the senses as opposed to the reading eye and the reflective mind. Now that the electronic age is upon us and, most especially, the age of television, he believes that the age of the printed symbol is largely over. The eye and the mind to him are related to one word at a time, to slowness, to the past as opposed to the exploding *Now* of the ear and the senses; the all-at-once drenching television pours over us so that we absorb impressions instantly through all of our pores. The youth of the future, he wrote about ten years ago, will no longer want to read and meditate and check up on facts and ideas; they will want to see and feel and act immediately. Electronic waves are what turn McLuhan on and whether we know it or not, he says, they are what turn all of us on. And so great is his joy in this phenomenon, so great is his trust in its power for good, in the computer, and in electronic circuiting, one would think that human beings had never been turned on by anything else before. He believes that what electronic waves project does not matter — that is, content doesn't matter — which is no doubt why he gets so excited about TV ads. That they do project, that we are constantly being bombarded by cool sensory impressions, is what is giving our age its character and its quality.

And in tune with what McLuhan calls the coolness of television, he himself is what one would no doubt call these days a very cool cat. He makes no value judgments; in fact, he is acidly scornful of them. He loathes philosophizing as much as he loathes having to stop and clarify his thinking for those who are skeptical of a good many parts of it: the vast overgeneralizations, the non-sequiturs, the jerry-built theories, the dogmatic assertions based on sheer error, the disorganized successions of parenthetical observations. What delights him is to comment rapidly on what he thinks is happening and what he is certain can be done with electronic circuits in order to orchestrate programs for the sensory life.

For instance, consider a culture such as Indonesia's. It can be shaped and worked, he says, according to what we think is best for it. He doesn't pause to reflect, apparently, upon whether the United States, or any other power in dire straits itself, might know what is best for Indonesia. He believes that we could write an ideal sensory program for Indonesia or some area of the world we "wanted to leapfrog across a lot of old technology," if we knew, first of all, its present sensory thresholds. But who is to judge what would be an "ideal" sensory program for Indonesia? And what if the Indonesians or people in some other area of the world didn't want to be leapfrogged but just wanted to be left alone? McLuhan doesn't go into this. He never explains values. What one feels above all is his extreme objectivity, his brushing aside of individual preferences, his complete lack of interest in bothersome details, in the slow and painful process.

And this leads me once more to Eudora Welty before I go on to a certain children's book I have in mind, *Charlie and the Chocolate Factory* (Knopf). As opposed to McLuhan's enormous admiration for instantaneousness, Miss Welty's *Losing Battles* took nine years to write. And as opposed to the superficial quality of most TV shows, what I was constantly aware of in it — what I am always aware of in those children's books I put on my special shelf — was the extreme individuality of the style, the subtle, unovert way in which the characters through their dialogue gradually but forcefully moved in on me, the pervading humor in the midst of sadness, and the sharp conveyance of a special time and place by means of brief but telling images. And because of this I was compelled to go back once again to her fine little monograph *Place in Fiction*. In this small book Miss Welty sets forth her belief not only in the power of place in any created work but in the ways in which place exerts control over character portrayal, of how exceedingly important is explicitness of detail and a steady lucidity and uncompromise of purpose. She speaks further of how place has deeply to do with three kinds of goodness in fiction: the goodness and validity of the raw material, the goodness of the writing, and the goodness of the writer himself, his worth as a human being. And this worth is always mercilessly revealed in his writing, because there we discover his roots or lack of them, the place where he stands, his point of view or lack of it.

We come now to Charlie, that starved child Roald Dahl

dreamed up to go and live forever in pure bliss in Mr. Willy Wonka's chocolate factory. The more I think about Charlie and the character of Willy Wonka and his factory, the more I am reminded of McLuhan's coolness, the basic nature of his observations, and the kinds of things that excite him. Certainly there are several interesting parallels between the point of view of *Charlie and the Chocolate Factory* and McLuhan's "theatrical view of experience as a production or stunt," as well as his enthusiastic conviction that every ill of mankind can easily be solved by subservience to the senses.

Both McLuhan's theories and the story about Charlie are enormously popular. *Charlie and the Chocolate Factory* (together with *Charlotte's Web* [Harper]) is probably the book most read aloud by those teachers who have no idea, apparently, what other books they might read to the children. *Charlie*, again along with *Charlotte's Web*, is always at the top of the best sellers among children's books, put there by fond aunts and grandmothers and parents buying it as the perfect gift, knowing no better. And I do think this a most curious coupling: on the one hand, one of the most tasteless books ever written for children; and on the other, one of the best. We are reminded of Ford Madox Ford's observation that only two classes of books are universal in their appeal: the very best and the very worst.

Now, there are those who consider *Charlie* to be a satire and believe that Willy Wonka and the children are satiric portraits as in a cautionary tale. I am perfectly willing to admit that possibly Dahl wrote it as such: a book on two levels, one for adults and one for children. However, he chose to publish *Charlie* as a children's book, knowing quite well that children would react to one level only (if there *are* two), the level of pure story. Being literarily unsophisticated, children can react only to this level; and as I am talking about children's books, it is this level I am about to explore.

Why does *Charlie* continually remind me of what is most specious in McLuhan's world of the production and the stunt? The book is like candy (the chief excitement and lure of *Charlie*) in that it is delectable and soothing while we are undergoing the brief sensory pleasure it affords but leaves us poorly nourished with our taste dulled for better fare. I think it will be admitted of the average TV show that goes on from week to week that there is no time, either from the point of view of production or the time allowed for showing, to work deeply at meaning or characterization. All interest depends upon the constant, unremitting excitement of the turns of plot. And if character or likelihood of action — that is, inevitability — must be wrenched to fit the necessities of plot, there is no time to be concerned about this either by the director or by the audience. Nor will the tuned-in, turned-on, keyed-up television watcher give the superficial quality of the show so much as a second thought. He has been temporarily amused; what is there to complain about? And like all those nursing at the electronic bosom in McLuhan's global village (as he likes to call it), so everybody in Willy Wonka's chocolate factory is enclosed in its intoxicating confines forever: all the workers, including the little Oompa-Loompas brought over from Africa and, by the end of the book, Charlie and his entire family.

To McLuhan, as Harold Rosenburg has pointed out, man appears to be a device employed by the television industry in *its* self-development. Just so does Charlie seem to be employed by his creator in a situation of phony poverty simply as a device to make more excruciatingly tantalizing the heavenly vision of being able to live eternally fed upon chocolate. This is Charlie's sole character and being. And just as in the average TV show, the protagonists of the book are types, extreme types: the nasty children who are ground up in the factory machinery because they're baddies, and pathetic Charlie and his family, eternally yearning and poor and good. As for Willy Wonka himself, he is the perfect type of TV showman with his gags and screechings. The exclamation mark is the extent of his individuality.

But let us go a little deeper. Just as McLuhan preaches the medium as being the massage — the sensory turn-on — so *Charlie and the Chocolate Factory* gives us the ideal world as one in which a child would be forever concerned with candy and its manufacture, with the chance to live in it and on it and by it. And just as McLuhan seems to have lost sight of the individual and his preferences and uniquenesses, so Willy Wonka cares nothing for individual preferences in his enthusiasm for his own kind of global village. Just as McLuhan puts before us the question of leapfrogging Indonesia into whatever age we think best for it, so the question is asked why Mr. Wonka doesn't use the little African Oompa-Loompas instead of squirrels to complete certain of his processes. Brought directly from Africa, the Oompa-Loom-pas have never been given the opportunity of any life outside of the chocolate factory, so that it never occurs to them to protest the possibility of being used like squirrels. And at the end of the book we find the bedridden grandparents being snatched up in their beds and, though they say that they refuse to go and that they would rather die than go, they are crashed through the ruins of their house, willy-nilly, and swung over into the chocolate factory to live there for the rest of their lives whether they want to or not.

What I object to in *Charlie* is its phony presentation of poverty and its phony humor, which is based on punishment with over-tones of sadism; its hypocrisy which is epitomized in its moral — stuck like a marshmallow in a lump of fudge — that TV is hor-rible and hateful and time-wasting and that children should read good books instead, when in fact the book itself is like nothing so much as one of the more specious television shows. It reminds me of Cecil B. De Mille's Biblical spectaculars, with plenty of blood and orgies and tortures to titillate the masses, while a prophet, for the sake of the religious section of the audience, stands on the edge of the crowd crying, "In the name of the Lord, thou shalt sin no more!"

If I ask myself whether children are harmed by reading *Charlie* or having it read to them, I can only say I don't know.* Its influ-ence would be subtle underneath the catering. Those adults who are either amused by the book or are positively devoted to it on the children's level probably call it a modern fairy tale. Possibly its tastelessness, including the ugliness of the illustrations, is, in-deed (whether the author meant it so or not), a comment upon our age and the quality of much of our entertainment. What both-ers me about it, aside from its tone, is the using of the Oompa-Loompas, and the final indifference to the wishes of the grand-parents. Many adults see all this as humorous and delightful, and I am aware that most children, when they're young, aren't par-ticularly aware of sadism as such, or see it differently from the way an adult sees it and so call *Charlie* "a funny book."

I believe it is a pity that considerable sums, taken out of tight library budgets, should be expended on sometimes as many

*"The author of a work of imagination is trying to affect us wholly, as human beings, whether he knows it or not; and we are affected by it, as human beings, whether we intend to be or not." T. S. Eliot, *Essays Ancient and Modern.* New York: Harcourt, 1936, p. 102.

as ten copies of *Charlie and the Chocolate Factory* (Knopf) and that hard-won classroom time should be given over to the reading aloud of a book without quality or lasting content. And especially when there are really fine humorous tales such as Robert Lawson's *Ben and Me* (Little); Sid Fleischman's *By the Great Horn Spoon!, Chancy and the Grand Rascal,* and *The Ghost in the Noonday Sun* (all Atlantic-Little); E. C. Spykman's *A Lemon and a Star, Edie on the Warpath* (both Harcourt), and other chronicles of the Cares family; or, to go back in time, *Pinocchio* and certain deliciously funny chapters in *The Wind in the Willows* (Scribner). But children do not always have to be made to laugh, though certainly the books I have mentioned bring more to their readers than laughter. Classroom reading, it seems to me, should be a treasurable time, in which the discerning teacher can introduce books the children might never discover on their own, such a book, for instance, as Randall Jarrell's *The Animal Family* (Pantheon). A sixth-grade teacher tried it out on a group of boys more interested in sports than in anything else; and when she had finished, one of the roughest and most unlikely candidates as audience for such a poetical tale begged her, "Read it again! Please read it again!" And I think it extremely regrettable that the same children should hear *Charlotte's Web* (Harper) term after term, because this is one of the few books elementary schoolteachers know about; for, once it is introduced, the children can go back to it as many times as they like. However, as a contrast to *Charlie,* let us test *Charlotte's Web* by referring its various elements to standards set by some of the finest critics and writers of adult literature.

We remember Jack Kroll, in reviewing Welty's *Losing Battles,* speaking of the epic side of truth and wisdom dying out in adult fiction. We remember Eudora Welty herself noting three kinds of goodness that contribute to the stature of a novel: the goodness of the raw material, the goodness of the writing, and the goodness of the writer himself, which involves his roots, his point of view, his worth as a human being. Elizabeth Bowen, the great English writer, has spoken of a particular plot as being something the novelist is driven to, rather than its being a matter of choice; he is, she says, confronted by the impossibility of saying what he has to say in any other way. And she charges characterless action as not being action at all, in the plot sense, for the act cannot be divided from the actor, nor the qualities and likelihood of an act from a particular actor. Without this kind of truth, action is without force or reason. In *Literature and the Sixth Sense*, the critic Philip Rahv lists his own criteria for a work of literature: the criterion of language or style, the criterion of character creation (disclosing the depth of life out of which a novelist's moral feelings spring), and the criterion of plot constructed in such a way as to invest the interplay of experience with the power of the inevitable. The American novelist Flannery O'Connor has written that for the writer of fiction everything has its testing point in the eye, an organ which eventually involves the whole personality and as much of the world as can be perceived by it. For her, "the roots of the eye are in the heart."

As I do not know E. B. White personally, I cannot give inside information as to why Mr. White was driven to the particular plot of *Charlotte's Web* in order to say what he had to say. But I do know from his essays that he lives on a farm, that the natural world is of the greatest importance to him (which is perhaps why he has chosen to live on a farm rather than in the city), and that this importance is expressed throughout his book with a pervading, humorous tenderness. White's whole attitude toward the world of plants and animals, toward the rhythm of the seasons and of life and death is expressed in the story of a pig who forms a close friendship with a spider, whose death ends the tale.

"I am not a fast worker," White has said. Certainly his book did not come quickly, for the article that was its donnée was written in 1948*, and *Charlotte's Web* was not published until 1952. That article, which tells how White failed to save the life of a sick pig, gradually turned into the story of how the child Fern Arable out of love, the rat Templeton out of greed, and the spider Charlotte out of friendship managed to save Wilbur from becoming bacon in the autumn pig-killing. Now, in the course of this apparently simple tale, we are shown the truth of Eudora Welty's conviction that "[t]he moment the place in which the novel happens is accepted as true, through it will begin to glow, in a kind of recognizable glory, the feeling and thought that inhabited the novel in the author's head and animates the whole of his work."*

You may recall White's loving description of the barn, which is the main scene of the book:

*E. B. White, "Death of a Pig." *The Atlantic Monthly*, 181:30-33, January, 1948.

*Eudora Welty, *Place in Fiction*. New York: House of Books, 1957, O.P. pp. 9-10.

The barn was very large. It was very old. It smelled of hay and it smelled of manure. It smelled of the perspiration of tired horses and the wonderful sweet breath of patient cows. It often had a sort of peaceful smell — as though nothing bad could happen ever again in the world. It smelled of grain and of harness dressing and of axle grease and of rubber boots and of new rope. And whenever the cat was given a fish-head to eat, the barn would smell of fish. But mostly it smelled of hay, for there was always hay in the great loft up overhead. And there was always hay being pitched down to the cows and the horses and the sheep.

The barn was pleasantly warm in winter when the animals spent most of their time indoors, and it was pleasantly cool in summer when the big doors stood wide open to the breeze. The barn had stalls on the main floor for the work horses, tie-ups on the main floor for the cows, a sheepfold down below for the sheep, a pigpen down below for Wilbur, and it was full of all sorts of things that you find in barns: ladders, grindstones, pitch forks, monkey wrenches, scythes, lawn mowers, snow shovels, ax handles, milk pails, water buckets, empty grain sacks, and rusty rat traps. It was the kind of barn that swallows like to build their nests in. It was the kind of barn that children like to play in. And the whole thing was owned by Fern's uncle, Mr. Homer L. Zuckerman.[†]

It may seem that in quoting this passage I am following in the path of those teachers I complained of for repeating what is already well-known. But I quote it because it explains to those critics who feel that long descriptions are apt to be static and so have no place in children's books that the value and desirability of any description depends wholly upon the language, upon how the description is written; and, in this case, we see that it is anything but static and passive. I quote it, too, because we are reminded by the beautiful precision of White's evocation of the Zuckerman barn (which he enriches from chapter to chapter almost without the reader's being aware of it, as he does the whole life and appearance of the countryside) of another of Eudora Welty's convictions. "No blur of inexactness, no cloud of vagueness, is allowable in good writing; from the first seeing to the last putting down, there must be steady lucidity and uncompromise of purpose."[*] We are reminded also by White's description, which I have called *loving*, of Flannery O'Connor's words, "the roots of the eye are in the heart."

As for the protagonists themselves, they exemplify still another of Miss Welty's statements. "Place, then," she says,

†E. B. White, *Charlotte's Web*. New York: Harper and Brothers, 1952. pp. 13-14.

*Welty, *op. cit.*, pp. 15-26.

"has the most delicate control over character too: by confining character, it defines it." [†] E. B. White has not only given us a revelation of farm life as much from the point of view of his animals as from that of his human beings, but has also created his protagonists with absolute truthfulness, each to his kind. These animals and people illustrate to perfection Elizabeth Bowen's statement that characterless action is not action at all, for the act cannot be divided from the actor, nor the qualities and likelihood of an act from a particular actor.

Wilbur, the runt pig, who is saved in the beginning by Fern's love for him, never ceases throughout the progress of the story to be anything but naïve and ingenuous, completely unsophisticated in a plump, pig-like way, dependent upon others for comfort and spiritual sustenance and upon plenty of food and sleep and sunny weather for day-to-day happiness. Like many a naïve and ingenuous person, he is deeply influenced by the opinions and moods of others; he is always the innocent who is acted upon in order that he shall be saved, rather than the hero who acts independently and with assurance to save himself.

The real hero of the book is Charlotte, the spider, "brilliant, beautiful, and loyal" — so Wilbur characterizes her: controlled in the face of Wilbur's hysterics and desperation, acutely perceptive of the nature of mankind (as shown in her awareness that Wilbur's salvation lies in her one chance of working upon the gullibility of human beings), patient as spiders have need to be, and completely unsentimental when it comes to the prospect of her own death at the peak of her forces. All this is in marked contrast to Wilbur's own behavior under the same circumstances. Female spiders always die after they have hatched their eggs, and there is nothing to do — Charlotte knows — but to accept the fact with dignity. Yet E. B. White does not hesitate for a moment to tell the complete truth about his appealing heroine: that in addition to possessing the above excellences, she is bloodthirsty. Wilbur cannot bear this, but " 'It's true,' " Charlotte tells him, " 'and I have to say what is true.' "

Nor does White hesitate to tell the truth about Fern, even though it may not show her in a very favorable light. After the story opens, with Fern saving the piglet from being killed because he is the runt of the litter, Fern spends all her free time during the following months sitting at Wilbur's pen, listening to the

[†]Ibid. p. 11.

animals' conversation, and watching Wilbur grow. Next to Charlotte, she is his most devoted friend. And yet, because Fern is human and a child, she changes. During the opening chapters, Fern's whole life is Wilbur and the events of the barn, for she is at that particular age when imaginative children quite easily convince themselves that not only do birds and animals talk, but that they themselves understand them. And it is a nice little detail that never once does Fern enter into these conversations among the animals, but only reports them afterwards, quite matter-of-factly, to her mother and father, seeing nothing unusual or surprising in her understanding of bird and animal talk. Thus the halcyon summer passes. But then something happens to Fern. For the first time in her childhood she becomes disturbingly aware of a member of the opposite sex, one Henry Fussy. And at the very moment when Wilbur is winning his prize at the county fair, when he has become that pig which long, long ago (in other words, three or four months ago) she had envisioned him becoming, she is off with Henry, aware only of Henry. Nor does she ever come regularly to the barn again because "She was growing up, and was careful to avoid childish things, like sitting on a milk stool near the pigpen."

On the other hand, Wilbur never forgets Charlotte, nor can his love for her children and grandchildren ever supplant his love for her nor his gratitude to her. And it was quite moving to me to find in a library copy of the book a heavy black pencil line, rather wobbly, which some child had felt compelled to draw around the words, "Charlotte died. . . . No one was with her when she died." I had an idea that, like Wilbur, that child would never forget Charlotte.

It is the burden of feeling and meaning in *Charlotte's Web* which makes it memorable, which will speak to all times and not just to our own time. It is that burden which gives all the great children's books their greatness, a burden which is the natural result of their author's ability to invest a tale for children with wisdom and truth. It is this burden of feeling and meaning which speaks not only of the goodness of the raw material and the author's handling of it, but of the essence of the writer himself: his point of view, the roots from which he has sprung, roots which in White's case go deep into the natural world and are responsible for the tone and import of his book.

At a dinner in San Francisco where medals were being given

to various California authors who had published outstanding books in 1969, Theodore Taylor's *The Cay* (Doubleday) was given a silver medal for the best children's book. And I was amused when the master of ceremonies "complimented" it by saying that "even though it was for children" he would recommend it to the assembled guests and that they need not be ashamed of reading it. I don't know if it would have made any difference to anyone there that though *The Cay* was written in a remarkably short time, Taylor had brooded his material for ten years. If you step from books written for adults down to teenage books, you ought — I suppose — to feel self-conscious no matter how good such books might be. But if you step down further still into children's books and are caught reading them, you ought apparently to be nothing less than mortified. Yet, it intrigues me that, year after year, I find four or five children's books — real children's books, I mean — in which I find those qualities I pointed out in *Charlotte's Web*, but much more rarely do I find a rich and satisfying combination of these qualities in the creations — so often neither fish, flesh, nor fowl — which we call junior novels.

Nat Hentoff has written two novels for teenagers: one good, *Jazz Country* (Harper); and one, to my mind, a failure, *I'm really dragged but nothing gets me down* (Simon). In his essay "Fiction for Teenagers," Hentoff says, "Is it possible, then, to reach these children of McLuhan in that old-time medium, the novel? I believe it is, because their primary concerns are only partially explored in the messages they get from their music and are diverted rather than probed on television. If a book is relevant to those concerns, not didactically but in creating textures of experience which teenagers can recognize as germane to their own, it can merit their attention."*

What troubles me is that, in Hentoff's intense concern to reach teenagers, the difference between bibliotherapy and literature is lost sight of. I'm sure Hentoff knows the difference between the two: that literature was never written with the purpose of providing a tool or a release for the desperate. It is written because someone must make palpable and seen and understood his private vision of the universe. What we call literature gives the reader an intensified sense of existence, a revelation, gives him people with idiosyncrasies and habits and beliefs, people with

* Nat Hentoff: *Fiction for Teenagers*. The Atlantic Monthly (December 1967).

histories and possible futures which the reader cannot help dwelling upon when the last page is turned. People, I should think, at the opposite pole to those faceless ones, the message carriers (most of them depressingly, boringly alike in their involvements and rebellions and obsessions) presented us by the writers of the catering and problem type of teenage novel. Reading a stack of them becomes tedious beyond endurance, especially when they are written in the first person, purportedly by a teenager.

And yet Hentoff, desiring, I am sure, to write an admirable novel, one with quality, has given us exactly what he speaks against — didacticism, an arrangement of ideas already well-known to teenagers — but has not given us what he created in *Jazz Country*, a texture of experience. This, it would seem to me, ought of necessity, given the nature of the human body, to include Flannery O'Connor's all important eye. Yet very rarely does *I'm really dragged* give us the look either of human beings or of places; we are not, strangely enough, made aware of any particular place. And in losing the particularity of place, we lose somehow the sense of reality, and I mean an intense sense of reality. We are all but blind — like the chambered mole. Nor do we feel the surfaces of solid objects; they seem scarcely to exist. We never smell anything. As readers, we seem stripped of all senses except hearing, and remember McLuhan's saying, "For the eye has none of the delicacy of the ear."

I'm really dragged is like a play, with the characters coming through to us only in their speeches about subjects of interest to contemporary teenagers. You experience Hentoff's people as you do those in a play, only the strictly pertinent core of them rather than the accomplished novelist's exploration of facets of personality. And you can go through the short chapters and assign a title to each just by running an eye down the dialogue: Chapter One, the draft and blacks vs. whites; Chapter Two, father vs. son; Chapter Three, drugs, to smoke pot or not to smoke it; Chapter Four, father vs. son; Chapter Five, blacks vs. whites; Chapter six, father vs. son; Chapter Seven, the generation gap; Chapter Eight, parents and school; and so on. Is *this* what Hentoff calls "textures of experience"? But surely that texture we call "the novel" gives us, at its most treasurable, a passionate, sometimes rapturous meeting between the artist's private vision and the haunting, ambiguous, paradoxical world of feelings and objects — all interlaced. And these interlacings open up for us intimations about ourselves and the world we had not guessed at before, or had not seen, nor been able to put into words for ourselves.

Because of their loss of literature today, the young, writes Gore Vidal, "are quite unable to comprehend the *doubleness* of things, the unexpected paradox, the sense of yes-no without which there can be no true intelligence, no means, in fact, of examining life as opposed to letting it wash over one."*

The great makers of literature are door-openers, and teenagers especially need to be given not what they already know but what they have not yet divined.

Perhaps some will not agree with me that the number of real *children's* books — like the Borrower and the Green Knowe books, the Little House and the Moffat books, *Charlotte's Web* (Harper), *Island of the Blue Dolphins* (Houghton), *The Return of the Twelves* (Coward), *The Gammage Cup* (Harcourt), the books of Philippa Pearce — those that sit securely as classics in the realm of memorable literature, outnumber the ones you find memorable for teenagers. But for my own satisfaction I want to try to get to the bottom of why this should appear to me to be so.

For one thing, the average writer for teenagers seems to find himself caught between wanting to present a world in which the burgeoning awareness of sex and of sexual desire is overpowering, and at the same time feeling himself inhibited because he is not, after all, writing books to be published for adults and so cannot feel perfectly free and unconfined. Chekhov pointed out that the great writer has a sense of absolute freedom within the discipline of his craft, within his moral point of view, his sense of aesthetic distance. He has reached that point where he can be himself to the utmost degree and can say what he wants to say in exactly the way he wants to say it without descending to the meretricious, the vulgar, or to a cheap voyeurism. And I think that it is this sense of restriction — of not feeling perfectly free to express all he knows to be true of teenage sexual feelings and the teenagers' deepest attitudes toward them — that so often pulls the quality of the writer's work for this age down to the level of the bland and the superficial, to what Josh Greenfeld, in a review of Emily Neville's *Fogarty* (Harper), called "the cultivated cop-out." That cop-out, he said, is what is the matter with most

*Gore Vidal, *Two Sisters*. Boston, Little, Brown, 1970. p. 41.

children's books. But what he meant by "the cultivated cop-out" in reference to Emily Neville's novel was her failure to communicate any real understanding of Fogarty as a man desiring a woman. She closed the door on that scene, and on Fogarty's emotions in that moment because she possibly hadn't the knowledge or the power or the courage to face them and delineate them in a way she could handle. And I was sharply resentful at finding a novel about a twenty-three-year-old man reviewed with children's books (and called by Greenfeld a children's book) simply because Emily Neville usually writes for teenagers. But resentful above all because "the cultivated cop-out" in a child's book would have nothing at all to do with lack of frankness about sexual love, but would result in an avoidance of truth regarding some facet of a child's complex emotions before the age of puberty.

Furthermore, the writer for teenagers so often restricts himself as to implications about life in general. Very seldom do we get the reverberations called up by a sense of the past in teenage stories about contemporary life. The past seems scarcely to exist. More often than not, he avoids complexity of structure and of characterization and meaning. It is as if the writer for older youth is scared to death of losing his rock-tuned, TV-engrossed reader, so that he keeps telling himself, "Keep it simple! Keep is simple!" In an exploration of Alan Garner's *The Owl Service* (Walck)* I have told why I feel that it fails in its overall impact, and yet by comparison with Neville's characterization of Fogarty, and with most of Wojciechowska's, Hentoff's, and Zindel's characterizations and structures, I salute the intricacy and handling of Garner's conception, and the fine characterizations of his Welsh protagonists, Huw Halfbacon and Nancy and Gwyn.

Not only does the writer for youth seem, on the whole, to be incapable of complexity of characterization and meaning, but of subtlety and wit and individuality of style as well. Most of the junior novels sound exactly alike, and many are written in the first person, as Zindel's are. It is as if the writers felt that only a banal, flat-flooted, unevocative way of writing — utterly lacking in the overtones and elliptical expressions the accomplished writer takes pleasure in — would be tolerated by his audience. But surely there can be no more unrewarding prose than is found in these books, written as if by the teenagers themselves. Scarcely

*Eleanor Cameron, "The Owl Service: A Study." *Wilson Library Bulletin*, December 1969. pp. 425-433.

ever do their writers educate the ear, give it a chance to become fine-tuned, expand its experience of word play, or provide the reader any opportunity to reach into subtle comprehensions or to grow aesthetically. On the contrary, they offer only those word arrangements teenagers themselves use every day of their lives, which are most often extremely limited modes of expression.

I make no blanket condemnation of *I* books. For Mark Twain's *Huckleberry Finn* is literature and was written in the first person, a remarkable accomplishment when you consider that Huck is unlettered. But so deeply did Mark Twain enter into Huck, into the uniqueness of his personality, and so great was Mark Twain's own individuality, so sensitive his ear, that he could with integrity bring to his book unforgettable poetic feeling, projected as through Huck's own sensibility. Joseph Krumgold's three novels for young people are written in the first person, and especially is . . . *and now Miguel* (Crowell) rewarding as to style because of Krumgold's fidelity to all that is profoundly true of Miguel. Adrienne Richard's *Pistol* (Atlantic-Little) is told in the first person, but in the plainness of style there is no banality; rather there is great dignity and expressiveness and a certain cumulative power.

Benjamin DeMott, in an essay review of Saul Bellow's *Mr. Sammler's Planet,* has noted what literature possesses for him: "[h]igh spirits, humor, strong narrative rhythms, responsiveness to place as well as person, a swift idiomatic speaking voice, the power to nudge open a door upon common life without instantly banishing delight and wonder."* You might think he was speaking precisely of the Cleavers' *Where the Lilies Bloom* (Lippincott), for it answers well to each of DeMott's requirements. It is told in the first person, but the Cleavers have, above all, the "swift idiomatic speaking voice," whose attributes in this case are dryness, irony, understatement, and humor in the midst of desperation.

But these people — Huck, Miguel, Pistol, and Mary Call Luther of North Carolina in *Where the Lilies Bloom* — all inhabit worlds which have nothing to do with the world of acid rock and drugs and TV. They are remote in time or space from all this and speak our language each in his own way. Certainly the great

*Benjamin DeMott, "Saul Bellow and the Dogmas of Possibility." *Saturday Review,* February 7, 1970. p. 25.

challenge the writer about youth faces is to express the speech of towns and cities in their various uniquenesses and rhythms. June Jordan's *His Own Where* (Crowell) is such an expression, specifically the private, poetic expression of black people, and one hopes that from this first adventure Miss Jordan will go on to books of greater depth and power. One recalls here Flannery O'Connor's advice to young writers of her own region concerning the use of what is timeless and indigenous in the tone and twist of speech in their locality. "In one of Eudora Welty's stories," she notes, "a character says, 'Where I come from, we use fox for yard dogs and owls for chickens, but we sing true.' Now there is a whole book in that one sentence; and when the people of your section can talk like that, and you ignore it, you're just not taking advantage of what's yours. The sound of our talk is too definite to be discarded with impunity, and if the writer tries to get rid of it, he is liable to destroy the better part of his creative power."*

On the whole, it would seem that in the case of the average writer of novels for older youth there has been a failure not only of the ear (listening to others and to his own deepest self) but of perception as well. Such perception involves two kinds of seeing: the physical act of seeing, doing justice to the visible universe, and the kind of spiritual seeing that leads the writer into every vista of his fictional conception in order to comprehend creatively all of its possibilities. Henry James' aesthetic distance is of importance here. Lack of aesthetic distance results in emotional imbalance, exaggeration, a distorted view disclosing little but some current preoccupation, and that superficially. The gaining of aesthetic distance brings insight into one's story, which means living with it long enough to see into its unique and expanding meaning, the opposing of "how true" to "how new." We have only to compare Wojciechowska's *Shadow of a Bull* (Atheneum) with her later novels, *The Hollywood Kid* (Harper) and *Tuned Out* (Harper), and Hentoff's *Jazz Country* (Harper) with *I'm really dragged but nothing gets me down* (Harper) to illustrate the point. Even the titles are revealing.

At the far, opposite pole from such teenage problem novels as *The Hollywood Kid, Tuned Out*, and *I'm really dragged* are Isabelle Holland's *The Man Without a Face* (Lippincott) and

*Flannery O'Connor, *Mystery and Manners*. New York: Farrar, Straus & Giroux, 1961. p. 105.

116

Sharon Bell Mathis' *Teacup Full of Roses* (Viking). I spoke of the writer's reaching that point at which he has become so completely himself that he can speak freely of any aspect of human nature. Isabelle Holland writes with the utmost frankness of the sexual response of a fourteen-year-old boy to a homosexual, a response which the boy himself knows to be a momentary, overwhelming release brought about by the desperate need to love and be loved, to trust and be trusted. It is a strong, assured piece of writing that goes directly to the heart of a boy's deepest wretchedness and his bewildered reaction to a man whose complex nature and private searchings he cannot begin to understand.

I spoke of the lack of style, the lack of intricacy and depth of characterization and situation in the junior novel, resulting from a want of two kinds of perception. Sharon Bell Mathis has perception, and she is incisive, selective, precise. Her style is lean and taut in a book that is composed chiefly of dialogue which not only evokes, without explanation, the identity of the person speaking, but develops his singularity and furthers the action. Movingly, with a beautiful sense of aesthetic distance, Sharon Mathis brings all her characters alive in a situation which speaks truth in a black world, but which would speak truth just as clearly were this novel about a white family. For what she is talking about is the human condition.

But such novels are rare among those for older youth, and most teenagers prefer books published for adults. But then who reads the teenage books? I think that their readers must be younger and younger each year, but what a pity that children should be getting less, spiritually and aesthetically, than they did when they were reading children's books. On one level alone—that of subject matter — is the novel for older youth more "sophisticated."

I wonder if one could, with any hopefulness, recommend certain titles that have seemed to this reader to be moving and penetrating fictional creations by writers who have freely and with artistic assurance explored youthful lives between the ages of eleven and sixteen, as Carson McCullers did in *The Heart Is a Lonely Hunter* (Houghton) and *A Member of the Wedding* (Houghton). These and the books I have in mind have all been published as adult fiction, and I am led to wonder if perhaps editors should determine to publish no manuscript which will appear in their catalogues "for teenagers" unless they believe it could make its way aesthetically, if not financially, as an adult novel. It is significant in this respect that *Harper's Magazine* published a portion of *Pistol* in its pages before it was completed as a book. And Jean Renvoize's *A Wild Thing* (Atlantic-Little), handling with artistry a most difficult subject and written with admirable style, was brought out as a novel for adults in Great Britain. Its American editor, knowing it must be published, realized it would be lost in the adult market in this country, and so presented it as a novel for older youth. In this category it has been so warmly received that its life will undoubtedly be a long one.

I have read and reread Elizabeth Bowen's *The Death of the Heart* (Knopf), the story of a sixteen-year-old girl sent to live in a household full of elusive corruptions which she has at first no way of understanding or suspecting, and as the full force of these corruptions is borne in upon her, she goes almost mad with bewilderment. The structure of the book is not particularly complex, but the precision, the minuteness and delicacy of exploration of the human beings involved is surely matched by only a handful of other novels dealing with the subject of a young girl's slow awakening to the actuality of corruption.

John Knowles' *A Separate Peace* (Macmillan) ranges with merciless clarity, yet with tenderness, the tempestuous friendships, loyalties, struggles, and misunderstandings of two sixteen-year-old boys. *A Separate Peace* is told in the first person, the first person of a man passionately reliving (not simply recalling) his sixteenth year with extraordinary vividness, and the following paragraph is typical of the way he gives us sights, sounds, smells, intimations, emotions, all interlaced throughout the progress of the story.

It was surprising how well we got along in these weeks. Sometimes I found it hard to remember his treachery, sometimes I discovered myself thoughtlessly slipping back into affection for him again. It was hard to remember when one summer day after another broke with a cool effulgence over us, and there was a breath of widening life in the morning air — something hard to describe — an oxygen intoxicant, a shining northern paganism, some odor, some feeling so hopelessly promising that I would fall back in my bed on guard against it. It was hard to remember in the heady and sensual clarity of these mornings; I forgot whom I hated and who hated me. I wanted to break out crying from stabs of hopeless joy, or intolerable promise, or because these mornings were too full of beauty for me, because I knew of too much hate to be contained in a world like this.[*]

[*]John Knowles, *A Separate Peace*. New York: Macmillan, 1959. p. 45.

Joanna Crawford's *Birch Interval* (Houghton, O.P.), also written in the first person, is the story of an eleven-year-old girl learning in a year of humor and shock that whenever we persist, driven by outside opinions, in acting against our own deepest instincts and convictions, it is almost inevitable that we will do harm and injustice to others. *Birch Interval* was written by a very young woman, but the moment we read on the first page, "My father was an Irishman, tall and melancholy, with too much wildness in him, like all good Irishmen," we know that Joanna Crawford is acquainted with ellipsis and compression and can use them. And though this is a first novel by a young writer, there is no restriction of treatment, or of subject matter, or choice of words; nothing but absolute honesty, toughness, uncompromise of purpose.

Finally, Glendon Swarthout's *Bless the Beasts and Children* (Doubleday) is an exhausting, magnificent story of six boys — ranging in ages from twelve to fourteen, disgusting failures in the eyes of their boys' camp society — who have been shuffled off into a cabin away from everyone else. Here they cry and boast and find comfort in one another until finally they are hounded and pressed and driven to the limit of endurance by Cotton, their leader, into stealing a truck so that they can drive into the depths of Arizona and save a corralled herd of buffalo from the guns of brutal city "hunters." It is a novel full of scenes that hit you in the pit of the stomach, lift you up, and wring you dry, and which you keep hearing and seeing after you have read the last words.

The morning sun was steadfast now, the air blithe as a cool bottle of cola, and the countenance of the earth was fair. But a sad wind sneaked out of the canyon below, moaning baby, baby, and the blues and trembling through the pines and fanning over the preserve in farewell. It grieved.

Squinting under big hats, the men advanced, their faces grim. Some of them wore state uniforms. Some were sixpack city sportsmen and carried merciless rifles. Then they stopped abruptly.

Before them, standing frightened and defiant at the very jaw of the Mogollon Rim, were five redeye, hayhead juvenile delinquents in dirty boots and jeans and jackets with BC on the backs, one of them hugging the head and horns of a bull buffalo and all of them in tears. Lawrence Teft, III, and Samuel Shecker and Gerald Goodenow and Stephen Lally, Jr., and William Lally were bunched up bawling in their sorrow and jeering in their triumph over what seemed to be the sound of a radio. "Yah! Yah! Yah!" they sobbed and jeered at the men in ridiculous hats. "Yah! Yah! Yah!"*

*Glendon Swarthout, *Bless the Beasts and Children*. New York: Doubleday, 1970. pp. 204-205.

Just as that child who drew a heavy black line around the words "Charlotte died. . . . No one was with her when she died" found in *Charlotte's Web* a wisdom and poignancy that could last a lifetime, so youth could find in *Pistol* and *A Wild Thing, The Heart Is a Lonely Hunter, A Separate Peace,* and *Birch Interval,* in *The Death of the Heart* and *Bless the Beasts and Children* illuminations, moments of dramatic truth. And this is what literature is for: to tell us that language matters and to bring us the piercing imagination, not as "an idea machine," but as an instrument of revelation, something that in the most subtle and unpredictable and sometimes hurting ways pushes us into new awarenesses of ourselves and of life. This, in the face of McLuhan's predictions of a bookless world, a world without the printed word, is why literature, at its best, is worth fighting for.

From *The Horn Book* for October 1972, December 1972, and February 1973

"CHARLIE AND THE CHOCOLATE FACTORY": A REPLY

By Roald Dahl

MRS. ELEANOR CAMERON (I had not heard of her until now) has made some extraordinarily vicious comments upon my book *Charlie and The Chocolate Factory* (Knopf) in the October issue of this magazine. That does not worry me at all. She is free to criticize the book itself for all she is worth, but I do object strongly when she oversteps the rules of literary criticism and starts insinuating nasty things about me personally and about the school teachers of America.

She quotes Eudora Welty — and she wouldn't quote her if she didn't agree with her — as saying, "three kinds of goodness in fiction . . . the goodness of the writer himself, his worth as a human being. And this worth is always mercilessly revealed in his writing." Having said this, she goes on to announce that *Charlie* is "one of the most tasteless books ever written for children." She says a lot of other very nasty things about it, too, and the implication here has to be that I also am a tasteless and nasty person.

Well, although Mrs. Cameron has never met me, it would not have been difficult for her to check her facts. My wife, Patricia Neal, and I and our children have had a good deal written about us over the years, including a full-length biography called *Pat and Roald*. We have had some massive misfortunes and some terrific struggles, and we have emerged from these, I think, quite creditably. I deeply resent, therefore, the subtle insinuations that Mrs. Cameron makes about my character. I resent even more the patronizing attitude she adopts toward the teachers of America. She says, "*Charlie* . . . is probably the book most read aloud by those teachers who have no idea, apparently, what other books they might read to the children." She goes on to praise *Gulliver's Travels*, *Robinson Crusoe*, and *Little Women*.

I would dearly like to see Mrs. Cameron trying to read *Little Women*, or *Robinson Crusoe* for that matter, to a class of today's children. The lady is completely out of touch with reality. She would be howled out of the classroom. She also says, "I should like to travel up and down the country going to elementary schools and saying to all the teachers: Find out about the good children's books." I myself would like very much to hear what the teachers' replies would be if the patronizing, all-knowing Mrs. Cameron ever tried to do this. The hundreds of letters I get every year from American teachers tell me that they are on the whole a marvelous lot of people with a wide knowledge of children's books. It is an enormous conceit for Mrs. Cameron to think that her knowledge is greater than theirs or her taste more perfect.

Mrs. Cameron finally asks herself whether children are *harmed* by reading *Charlie and The Chocolate Factory*. She isn't quite sure, but she is clearly inclined to think that they are. Now this, to me, is the ultimate effrontery. The book is dedicated to my son Theo, now twelve years old. Theo was hit by a taxi in New York when a small child and was terribly injured. We fought a long battle to get him where he is today, and we all adore him. So the thought that I would write a book for him that might actually do him harm is too ghastly to contemplate. It is an insensitive and a monstrous implication. Moreover, I believe that I am a better judge than Mrs. Cameron of what stories are good or bad for children. We have had five children. And for the last fifteen years, almost without a break, I have told a bedtime story to them as they grew old enough to listen. That is 365 made-up stories a year, some 5,000 stories altogether. Our children are marvelous and gay and happy, and I like to think that all my storytelling has contributed a little bit to their happiness. The story they like best of all is *Charlie and The Chocolate Factory*, and Mrs. Cameron will stop them reading it only over my dead body.

From *The Horn Book* for February 1973

A REPLY TO ROALD DAHL

By ELEANOR CAMERON

MR. DAHL STATES in his reply to my article "Mc-Luhan, Youth, and Literature": Part I (*Horn Book*, October 1972) that I have made a personal attack upon him. I had no intention of attacking Mr. Dahl personally. Concerning Eudora Welty, it is true that I believe in what she has to say about the three kinds of goodness in writing, which for her include the evocation of a point of view. And I can only say that I find a certain point of view (or is it the *lack* of a point of view?) felt in *Charlie and the Chocolate Factory* (Knopf) to be extremely regrettable when it comes to Willy Wonka's unfeeling attitude toward the Oompa-Loompas, their role as conveniences and devices to be used for Wonka's purposes, their being brought over from Africa for enforced servitude, and the fact that their situation is all a part of the fun and games. I find it regrettable, too, that Willy Wonka, through the cleverness of his advertising, can triumphantly convince Charlie that life lived forever inside the factory, enclosed as in a prison, is the height of all possible bliss, with here again no word said, nothing expressed, that would question this idea.

The book is wish-fulfillment in caricature, and as caricature, it is removed from reality. This does not imply, however, that it lacks meaning (a depressing one, when you consider Wonka's power and coolness) any more than a fairy tale lacks meaning because, being fantastical, it is removed from reality. But the situation of the Oompa-Loompas *is* real; it could not be more so, and it is anything but funny.

Mr. Dahl doesn't touch on this point, but speaks instead of his personal difficulties. I am genuinely sorry to hear of them, and of the accident to Mr. Dahl's son. But had I known of the book *Pat and Roald*, which I did not, it wouldn't have occurred to me to read it as a necessary preface to thinking about the various ideas and attitudes that compose *Charlie*. Mr. Dahl's personal life has nothing whatever to do with those ideas and attitudes as far as criticism of the book is concerned.

Mr. Dahl accused me of "insinuating nasty things . . . about the school teachers of America" when I commented on the fact that *Charlie* and *Charlotte's Web* (Harper) are the two most read aloud books in the country by those teachers who haven't a wide enough awareness of what else they might read. I said that I wished more teachers had a real working knowledge of children's books which they could use to rich advantage in their classes. Mr. Dahl's exaggeration of these two statements into "insinuating nasty things . . . about the school teachers of America" is incredible. One teacher, after hearing a talk on children's fiction, spoke of the burden of teaching children with reading disabilities and of the never-ending reports she is required to make. She felt strongly that she could use a reminder about every three months of the relationship between children's literature and the development of their imaginations, the advantages to the children inherent in a teacher's wide knowledge of children's books, and the need to read aloud to her classes. She said it was all so easily lost sight of under the pressure of daily schedules.

I asked a Reading-and-Language-Arts director, who travels from school to school, what percentage of the teachers know a few children's books and read them aloud, and she said perhaps fifty percent. I then asked how many teachers have a really good working knowledge of children's books, and the reply was, "About twenty-five percent."

At no point in my article did I suggest that *Little Women* and *Gulliver's Travels* be read aloud in class. I spoke of them, along with *Pinocchio* and *Alice*, as books that have had a long life, and wondered how many books being written today would last as long.

As for Mr. Dahl's book, nobody is going to stop his son from reading it. Who would? This is preposterous. Thank God, both here and in the United Kingdom, we can read whatever books we like. Meanwhile, those who are involved with children's books and reading, those charged with making judgments, must bring all of their reflective powers to bear as well as a sense of aesthetics, because popularity and the literary value of a book are so often confused. Popularity in itself does not prove anything about a book's essential worth; there are all sorts of poor and mediocre creations which are enormously popular simply because they are wish-fulfilling.

Certainly, it is true that in the process of discriminating, some people may come to differing conclusions, as many of us have about *Charlie*. Still, those who are concerned with children's reading realize that they must think about a book as well as have feelings about it, even though criticism — indeed, *because* criticism — like poetry, begins with emotion.

From *The Horn Book* for April 1973

V

THE CURRENT SCENE

For the past decade or so, children's literature has enlarged its domain and opened itself up to a host of controversies. The rise of the so-called New Realism gave the writer freedom to explore sociological, psychological, and sexual problems formerly considered taboo. On the printed page, the ban of gentility was removed from words once judged to be coarse or obscene. One was made aware of a generation gap, of sexism, and of racism; and the social turbulence of the sixties was reflected in children's books by an awareness of the experiences of ethnic minorities.

The essays which follow send searching beams from many different directions over the current scene. Dealing with American realistic fiction of the 1960s, Sheila Egoff reminds us that "[c]hildren's books . . . have always reflected the values and the mores of the society that produced them." Isabelle Holland comes to the interesting conclusion that art needs limitations to be effective and realizes that the removal of taboos may be aesthetically self-defeating. Sylvia Engdahl refreshingly expresses her confidence in writing seriously for teenagers — "the young people who read at all are too sophisticated to read anything that lacks adult interest." By bypassing the folkloristic approach to ethnic differences, Eric Kimmel stresses the cultural, philosophic, and ultimately religious significance of the Jewish heritage; and Virginia Hamilton — although she invokes High John, a hero of black slave folklore — propounds a universal rather than a particularistic point of view: "For the experience of a people must come to mean the experience of mankind. . . . I am confined only by the measure of my knowledge."

CHILDREN'S BOOKS: A CANADIAN'S VIEW OF THE CURRENT AMERICAN SCENE

By Sheila Egoff

WHAT I FIRST HAD IN MIND was a completely objective examination of American children's books — the sort of dispassionate and impartial scrutiny that they would get from, say, a Martian or a Venusian who had examined your society and your literature. Unfortunately, I have neither pointed ears nor six tentacles, nor am I without an ax to grind. I also remembered an old Canadian aphorism: "A man that has *too* many irons in the fire is plaguy apt to get some of 'em burnt." So this paper will not be an interplanetary analysis of children's literature, but just *Children's Books: A Canadian's View of One Aspect of the Current American Scene.*

We Canadians are probably the most assiduous American-watchers in the world — and with reason. We are close to you, influenced by you, protected by you, deluged by you, dependent on you, and — yes — often alarmed by you. Americans, we say, know little of Canada and so tend to be favorably disposed toward it. Canadians, on the other hand, know a lot about the United States and are often *not* so favorably disposed. Recently a major American publisher of children's encyclopedias put out a new volume that showed pictures of children around the world. I took a poll among my colleagues. "What do you think they chose to represent Canada?" I asked. "We know," they said wearily. "Eskimo children playing in the snow." Which is exactly what they did show. In my opinion, there is much truth in the remark of that shrewd nineteenth-century Yankee trader, Sam Slick: "It is the authors of silly books, editors of silly papers and demagogues of silly parties that keep us apart."

The irresistible flow of communication northward (and occasionally southward) across the border has made our similarities greater than our differences. Indeed, I believe that eastern Canada and western Canada are more significantly different from each other than either is from its immediate American neighbors. But if our differences are only slight, Canadians still manage to make much of them, particularly the cultural differences. To maintain our own identity in the cultural sense as well as in the political

Originally given at a talk on the occasion of the award of the Rutgers Medal to Lynd Ward, November 14, 1969, at the Graduate School of Library Service, Rutgers, the State University, New Brunswick, New Jersey.

one, we have had to become aware of how we differ from you, and this has meant getting to know you very well. You are the *Big Brother* in this relationship, but *we* are watching *you*.

In my case I have done more than watch you. As a Canadian I have made American literature perhaps as much a part of my background as you have, and as a librarian I have tended to rely on books — particularly fiction — rather than on the mass media to learn about your society. When I speak, then, in a critical way of recent American fiction for children, I do so out of a lifelong devotion to your country and your literature. But I offer you one important caveat. I speak *as* a Canadian, but not *for* Canadians, only for myself. I make a point of this because of a vivid recollection. Some years ago one of our TV personalities made the statement that Canadians were not interested in a visit from the Queen. There was a great and immediate public outcry — not so much over the lese majesty, but because one person had presumed to speak for all Canadians. The TV star had to go into exile in the United States, where she fared rather well, by the way, marrying a millionaire and living happily ever after — a delightful outcome that makes the episode the very opposite of a cautionary tale, now that I think of it. Nonetheless, I repeat that my opinions are just my own.

There are two ways of looking at children's books. You can read them as children themselves do, one at a time, purely for enjoyment, without heeding their interrelationship or what they stand for as a group. But we librarians, reading many books and trained to seek generalizations, can find another whole dimension in children's books. We can see them as indicators of the society that produced them, as a group portrait of the children and adults pictured therein, and as a potent influence on the generation that reads them. It is this second point of view that I will be taking, and if some of my broad judgments seem to be ill-founded, please remember that generalizations inevitably err — but then I have never been one to stand back from a generalization.

Let me begin with the statement that children's books (and by children's books I mean those deliberately intended for the young) have always reflected the values and the mores of the society that produced them. Much of this self-revelation has been quite deliberate. Every generation has used children's books to inculcate adult values and to train children in the mores espoused by adults. Perhaps this intention was never so flagrantly apparent as in the early nineteenth century.

In a little book of 1801 called *Pleasant Tales, to Improve the Mind and Correct the Morals of Youth* (no irony is intended in the word "pleasant"), we meet Patty's cousin, who was haughty and arrogant, and who, having the misjudgment to marry her father's valet, was thrust out into the snow in true *East Lynne* style. The book ends thus:

Patty put her poor cousin to bed, where she lingered a few hours, and then expired, saying — "had I been GOOD, I should have been HAPPY; the GUILTY and the UNFEELING can never taste of PEACE." Patty lived long and happily, a striking example to the world, that HONESTY, FILIAL DUTY, and RELIGION, are well-pleasing in the sight of the Almighty, who is the punisher of VICE, and the liberal rewarder of VIRTUE.

Many literary revelations of a society have been inadvertent. In endeavoring to simplify for children, to present themes in terms of right and wrong, good and bad, to winnow character and hone plot, adults have, as it were, "given themselves away" and have told more about themselves and adult life than they intended. Mrs. Sherwood, for example, in *The Fairchild Family* (1818), intended to show children the importance of a religious education. What emerges is the picture of an adult society that is obsessed with religion to the point of distortion and with maintaining power over children, particularly retaliatory power. It is hardly a society that any right-minded children would want to join, and, of course, they eventually did not — not in the religious, social, or literary sense. Just as the writers of Mrs. Sherwood's day did not have any objectivity about what they wrote, it is likely that the picture of American society that is emerging in current writing is least evident to those who are producing it.

Fiction has been more of a vehicle for the transmission of adult attitudes towards children than nonfiction, and it is particularly through the so-called realistic novel for children that the overall public pattern of a society emerges. Therefore, in this capsule survey I would like to concern myself chiefly with American realistic fiction of the 1960's intended for the older elementary schoolchild and the younger adolescent. I include the latter because in Canada, at any rate, if these books are used at all, they tend to be used in children's departments.

I have asked myself the following questions: What is American society like as it is revealed in current realistic fiction for children? What are adults like? What are children and young people like? What is the writing like? Will these books last?

What is the society like? Well, it is not "la vie en rose." It is a society in transition and upheaval with overtones of violence. Violence, when it is presented, is not part of the great universal struggle between good and evil as in the great folk tales and fantasies but is sudden, direct, and personal — as depicted in the books dealing with gang warfare and race relations.

It is an urban society. The megalopolis has replaced the country-side. (In the forties and fifties you could hardly find a book about city life.) No longer are children off on summer holidays in the country. They are seen in their daily life in the city where apartments have replaced houses, trouble at school has replaced the visits to Grandma, and where making friends, dating, coping with problems, and — particularly — coping with adults has replaced having an adventure.

It is a highly personal and individualistic society. Children and young people "go it alone" without too much help from parents, friends, school, religion, traditional customs.

It is an introspective society. The physical frontiers are gone — man is on a moral and ethical frontier. Success is internal self-knowledge rather than a rise from log cabin to White House.

It is a serious society. *Homer Price* (Viking) has gone and so has *Junior Miss* (Doubleday). Even in a book that is more enter-taining than usual for the 1960's, *About the B'nai Bagels* (Athe-neum), Little League baseball is a serious business — at least for mothers.

It is a concerned society, one that sees itself as responsible for the malaise of the young and one that makes an effort to state their problems for them. The themes of modern American real-istic fiction for children and young people are almost exclusively concerned with the personal problems of the young: growing up, coming to terms with oneself, alienation, the generation gap; and with social problems: divorce, alcoholism, poverty, prejudice, and drugs.

It is a society that is somewhat intimidated by the young. The adult view of life — rationality as opposed to emotion, sense as opposed to sensibility — is rarely allowed to have a voice (in deference to the feelings of the young); and if this is expressed at all, it is done so without depth or sympathy.

It is a society that is unsure of itself. Many of the problems raised in these books are skirted, not solved. The frequent ab-sence of a definite and convincing solution indicates uncertainty in American society. Where there is a resolution, it often moves uneasily between conformity and nonconformity.

What are the adults like as presented in these books?

They are chiefly ineffectual. Such are the parents in Nat Hentoff's *I'm really dragged but nothing gets me down* (Simon), Maia Wojiechkowska's *Tuned Out* and *The Hollywood Kid* (both Harper), Louise Fitzhugh's *Harriet the Spy* (Harper), Barbara Wersba's *The Dream Watcher* (Atheneum), Paul Zindel's *The Pigman* (Harper), Annabel and Edgar Johnson's *Count Me Gone* (Simon), Regina Woody's *One Day at a Time* (Westminster), Vera and Bill Cleaver's *Ellen Grae* and *Lady Ellen Grae* (both Lippincott), Marilyn Sachs's *Veronica Ganz* (Doubleday) and a host of others. You do not find the firm, loving parental authority that is still shown in most British and Australian books, and if the parents are presented as quite decent types, as in Lee Kingman's *The Year of the Raccoon* (Houghton), E. L. Konigsberg's *From the Mixed-up Files of Mrs. Basil E. Frankweiler* (Atheneum), and Louis Muehl's *The Hidden Year of Devlin Bates* (Holiday), the children still remain unhappy. Interestingly enough, it seems to me that black parents are presented as kinder, firmer, and more understanding than white parents.

In their desire to adopt and adapt themes for children's books, American writers are hurrying children into adulthood. Yet adulthood is by no means presented as a felicitous state. In books, children and young people solve their own problems, chiefly because adults seem incapable of problem solving. The young come to see the flaws in adults and in so doing move on to a plane of adult understanding themselves. In their wisdom, they become superior to adults. Since adults represent authority, it is logical to argue from the evidence given in these books that authority is ineffectual.

What are the young people like? They appear to be the unhappiest, most upset, distressed, suspicious, alienated, introspective generation the world has ever known. They are existentialist heroes and heroines who make a decision — on the last page — to "go it alone," either by growing up or dropping out, and it is even suggested that they will have to grow up by themselves. They say to the adult world, "Tell us no lies, pass us no platitudes, we will test truth by our own experience." They say, "Respect us." They often take their revenge on society and particularly on their parents by threats and desperate actions. Devlin Bates says, "I will give them exactly one year to change — or else." Claudia in *The Mixed-up Files of Mrs. Basil E. Frankweiler* runs away. Ellen Grae in *Lady Ellen Grae* deliberately allows herself to be injured so that she can get her way with her father. Rion in *Count Me Gone* says, "Maybe I'll get back to the books someday, but if I do, I'll be buying the deal myself. I'll figure it out, why I'm there, and it will be up to them. . . ." The young hero of Glen Swarthout's *Whichaway* (Random) rides for miles with two broken legs to prove to his father that he is a man. It is a question whether these things represent courage, martyrdom, or narcissism. When young people do make a link with an older person, it is never with a member of their family but with an oddball adult, considerably removed from the family circle, who is himself somewhat inadequate in his own world. The rather senile Mr. Pignati in *The Pigman*, the eccentric old lady in *The Dream Watcher*, the janitor in Constance Greene's *A Girl Called Al* (Viking) who has rejected his own family, the old lady arsonist in *The Hidden Year of Devlin Bates*, the petty criminal in *Count Me Gone* — all come to the aid of troubled youth. All but one of these particular understanding adults die — as though without this termination of their friendships the young protagonists could not "grow up" or "come to terms" with themselves.

These young people are concerned with themselves exclusively. They do not join demonstrations or groups (except perhaps for the hero of Hentoff's *I'm really dragged but nothing gets me down*). Most of the time they are smothered in their own unhappiness and for fairly ordinary reasons. They are upset because they are not doing well at school or because they do not want to join a group. They are upset because they are the youngest child, or the oldest child, or the middle child, or an only child. Gus in Paula Fox's *The Stone-Faced Boy* (Bradbury) is stone-faced because he is the third child in a family of five. American children are far from being childish, but they are certainly not childlike: Their ruminations would sound more plausible if they emanated from a psychiatrist's couch. A genuinely precocious or self-sufficient child tends not to be presented sympathetically; Harriet and Janie in *Harriet the Spy*, and Claudia in *The Mixed-up Files* are examples. Finally, with the exception of a few books — such as Zilpha Snyder's *The Egypt Game* (Atheneum) — the writer's attention is always focused on a single child, not on a group of children.

What is the writing like? First of all, the writers cannot or do not want to write in a traditional manner; in other words, they eschew the developed plot in which characterization and denouement spring from the inevitability of events. Plotless character studies are the order of the day; the problem is all. In many cases the writing is staccato and sometimes incoherent. The narrow egotism of the books is plainly reflected in their titles: *Me, Cassie* (Dial); *Irving and Me* (Harper); *Count Me Gone; I'll Get There, It Better Be Worth the Trip* (Harper); *I'm really dragged but nothing gets me down.* They are also extremely didactic, though the attempts to treat tolerance, growing up, and coming to terms with oneself definitively are simplistic and misleading. It seems as if the history of children's literature has come full circle: The religious and moral didacticism of the seventeenth to early nineteenth centuries has been replaced by the social and personal didacticism of the 1960's.

Current American children's books make a point of spurning and scorning commercial success, almost as though they were written in deliberate opposition to Horatio Alger. Yet it sometimes seems to me that it is precisely commercialism that dictates their whole approach. I have the feeling that most American problem fiction is contrived for the market place. Like the mass media, where sales appeal rules over intrinsic merit, many children's books ride the bandwagon of themes that are currently "in" — alienation, drugs, dropout, generation gap, race relations, and what have you. They emphasize news value rather than story value. They are instant, slick, superficial, and as prone to style change as your automobile. The writers of this so-called realistic school never heard of or have forgotten the words of Christopher Morley: "When you sell a man a book you don't sell him just twelve ounces of paper and ink and glue — you sell him a whole new life."

Most of them will not last. But does this matter? The problems they deal with are important and perhaps the very stating of a problem is a step towards its solution. If these books do indeed improve human understanding, should one complain?

That problems should provide themes for children's literature is not being questioned, for they should if literature is to reflect life, but it is clear that in most cases the demand for problem books is being filled by highly superficial and mediocre writing.

One view of the problem books — that if a problem exists it should be presented to the young reader in as realistic a way as possible — often implies that such literary values as style, characterization, plot, and the welding of a philosophy of life to a literary form must take second place. The opposite view is based on a literary standard and all that it demands. Generally speaking the modern American realistic school of writing is almost aggressively unliterary. Most authors appear to be amateur writers dragged into active existence by the great demand for the problem book, not because they have something to say to the young and can say it well. Their plotless efforts read like sociopsychological case studies that are entirely devoid of interpretation and significance. Is bibliotherapy really an excuse for poor literature even though the problems — racial inequality, drug addiction, unmarried mothers, alcoholic fathers — are important ones? What answers do these books give to the problems they set up? Whatever they are, they tend to be one-dimensional answers to multidimensional problems. To explain to children the deep and complex roots of prejudice is no easy matter, especially when most adults have failed to come to terms with prejudice themselves. Most children's books about black people make a special point of presenting them as good, kind, intelligent, religious, and so on. This is oversimplifying and overcompensating to the point of negating the very purpose sought. One looks in vain for a book that indicates the plain truth: "Look, we are all human beings. This is why we have rights; this is why we should cherish one another." It can be argued that in the hands of a real writer the problems of a fifteen-year-old with a famous movie-star mother could be made absorbing and significant. So they could, but only if the writer can make pain and sorrow and joy universal, so that every reader can say of the protagonist "That's me!" and of the theme "I know it's true."

Will they last? No. And I must deduce that the writers, publishers, and editors do not care whether they do or not. They may see the advantages in deliberately built-in obsolescence.

The reading tastes of children are changing. Books of fantasy appear to be declining in numbers, quality, and readership. Books about "real life" are on the increase. But these "outer-directed" works of fiction that offer thinly disguised instruction on psychological and sociological themes — hastily written, speedily published, whose only interest derives from the topicality of their subjects — are no more realistic than soap operas.

Painfully and ironically enough, this vogue for nonliterature comes at a time when we have produced young people who are better informed, more sophisticated, and more troubled by adult

135

values than any other generation in history. They sit with their parents around the same television screen and watch the same programs, they read the same newspapers, and in many cases they own the same paperbacks, for they are reaching out for adult books just as they have done in the past whenever their own literature did not satisfy them. They present a challenge to children's literature that to date writers and publishers have not yet met nor fully comprehended.

Now, before you have second thoughts about our undefended border, may I remind you again that I am not talking about the great body of American children's literature, most of which we have adopted in Canada and much of which matches the best in the world. The best of the American picture books, for example, are unsurpassable. Many of them are realistic — but they also reveal joy, love, and understanding. They bring a smile and a laugh; they lighten our hearts. And they also show this great land in its teeming variety and in its changing moods.

Every country has its own ethos and tradition from which its particular genius derives. Canada, for example, is often described as gray and colorless — without character. Yet our conservatism, caution, and compromise have produced a society that most of us agree suits us. The great United States is far more complex. It often seems to us Canadians fascinatingly vivid, emotional, prone to large and quick swings of viewpoint; it is most of all "open" and highly visible. Your debates are conducted before the world and in a very real sense you are more radical than we on both sides of any issue. It seems to me that many recent American children's books express restlessness, confusion, and a search for novelty. They want to say large things quickly; they may say things with intensity, but they often say them carelessly. Few of them express the best that I feel the United States has to offer the world. There is little to show your long, hard, slow climb to some pinnacle of success, and I do not mean material success. If I may use a literary analogy, your recent realistic fiction expresses the Time-Life syndrome rather than the *Atlantic Monthly* or the *Harvard Review*.

We will continue to read your children's books in Canada just as we will continue to watch you with absorption, involvement, and affection — for we are all North Americans.

The undefended border is still there — the border that brings the culture, the emotions, the ideas of two hundred million people to bear upon twenty million. Good luck, Big Brother, for your sake and for ours.

From *The Horn Book* for April 1970

TILTING AT TABOOS*

By Isabelle Holland

*T*HE MAN WITHOUT A FACE (Lippincott) is about the relationship of a fourteen-year-old boy with a man who tutors him through a summer to pass a prep-school exam. The man is a disfigured recluse, something of a mystery in the New England village where the boy, Charles, is spending the summer with his family. The man, Justin Mc-Leod, is known only for his abrupt manners and generally misanthropic approach. The boy, Charles, starting from dislike, progresses through respect for Justin to affection and finally love. Ultimately, he discovers that Justin is indeed a homosexual and that what has happened to Justin in the past has gone into what he is at the present. There is one incident that is overtly — although by accident — homosexual. The boy turns from this in revulsion, leaves Justin, passes the exam, and goes to school — putting, he thinks, Justin out of his mind. But two months later he faces what has happened and goes back to see Justin, only to find that it is too late.

Now, I didn't set out to write about homosexuality. I started this book with only the idea of a fatherless boy who experiences with a man some of the forms of companionship and love that have been nonexistent in his life. Because the other side of Charles' dilemma or emotional history arises from his feeling of being both suffocated and rejected by the predominant female influence in his home — his four-times married mother and his older sister. His stepfathers have come and gone too fast for him to do anything but dislike them. Emotionally, Charles has lived his life as an armed camp, hanging onto a shadowy memory of his own father. Hence the revolutionary impact that Justin has on him.

I think I might diverge here and say something that has always interested me about the eternally fascinating subject of love: Into one person's love for another goes much of the love, either present or in default, that has gone, or should have gone, into other relationships. The title, *The Man Without a Face*, really has two meanings: It refers to the nickname by which Justin is called because of his facial disfigurement; but, on a deeper level, the man without a face is also Charles' father,

*Based on a speech presented on January 18, 1973, at the Educators' Conference, held at Framingham State College, Framingham, Massachusetts.

137

whom he can barely remember. But Charles has wrapped his memory of his father around himself as a shield against a world that he finds, on the whole, hostile. Behind that shield, Charles is emotionally starved. When Justin steps into his life, he brings three qualities that mythologically as well as psychologically have always been the archetypes of fatherhood: Justin is masculine, he is authoritative, and he is undemonstratively kind. He steps into the vacuum of Charles' emotional life, and the result is cataclysmic.

Now, all of this interested me far more than the almost incidental fact that the book is about love between two people of the same sex. The story could have been about a boy whose deprivations and needs were the exact opposite from Charles'. Given another kind of boy, with another kind of emotional background, the instigator of his youthful love could have been female — as in *Summer of Forty-two*. And if that had been the case, how much of the love could have been that of the male child for the missing or inadequate female parent, and how much that of the male adolescent in his first sexual encounter with a female? As with Charles, I don't think it's either-or. I think it's both.

An English psychologist (whose name I have forgotten, in a book whose title I can't remember) said that it was his personal observation and belief that the child of either sex took its identity from its father. Margaret Mead — this time I can remember — said back in the sixties that when the campus protesters and anti-war demonstrators were chanting "Ho, Ho, Ho Chi Minh," what they were really doing was asking for strong fathers with strong convictions. And that was what Justin was, a strong father with strong convictions who believed that discipline was a necessary element of affection, not its opposite.

Now, about taboos per se. Speaking solely from a storyteller's point of view, I think the sexual revolution has been a somewhat mixed blessing. And I say this even though I realize that without the dropping of taboos, *The Man Without a Face* could never have been published as a juvenile. But, in a way, it's also an example of what I mean. Because *The Man Without a Face* is a love story — an unusual love story, but nevertheless, a love story.

Art forms come and go. Every few decades there's a great brouhaha over what's happened to the novel — it's dying, it's dead, it's just been resurrected. Poetry changes radically. The one form that has remained constant since the days of the troubadours before reading and writing is the story — and by that, I mean the love story. Prince meets princess, boy meets girl, man meets woman, he (or she) travels over obstacles, either external or internal — and at the end the lovers meet. They may meet only to part or die (as do Romeo and Juliet, Tristan and Isolde, Lancelot and Guinevere) or meet to live happily ever after. But between the beginning and the end, there have to be obstacles, or there's no story.

If you look over any paperback rack, you will see, burgeoning into popularity over the last decade, the romance and the Gothic novel. Why? Because the oldest story of all, the love story, has virtually vanished from hard-core, hardcover literature. For one thing, major review media will rarely review it. It's considered middlebrow and old hat. And anyone who breaks that taboo — and it is a very real one — gets his knuckles rapped. Erich Segal may be crying all the way to the bank, but he is no longer teaching at Yale. The students who used to flock to his Latin class before his book was published, booed him when his sales soared. The intellectual establishment tore his skin off in strips. And all he'd done was to take one of the oldest stories of all, put it into modern jargon, and have it achieve tremendous success. If it had been a homosexual love story, or an interracial love story, or a lesbian love story, or an Oedipal love story, it would, if it were halfway decently written, have had serious consideration. But not a straight love story.

But to go back to my mixed feelings about the sexual revolution: It has destroyed — temporarily, I trust — the old-fashioned love story. A modern story might well have the hero and heroine exchanging smoldering glances across a crowded cocktail party, but they would be in bed by page ten, and what are you going to do with the next two hundred pages? You could still produce a set of obstacles so that hero or heroine would climb out of bed and stay out for a while before getting back in again, but it's not the same. The essence of the true love story, its real mystique, lies in the unattainability to each other, for at least two hundred pages, of the hero and heroine. When physical encounter is easy and casual, even though obstacles remain, the mystique is gone. That moment that used to occur a few pages before the end when the lovers have their first kiss was electric, not only for the participants, but for the reader, and it had all the more impact for being filled with all the yearnings of the preceding pages. Again, speaking entirely from the literary point of view, I think the multiple orgasm is a poor substitute. That is why I am not a tilter of taboos per se and on principle. As a storyteller, I need them.

While I was thinking about this subject, I remembered some of the books I read when I was at school. I grew up in England, and the books I got out of the school library or read in Welsh hotel rooms when we were on holiday would be incomprehensible to the children of today. This, of course, was before World War II. These books, many of them, were even a generation older and were pre-World War I. But I found them less antediluvian and grotesque than I think a child of today would find those written when I was growing up. However, I do remember one that — unsophisticated as I was, growing up in a small town in the north of England — gave me a case of the giggles, although I found it quite touching. It was, at least in one way, a sort of ground-breaking book for its time, because it was about a young lady — capital *L* lady — who went into training as a nurse at a time when it was considered socially very unacceptable. Anyway, after numerous mishaps, she finally had her big moment at the end with the young house surgeon, at which they reached an "understanding." The next line went something like, "[h]e did not kiss me, of course, because we were not yet engaged." We're a long way away from that. And yet — I don't regret those books even though they gave me an indelibly romantic streak.

I realize that in many ways, I had a longer childhood than most young people today who are reading of problems at thirteen that I never heard of until I was eighteen or older. And this, of course, both affects, and is affected by, their reading habits. There are times when it seems to me they go straight from *Peter Rabbit* to *Portnoy's Complaint*. On the other hand, the child of today seems to live the last of her childhood at the same time that she is living the first of her adulthood, so that she can and does switch from D. H. Lawrence to Louisa May Alcott and back again with a versatility that is, to me, dizzying.

To be truthful, I don't write books specifically for children. I just write the books as they come out, and they turn out to be for elderly children. Now that may well be the influence of my long childhood. At some inner depth I remain perpetually twelve. My first book, *Cecily* (Lippincott) — about a child in an English boarding school, one of her teachers, and the young man her teacher is engaged to — was actually published by the adult department, although the reason it's still in print is because it did quite well in the Young Adult category. The next book, *Amanda's Choice* (Lippincott), started out as an adult book but became a juvenile; and I have stayed with children's books ever since. As adult novels become more and more adult, I become firmer and firmer in my convictions that I am not yet old enough to write one.

And yet, *The Man Without a Face* has received very gratifying reviews outside New York where it was reviewed as an adult book. If I had written it six years ago, it would unquestionably have been published on the adult list. The line between adult and juvenile has moved. But it's a very wavering line even now, depending on geographical area. I am not as acquainted as I should be with other children's books, but I do know that the taboo against any mention or recognition of homosexuality was broken by my friend and neighbor John Donovan in his book, *I'll Get There. It Better Be Worth the Trip.* (Harper). Vera and Bill Cleaver have pushed the quality and the line higher so that some of the better children's books of today are in every way comparable in viewpoint and sophistication to the bulk of adult books of, say, twenty years ago. And there is no question but that the children of today — hearing nightly on television and daily in the classroom of the problems of war, race, and poverty — require of their books a social depth that the young people of my generation never dreamed of.*

Personally, I think the line between adult and children's books is largely artificial, anyway. *Alice in Wonderland* — one of my old favorites — is a children's classic. Yet, it was written by an eccentric professor of mathematics with a humor that is extremely adult. Someone once said erroneously that the charm of Alice lay in the fact that she was an imaginative child caught in a fantastic world. But Alice's charm is that she is a totally unimaginative, very literal-minded child caught in a fantasy; and her statements are funny because she responds to the fantastic, not with whimsy or imagination, but with irritable common sense. The humor is adult in concept because it is based on irony, the subtlest of all forms of humor.

*To anyone interested in this subject I strongly commend Patrick Merla's article in the Arts Section of the November 1972 *Saturday Review:* " 'What Is Real?' Asked the Rabbit One Day."

I sometimes amuse myself by wondering what would happen if some of the great favorites of adolescent years, *Jane Eyre*, for instance, were submitted to a publisher now for the first time. The first thing it would do would be to cause a battle between the juvenile and adult departments as to where the real area of interest lay, though I think the juvenile would win. But dividing books in this way is a relatively recent innovation — at least I think it is — except, of course, for the very young books. My father once told me that when he was twelve years old he got his first library card and took out his first book, *The Vicar of Wakefield* — certainly one of the dullest adult books ever written — and he swallowed it whole. But in his small Southern town's library there were only adult classics. In his whole life he never read what could be called a children's book. So what, strictly speaking, is an adult book? What is a juvenile?

As far as taboos are concerned, I have played devil's advocate on their behalf. To be honest I would be just as outraged as the greatest libertarian if I ran into a taboo standing in the way of something I wanted to do or say — that is, if there are any left. Has anyone written a moving story yet about incest? Other than Sophocles, that is? But unless they obstruct my way, I am forced to admit that taboos frequently help to make interesting stories: The prince still has to climb through the hedge of thorns to find his lady.

Now today's prince may be born in a ghetto or be Puerto Rican, a Chicano, an Indian (American or Eastern), be a mental or physical cripple, an alcoholic or a drug addict. His hedge of thorns may be his environment, justice or the lack of it, his parents, drugs, no job, or some other handicap. But in the sense that a love story is a journey of the heart and the mind as well as of the body, he has to make his journey from here to there, over or through or around his obstacles. And obstacles are frequently the result of, or contingent on, taboos.

What are taboos? Well, one used to be that you cannot portray homosexual love, certainly not sympathetically, certainly not in a children's book. But if there were no taboos, there would be no urgency. Let me say again that I am not speaking for or against a tabooless society. That is a social or moral or even theological question. I am merely talking of what is good for storytelling.

If you have any doubt about it, please consider: If Romeo Montague and Juliet Capulet had been members of the Now generation with no worn-out ideas about obedience to parents or the sanctification of marriage, they would simply have announced to their parents what they were going to do and then left together after the ball. There would have been no tragedy. There would also have been no play. And if Anna Karenina had lived in a society of easy divorce and remarriage, Tolstoy's masterpiece would have ended up being the essay pure and simple on land reform that I thought it was when I first began reading it.

I realize at this point that I could easily be heading for trouble. Because there is no doubt that if we had a tabooless society, many people would think that Utopia had arrived. If prejudice, poverty, greed, and individual and collective ill will had also vanished, then indeed the Kingdom of Heaven would be at hand. But what would have happened to storytelling? Well, perhaps we would all be on a such a perpetual alpha wave that we wouldn't need it — a dreary outlook for an author. Not having the hedge of thorns (our taboos, our inequities, our unfulfilled yearnings for our heroes and heroines to overcome and/or fulfill so that each may grasp his or her particular Grail), we'd have to invent taboos. Or we would depend upon the troubadours of the future who, to entertain the travelers as they sped from planet to planet, would begin . . .

"Once upon a time long, long ago, way back in the twentieth century, before people were able to see freely into each others' minds and hearts, there lived a fourteen-year-old boy named Charles Norstadt who had great trouble with his womenfolk and who yearned for the love of a man who could, among other ways of loving him, take the place of a father. Now, to understand the meaning of Charles' and Justin's story, you must realize they had something in those days they called a taboo against any expression of love between members of the same sex. Yes, I know it's hard to believe, but without that there wouldn't even be a story to tell . . ."

You see the conceit of the author: In interplanetary travel they will be explaining taboos so they can read my book.

So, back to our hero and his hedge of thorns, the taboos in his life. As I said at the beginning, my feelings about them and about abandoning them altogether are very mixed.

From *The Horn Book* for June 1973

WHY WRITE FOR TODAY'S
TEENAGERS?

By Sylvia Louise Engdahl

AT FIRST, when I was asked to address a workshop session
focused on recent changes in writing for teens, I questioned whether the subject would apply to someone who
has been writing as short a time as I have. Yet, on reflection,
I realized that it does; for if attitudes about what is suitable for
teenagers had not changed, I might never have become a writer.

Until four years ago other work kept me too busy to write; but
I have studied the field of children's literature periodically for
more than twenty years, and there have indeed been dramatic
changes in the past few — even since I began my first book.
While I was writing *Enchantress from the Stars* (Atheneum), I
had serious doubts that it would be publishable. I felt that it was
halfway between an adult novel and a children's book and was
unlikely to fit either the adult or juvenile market. In terms of the
usual juvenile I considered it too long, too philosophical, and in
some respects far too mature. Still, the story could not have been
written in any form other than the one it took, so I decided to try
my luck with it. Not only was the book accepted by the first
publisher to which it was submitted, but also — to my astonishment — it was a runner-up for the Newbery Medal. I think my
experience shows that, although as a matter of professional preparation one should become familiar with what has generally
been done in a field, one should not try to force a work of fiction
into an established mold. If a writer has something to say, he must
say it in the form that seems right to him.

I also think, however, that when a book that does not fit the
traditional categories is successful, its reception indicates there
are readers looking for something outside those categories and
a new category is in the process of being formed. We are seeing
evidence of such a situation in many of the recently published
books for young people. The change is often spoken of as *the
new realism*, but I believe that the factor of realism is merely one
aspect of a wider issue: Young people today are more serious-
minded than they used to be. They are interested in exploring
questions of values and of philosophy. And, at the same time,

adults who have become weary of current trends in fiction are discovering that some of the junior books, being less subject to the dictates of fashion than other novels, are more satisfying to them than a lot of the adult ones. In the artistic sense the distinction between the two is blurring.

It seems to me, therefore, that before a writer considers *how* to write for teenagers, he must first ask himself *why*. Why should he direct his books to young people instead of to adults? Writing for the young certainly is not easier; no one who has had contact with the field can remain under the misapprehension that it requires less skill. And there are few, if any, restrictions left on subject matter. Restrictions on style and vocabulary apply only to textbooks and specialized series. So what need is there to have teenage novels at all?

Obviously, if a serious writer chooses to write for teenagers, he feels that he has something important to say to teenagers — but young people do not welcome messages from adults. I myself feel strongly that I have things I want to communicate to the young, but these are not things that apply exclusively to them. To young people, I say the same things I would want to say to people of any age. I think I would be insulting today's youth if I were to do otherwise. So that is not really an answer to the question, especially since publishers are beginning to mark teenage books "ages ten to fourteen" because boys and girls over fourteen read mostly adult books anyway. Therefore, if I wrote adult novels, I could reach the teenage audience and adults, too. I could also reach the advanced readers among the ten- to twelve-year-olds, many of whom already read adult fiction and are the only subteens that do not find my junior books too difficult. From time to time I do consider the possibility.

I doubt that I shall go beyond considering, however. The true reason I direct my books specifically to young people is not that I would be unable to reach them through adult books, but that in the publishing field today I see more restrictions on what I can do in adult books than in so-called juveniles. That sounds like a strange statement; one might think that in the adult market there are no restrictions whatsoever any more. Yet actually, when the old taboos disappeared, new and different varieties took their place. Every era has its conventions, and I happen to be guilty of two of the most scorned heresies of ours: I have an optimistic view of the universe, and I just do not believe that sex is the most significant thing in life. These days, a novelist who concentrates neither on gloom-and-despair nor on sex has little chance of being taken seriously by the critics. Since I would rather be known as an author of "adult" juveniles than of "juvenile" adult novels, I therefore think writing for teenagers offers me the best opportunity to express my ideas.

An optimistic outlook is frequently cited as one of the few remaining differences between children's literature and adult literature. It is all too true that such an outlook is no longer thought appropriate for grownups. This, I think, is a sad commentary on the predominant viewpoint of our age. Moreover, I am troubled because it is sometimes implied that the optimism in junior books is inserted as a concession to the young: almost as if writers for young people were suspected of saying, "We will be realistic, but only to a certain extent; while we may depict life as it is, we will not go so far as to point out that its evils are futile and meaningless." I trust that most authors do not feel this way. I believe a writer has as much obligation to be honest with young people as with adults, and if optimism is a concession for him, he has no business putting himself in a position where he has to make it.

For me, it is not a concession. I consider today's tendency to equate realism with pessimism wholly invalid. In the climate of current opinion this viewpoint is, as I have said, very heretical indeed. Nevertheless, I feel that although some junior fiction may be unduly optimistic, our contemporary adult fiction is equally unrealistic and one-sided since it so often makes the assumption that all optimism is blind.

Let me emphasize that by optimism, I am referring not to the outmoded, sugar-sweet happy ending, but to the portrayal of whatever ordeals a story's characters have undergone, whatever griefs they are left with, as being in some way purposeful — as leading somewhere. Today's teenagers are well aware that reality is apt to prove unpleasant and that problems are not always resolved happily for everyone; they will not listen to us if we ignore these facts. They hear about the grimmer aspects of the human condition all the time through current events, if not through personal experience. What they do not hear is any suggestion that there may be grounds for hope. In making such a suggestion, I feel that it is necessary to take full account of the dark side in order to be believed. To call that side "real" and the concept of underlying purpose "unreal," however, is something else again, and the trend toward doing so, unfortunately, seems to be spreading even into the children's book field.

The only way I can see to counter this trend is to take grim reality and show it to be less grim than is commonly supposed. *The Far Side of Evil* (Atheneum), for example, deals with some of the grimmest topics that could be chosen: brain-washing, imminent nuclear war, and the sacrifice of innocent lives. At first, I feared it might be entirely too grim for a junior novel, but nobody seems to have been bothered on that score. Its view of the perils of our time is rather more hopeful than what one generally finds in adult books, but I am completely serious about that view; I did not make the book hopeful because I was writing for young people. On the contrary, I wrote it for young people because the theory I wanted to present was hopeful.

That theory happens to be concerned with the importance of space exploration to the survival of mankind, something about which I have felt very strongly since long before the first space satellites were launched. As a matter of fact, all four of the books I have written grew from unpublished stories that I wrote in 1956, when my theory was developed. I first conceived them as adult short stories, but their themes were far too complex for anything short of novel length and too optimistic — even then — for the adult market. Yet, at that time, they would have been considered too mature for juveniles. Now, since we are in the Space Age when anything connected with space is popular with the young, I am able to publish books that I doubt would have sold fifteen years ago even if I had been free to write them. To be sure, their subject matter has some bearing on this; today's young people have a sincere interest in the universe as a whole and in man's relationship to it, and I believe that they are a long way ahead of most adults in this respect. The implications of the shift in publishing trends, however, are equally applicable to other subjects.

Since I have said that I find fewer restrictions in writing for teenagers than I would encounter in writing for adults, there may be some question as to whether the field demands any compromises at all. Actually, I can think of only one necessary conclusion — aside from the exclusion of sensational sex, which I do not consider a handicap — and it pertains principally to the particular kind of story I write: I do have to oversimplify my theories somewhat. It would be impossible to explain all facets of them without slowing down the action too much, and even the essential aspects are too abstract and complex to suit everyone's taste. Still, adult tastes also differ. Modern teenagers, having a broader background than that of former generations, are as diverse in their preferences as their elders; a writer can no more expect to please all of them than he can expect to produce an adult novel with universal appeal.

I try, of course, to direct my work to young people of various tastes. Apart from the complexity inherent in stories concerning future or hypothetical worlds, my books are quite different from each other. Though many readers like them all, each story seems to have found an additional, and more or less separate, audience. On the whole, for instance, readers who are particularly impressed by *Enchantress from the Stars* don't like *Journey Between Worlds* (Atheneum) as well, and vice versa. I know a number of people, both teenagers and adults, who like *Journey Between Worlds* best because it seems more real and immediate to them and is less complicated, although from a literary standpoint it is not unique. It was not meant to be; I wrote it in order to say something about space to readers who are "turned off" by fantasy, and I think I achieved my purpose, for several older women with no prior interest in other planets have told me it made them believe that the colonization of Mars is possible.

This response illustrates why I feel a new category is emerging in fiction. On the one hand, young people are demanding more mature books than they once did; on the other, adults are beginning to realize that these books have something to offer that is rarely found in the standard contemporary novel. I have been told by librarians that *Enchantress from the Stars* is checked out by adults before the children can get hold of it, and I have had letters from strangers who were apparently unaware that it was published as a juvenile. *The Far Side of Evil*, like a good many recent teenage books, has been placed in the adult collection of some libraries as well as in the children's room. More and more junior novels are being reissued in paperback with no indication that they were originally written for young people, and they are finding readers of all ages. The official spokesmen of our time might call this escapism, but I sometimes wonder if it may not be a sign that adults know underneath that a positive outlook is, in fact, a truer representation of reality than the now-fashionable negative one.

As a writer for today's teenagers, then, I think the best approach one can take is to forget that one is writing for teenagers and to speak to them on one's own level. For the truth is that there is no unique teenage audience any more. Either a book appeals only to children under fourteen, or it must have enough substance to appeal not just to older teens but to adults; because the young people who read at all are too sophisticated to read anything that lacks adult interest. Through the changes of the past few years, the juvenile publishing field has given authors new freedom to be honest with young people. Consequently, it has developed into a field where a writer can express what seems true to him when his opinions are not in accord with the cynical bias of our era. He is free not only of the old requirement that he ignore aspects of life, but of the adult market's demand that he view those aspects in a sordid and sensational way — and to me, both of these freedoms are vital.

From *The Horn Book* for June 1972

JEWISH IDENTITY IN
JUVENILE FICTION:
A Look at Three Recommended Books

By ERIC A. KIMMEL

THE RECENT UPSURGE in racial and ethnic consciousness in American society has had a significant influence in the field of children's books. Titles in recent years have dealt with the problems of Blacks, Chicanos, Puerto Ricans, Indians, Chinese, Appalachians, and Jews—to name only the major groups. In one way or another, most of these books seem to revolve around a basic theme: The main character learns to find pride and worth in his racial or national identity while he reinterprets the social role of his group. Details in plot and setting develop from the particular situations in which different minorities find themselves. However, though the challenges of growing to maturity on an Indian reservation may be different from those faced in an urban ghetto, the basic problem is still learning how to establish a sense of human worth in the face of a not overly sympathetic society.

Any book claiming to deal with the situation of any minority group must deal with these challenges. It must present a realistic view of the important problems facing the minority and provide an opportunity for the characters to understand and acknowledge their identity.

As a Jew and a teacher, I have long been interested in books dealing with Jewish characters and themes. The selection in recent years has been better than ever before, both in quantity and depth. I. B. Singer's uniformly excellent books have opened a remarkable world of Hasidic and old-world legend to Jewish, as well as to Gentile, children. His *Day of Pleasure* (Farrar) is a gem, recreating the joys as well as the hardships and intellectual challenges of growing up in a Warsaw ghetto. Sulamith Ish-Kishor, another Jewish writer for children, is worthy of considerable attention. *Boy of Old Prague* (Pantheon) is still a basic book for a child's understanding of the medieval roots of anti-Semitism; and *Our Eddie* (Pantheon) — though I think it has often been misinterpreted through lack of basic knowledge of early twentieth-century Zionism and Jewish life and history — strikes right to the heart of the major Jewish intellectual crisis of our age: the choice between dedication to the Jewish people and the material riches offered by a secular, Gentile, Western society.

It is interesting that nearly all the best titles are set in the past. *Our Eddie* takes place at the turn of the century, as does *A Day of Pleasure*. *Boy of Old Prague* is set in medieval Europe. Also, excluding only the second half of *Our Eddie*, all take place in countries other than the United States. The All-of-a-Kind Family books, though hardly in the same class as the others, do give a good picture of the life of an immigrant Jewish family in New York City. Still, these are also set around World War I. It is a peculiar situation, as if the best children's books to deal with the Black experience were Borton de Treviño's *I, Juan de Pareja* (Farrar) and Armstrong's *Sounder* (Harper).

Yet, there are many problems in modern American Jewish life worth writing about, though these are somewhat different from those which Jews faced in the past and vastly different from those which other minorities face at present. American Jews, for the most part, are neither poor nor undereducated nor underprivileged nor culturally deprived. They feel the effect of open discrimination less than at any other time in their history, and far less in comparison with other minorities. The major challenge today is the struggle to keep Jewish identity, rather than Jewish bodies, alive. Being Jewish is more than wearing a button and a beard and cheering Rabbi Kahane. Is it possible to be a Jew without walling oneself into a Brooklyn ghetto, or packing one's bag and leaving for Israel? Is it possible to lead a satisfying Jewish life without following all the precepts of the Talmud and its Responsa? If one is to discard or alter certain practices, how does he go about it without damaging the entire framework of belief and observance? How does one relate to Western, Gentile society when thirty years ago a Western, civilized, Gentile society gassed millions of Jews like vermin? How does one relate to the State of Israel? Should all Jews really go there? What about intermarriage? Would a world without races and religions really be a better one? How does one deal with the idea of a Chosen People and a Messiah in the light of the twentieth century?

"S'iz shver tzu zayn a Yid!" It's hard to be a Jew! I certainly cannot claim to have solved most or even any of these problems for myself. On the other hand, I do not believe that they are so esoteric as to be beyond the understanding of children from upper

elementary to high-school age. It is for this reason — the failure to deal with the real problems of contemporary Jewish life — that I find three highly recommended books dealing with modern American Jews inadequate. These books are Emily Neville's *Berries Goodman* (Harper), Hila Colman's *Mixed-Marriage Daughter* (Morrow), and E. L. Konigsburg's *About the B'nai Bagels* (Atheneum). I hope that the reasons for their inadequacy will help to establish some sort of framework for judging the effectiveness of books for children that attempt to deal with the modern American Jewish condition.

The central issue of *Berries Goodman* is that of polite suburban anti-Semitism. The Goodman family moves from New York to a suburban community divided into Jewish and Gentile sections by an unspoken agreement among the local realtors. Berries, in spite of his name, is not Jewish; he does, however, have a best friend, Sidney Fine, who is. The slurs directed against his friend by Sandra (the rather unpleasant girl next-door) and her family, and the spineless acquiescence of his older brother and his mother to stupid remarks and subtle discrimination open Berries' eyes to the unpleasant fact of religious prejudice. The climax is reached when Sandra goads Sidney into a near-fatal fall down a dam spillway. The book ends with the hurried move of the Goodman family back to the city after a misunderstanding results in the sale of the Goodman house on the right side of town to the wrong sort of Goodman.

Ms. Neville cannot really be criticized for not presenting a very clear picture of the central issues of Jewish life, for the main action does not involve Jewish characters in any roles other than secondary ones. Still, some points should be noted. Sidney Fine falls victim to a malady common to minority characters in similar situations. Because of the structure of the plot, it is important that he be seen as a sympathetic, regular guy, so nice that any dislike of him is revealed as foolish and unjustified. What really happens in this case and in similar ones is that the character becomes flat. Although Ms. Neville is especially gifted in capturing the speech and thought of children and adolescents, Sidney seems to have nothing to say about what it means to be Jewish in a hostile Gentile environment. A conversation between Berries and Sidney on this subject would have been memorable. However, it never occurs.

Sidney's mother is more interesting, bent on over-protecting her son from what she sees as an overtly hostile environment. But again, we never get a rational statement about her motives. We merely see her reacting, or over-reacting.

A far more serious criticism involves the handling of the issue of anti-Semitism, the book's main theme. We are shown the effects of anti-Semitism, but we never get down to its basic causes. The bigoted characters speak of Jewish ostentation, wealth, and pushiness. These are, obviously, pseudo-reasons. Poor, humble, clannish Jews are not liked any better. Yet, Ms. Neville never really deals with this rationalization directly, other than to try to link it to Hitler's ovens. Her refutation takes the view that since Jews are nice people who behave like everyone else, it is foolish to regard them as different and to dislike them for it. Such a view, adequate for 1952, is out-of-date today. It is as if one tried to explain away racism by stating that Blacks are like everyone else, except for a deeper tan.

Hila Colman's adolescent romance, *Mixed-Marriage Daughter*, deals directly with the problem of defining and establishing a personal Jewish identity. When her father accepts the job of principal of the local elementary school, Sophie Barnes, a seventeen-year-old high school junior, must leave New York and her fashionable private school for the small New England community where her mother's family lives. Sophie is the child of a mixed marriage. Her mother is Jewish, while her father is not. The marriage was apparently not greeted with any great delight by either side, but until this time her mother's Jewishness has meant little to Sophie, and to her mother as well. However, once in a small town environment, Sophie finds out that local prejudices effectively determine what crowd you will go with. She is caught in the middle, barred from the Gentile cliques, yet unable to relate to the girls in the Jewish one. Ignoring the warnings of her family and a Catholic girl friend, she decides to strike out on her own and soon complicates the situation even further by taking up with a boy who happens to be the son of the town's leading citizen and Jew-hater. As if all this were not enough, her mother's family, the Goldens, expect her to conform to Jewish religious customs, and — most important of all — not butt in where Jews are not wanted. Poor Sophie must face the fact that regardless of her own ideas or feelings, the whole town regards her as a Jewish girl.

Ms. Colman, while not an exceptional writer, does have the

153

ability to get down to the basic issues. Her main character is faced with the problem of developing a Jewish identity. But what is that? The author takes an extremely ethnic viewpoint. The Jews are a distinct national-cultural group, and being Jewish is feeling that one is a part of that group.

And yet, she decided, there must be something more than oppression and discrimination that has made these people stick together in this predominantly Jewish community. There must be something positive behind the struggle to remain Jews, and maybe for the first time in her life she was feeling it. Her mother had said it was a tribal feeling, and Sophie could not think of a better way to express it.*

According to the tribal definition, Jewishness is a precious heirloom, passed down from distant generations only through extreme dedication and sacrifice. It is the duty of each present inheritor to carry the torch and pass it on to the next generation. Apparently Ms. Colman has accepted this definition and built her novel around it.

However, it is not the only interpretation of the Jewish experience, and certainly not the most satisfying one for those who believe that the Jewish tradition is a living one. This tribal view makes our heritage into a vast museum. We are surrounded by endless, dusty donations from the past, which have no practical use but are regarded as being too ancient to be questioned and too precious to be discarded. Being Jewish, according to Ms. Colman's presentation, means not eating ham, lighting candles on Friday night, munching matzoth instead of bread on Passover, and putting the menorah in the window on Hannukah. Secondary rites involve intoning *"Oi vay!"* and eating pastrami. Being Jewish is cute and quaint — and irrelevant — but because the Goldens are such nice people, we're not supposed to think that.

Why should anyone go to the trouble of preserving all these customs? Apparently because they make one conscious of being Jewish. And why should one want to be conscious of that? Just to spite the Gentiles? Here the tribal view comes to a dead end. Nowhere is there a hint that there might be a religious philosophy or a distinct ethical outlook behind any of the practices. Ms. Colman raises the issue of establishing a Jewish identity, but she does not know how to resolve it.

The Jews in the book, nice as they are, are on their way out the tribal door. All they seem to know about their tradition are fragments of ritual and folklore, which they practice in a more or less

*Hila Colman, *Mixed-Marriage Daughter*. New York: William Morrow & Company, 1968. p. 158.

contradictory fashion to greater or lesser degrees of rigidity. However, the theological, cultural, and historical reasons making the customs meaningful have been forgotten. Not one character can speak on any other level than the folkloric. For example:

Sophie could not follow or understand the many contradictions in her grandparents' household. Why did her grandmother light candles with a prayer every Friday night but at the same time have no compunction about riding in a car or turning on an electric light, which, it was explained to Sophie, Orthodox Jews did not do on Shabbas? Why did her grandmother never serve butter or dairy dishes with meat, according to the kosher law, but sometimes go to a restaurant for lobster, which was forbidden? . . . Grandma, who looked young and dashing to be the head of such a brood, was flustered by Sophie's questions. "As if you could learn about being Jewish from a book," she said with exasperation.*

The grandmother's statement is preposterous. Unless one regularly has Friday night dinner with the likes of Scholem, Finkelstein, Soloveitchik, Rosenzweig, or Buber, one can learn far more about being Jewish from books than by moving in with the Goldens. The whole pattern of observance in the household is extremely flabby. No cogent explanation is given for either observing or violating a ritual law. We are in a world of muddled habit, with no one to ask the merciless but absolutely necessary "Why?" that would bring the whole façade crashing down.

In *Mixed-Marriage Daughter*, we are operating solely at the folklore level. Where in New York does Sophie go to find her Jewish roots? To the Jewish Museum, or the Theological Seminary, or a Hasidic yeshivah, or a Havurah meeting, or a Shlomo Carlebach concert? No. She walks into a delicatessen and partakes of what she believes to be some sort of Jewish communion — the sacred knish and pastrami sandwich, as if these were the body and blood of Jewish existence.

The problem of being unable to resolve an issue which she raises with great skill also besets Ms. Colman's handling of anti-Semitism. Bitter feelings in the town reach an unpleasant peak when swastikas are placed on the lawns of the Jewish families. Although the culprit is not caught, such blatant hostility shocks the Gentile community, which at the end of the book appears to be beginning to examine its basic attitudes with a more critical eye. The author touches on a very significant point. Pogroms and mass murder do not come out of the sky. Their way is paved by the attitudes and prejudices of polite, refined people. But here

*Colman, op. cit., pp. 61-62.

again, just as in *Berries Goodman*, we fail to get at the root of the problem. In *Mixed-Marriage Daughter*, anti-Semitism is largely a matter of social snobbery. Is the community's shock at the swastikas due to surprise that anyone hates Jews so intensely, or to disapproval at a gross social faux pas: It is acceptable to bar Jews from the country club, but one doesn't go about placing swastikas on their lawn?

The main problems with *Mixed-Marriage Daughter* lie in the fact that though Ms. Colman can raise issues important to both her Jewish and Gentile characters, she seems unable to challenge their attitudes fully or to examine them with a ruthless eye. Thus, instead of reaching a new synthesis, all we get are basically untenable, unrealistic solutions.

The inability to tie folk customs and rituals to any sort of historical or religious rationale, a severe flaw in *Mixed-Marriage Daughter*, becomes an incessant shriek in E. L. Konigsburg's *About the B'nai Bagels*.

The story is told by Mark Setzer, a Long Island Jewish twelve-year-old whose main aims in life are to play baseball on a winning Little League team, to own a *Playgirl* magazine, and to become bar mitzvah — in that order.

On the whole the Setzers are a nice family, though more than a little reminiscent of the Portnoys. Mrs. Setzer talks to God in the light fixture or up in the sky, makes stuffed cabbage, sighs a lot, and sends Mark off to the synagogue every Saturday morning. The father is an accountant who is usually busy somewhere else, and Spencer, the oldest boy, is a know-it-all college student. All in all, the author would have us think, a nice Jewish family.

The trouble is that the Setzers are typical only of a certain type of Jewish family; one operating on the ethnic level of Jewish consciousness, which manifests itself in the form of a garbled observance of religious festivals and an incessant fixation with bagels. Mark and his family eat bagels by the bushel. The team which Mrs. Setzer coaches is called the B'nai Bagels. Mark even gives a bagel to his Spanish girl friend as a symbol of his affection.

Ms. Konigsburg also takes pains to surround the reader with Jewish religious folklore, but absolutely fails to link these peculiar customs together in any sort of rational order. Mark is packed off to the synagogue on the Sabbath, but his mother stays home to pore over Little League batting averages as Mr. Setzer works on his ledger. Mark never complains about the hypocrisy of this. Rather, he has established his own peculiar routine. He insists on not carrying money on Sabbath, a minor regulation, but thinks nothing of skipping synagogue altogether week after week to run down to the housing projects to play baseball. Similarly, Mrs. Setzer borrows from the *khometz* closet over Passover; after all, Mark says, the main thing is not to eat bread, isn't it? The Catholic equivalent of this statement would be that of a priest excusing the fact that he has a mistress by saying that the main thing is for the clergy not to marry. It is a very sad thing that a boy about to become bar mitzvah sees Passover as merely doing without bread. The point of the holiday is to cleanse ourselves and our homes of leavening, of ferment, of rottenness and impurity. For this reason, the everyday utensils are stored away in sealed closets, so that there should be not even a speck of leavening present during the holiday period. To *borrow* from a closet that has been sealed for this purpose is to negate the purpose of the whole holiday. That someone would even do so is conceivable only if that person had no idea of what the Passover season was about in the first place, and was merely following an old custom blindly. This is precisely how the Setzers function as Jews.

Mark's training for his bar mitzvah makes it appear as if the household madness has infected the entire community. His rabbi must be the dreariest, least inspired teacher of children outside of a Sholem Aleichem story. That he could exist in suburban Long Island and hold a pulpit for more than a week is very unlikely. His idea of a Jewish education is to have boys shout out their *haftorahs** while he makes snide remarks about their singing. If they ever discuss anything about Jewish ethics, history, or culture, Mark makes no mention of it. He never even tells us what his *haftorah* is, what book of the Bible it comes from, in what context it lies, or how it is connected to the main reading of the week. I doubt if he even knows. According to the view Ms. Konigsburg gives us, all bar mitzvah means is yelling a babble of foreign words from a podium to give the parents a chance to throw a lavish party. Philip Roth effectively demolishes this sort of decadence, but the shocking thing about *About the B'nai Bagels* is that everyone seems to accept this mockery of a Jewish education as perfectly normal.

*A formal bar mitzvah ceremony involves the boy's chanting a *haftorah*, a specified portion from the Prophets or from other biblical writings chosen to supplement the portion of the Pentateuch read that week during the Sabbath service.

Mark also encounters anti-Semitism. An exceptionally un-pleasant member of the team, Botts, who sells the other boys peeps at a *Playgirl* magazine for a nickel, makes some nasty remark to Mark. Mark broods about it, but it doesn't seem to open up any wells of Jewish feeling within him. The main crisis seems to be whether or not he should tell his mother. The epi-sode is a minor one, and the handling of the issue is superficial.

Whatever the merits of *About the B'nai Bagels* as a growing-up or a baseball story, from the Jewish point of view the Setzers represent a dying Jewishness. The understanding that gives meaning to folkways has long since leaked out of their lives. It is very significant that in Singer's *A Day of Pleasure*, the older brother argues the relevance of Judaism in a modern society with his mother, while in Ms. Konigsburg's book, Spencer, who has nothing to do with anything Jewish, argues with his mother about the proper way to cook stuffed cabbage.

There is more to modern American Jewish life than knishes, pastrami, and bagels. An author choosing to deal with the sub-ject must take into account the fact that Jewish identity is reli-gious as well as ethnic, mystical as well as national, logical and — at the same time — contradictory. Books dealing with Jewish themes must be evaluated according to how well they present these characteristics. At present, many children's books on the topic fail to penetrate beyond the ethnic level.

From *The Horn Book* for April 1973

HIGH JOHN IS RISEN AGAIN

By Virginia Hamilton

E WALKS THE COUNTRY AGAIN, the one who was a slave to a black obsession but a master at biding his time. The timeless ally and confidant of oppressed and depressed dark-skin folk is risen for a second coming, so they say. They speak of High John de Conquer, who has not walked the miles of America since his people had their freedom over one hundred years ago. Since the time the people bartered that freedom for all of the things they thought they wanted, such as a bit of money and land, education, and some amount of acceptance, High John de Conquer had vanished into the soil of the South to wait.

Now, he is back. We know he is back. We can turn on the educational television channels any time and hear our most notable folk-blues bards sing of our remarkable folk hero:

"I got my mojo workin'/ My John de Conquer is workin' true."

We might just as soon call de Conquer Spade (black as the ace of spades), or Cue, he wouldn't care:

My name's Cue — John H. Cue. I got a strong back and strong arms. I got freedom in my heart. I got a first name and a last name and a middle name. . . . I got a tale to tell my people.[1]

They said he would come walking out of southern soil whenever his people were in need of him again: "White America, take a laugh out of our black mouths, and win! We give you High John de Conquer."[2]

Black writers after the Civil War wrote of the plantation tradition, ignoring for a time the rich vein of race relations and the race question for their subject matter. When Zora Neale Hurston, writer and folklorist, first wrote of High John de Conquer in the mid-1930's, there were still sons and daughters of ex-slaves who remembered the stories of High John:

[1]Stephen Vincent Benet, *Selected Works of Stephen Vincent Benet*, Volume II (Holt, 1942), p. 59.

[2]Zora Neale Hurston, "High John de Conquer," in *Book of Negro Folklore*, edited by Langston Hughes and Arna Bontemps (Dodd, 1958), p. 102.

First off, he was a whisper, a will to hope, a wish to find something worthy of laughter and song. Then the whisper put on flesh. His footsteps sounded across the world in a low but musical rhythm as if the world he walked on was a singing-drum. The black folks had an irresistible impulse to laugh. High John de Conquer was a man in full, and had come to live and work on the plantations, and all the slave folks knew him in the flesh.[3]

De Conquer was no messiah come from on high, although he surely had come from somewhere to save the black folk. Rather, he was a working, dues-paying black man with the same weaknesses and strengths as everyperson. And when Old Massa and Old Miss caught him dallying or resting or (mercy!) organizing, High John got himself out of trouble through his wit. Finally, John became a trickster-hero as well as a conqueror. While individual black slaves may not have had the chance or spirit to run (of 3,100,000 slaves in 1850, 1,000 escaped into free states), they conjured a being who released power unto them. High John gave them strength and made them laugh; he freed their spirit if not their bodies.

Black slaves who brought their art of storytelling with them from the motherland now created in America ever more subtle tales in terms of racial oppression. They created towering beings as well as animal figures whom they could recognize easily as representations of themselves (Old Massa thought the tales, spirituals, and sermons mere entertainment), and who personified their experiences of defeat, triumph, and hope. The concept of the weak overcoming the strong was always of steady, fascinating consequence to the slave, just as self-identity is of certain consequence to the inheritors of the slave art of storytelling. We who hope to find alternatives to culturally prescribed ways of writing about black- and white-living must reach far back and learn to know again and to trust the sensibilities of slave ancestors.

The slave art of storytelling through and beyond oppression has been translated into American entertainment and literature, both black and white, from minstrel offerings at the turn of the century through the works of Hurston, Toomer, Benet, Faulkner, Ellison, and now the wit of Ishmael Reed:

Folks. This here is the story of the Loop Garoo Kid. A cowboy so bad he made a working posse of spells phone in sick. . . . This was

3Ibid., p. 93.

one lonely horse. The male horses avoided him because they thought him stuck-up and the females because they thought that since green he was a queer horse. See, he had turned green from old nightmares.[4]

American literature often echoes slave art but with peculiar reverberations. In Ralph Ellison's novel, *Invisible Man* (Random), the protagonist is nameless, as are the protagonists in William Armstrong's *Sounder* (Harper) and the slaves — and for a time the slave lad — in *The Slave Dancer* (Bradbury) by Paula Fox. When in *The Slave Dancer* we are finally told the name of the slave lad, which is Ras, it is a startling echo of the name of one of Ellison's memorable characters from *Invisible Man*, Ras the Destroyer.[5] Ras the Destroyer obeys the absolute doctrine that all blacks must hate all whites. He is a prototype of the avenging black angel just as Ras the slave lad in *The Slave Dancer* is a prototype of the suffering, obedient slave. Both Rases are figures modeled after certain historic individuals whose responses may at one time have been spontaneous although confined by existing cultural limits.

Certainly Ellison's nameless protagonist in *Invisible Man* is not a prototype as is Ras the Destroyer. And through his image, Ellison projected a non-white literature in which the right to be different was a profoundly American right. Such literature has been abundant since 1930, before which social literature was one either of subservience or of transition from self-sacrifice to self-assertion. *Invisible Man*, of the reactionary 1950's, completes the transition in the clearest of terms. By disappearing underground, the nameless one has created conditions by the end of the book for discovering his own identity. The crux then is the preservation and advancement of the individual in non-white literature through self-assertion — not necessarily self-sacrifice and self-destruction — and through new art forms wherever possible.

Just as slave art created High John de Conquer and all manner of other beings out of devastating oppression, so must non-white literature project its own ethos from today's subtle encounter. Our present experience is not one and the same with

---

[4]Ishmael Reed, *Yellow Back Radio Broke-Down* (Doubleday, 1969), pp. 9, 10.

[5]It is likely that in both instances the name Ras is derived from Ras (meaning Prince) Tafari, which was former Emperor Haile Selassie's pre-coronation name. The politico-religious movement of the Jamaican Ras Tafarians considers Selassie the Messiah. Moreover, the Ras Tafarians believe themselves captured by an evil white race; but they will be freed through repatriation to an African heaven on earth.

the oppression of slave time. While we are not wholly free, neither are we totally captured. For never before has black creative intelligence coincided so opportunely with the development of black pride, the advancement of political-cultural awareness, independence, and style to affect black art. Not in our Renaissance of the 1920's was so broad a base of black people ever so involved in self- and group-assertion.

At the end of the nineteenth century, blacks were still stereotyped as "darkies" — smiling, happy, and subhuman. Remnants of such past attitudes in the present caused the poet, the late Conrad Kent Rivers, to cry out in anguish, "Must I shoot the/ white man dead/ to free the nigger/ in his head?"[6] But by the 1920's and the Harlem Renaissance, black people had become *It*, the fighter, the martyr for justice and freedom. *It* was The New Negro, a dramatic superhuman, just as unreal for white Americans and Europeans as had been the stereotyped subhuman.

For the American culturists of the 1920's, all things Negro had come into vogue. And nothing so reveals the danger of popularity based on misunderstanding than the artificial fall of Paul Robeson in the late forties after his extraordinary rise in the twenties. The Robeson experience was unique to America, as was his genius. He influenced our culture to the good as no other black artist had. Always knowing what he believed, Paul Robeson was a man who said what he thought. But society mistook his identity for a symbol of what a race could become if given the opportunity. The culturists ignored the race and elevated the symbol of the African transformed by American freedom and democracy. The figure of the noble savage rose smiling to the top of the heap — with the support of white liberalism and money, of course. That Robeson deserved such acclaim for his superb talent is beyond question. But the fact that the poorly educated, fairly ordinary, decent remainder of black Americans would never have his opportunities was a tragedy the culturists were not wont to notice. Paul Robeson saw and never forgot. The condition of the black masses tortured him and marred for him the success of the Black Bourgeoisie of the Renaissance, as well as his own symbolic personal success.

[6]Conrad Kent Rivers, "Watts" from *The Still Voice of Harlem* (London: Paul Breman, Ltd., 1968).

Nevertheless, the steady assertion of a multifaceted black identity within America by individuals such as Robeson and the late Mary Bethune, educator and President of the National Association of Colored Women, did much to impress gradually on the country the thorough humanness of its black population. Both Mrs. Bethune and Mr. Robeson struggled daily, with courage and talent, to achieve an enormous amount that was of value to their people. Bethune-Cookman College in Florida, which Mrs. Bethune built virtually alone, is her testament. And ever so slowly, the monochromatic image of a black superhuman hero retreated before the vanguard of "second-class" multitudes clamoring for human dignity.

From this vantage, enter an ethnic literature of assertion and authority and of unique black ethos. Non-white literature is itself a vanguard, a continuing revelation of a people's essence and individuality. It has grown and developed as the struggle of the race to be dealt with as human has grown.

Some years ago, I realized that during the month of February I am in greater demand as an author than at any other time of the year. February is, of course, the month when Americans pay tribute to the historical accomplishments of black Americans. School children in all-white, all-black, and racially mixed schools diligently read my books for Black History Week or Month. I dutifully make appearances in classrooms to discuss my fictional trials. Upon asking a group of students by what means they came to read my books, they informed me that in February they had to read "black books," but the rest of the year, they were free to read anything they wanted! However much I value black history, and I do, I am appalled that reading books written by and about blacks substitutes for true evaluation of non-white literature — one month a year.

Black studies programs in schools and colleges often fail to attract the numbers of black students they deserve because students soon realize that they are guinea pigs in some "final solution" experiment. Rather than presenting non-white literature as part of survey offerings in American Literature, such courses have often purposefully become segregated in black studies programs and are ignored by chairmen of so-called American Literature departments. When the present financial crunch began taking its toll, studies in black cultural heritage disappeared throughout the country. How tragic that no preparation was made to include black studies in American Literature programs. And it is surely ironic that economic recession could well have provided an opportunity for curriculum integration.

So it has been with interest that I've observed the growth of new language arts programs in our public schools. Numbers of writers find that their books or parts of their works are used not only as teaching material for writing courses, but for reading and literature programs as well. I, too, have lent myself to the cause of thorough education — often as not with the spirit of cooperation, but occasionally with a distinct feeling of apprehension. I have told how and why I write, having bared my life in two hundred words or less. My fiction is being anthologized, analyzed, dissected, explicated, and distilled in tens of not-so-provocative end-chapter questions. Even my first drafts have been utilized to demonstrate, I suppose, to students that a poor speller can be taught proper writing.

One reading specialist wrote me that my stories have the reality of today's world. Their less-than-happy endings, she suggested, were just the sort of thing children would be needing to grow up whole. I'll submit that children don't need books to know the reality of today's world — fathers and mothers laid off from jobs, less food for the table, less petrol for the family car.

As a writer, my concerns begin at some point on the far side of reality. One will find in my books no documentary history of non-white America in the 1970's. No exact rural language or street language and no behavior that one could say is precisely the way people speak and act at the moment. What I am compelled to write can best be described as some essence of the dreams, lies, myths, and disasters befallen a clan of my blood relatives whose troubled footfall is first discernible on this North American continent some one hundred fifty years ago. Some essence, then, of their language and feeling, which through space-time imagery I project as the unquenchable spirit of a whole people. The fact that others recognize my projection as reality simply reveals how similar is the spiritual struggle of one group to that of another. I claim the right (and an accompanying responsibility) by dint of genealogy to "plumb the line" of soul and ancestry.

But how is one to approach teaching an animating principle of a race? The very abundance of programed learning materials in our schools — teaching machines, kits and kaboodles of

164

answer cards — may well signal our perplexity. We seem to trust nothing unless it is boxed, keyed, and cross-referenced, or otherwise stamped with approval. Perhaps we trust ourselves least of all to guide and interpret, and to bring our own experiences to bear on the reading of books.

Librarians brought me knowledge of literature and made it seem significant through the crucible of their mature opinions and understanding. Teachers taught me to cherish reading through their enthusiasm for the sport and their ability to pass their love for it on to me. However, through their literary offerings, I came in contact with no non-white literature. That was the situation of the times and the state of American life. It was an all-too-familiar period when individuals such as Mary Bethune, Richard Wright, and Paul Robeson were internationally renowned, while at the same time they and the rest of their race remained segregated at home.

It is no mystery that the segregated experience continues to revive throughout our history — as does book banning. So, again and again we must reassert the duality of non-white literature, not only as minority group literature but as American literature. In a world in which the majority of peoples is non-white, the term *minority*, with its connotations of less and of less importance, is a misnomer detrimental to the education and self-image of non-white children. So too it is detrimental to offer children white literature only — as happened in my youth and is still happening today — or one type of non-white book by one kind of author.

I am bored by proponents (white as well as black) of the "Black of the Month" or "Indian of the Year" clubs who cannot conceive of a vanguard, but insist on only one kind of non-white book or non-white writer existing at any given time. They will condemn books that do not conform to the image of an experience popular at the moment and thus narrow the myriad of marvelously diverse possibilities of non-white literary contribution. Too often, we waste time worrying whether one book is written in Black English or if another is authentically something-or-other, rather than setting our sights on good writing no matter what the source, the idiom, argot, or social dialect. We need good literature for young people that will bring characters and the past and the present to life through uncontrived situa-

165

tions. I don't care whether this is accomplished through so-called street language or an oneirocritic's nightmares. I would read both, and if I found story and writing truely plumbed, I would present both to my children.

In my own writing, I attempt to recognize the unquenchable spirit which I know exists in my race and in other races in order to rediscover a universality within myself. My assumption, of course, is that non-white, although different, is as essential as white — that non-white literature, defined through its diversity, is as American as white. The experience of a people does not exist for me merely in present time, nor in past or future, but in a time I appropriate from all of these. It is my time, a continuing stream. It is the right time for me, and my time is of the *essence*. Therefore, I wouldn't think twice about taking possession, for a group of my characters, of the survival instinct that created High John de Conquer, nor about appropriating the Babylonian concept of lex talionis to limit another group of my character's retaliatory zeal. For the experience of a people must come to mean the experience of humankind. I am free to write about the time of the world as I wish; I must be; and I am confined only by the measure of my knowledge. For all writers this must be so, and never should they be intimidated into believing otherwise.

And yet, there is nothing so jarringly real as reality. If we discover the knowledge that we think is true is not nearly so, we are apt to hear the thunder and to weather the storm of those who know more. But then, nothing ventured, nothing risked. Writers need to take chances, as should we all. Chance love, chance terror, chance misunderstanding, chance truth. But chance.

My seven-year-old risks his mother's ire each time he takes up a small, hard, green block and throws it inside the house, with all of his might, two inches to the left of my shoulder. He has transformed the block into a pigskin missile. He is the star quarterback throwing expertly to his favorite receiver. He knows I'm there and that I'm sure to scream and reprimand him even when he doesn't hit me by mistake. But a vast, tantalizing playing field has materialized just beyond me behind the couch. His receiver is only a couple of yards from the end zone. So he risks it — whiz . . . wham-o! The running back glides in for the touchdown (magically, my son's receiver is never tackled). Seemingly content, he stands listening attentively, if not contritely, to a severe reprimand. The risk had to be worth it.

Another boy, older, called M.C., wanted something higher than anything to sit on. So he risked swimming a dangerous river in order to get a forty-foot pole because such a pole is better to sit on than anything, even better than a mountain. M.C. sits up there to make certain each day is still perfect, still beautiful, the way he wants each day to be. And every day, he risks falling off the pole; still, he climbs and sits because seeing that way is always worth the chance of falling. Almost every moment of M.C.'s life is one risk or another. He risks catching skunks by setting traps for rabbits; or he risks his father's rage by playing with a forbidden companion because friendship has to be more important than the chance of discovery and punishment. M.C.'s final risk is to build a wall which may or may not stop a spoil heap. I'm inclined to think it is unimportant whether the wall will stop the heap. It's probable that nothing can halt the momentum of tons of falling debris. Still, M.C. must risk it, for no wall at all means certain destruction. At least with a wall, there is that one chance of a lifetime.

We find ourselves having come full circle from High John de Conquer, who for his people will ever risk an unalterable consequence to give freedom the advantage in the world. So it has always been, whether the name is High John, Long John, or John Henry of fiction or Sojourner, Malcolm, or Mohandas of reality. As Zora Hurston revealed:

If the news from overseas reads bad, and the nation inside seems like it is stuck in the Tar Baby, listen hard, and you will hear John de Conquer treading on his singing-drum. You will know then, that no matter how bad things look now, it will be worse for those who seek to oppress us. Even if your hair comes yellow, and your eyes are blue, John de Conquer will be working for you just the same. From his secret place, he is working for all America now.[7]

I want to believe it. While I go about doing what I know how to do, I listen hard. And plumb the line.

[7]Book of Negro Folklore, op. cit., p. 102.

From *The Horn Book* for April 1975

VI

IN DEFENSE OF FANTASY

"We who hobnob with hobbits and tell tall tales about little green men are quite used to dismissal as mere entertainers, or sternly disapproved of as escapists. But I think that the categories are changing like the times. Sophisticated readers are accepting the fact that an improbable and unmanageable world is going to produce an improbable and hypothetical art. At this point realism is perhaps the least adequate means of understanding or portraying the incredible realities of our existence.

"A scientist who creates a monster in his laboratory; a librarian in the Library of Babel; a wizard unable to cast a spell; a spaceship having trouble getting to Alpha Centauri; all these may be precise and profound metaphors of the human condition. The fantasist, whether he uses the ancient archetype of myth and legend or the younger ones of science and technology, may be talking as seriously as any sociologist — and a great deal more directly — about human life as it is lived, and as it might be lived, and as it ought to be lived.

"For, as a great scientist has said and as all children know, it is by the imagination, above all, that we achieve perception, and compassion, and hope."

From the Acceptance Remarks of Ursula Le Guin on receiving the 1973 National Book Award in Children's Books for *The Farthest Shore* (Atheneum)

From *The Horn Book* for June 1973   URSULA LE GUIN

HIGH FANTASY
AND HEROIC ROMANCE*

By LLOYD ALEXANDER

THE WHITE QUEEN proudly told Alice she had learned to believe six impossible things before breakfast. We do much better. Science appears on the verge of discoveries that may let us live forever, at the same time perfecting ways to get rid of us altogether. We can fly to any place in the world in a matter of hours, if we can find a parking space at the airport. We have a beachhead on the moon — for the moment free of beer cans and oil slick. We have the material benefits of labor-saving machines, along with the cultural benefits of Jacqueline Susann and her *Love Machine*. As time goes on, Lewis Carroll seems more of a realist than ever.

When our own world is so fantastic, I am amazed and thankful we can still be deeply moved by worlds that never existed and touched by the fate of people who are figments of our imagination. Perhaps our daily diet of impossibilities and incongruities is lacking some essential ingredient. Our systems of information retrieval still have not retrieved the one vital bit of information: How shall we live as human beings? The same questions that preoccupied the ancient Greeks preoccupy us today. Shakespeare is truly our contemporary. Or we, perhaps, are not as modern as we like to think we are.

The arts, surely, are not as modern as we might believe — despite *Oh! Calcutta!* If not quite sisters, Lysistrata and Lena of *I Am Curious (Yellow)*, are distant cousins under the skin. However much their forms and functions have changed, the arts show a line of organic growth from a common ancestry. Poetry, dance, theatre, comedy, and tragedy have roots in the most ancient religious rituals. The first language of art was the language of magic and mythology. And decoding this language has long been a study — for poets, philosophers, philologists, and psychiatrists.

Most recently, the structural anthropologist Claude Lévi-Strauss in *The Savage Mind* and in *The Raw and the Cooked* has

*Originally given at the New England Round Table of Children's Librarians, October, 1969.

tried to analyze man's capacity for myth-making and the processes at work in primitive thought. Despite speculations and insights, the original meanings of a great many, perhaps most, of our earliest legends are still as shadowy as the ancient ceremonies they mirror. We glimpse the seasonal progress of sacred kings in a calendar of birth, death, and resurrection. But the substance of these mysteries is long lost, or preserved only in fragments: A fairy tale may hint at figures in forgotten dramas, or a child's game of hopscotch pattern the Minotaur's labyrinth.

While its full meaning remains tantalizingly unknown, we can still trace mythology's historical growth into an art form: through epic poetry, the *chansons de geste*, the Icelandic sagas, the medieval romances and works of prose in the Romance languages. Its family tree includes *Beowulf*, the *Eddas*, *The Song of Roland*, *Amadís de Gaule*, the *Perceval* of Chrétien de Troyes, and *The Faerie Queene*.

In modern literature, one form that draws most directly from the fountainhead of mythology, and does it consciously and deliberately, is the heroic romance, which is a form of high fantasy. The world of heroic romance is, as Professor Northrop Frye defines the whole world of literature in *The Educated Imagination*, "the world of heroes and gods and titans . . . , a world of powers and passions and moments of ecstasy far greater than anything we meet outside the imagination."*

If anyone can be credited with inventing the heroic romance as we know it today — that is, in the form of a novel using epic, saga, and *chanson de geste* as some of its raw materials — it must be William Morris, in such books as *The Wood Beyond the World* and *The Water of the Wondrous Isles*. Certainly Morris showed the tremendous strength and potential of the heroic romance as an artistic vehicle, which was later to be used by Lord Dunsany, Eric Eddison, James Branch Cabell; by C. S. Lewis and T. H. White. Of course, heroic romance is the basis of the superb achievements of J. R. R. Tolkien.

Writers of heroic romance, who work directly in the tradition and within the conventions of an earlier body of literature and legend, draw from a common source: the "Pot of Soup," as Tolkien calls it, the "Cauldron of Story," which has been simmering away since time immemorial.*

*Northrop Frye, *The Educated Imagination* (Bloomington, Indiana, Indiana University Press, 1964), p. 100.

*J. R. R. Tolkien, *Tree and Leaf* (Boston, Houghton Mifflin Company, 1965), p. 26.

The pot holds a rich and fascinating kind of mythological minestrone. Almost everything has gone into it, and almost anything is likely to come out of it: morsels of real history spiced — and spliced — with imaginary history, fact and fancy, daydreams and nightmares. It is as inexhaustible as those legendary vessels that could never be emptied.

Among the most nourishing bits and pieces we can scoop out of the pot are whole assortments of characters, events, and situations that occur again and again in one form or another throughout much of the world's mythology: heroes and villains, fairy godmothers and wicked stepmothers, princesses and pig-keepers, prisoners and rescuers; ordeals and temptations, the quest for the magical object, the set of tasks to be accomplished. And a whole arsenal of cognominal swords, enchanted weapons; a wardrobe of cloaks of invisibility, seven-league boots; a whole zoo of dragons, helpful animals, birds, and fish.

But — in accordance with one of fantasy's own conventions — nothing is given for nothing. Although we are free and welcome to ladle up whatever suits our taste, and fill ourselves with any mixture we please, nevertheless, we have to digest it, assimilate it as thoroughly as we assimilate the objective experiences of real life. As conscious artists, we have to process it on the most personal levels; let it work on our personalities and, above all, let our personalities work on it. Otherwise we have what the computer people delicately call GIGO: garbage in, garbage out.

Because these conventional characters — these personae of myth and fairy tale, though gorgeously costumed and caparisoned — are faceless, the writer must fill in their expressions. Colorful figures in a pantomime, the writer must give them a voice.

Since I have been talking about the "Cauldron of Story," I am now reminded of the Crochan, the Black Cauldron that figured in one of the books of Prydain. Now, cauldrons of one sort or another are common household appliances in the realm of fantasy. Sometimes they appear, very practically, as inexhaustible sources of food, or, on a more symbolic level, as a lifegiving source or as a means of regeneration. Some cauldrons bestow wisdom on the one who tastes their brew. In Celtic mythology, there is a cauldron of poetic knowledge guarded by nine maidens, counterparts of the nine Greek muses.

There is also a cauldron to bring slain warriors back to life.

The scholarly interpretation — the mythographic meaning — is a fascinating one that links together all the other meanings. Immersion in the cauldron represented initiation into certain religious mysteries involving death and rebirth. The initiates, being figuratively — and perhaps literally — steeped in the cult mysteries, emerged reborn as adepts. In legend, those who came out of the cauldron had gained new life but had lost the power of speech. Scholars interpret this loss of speech as representing an oath of secrecy.

One branch of *The Mabinogion*, the basic collection of Welsh mythology, and one of my own prime research sources, tells of such a cauldron of regeneration, and how it ended up in the hands of the Irish. And, in the tale of Branwen, the Welsh princess rescued from the Irish by King Bran, a great number of slain Irish warriors came back to life. Naturally, this cauldron posed an uncomfortable problem for the Welshmen, who were constantly finding themselves outnumbered; until one of the Welsh soldiers sacrificed his life by leaping into the cauldron and shattering it.

This incident gave me the external shape of the climax of *The Black Cauldron* (Holt). Though changed and manipulated considerably, the nub of the story is located in the myth — except for one detail of characterization: the essential *internal* nature of the cauldron, its inner meaning and significance beyond its being an unbeatable item of weaponry.

And so I tried to develop my own conception of the cauldron. Despite its regenerative powers, it seemed to me more sinister than otherwise. The muteness of the warriors created the horror I associated with the cauldron. Somehow, I felt that these voiceless men, already slain, revived only to fight again, deprived even of the oblivion of the grave, were less beneficiaries than victims.

As the idea grew, I began to sense the cauldron as a kind of ultimately evil device. My "Cauldron-Born," then, were not only mute but enslaved to another's will. If they had lost their power of speech, they had also lost their memory of themselves as living beings — without recollection of joy or sorrow, tears or laughter.

They had, in effect, been deprived of their humanity: a fate, in my opinion, considerably worse than death. The risk of dehumanization — of individuals being manipulated as objects instead of being valued as living people — is, unfortunately, not confined to the realm of fantasy.

173

Another example of the same kind of creative invention on the part of a writer has to do with the birth of a character; and in this case a most difficult delivery. Writing *The Book of Three* (Holt), the first of the Prydain chronicles, I was groping my way through the early chapters with that queasy sensation of desperate insecurity that comes when you do not know what is going to happen next. I knew vaguely what should happen, but I could not figure out how to get at it. The story, at this point, needed another character: Whether friend or foe, minor or major, comic or sinister, I could not decide. I only knew that I needed him, and he refused to appear.

The work came to a screaming halt: the screams being those of the author. Day after day, for better than a week, I stumbled into my work room and sat there, feeling my brain turn to concrete. I had been reading a very curious book, an eighteenth-century account of the various characters in Celtic mythology. One of them stuck in my mind — a one-line description of a creature half-human, half-animal. The account was interesting, but it was not doing much to solve my problem.

I was convinced, by now, that I had suffered severe brain damage; that I would never write again; the mortgage would be foreclosed; my wife carried off to the Drexel Hill poor-farm; and I — quivering and gibbering, moaning and groaning — I did not even dare to imagine what would become of me. The would-be author of a hero-tale had begun to show his innate cowardice, and I was feeling tremendously sorry for myself.

At four o'clock one morning, I had gone to my work room for what had become a routine session of sniveling and hand-wringing. I had decided, one way or another, to use this hint of a half-animal, half-human creature. The eighteenth-century text had given him a name — Gurgi. It seemed to fit, but he still refused to enter the scene. I could see him, a little; but I could not *hear* him. If I could only make him talk, half the battle would be over. But he would not talk.

And so I sat there, expecting to pass the morning as usual, crying and sighing. All of a sudden, for no apparent reason whatever, I head a voice in the back of my mind, plaintive, whining, self-pitying. It said: "Crunchings and munchings?" And there, right at that moment, there he was. Part of him, certainly, came from research. The rest of him — I have a pretty good idea where it came from.

My point, in these examples, is simply this: A writer of fantasy, like any writer, must find the essential content of his work within himself, in his own personality, in his own attitude and commitment to real life. Whatever form we work in — fantasy or realism, books for children or for adults — I believe that the fundamental creative process is the same. In his work, the author may be very heavily disguised, or altogether anonymous. I do not think he is ever totally absent.

On the contrary, his presence is required; not as a stage manager who can be seen busily shifting the cardboard scenery, but as the primary source of tonality and viewpoint. Without this viewpoint, the work becomes more and more abstract, a play of the intellect that can move us only intellectually. It may be technically brilliant, but it becomes sleight of hand instead of true magic. If art — as Plato defined it — is a dream for awakened minds, it should be, at the same time, a dream that quickens the heart.

High fantasy indeed quickens the heart and reaches levels of emotion, areas of feeling that no other form touches in quite the same way. Some books we can enjoy, some we can admire, and some we can love. And among those books that we love as children, that we remember best as adults, fantasy is by no means least. It would be interesting to calculate how many of the classic works of children's literature are works of fantasy.

The logical question is: What makes fantasy so memorable? Unfortunately, art is not always susceptible to logical analysis, or at least not to the same patterns of logic that apply in other areas. Instead of provable answers, we have possibilities, hints, and suggestions. The most obvious answers are the least accurate. Fantasy can be considered an escape from complex reality to a more simplistic world, the yearning for a past that never existed, or a vehicle for regression. Attractive as these answers may be, fantasy offers no such escapes from life. It can refresh and delight, certainly; give us a new vision; make us weep or laugh. None of these possibilities constitutes escape, or denial of something most of us begin to suspect at a rather early age: that being alive in the world is a hard piece of business.

There may be subtler forces at work. In even the wildest flights of fantasy, there seems to be an undercurrent of rationality. On its own terms and in its own frame of reference, the fantasy world makes a certain kind of sense. If there are ambiguities, they are recognizable as such. The fantasy realm includes superb villains—utterly fiendish and irretrievably wicked—but no neurotics. The story does not move as the result of irrational behavior, capriciousness, or sudden whim. The "bad guys" have very good reasons for perpetrating whatever villainy they have in mind.

And there is always the possibility of effective action. The hero wants to do something, he can do something, and he actually does do something. So much of current adult literature offers us the anti-hero: I might say the hero as clodpole, the hero as a crashing bore, or as an existential loser. The fantasy hero may lose, too. But in the process, at least, he has made some effort to cope with his environment. He may be a sacrificial figure but never a passive victim.

The fantasy hero is not only a doer of deeds, but he also operates within a framework of morality. His compassion is as great as his courage — greater, in fact. We might even consider that his humane qualities, more than any others, are what the hero is really all about. I wonder if this reminds us of the best parts of ourselves? A reminder, as Lewis Mumford says, that our potential is greater than our achievement. An ideal, if we choose to call it that; but an ideal that may actually be within our reach. We cannot know for sure unless we do try to reach out for it.

Or, does the vitality of fantasy come from a deeper source: from its deliberate use of the archaic, the imagery of our most ancient modes of thought? Jung believes it does, and spoke eloquently about "primordial images," which at times overpower us and make us aware of what is universal, and therefore eternal. In practice, this point of view seems to have a great amount of truth in it. Whether this also implies, as Jung believed it did, a common racial memory, a collective unconscious, is open to speculation.

We are now starting to wade into some rather deep metaphysical waters. But the "Cauldron of Story," we realize, does not serve up No-Cal carbonated beverage. The brew is considerably stronger. But certainly not too strong for children. They love it and thrive on it; and I believe they need the experience of fantasy as an essential part of growing up.

Strong emotions, moments of triumph or despair, are surely familiar to children. They respond to them and identify with them because these feelings are already a part of their inner lives — lives which, as we are continually discovering, are richer and more complex than we might have imagined, on both an unconscious and conscious level. Graham Greene touches on this in his essay "The Lost Childhood," when he says: "A child . . . knows most of the game. . . . He is quite well aware of cowardice, shame, deception, disappointment." I think these statements are true. And equally true that the child is aware of courage, pride, and honesty. Greene continues with what I think is the operative phrase: "it is only an attitude . . . that he lacks."* And here, on this point of attitude, the goals and values of high fantasy merge with those of all literary and artistic forms. Each work of art, in its own way, suggests a possible attitude toward life: a variety of life-styles, ways of seeing ourselves and others.

George Steiner, in his book *Language and Silence*, says: "the critic. . . . must ask of it [contemporary literature] not only whether it represents a technical advance . . . or plays adroitly on the nerve of the moment, but what it contributes to or detracts from the dwindled reserves of moral intelligence." High fantasy as we write it today must, of necessity, be included as contemporary literature, whether its apparent content pretends to look back to an imaginary past or ahead to a future (that may or may not be altogether imaginary). It must be able to answer the question that Steiner also raises: "What is the measure of man this work proposes?"†

The question is not an abstract one, of merely literary judgments, but fundamentally one of how we choose to see ourselves. Shall we measure only our present condition, which is far from a happy one? Or is there some larger scale — not only to measure man, but which man can measure up to? Fantasy imagines there is. And if we can dream, maybe we can really measure up to the dream.

*Graham Greene, *Collected Essays* (New York, Viking Press, 1969), p. 16.
†George Steiner, *Language and Silence: Essays on Language, Literature, and the Inhuman* (New York, Atheneum, 1970), p. 9.

From *The Horn Book* for December 1971

"REALISM PLUS FANTASY EQUALS MAGIC"

By ROGER W. DRURY

I

REALISM PLUS FANTASY equals Magic. It sounds like simple arithmetic, but, in the doing, it comes nearer to cookery or chemistry. Quantities matter. How they are combined is terribly important; and most important is the use of fresh ingredients. There are endless possible combinations of realism and fantasy, but you can boil most of them down to two types: real people in fantastic situations, and fantastic people in real situations. I should like nothing better than to discuss these situations, but it might be profitable instead to do a little burrowing into the nature of fantasy.

We all know what realism is. But just what is fantasy, and where do we find it? What is this ingredient which causes a story to light up with the special glow of magic? Webster says fantasy is "a product of imagination." Yes, so it is, sometimes. But that definition implies invention by a human mind. Fantasy, however, is not always a product of the human imagination. I prefer a definition which suggests that some things are fantasy which are merely waiting to be found.

How precise can we be about the realm of fantasy? The boundaries keep crumbling — consider four-minute miles, voyages to the moon, and porpoises trained to carry messages in the deep ocean. Every day, it seems, things happen that would have seemed purely imaginary the day before. And not only are the boundaries between the real and the fantastic as wobbly as painted lines on asphalt roads in summer; the boundaries also insist on moving to or fro to suit the vision of each observer.

For example: Is there any more vivid image of reality than a clock? Whether an alarm clock with its ghastly gong that cuts off our dreams, or a time-clock measuring with icy objectivity our arrival and departure from the production line. Whatever sort it may be, a clock has anchors in reality that nothing can dislodge. Now, come away a few steps. You will agree with me, I think, that a clock intact inside a crocodile is still possible (at least, in a crocodile which never learned to chew everything before he swallowed). On the other hand — come a mile or two further — a clock which can be heard ticking inside a crocodile is not very likely. And a clock which was ticking inside a crocodile before the story began — and which keeps on ticking, without running down and without being rewound, until almost the end of the book — is certainly fantastic! But where did the fantasy begin? Where do you draw the line?

In traveling away from the center of our experience, we make a gradual transition from the probable, to the unlikely, to the downright impossible. We get there by imperceptible stages. Do we cross a boundary? Perhaps. But where the boundary is drawn depends on the traveler. It is not exactly a question of his credulity, but more a matter of the "willing suspension of disbelief which constitutes poetic faith." I happen to be very willing to suspend my disbelief. On the map I use, reality is a far-flung kingdom. It embraces many provinces of possibility, which become tinged with fantasy long before they touch the frontier of unexplored lands.

In my home town, most of the roads are named for early property owners — roads with sober names like Barnum Street, Foley Road, Cook Avenue. But one of our roads (would you believe it?) is named Bow Wow Road. Was it named for a dog? No one knows. Anyway, on Bow Wow Road there lives a man — you will not believe this — who is embarrassed by what he calls his undignified address. I call that fantastic.

Someone recently crossed the Atlantic Ocean in a rowboat — actually rowed himself across in a rowboat! Fantastic! Mark my words: Someone will go to sea in a sieve before the seventies are out. How long the voyage will be, I don't predict, but will the Three Wise Men of Gotham then be any the less fantastic?

A third example: In Blayon, England, our newspaper reported, "Edward Stainer lifted the floorboards in his living room in an attempt to trace the source of a worrisome draft. He found a hole 1,000 feet deep. 'There was just no ground there,' said the horrified Stainer, who has lived in the house in this County Durham mining village for twenty years. He moved his furniture out of the room, barricaded it off from his two children and called in the local expert on holes in the ground, the National Coal Board. It [the Board] said Stainer's find was a 200-year-old mineshaft, and informed him the house could have collapsed if the hole had been wider. Coal Board officials plan to try to fill the hole with concrete, hoping it won't get any wider." Fantastic.

Just how fantastic Bow Wow Road, or a man rowing alone across the ocean, or the thousand-foot hole under the living room will seem, depends on where you read or hear of it. If a writer seems more or less trustworthy, will you insist these things are nothing but real? Please, no. The real world is full of fantastic events and combinations. Some of them have already been reported in the newspapers, while others have—so far—happened only in children's books. (I am not so naïve as to think the real world produces fantastic dramas as artful as those you find in children's books. Yet, they are related. They are cousins.) I accept this axiom: Fantasy begins far closer to the real than we are used to supposing, and it extends as a tantalizing fringe of the probable many, many leagues out, blending at last imperceptibly into the impossible.

II

Now, let us dig a little further. Why do most childen inhabit this on-again, off-again borderland with such self-confident delight? I am no expert, no psychologist. Perhaps I should not try even a worm's eye peep into their territory, but I did help rear four children, and years ago, unforgettably, I was one. All of a child's experience is new. Every bit of color, motion, and sound around him; every sensation he feels; every thought that flies through his mind — is a surprise. Some of this experience comes to him awake, some in dreams. At first he takes both worlds to be equally real, and at first the stuff of his waking experience is just as magical as the dreams. From hour to hour, wrapped in an infinite variety of impressions, he finds everything wonderful, anything possible; and he is on the watch for more of the same.

That expectation dies hard. But as experience repeats itself, all of us — more or less — suffer the sad disappearance of magic from a wonderland that has become habitual. (Would it, I wonder, be cynical to define the real as the habitual, the expected, the predictable?) At all events, we keep the old hunger for magic. We go on searching for the once-known rainbow. Not only children do this; we adults do it, too. We long to be surprised. Continually, we itch to explore the fringes of reality. And the boldest of us make border raids into those unexplored provinces beyond the probable: the unlikely, the invisible, the impossible.

Here we come to that perennial question: Is such play with fantasy good for children? Will it hopelessly tangle the strands of their reality? Will it make them into undisciplined dreamers, schizophrenics, malcontents? Will it — God forbid — lead them to take drugs?

If a child has a very insecure home base, I suppose the fantastic might for him have the attraction of a secret refuge. But, just as likely, the fantasy he finds in children's books will make him uneasy and repel him by its casual treatment of the few landmarks he knows.

But with a normal, healthy child, it is a matter of ducks and water. Such a child seems positively obsessed by a need to experiment with ways of looking at the world, to rearrange place and time, to challenge the stable and predictable frame of experience. He sits on a swing and makes the landscape rock like a pendulum under him. He hooks his knees on a branch and turns the world upside down. He spins round and round and then stands still to watch the world reel. He borrows (and parodies) the roles of his parents, teachers, doctors, and adult neighbors. He sticks out his tongue in front of S-curved mirrors.

From such eccentric dealings with the known and predictable, he proceeds to follow little girls down rabbit holes, to ride with Toad in his new motor car, or to gawk at Nate Twitchell's enormous egg and speculate on what sort of critter will hatch from it. Like all of a child's experience, these explorations help to shape his character. They teach him to expect and relish the unlikely, to miss none of life's surprises, but to be astonished by nothing. He may learn through this training how to leap spontaneously from one way of thinking to another — an ability which is the heart and soul of humor. If he is lucky, he will be one of the elect who can treat appearances playfully.

Think of it! All these benefits from exercising one simple formula: "What if?" — the words that bring magical results, as surely as rubbing a lamp brought them to Aladdin. You know from your own travels on the magic carpet, I am sure, that one comes home refreshed, to the firm ground where people must add two and two, carry in firewood, stamp dates in books, and tie their shoelaces in the morning.

IV

By now, you may be expecting me to claim that a good diet of fantasy in childhood is the royal road to success, to the White House, to heaven knows what. Better than that, this exploration of the frontier of the real is a child's best way to enlarge the boundaries of whatever world he will inhabit as an adult. They are enlarged from within. In Shakespeare's words, he can be "bounded in a nutshell and count [himself] a king of infinite space."

Here I must pause for a moment to note that a certain proportion of mankind grows up shy of fantasy, suspicious of its motives, and fearful of its consequences. They prefer to locate their lives in a narrow frame of the real and the possible. They inhabit a world in which events are all predictable, in which cause and effect run on railroad tracks and arrive on time. Clocks again!

In that world, any rumor of an unseen realm is relegated to churches and mental hospitals, or allowed in a well marked cage in children's books. As children, these fantasy-shy people had the valuable ability to perceive instantly that the emperor had no clothes. I do not mean to belittle or to poke fun at them. They are conscientious parents. Though they avoid the overtly fantastic, they do supply their children with solid biographies of Helen Keller, Madame Curie, Martin Luther King, and Abraham Lincoln; histories of the American Revolution, the Pyramid builders, and the Gold Rush; expositions of the atom, chlorophyll, and electric wiring.

But it must not surprise you if I show a little bias towards those others, the pixilated children who are always more or less charged with expectation of the unlikely; the children who grow up to put as flexible a frame as possible around their adult world.

We all remember our days of priceless discovery. One of mine came thirty-five years ago at college. I suspect that permanent wrinkles were made that day in my brain by this magic sentence from Coleridge's notebook: "If a man could pass through Paradise in a dream, and have a flower presented to him as a pledge that his soul had really been there, and if he found that flower in his hand when he awoke — Aye! and what then?"

"If . . . what then?" Because of their inability to let such tantalizing questions alone, because of their experimentation with unheard-of arrangements of reality, these fringe-fanciers —

these fantasts — form a tribe which fathers more than its share of the world's explorers, inventors, humorists, poets — and writers of children's books! They turn facts over, as anteaters turn rocks over, looking for the scurrying meanings beneath. They too see that the emperor is naked, but they see more than the shocking fact: They see the absurdity. When the floorboard is lifted and a thousand-foot hole is discovered, do you think these acrobats of the imagination will be caught off balance? Not they! They have been looking for something like this all along. Do they call in the Coal Board? I should say not. They get pencil and paper and start to write a children's book.

They are the ones — I rather think — who saw the star of Bethlehem and knew what to do about it. I suspect they are the ones who have given us timely warning of new dragons at large — uncontrolled population, humanity entombed in its own trash. For only a certain familiarity with dragons will keep us from saying "Pooh, pooh!" when a dragon appears, or — just as imprudent — wasting time with rat poison. They are the finders of four-leaf clovers, and Indian arrowheads, and winding backroads that lead off the edge of the map straight into mystery.

V

This raises a question. If I am right, if the fringes and unexplored provinces beyond reality are a playground of healthy childhood, and a training ground for creative adult life, should we not be concerned about the child who avoids fantasy, who prefers to stay in a narrow, putting-green world where there is no hiding place for the unexpected?

Yes, I think perhaps we should. Chiefly, I think it because I value so highly the flexibility of outlook won by a well exercised imagination. The real world has dragons, and sleeping princesses, and outlandish words escaping from dictionaries, and terrified gardeners repainting the roses — yet the putting-green child may grow up unable either to identify or to enjoy them.

Think now, in conclusion, of a memorable image near the end of *Peter and the Wolf*. The boy Peter has, of course, wandered farther afield than his grandfather thought wise, and he has been chased up a tree by the wolf. But watch Peter! He dangles a crafty noose from his tree and snatches the wolf into the air by one lassoed hind leg — and simultaneously out of the woods march the hunters, indiscriminately shooting as they come. In this tight spot, it is Peter whose imagination tells him the most practical and, incidentally, humorous thing to do. The best the others can contrive is to aim blindly and make a big noise. I feel certain that Peter was raised on a good mixture of realism and fantasy. Place your bets on him. In an unpredictable world, Peter is the best traveling companion you can have.

Some of you may be reading all this with a certain skepticism, wondering whether these are truly my reasons for writing stories that mix fantasy with realism: Because they make children creative; because children reared on such stories grow into resourceful adults, who are never bored or cornered. Well, not entirely. Let's confess it. I write such tales because I like them that way. My realism comes naturally with a wide fringe. I was, and still am, grateful for this chance to stop and ask why; to look for reasons — if the desire to make magic (in books or in daily life) requires reasons. But you should be warned. Writers are writers, no matter what pose we adopt. We make no special claim as philosophers, or as psychologists, or as gurus of any esoteric knowledge. Our books must speak for us. When we write about our books, we should accept gracefully the not-at-all-fantastic thought that our profoundest analyses and self-justifications may be only — gossamer.

From *The Horn Book* for April 1972

THE WEAK PLACE IN THE CLOTH:
A Study of Fantasy for Children

By JANE LANGTON

ANALYZING BOOKS of fantasy for children is like explaining a joke after everyone has laughed. Who cares how *Stuart Little* (Harper) differs from *Mary Poppins* (Harcourt)? If you've read them, that's all that matters. But, as a writer of fantasy for children, I want to find out exactly what I've been trying to do so long by intuition and imitation. So I've been sorting and categorizing a lot of old and new favorites to see if I can make some sort of sense out of them. The result is a modest set of conclusions concerning the three primary questions which each fantasy asks and answers: *What if? Then what? So what?*

WHAT IF?

What if rugs could fly? What if pigs could talk? Every writer of fantasy poses a *what-if* question that is the theme of his book. He can ask it in many ways, and all of these ways are different approaches to the dividing line between truth (the real world) and fantasy (the unreal world). For E. Nesbit, the dividing line was a piece of cloth.

> There is a curtain, thin as gossamer, clear as glass, strong as iron, that hangs forever between the world of magic and the world that seems to us to be real. And when once people have found one of the little weak spots in that curtain which are marked by magic rings, and amulets, and the like, almost anything can happen.[1]

There are at least eight different uses which have been made of this cloth by writers of fantasy. In the first, the fabric remains whole. It is merely stretched a little out of shape. The entire story happens on the real-world side of the curtain. These books are tall tales. Who's to say they couldn't happen? What if, for example, someone imitated the Pied Piper and invented a contraption to trap mice with music?

> Through the streets of Centerburg rolled Mr. Michael Murphy. . . . The mice came running from every direction! . . . They all went run-

ning up the ramps and runways and disappeared in Michael Murphy's musical mouse trap.[2]

A musical mousetrap? Unlikely, but not impossible, not beyond the stretch of the fabric we're talking about. The cloth may be getting a little thin in spots, but it's still whole.

In a second kind of book, the cloth is punctured. The characters leak through the hole into another world. Somewhere near the beginning of all of these books there are episodes like these.

In another moment Alice was through the glass, and had jumped lightly down into the Looking-glass room.[3]

"This must be a simply enormous wardrobe!" thought Lucy, going still further in and pushing the soft folds of the coats aside to make room. . . . A moment later she found that she was standing in the middle of a wood . . . with snow under her feet.[4]

Sometimes the weak point in the cloth is not a place but a thing, a device, a charm of some sort. For the children in one of my books, it is the Astonishing Stereoscope.

There was a great clanging sound. The lenses in front of his eyes rushed outward on all sides, the papery specks and cracks on the surface of the picture disappeared, and Eddy suddenly found himself *inside the stereoscope.*[5]

Edward Eager's children find an extraordinary book on the bottom shelf of the fairy-tale section in the library, which turns on some Seven-Day Magic.

Barnaby nodded excitedly: "It all adds up. Think of it sitting there all those years, with the magic from all those other books dripping down onto it! . . . And we came and wanted a magic story; so that's what it turned into."[6]

Eleanor Estes invented one of the cleverest devices for tearing a hole in the fabric. The two little girls in her *Witch Family* (Harcourt) draw pictures with crayons, and it is the pictures themselves which create and control what happens on the other side of the cloth. In some of the most celebrated books of fantasy for children, the knife that rips the cloth is not a place nor a thing but a magic person. Peter Pan is one; Mary Poppins is another.

Jane and Michael edged toward Mary Poppins. . . . "How did you come?" Jane asked. "It looked just as if the wind blew you here." "It did," said Mary Poppins.[7]

It is interesting to see how carefully all the writers who tear holes in the fabric of reality patch it up again at the end of the book. The magic volume goes back to the library; the stereoscope is put back under Eddy's bed; the children tumble out of the wardrobe. Mary Poppins flies away; so does Peter Pan. But the reader is often left with the pleasant suspicion that the stitching on the patch isn't very good and that the hole will fray through again.

In a third kind of fantasy, the cloth dividing *here* from *there* is invisible and totally permeable. The two worlds live side by side. No device is needed to turn peculiar events on and off or to escape into the unreal world. It is there all the time, hidden from view. Its inhabitants live uneasily just out of sight of ordinary human beings. In T. H. White's *Mistress Masham's Repose* (Putnam) his young heroine, Maria, stumbles upon a hidden colony of the descendants of Lemuel Gulliver's Lilliputians.

She saw: first, a square opening, about eight inches wide, in the lowest step . . . next, she saw a seven-inch door in the base of each pillar . . . finally, she saw that there was a walnut shell, or half one, outside the nearest door. . . . There was a baby in it.[8]

Mary Norton's pocket-sized people, the Borrowers, go to great lengths not to be seen by the human beings from whom they borrow.

"Stillness . . . that's the thing," Pod whispered to Arrietty the first time he saw Miss Menzies crouching down behind her thistle. "They don't expect to see you, and if you're still, they somehow don't. And never look at 'em direct — always look at 'em sideways like. Understand?"[9]

Of necessity, perhaps, the inhabitants of all of these secret side-by-side worlds seem to be small in scale.

The fourth kind of *what-if* fantasy has its origin in myth, folk tales, and fairy tales. It is the opposite of the first kind. Again the fabric is whole and unbroken, but this time we are on the other side of it. We do not have to find a way through to some fantastic place where anything might happen, because we are there already. We know from the beginning of the story that we are in Once-Upon-a-Time. This realm is no Centerburg nor Cherry-Tree Lane nor domestic establishment under the kitchen floor, but it is a kingdom we all know and recognize and feel at home in. If we were to place it vaguely in space and time, we would attach it to northern Europe sometime between the fall of Rome and the invention of the internal-combustion engine, and populate it exclusively with wizards, witches, jesters, goose-girls, youngest sons, aristocrats of royal blood, absolute monarchs, and a scattering of peasantry.

"That may be as may be," said the Swan Maiden. "For listen! I serve the witch with three eyes. She lives on the glass hill that lies beyond the seven high mountains, the seven deep valleys, and the seven wide rivers; are you man enough to go that far?" "Oh, yes," said the prince, "I am man enough for that and more too."[10]

The next morning she asked the princess how she had slept. "Slept!" cried the princess. "I didn't sleep a wink!"[11]

Perhaps it is presumptuous to say anything against a form which has survived so long and which still has so many distinguished exemplars, but in my opinion it is difficult in the age of television to say anything fresh in this format. Ten thousand TV cartoons have cranked the life out of it, often cleverly.

THWUP! The beautiful princess turned into a toad.
"YUK!" said the handsome prince.
"But, dearie," said the toad, "I'm still a princess deep down inside."
"Princess, schmincess," said the prince."

The fifth kind of fantasy asks the question, "What if beasts could talk?" In this sort of book, loquacious animals from the other side of the dividing membrane punch their way through into the real world and take over. There is no magic; there are no spells. Everything is perfectly normal with the single exception that animals behave like human beings. Kenneth Grahame's Mole and Rat, for example, behave exactly like a pair of polite Edwardian gentlemen living on comfortable incomes of a few hundred pounds a year. And listen to this white mouse, conducting a meeting of the Mouse Prisoner's Aid Society, in Margery Sharp's Miss Bianca (Little).

"And now," said Miss Bianca, consulting her notes, "we come to the main item on the Agenda. . . . Can everyone hear me at the back?"[12]

In Hugh Lofting's stories about Dr. Dolittle, Polynesia the parrot is a kind of Rosetta Stone.

Being a parrot, Polynesia could talk in two languages — people's language and animal language. She was able to explain to the Doctor the meanings of the nose-twitching, ear-scratching and tail-wagging signals that make up the language of animals.[13]

This, of course, is the reverse of animals talking like human beings, since it is Dr. Dolittle who talks like animals, but the sober domesticity of Hugh Lofting's beasts is altogether human. All of these books, too, have ancient beginnings.

But unfortunately, the Hare overslept himself; therefore when he awoke, though he ran his best, he found the Tortoise was already at the goal. He had learned that "Slow and steady wins the race."[14]

In the sixth kind of fantasy, there are overlays in time. In some of these stories the present moment dissolves and becomes the past; in others someone from an earlier period in history bursts through the fabric dividing *now* from *then* and emerges among us, to be astonished by washing machines and Chevrolets. In *A Traveler in Time* (Viking) Alison Uttley uses the device of an Elizabethan house as the permanent background for shifting sets of occupants. A child opens doors to find ancestors in ancient rooms, and then returns to the present. But no one merges past and present more seamlessly and masterfully than William Mayne. In some of his settings, the past is embodied in relics and monuments which litter the landscape, it incarnates itself in optical effects of light, it spills out of the cracks in the sky, it moves restively under the soil, it maintains a kind of urgent pressure on the present day. Witness the emergence into the *here* and *now* of Nellie Jack· John, Mayne's eighteenth-century drummer boy, in *Earthfasts* (Dutton).

The ground stirred. The stirring did not extend beyond the swelling in the turf. But there was movement, a lot of movement. It was as if someone were getting out of bed. And with the movement came clear drumming. . . . There was light, increasing light, pure and mild and bleak.
David tried to say that it was the last of the day shining on moving water, but the words would not form themselves, because his jaw was trembling. . . .
It was not light on moving water. . . . The light was from a little flame. The little flame came out from the hillside, and balanced in the air, and the wind bent the flame over but did not blow it out. . . .
There was a shadow before their eyes, against the hill. . . . In the dusk the little flame was brighter than they had imagined. It was not standing in the air by itself. It was being held there by a person, and that person was drumming on a side drum, and looking round, and smiling. . . .
"I wasn't so long," said the drummer. "But I niver found nowt."[15]

In a seventh kind of fantasy (ghost stories), the dividing piece of cloth is a shroud, a veil between life and death. The dead pluck at the curtain, draw it aside with their wasted hands, and enter among the living. Behold Sir Edmund Orme.

He stood there without speaking — young, pale, handsome, clean-shaven, decorous, with extraordinary light blue eyes and something old-fashioned, like a portrait of years ago, in his head, his manner of wearing his hair. . . . He looked again strangely hard at me, harder than anyone in the world had ever looked before; and I remember feeling rather cold and wishing he would say something. No silence had ever seemed to me so soundless.[16]

Henry James has tempted me away from the subject of children's books, but, of course, there are masters of the same tradition writing for young people. Leon Garfield is one.

The phantom stood in the merciless sunshine: a little boy of seven, dressed in an old-fashioned sailor's suit. Its hair was fair and curling; its face was of an unearthly pallor. The clerk gave a harsh scream and clutched onto the area railings. He glared down in rage and terror at the ghost of his childhood.[17]

In this catalogue of an uncataloguable subject there is an eighth and final item, science fiction: a vast body of literature irreducible to a single example. One can only suggest that in such works of the fantastic imagination the curtain hangs between a finite present and a kind of infinite future, a time in which the possibilities of knowledge will be infinitely extended or in which nature itself will be discovered to be infinitely varied.

THEN WHAT?

"When once you have thought of big men and little men," said Samuel Johnson of *Gulliver's Travels*, "it is very easy to do all the rest." He was wrong. It took a Jonathan Swift to decide that the best way to capture a sleeping giant was to attach to the ground every hair of his head. "Big men and little men" was Swift's *what-if*. The Lilliputians' technique for capturing Gulliver was part of his *then-what*. While it is true that the *what-if* question establishes the axiomatic ground-of-all-being for each book and that in itself it must be fresh and interesting, the consequences of this *what-if* — Well, what happens then? — must be worked out successfully. Samuel Johnson to the contrary, it isn't easy. But the more diligently, searchingly, carefully, and cleverly the author figures out what happens, the more convincing and absorbing his book will be.

190

To ask the question, "Then what?" is to ask what corollaries follow from the original axiomatic "What if?"

AXIOM (*what-if*): What if a New York City mouse went to visit a friend in the country?

COROLLARY (*then-what*): Like the hero of George Selden's *Tucker's Countryside* (Farrar), he might get hay fever; and, lacking citified things like Kleenex, he would have to blow his nose on a fern.

AXIOM: What if a little girl discovered a secret colony of Lilliputians?

COROLLARY: She might fly one of them in her toy airplane, with disastrous results. (In *Mistress Masham's Repose*, T. H. White thinks up some of the most brilliant *then-whats* of all.)

AXIOM: What if a girl woke up one morning and discovered she had turned into her mother?

COROLLARY: She might stay home from school, watch television, and fire the cleaning lady, as did Annabel in Mary Rodgers' *Freaky Friday* (Harper).

It is important to see that once the fabulous axiom has been stated, the writer must cleave to logic. He must rack his brain to answer the question, "Given such-and-such a situation, what would really happen?" It is the *really* that is to be stressed. *Realism sharpens fantasy*. Take a magic boy, take a Neverland, take some flying children, take a fairy, take all of these fabulous things — what is it that makes this mishmash work? Homely touches that have the feel of truth: The fairy is jealous of Wendy; when Peter Pan loses his shadow, it is sewn back on with a needle and thread.

Of course, the most important key to the *then-what* question is the realness of the characterization. Sharply-drawn characters — whether children, miniature people, elves, or animals — make the cleanest rip in the cloth of reality. Commonsensical Alice, for example, is the handle by which we are able to grasp at Wonderland. Her down-to-earthness throws the Mad Hatter into wild relief. Without her solidity the nonsense would be tenuous and meaningless. And it is the human qualities of Milne's animals that make his Hundred-Acre Wood an enchanted place: Pooh's kindness and humility, his gluttony and courage.

And meet in person young Maria, who stumbles upon the Lilliputians. She nearly rears up off the page in passages like this one.

She was one of those tough and friendly people who do things first and think about them afterward. . . . Her happiest times were when the Vicar was in London and Miss Brown was in bed with a headache. Then she would be mad with pleasure, a sort of wild but earnest puppy rushing about with the slipper of her imagination, tearing the heart out of it.[18]

Thus when the Lilliputians turn up, we believe in them instantly, because we believe so wholeheartedly in Maria.

Any experienced plotter of books for children knows another dread necessity, another *then-what* question to which he must provide an answer right off-the-bat. The child reading the book must be made to care what happens next, to read on, to be caught on a hook of suspense. The writer must set his stakes high, as soon as possible. In *Rabbit Hill* (Viking) Robert Lawson gets you worrying about his young rabbit hero, Little Georgie, by having him recite for his father a list of the dogs on the route of a journey he must make.

"House on Long Hill: Collie, noisy, no wind — Norfield Church corner: Police Dog, stupid, no nose — On the High Ridge, red farmhouse: Bulldog and Setter, both fat, don't bother — Farmhouse with the big barns: Old Hound, very dangerous."[19]

You can bet Little Georgie is going to encounter that old hound, and so you read on eagerly. Here's another, a terrifying conversation between a tactless sheep and E. B. White's young spring pig in *Charlotte's Web* (Harper).

"Well, I don't like to spread bad news," said the sheep, "but they're fattening you up because they're going to kill you. . . ." "They're going to *what*?" screamed Wilbur.[20]

So What?

Two young friends of mine read a thousand books between them one summer when they were about twelve. They will forget most of them, but they will remember some. What is it that makes a book unforgettable? What does it all add up to, the *what-ifs* and the *then-whats*? After all the invention and the action and the pretty devices, *so-what*? What makes for quality?

I can think of two things that set some books of fantasy apart. The first thing, surely, is a strongly realized personal vision. It is the writer himself and his interests and obsessions that count, not simply his vague fondness for children or for the good idea he has systematically worked out. William Pène du Bois is a writer with an obsession. Here he talks about Auguste Piccard's attempts to go a mile up into the sky and a mile down into the sea.

There was something in this ambition of his which excited me . . . turned me on. . . . Thus in my books the most often found prop is the ladder. Peggy Moffit falls down coal holes. Peter Graves goes up, straight up — all of my nuts go up and down. Otto digs dinosaurs. The three policemen go to sea in fish suits. Angels fly to work pulled by kites. The star performer in my latest book, *Bear Circus*, shoots straight up through a hole in a circus tent.[21]

The obsession comes first, and the books come after. The result is a succession of books with a special quality all their own. When you open one of them and turn the pages, you are traveling in a place invented by William Pène du Bois, one that belongs to him and to nobody else. Other writers have discovered and mapped their own personal geographies, and they are places as real to us now as Iowa or Tibet or the Bronx: Laurent de Brunhoff's Celesteville, where Babar is king; the Cherry-Tree Lane of P. L. Travers and Mary Poppins; Maurice Sendak's land where the Wild Things are; C. S. Lewis's Narnia; the foolish villages of Isaac Bashevis Singer; Milne's Hundred-Acre Wood; Antoine de Saint Exupéry's Asteroid B-612, inhabited by the Little Prince; Edward Lear's Terrible Zone and the hills of the Chankly Bore; Tolkien's Middle Earth; Tove Jansson's Moominland; Hugh Lofting's Puddleby-on-the-Marsh; Margery Sharp's Black Castle and Diamond Palace; the various hilarious provinces of Dr. Seuss. This gazetteer could go on and on. Each of these places is somehow whole and perfect and entire — *real-ized* and altogether there. With the borders of these imaginary territories placed end-to-end, a child's mental dominion can stretch all the way to Homer's Ithaca or Shakespeare's forest of Oberon. A world like this is rich freight to carry around inside any child's head.

The other quality that sets apart some books of children's fantasy is, of course, a second level of meaning — significance, symbolism, allegory; a stab at a moral, a message, a lesson. The meaning may be as bald as the last sentence in one of Aesop's fables ("slow and steady wins the race") or as unpretentious and delicate as the distillation from the modest adventures of Milne's animals (what it means to be a friend). Meaning is not easy. Sometimes the attempt at it is too vaguely vast, too preachy-teachy, too thin and scant. But when it works, the book gains a value that may outlast the short time-span during which a young reader is available to us. It may last him all his life.

James Thurber's *Wonderful O* (Simon) is an example. It is an artful allegory that explains what freedom is. And the famous chapter in *The Wind in the Willows* (Scribner) about the piper at the gates of dawn interjects into the story about Rat, Mole, and Toad an experience of God.

[A]nd, then, in that utter clearness of the imminent dawn, while Nature, flushed with fullness of incredible colour, seemed to hold her breath for the event, he looked in the very eyes of the Friend and Helper; saw the backward sweep of the curved horns, gleaming in the growing daylight. . . . Then the two animals, crouching to the earth, bowed their heads.[22]

Hugh Lofting's Dr. Dolittle embodies a Schweitzer-like reverence for life. Dr. Seuss's elephant Horton discovers that a person's a person no matter how small. And Seymour Leichman's book, *The Boy Who Could Sing Pictures* (Doubleday), praises art, poetry, and storytelling.

It was like no song they had heard before. His voice was high, sweet and clear. He sang about the farmer and he sang about the land and he sang about the doves and he sang about the river and the rainbow. . . . He knew he would sing forever against the sadness. The miracle did not happen all at once. It happened first when he sang about the doves. And they appeared. And the people saw them. Then the rainbow. And the people saw it. They could see in the air above them, everything that he sang.

Ben saw it too, and more. He looked into their faces, into their eyes and the sadness was gone. They had seen a beautiful thing. Ben left the stage.

No one cheered. You do not cheer a miracle.[23]

You do not itemize and analyze a miracle either, which is what I have been trying to do. And it has leaked through my fingers, spilling numbered headings and subheadings. Now I want to pick it up and rearrange it differently, because there is one thing that hasn't been said. Perhaps it is the only thing that can truthfully be said of all of these books, and it is the secret of their deathless charm.

They are all dreams. They are waking dreams. They make up to us for the sense of loss we feel when we wake up and find our dreams shrinking out of memory. A literary fantasy gives us a dream back to keep. Here is one of Lewis Carroll's, straight from the edge of the bed.

> *"He thought he saw a Banker's Clerk*
> *Descending from the bus:*
> *He looked again, and found it was*
> *A Hippopotamus."*[24]

Most children's fantasies are not as midnight-pure as that, but surely the reason why we are so inexhaustibly delighted by mice that talk and spells that work and the Dong with the Luminous Nose is that we spend a third of our lives asleep, with bankers' clerks dissolving into hippopotamuses. Nonsense pleases. We want the laws and verities to be different from the ones by which we are trapped during the day. Like Dr. Seuss's foolish king we want something new to come out of the sky, not just this everlasting sunshine, rain, and snow, even if the new thing turns out to be sticky green Oobleck, and a disaster. And when the writer of a literary fantasy adds real children to this surreal landscape, when he inserts a flesh-and-blood Alice into his Wonderland, we are given in one package both ends of our daily experience. It is a mixture of waking and dreaming, and that has a pungency that satisfies. It feeds a hunger we didn't know we had.

SOURCES REFERRED TO IN THE TEXT

1. E. Nesbit, *The Enchanted Castle.*
2. Robert McCloskey, *Homer Price* (New York: Viking, 1937, 1971), pp. 113-116.
3. Lewis Carroll, *Through the Looking Glass and What Alice Found There.*
4. C. S. Lewis, *The Lion, the Witch and the Wardrobe* (New York: Macmillan, 1950), p. 5.
5. Jane Langton, *The Astonishing Stereoscope* (New York: Harper, 1971), p. 38.
6. Edward Eager, *Seven-Day Magic* (New York: Harcourt, 1962), pp. 24-25.
7. P. L. Travers, *Mary Poppins* (New York: Harcourt, 1934, 1962), p. 10.
8. T. H. White, *Mistress Masham's Repose* (New York: Putnam's, 1946), p. 18.
9. Mary Norton, *The Borrowers Aloft* (New York: Harcourt, 1961), p. 48.
10. Howard Pyle, *The Wonder Clock.*
11. Hans Christian Andersen, "The Princess and the Pea."
12. Margery Sharp, *Miss Bianca* (Boston: Little, Brown, 1962), p. 4.
13. Hugh Lofting, *Doctor Dolittle's Puddleby Adventures* (New York: Lippincott, 1925, 1952), p. 1.
14. Aesop, *Fables.*
15. William Mayne, *Earthfasts* (New York: Dutton, 1966), pp. 6-7.
16. Henry James, *Sir Edmund Orme.*
17. Leon Garfield, *The Ghost Downstairs* (New York: Pantheon, 1971), p. 51.

18. T. H. White, *Mistress Masham's Repose* (New York: Putnam's, 1946), pp. 9, 12.
19. Robert Lawson, *Rabbit Hill* (New York: Viking, 1944), p. 37.
20. E. B. White, *Charlotte's Web* (New York: Harper, 1952), p. 49.
21. Letter to Jane Langton from William Pène du Bois, dated August 8, 1971.
22. Kenneth Grahame, *The Wind in the Willows* (New York: Scribner, 1908, 1933, 1953), pp. 135-136.
23. Seymour Leichman, *The Boy Who Could Sing Pictures* (New York: Doubleday, 1968), p. 37.
24. Lewis Carroll, *Sylvie and Bruno.*

From *The Horn Book* for October 1973 and December 1973

VII

HUMOR

Critical discussions of humor in children's literature are few and far between. The writer often hesitates to pursue the subject too far, too analytically, for fear of incurring solemnity or — a worse sin — of ending up humorless. It is not necessary, however, to be jolly while discussing the comic spirit any more than it is necessary to be lugubrious while discussing tragedy. Of course, delicacy and tact are needed in uncovering the mainsprings of humor; and the observations of experienced and intelligent practitioners tell us something about children as well as about children's books.

Sid Fleischman observes, "Laughter is the naural sound of childhood, but one would hardly suspect it from reading children's literature," and he touches on the paradoxical concept that "[c]omedy is tragedy; but it is tragedy in motley." Alvin Schwartz explores the mechanisms of humor by considering such traditional forms as word play, conundrums, riddles, and hyperbole and goes so far as to probe the source of racial and ethnic jokes. Both writers stress the part played by folklore in the creation of humor. Perhaps it should not be forgotten that comedy often lies next door to fantasy: Lewis Carroll, the master of topsey-turvey logic, embodied his preposterous notions in phantasmagoric verbal images.

LAUGHTER AND CHILDREN'S LITERATURE*

By SID FLEISCHMAN

PAUL HAZARD once wrote, "England could be reconstructed entirely from its children's books."

I wish the same observation could be made about our own country in this Bicentennial year. I'm afraid that a key shard of American life would turn up missing. Except for the works of Mark Twain it would be almost impossible to reconstruct the American sense of humor.

Laughter is the natural sound of childhood, but one would hardly suspect it from reading children's literature. I am reminded of a comedy sketch performed by the late Ernie Kovacs. Browsing silently along a library shelf, he pulled out *Camille* and opened it. The sound of coughing arose as if from the pages. He moved on to *The Three Musketeers*. The clank and clash of a sword fight was heard. And so on.

Can you imagine yourself browsing through the children's room of any library and opening books for the sound of laughter? One would go to the C's, obviously, for Clemens. And Cleary. To the K's for Konigsburg. The R's would yield Raskin. There are others (and I would hope you'd have some luck in the F's). But, by and large, it would be an exercise in futility.

The reason, at first glance, seems obvious. Laughter, surely, cannot be taken seriously — more about that in a moment. It is frivolous and confectionary and it belongs in the nursery.

Mother Goose is rich in broad comic images: a woman living in a shoe; a cow jumping over the moon; blackbirds flocking out of a pie. My earliest literary memories are funny ones. I remember most vividly the woodman's wife with the link sausages attached to her nose in "The Three Wishes." That had me rolling in the aisles — or on the living-room carpet. A little later came Lewis Carroll's Cheshire Cat and the mad Hatter.

*Based on speeches given at the 43rd Annual Claremont Reading Conference, Claremont, California, on February 7, 1976, and at the 14th Annual Symposium on Children's Literature sponsored by the School of Librarianship, University of California at Berkeley, on July 14, 1976.

Contemporary comic talent in the picture-story field comes easily to mind — Maurice Sendak, Arnold Lobel, Don Freeman, Bill Peet, David McPhail, Judith Viorst. But once we leave the nursery behind we are expected to shelve childish laughter like outgrown toys. Novels in the eight-to-twelve group seem to tell us that it is time to face real life. And if you remember your Longfellow you know what *that* is. "Life is real!" he wrote, complete with exclamation points in case you weren't paying attention. "Life is earnest!"

These were certainly the academic mantras of my boyhood. I was assigned "Evangeline" and not long after, *Silas Marner* and *Ivanhoe*. If you can find a laugh in any of these works, you have a better sense of humor than I. I was almost fully grown before I discovered that real life may also wear baggy pants and carry a slapstick.

But the writer offers this view of reality at his own risk. Comedy is easily misread as the mere vaudeville of literature. Mark Twain was routinely passed over for the Nobel Prize. Rarely since the 1920's and *Dr. Dolittle* have the Newbery judges given recognition to humor. In *Newbery and Caldecott Medal Books 1966-1975* (Horn Book), John Rowe Townsend, the English critic, writes, "One lack is very evident in chil-. dren's books generally. . . . That is the absence of fine, sustained comic writing."

The trouble, I think, is that laughter is not quite respectable — a little vulgar, perhaps. That was certainly the stately view of George Meredith, who felt uneasy at anything above a smile. Walter Kerr has said that Meredith was "distressed that Oliver Goldsmith should have stooped so low to conquer" with " 'an elegant farce for a comedy.' " Perhaps that's why Goldsmith is still read and Meredith merely quoted. And not very often at that.

I had better confess that I conceived *Jingo Django* (Atlantic-Little) as a dark and earnest novel. It was time to become respectable, I thought; I still accepted the majority view that comedy was the lesser of the Greek masks. In this story I was going to deal with a child ruthlessly abandoned by a truly sinister father. Oedipal hatred, orphan house cruelty, a painful and mysterious problem of identity — what raw materials could be more serious?

But a funny thing happened on the way to the typewriter. My resolve gave way to one caprice after another. Only after finishing the novel — it turned out to be a broad, farcical adventure — did I discover for myself the Great Truth. Comedy is tragedy; but it is tragedy in motley.

A stunning example of this is cited by Charles Chaplin in his autobiography. Perhaps the funniest scene ever put on film occurs in *The Gold Rush* when the starving Chaplin and a fellow miner dine on a hob-nailed shoe. Then his table companion hallucinates, seeing Chaplin as a huge, plump chicken to be similarly parboiled. The inspiration for this scene, as Chaplin reveals it, is a hair-raiser. He had been reading about the snow-trapped Donner Party driven by starvation to eating its footgear and to cannibalism.

Comedy, then, is alchemy; the base metal is always tragedy. War has excited the comic imagination from Aristophanes to Joseph Heller. It was only while preparing this paper that I realized, having written such tall tales as *McBroom's Ghost* (Norton) and *The Ghost on Saturday Night* (Atlantic-Little), that the ludicrous subject was death itself.

It was no accident that the tall tale flourished on the frontier, providing me with the raw material for the various McBroom stories. In laughter, pioneers found a way of accommodating themselves to the agonies that came with the land. Bitter cold? Even words froze in the air. Blowtorch summers? Chickens laid hard-boiled eggs. Raging winds? To pluck a chicken, hold it out a window. Tornadoes, plagues of grasshoppers, swarms of mosquitoes — all were natural subjects for tall-tale humor.

I have found that writers of comedy don't like to probe too deeply into their elusive and sometimes mysterious sources. They are in the position of the centipede asked by an admiring frog how he (she?) moved all those legs with such grace and precision. Since it came naturally, the centipede had never before given the matter a thought. Trying to figure out which leg to move when, the centipede entirely lost the fine art of walking.

But I will take a limited risk. I know where some ideas in my books come from. I remember my surprise, after writing *By the Great Horn Spoon!* (Atlantic-Little), at being credited with the most outrageous imagination when I served up the notion that the forty-niners shipped their starched shirts to

China for laundering. I thought everyone knew that. It's true. While saloons were in ample supply in boom-town San Francisco, no one felt a special calling to go into the laundry business. In due time a few Cantonese sailed to California and the source of the soiled haberdashery; others followed, and I suspect that out of this historical fluke arose the stereotype of the Chinese laundryman.

I had always regarded history as dignified as all get-out, but with this incident I discovered that the past assays out fairly rich in comic ore. In an old copy of the *Missouri Historical Review* I sifted out an incomparable petty schemer, a man caught stealing his neighbor's land by moving the rail fence at night, a few inches at a time. He became a key, though off-stage character, in *Jingo Django*, when Jingo and Mr. Peacock-Hemlock-Jones go tumbling across the country in search of a cache of Mexican gold coins buried under a fence post. You can imagine what happens and why, when my heroes go rooting around in *that* post hole.

In the last century the Missouri River jumped its bank in an act of pure comedy. A thriving tavern on the Missouri side awoke to find itself in dry Kansas. This provided me with the first faint stirrings of *Humbug Mountain*, a novel-in-progress. I have enlarged upon the incident, cross-pollinating it with the history of mad speculation in town-building and lot-selling on the frontier. As you might guess, my raffish entrepreneur makes the mistake of staking out his rip-roaring metropolis-to-be on the Missouri. At the moment he's still trying to unload those cursed dry Kansas lots.

Folklore is rich in humor. The old belief that one born at midnight has the power to see ghosts set me on this train of thought. What if pirates threw their murdered captain into the same pit with buried treasure? What if they lost the map? It's another superstition that the murdered rest uneasy and walk their grave sites until avenged. Now I had it. What if my young hero were born at the stroke of midnight? Using his ghost-seeing gift, the pirates would know where to dig for the lost treasure. The result of this assortment of folklore and "what ifs" was *The Ghost in the Noonday Sun* (Atlantic-Little).

My favorite scene in *Chancy and the Grand Rascal* (Atlantic-Little) occurs when my heroes come across a chuck-wagon cook about to drown a sack of kittens. Uncle Will, the grand rascal, declares that one can tell the time by reading a cat's eyes. This is a folklore belief. The cook is persuaded and holds out one kitten as a timepiece. But what of the rest of the litter? The grand rascal advises the man to hang on to the entire litter. "I've known cats to run slow and run fast," he says.

Folklore once again provided me with the basic idea for *Longbeard the Wizard* (Atlantic-Little), a picture book. I was reading a museum-published biography for an exhibit of the paintings of Chaim Soutine. A sentence leaped out at me. Soutine was affected by a folk belief that we are born to speak a certain and unknown number of words; when we use them up, we die. An irresistible idea. Enter Queen Gibble-Gabble, unaware that she is chattering her way into a sudden grave. Trivia? I think not. The magic power of words runs through all cultures.

It is American folklore that betrays our unconscious rather than our formal literary taste. I find that this common lore breaks down into three general areas — the supernatural; hero tales; and, writ especially large, HUMOR. And these are the delights of childhood. To be safely frightened. To identify with larger-than-life heroes. To laugh. Curiously, tragedy in tragic terms is dealt with almost exclusively in ballads. John Henry, for example, and Casey Jones.

Why, then, has there been so little laughter in children's books? The trouble seems to stem from a traditional judgment that humor is unpredictable. What some find funny, others may not. That's true, of course. But the premise is faulty. Why must we like the same books, the same paintings, the same music — the same humor? I was recently told of a boy, somewhat miffed and insulted by one of my McBroom tall tales. "If that story is true," he protested, "I'm stupid."

I am happy to be able to say that, while I have not been beating a dead horse, it appears to be a moribund one. If my mail is any indication, editors are now actively seeking out humor. In some schools in California, and perhaps elsewhere, a unit on tall tales is being taught as a legitimate aspect of frontier social history. And last year the National Council of Teachers of English/Children's Book Council joint conference in San Diego scheduled a session on humor in children's books.

Laughter is the humorist's applause, and I would like to end with that sweet sound. I am working on a character exhumed from a two-inch display advertisement that appeared during the nineteenth-century in a Fresno, California, newspaper. Here's history wearing a putty nose.

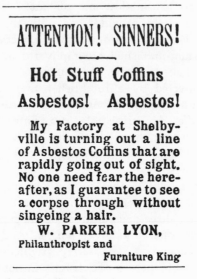

From *The Horn Book* for October 1976

CHILDREN, HUMOR, AND FOLKLORE*

By ALVIN SCHWARTZ

SOME TIME AGO somebody counted the books which undertake to explain humor. He found three hundred sixty-three with names on them like Max Eastman, Arthur Koestler, Sigmund Freud, Immanuel Kant, and Aristotle. In examining this collective wisdom, one also finds that much of it does not agree, for humor is a slippery subject. Put simply, humor is the comic quality in a person, experience, or idea that makes one laugh.

Consider some of the material I have collected from children — material that they regard as funny. This rhyme from a boy named Henry Millner of East Windsor, New Jersey:

Row, row, row your boat gently down the stream,
Throw your teacher overboard, then you will hear her scream.

And these conundrums from various places:

What is round and purple and hums? An electric grape.
What do you do with a dog that barks all the time? Put it in a barking lot.
What is green and white, and green and white, and green and white? A pickle rolling down a snow-covered mountain.

And this traditional catch:

Take a number. Add 10, subtract 4, divide by 2. Now close your eyes. Dark, isn't it?

Why do people laugh at such things? Because they have been tricked. Scholars who study the mechanism of humor say that much of the joking we encounter involves a trick played on the mind. One expects that something rational, or normal, is going to happen — but it doesn't. Instead, something absurd happens or something nonsensical, eccentric, or untoward. Thus, a rhyme does not follow an anticipated pattern. Or a conundrum does not lead to a logical conclusion. Or a problem in arithmetic does not produce a proper answer. And if you are in a playful mood, you laugh at having been had.

Of course, not all humor involves a trick. There are times

*Based on a speech delivered at the conference of the NCTE, November 26, 1976.

when we laugh out of the sheer pleasure of encountering the work of a humorously creative mind, whether words or illustrations are involved. In either case, what is critical is whether you are in a playful mood. Children tend to be more playful than adults; as a result, they are inclined to laugh more readily and more frequently. They also tend to laugh in situations where laughter does not seem appropriate — unless you, too, are in a playful mood.

A playful response evokes laughter that is usually good for the soul. However, there are exceptions and I shall return to these. E. B. White once observed that laughter is like breaking into tears. It does for you just what tears do. "My life as a humorist began," he wrote, "in a Child's restaurant when a waitress spilled buttermilk down my neck. That great smear of white wet coming down over a blue serge suit, and her words, 'Jesus Christ!' were the turning point in my career."

One of the fascinating aspects of the humor children use and respond to is the number of discrete and surprising forms involved. Some of them are very old, and most are in use virtually everywhere, for the basic needs that humor satisfies — the needs for pleasure and for release — are universal.

A fair amount of the joking children do involves word play. One form they especially like is the tongue twister, an ancient device used to play a trick on the tongue. In this case, a pattern of consonants and vowels constitutes the trick, not a pattern of reasoning. For example, try to recite "Slim Sam slid sideways" three times — fast. The trick is, of course, the confusion created by the sound *sl* when used with the sound *s*; the joke is how foolish it makes you seem.

Punning is another technique which is widely used by children. Oliver Wendell Holmes did not like puns at all. "He who makes a pun will pick a pocket," he warned. But this admonition does not seem to have deterred anybody. One finds punning in most of the joke forms to which children are attracted. This chain tale that I learned as a child in summer camp and encountered years later in a folklore archive in Cooperstown, New York, is one example:

A petunia is a flower like a begonia.
A begonia is a meat like a sausage.
A-sausage and battery is a crime.
Monkeys crime trees.

Trees a crowd.
The rooster crowd and made a lot of noise.
The noise is between the eyes.
Eyes are the opposite of nays.
A horse nays.
A horse has a colt.
You may go to bed at night with the windows open —
    and wake up in the morning with a colt —
    if you are not careful.

There also are joke cycles which rely heavily on the pun. One is the *Confucius Say* joke, which first appeared in the 1930's and still circulates. Among other things, Confucius say now, "Man who put face in bowl get punch in nose." I have also encountered two Tom Swifties out of the 1950s. "I will have four hot dogs," said Tom frankly, "and also two Cokes," he said coaxingly. The Little Moron joke is another example of a joke cycle which depends on punning; to some extent, so is the conundrum.

In fact, the conundrum is probably the most widely disseminated of any of the joking forms which depend on word play. It is so popular, I suppose, because it is so silly. But it also can be constructive. Collecting conundrums, I have learned these things:

A ringleader is the first one in a bathtub.
A meat thief is a hamburglar.
A watchdog that runs in circles actually is winding itself up.
Rhubarb is celery with high blood pressure.
And ignorance is when you don't know something and somebody finds out.

I did not realize the great continuing appeal of the conundrum in our culture. A few years ago I talked with many people in their eighties and nineties who recalled with zest the conundrums of their youth. Even then, "What is black and white and red all over?" was circulating widely. In those days the answer was, of course, "A newspaper." Nowadays it also is "A skunk with diaper rash," "A sun-burned penguin," "A blushing zebra," or "A chocolate sundae with catsup on it" — all of which suggests, if nothing else, an increased sense of the ridiculous and increased freedom in the use of language.

Frequently, children and adults confuse conundrums with true riddles. To solve a true riddle one must use reason. Thus,

What do you give away and still keep? A cold.
What is taller when it is sitting than standing? A dog.

And this . . .

A riddle, a riddle, I suppose,
A thousand eyes and never a nose. A kitchen sieve.

If one is smart enough one might be able to figure these out. But to solve a conundrum — the electric grape conundrum, the elephant conundrums, or the "knock, knock" conundrums (Knock, knock. Who is there? Dishes. Dishes who? Dishes me. Who ish you?) — one must know the answer; for there is no logical connection between the question and the required response.

Folklorists call conundrums *catch riddles*. In some respects, these catch riddles are attenuated versions of catch tales or hoax tales, which no longer circulate to any extent but which children like. Here is one example out of Brown County, Indiana.

There was this rich old miser who died. And he had it in his will to have a lot of money spent on his funeral because he really wanted something grand. So to be fancy his relatives bought him a big, heavy coffin and got a big, white cart to carry it and a big, white horse to pull the cart.

Well, the cemetery was on a high hill outside of town at the end of a steep gravel road. And when his relatives got part way up, they decided to stop and rest. But when the horse stopped, something frightened it, and it reared up on its hind legs and jerked the cart so hard the coffin slid off onto the road.

And when this happened, the coffin began sliding back down the hill into town, going faster and faster and faster. Finally, it tore around a bend in the road, smashed through the window of the drugstore, plowed into the medicine counter, and stopped. Then the lid popped open, and the miser sat up. "Do you have something to stop this coffin?" he asked.

In my research with children, I also encounter what may be classified as the nonsense of humor. It ranges from the sublime to the ridiculous. Yet it often possesses a disconcertingly clear perspective of the curious nature of reality. There is tangletalk such as this:

'Twas a moonlit day in August,
The snow was falling fast.
A barefoot boy with shoes on
Stood sitting in the grass.

The moon shone over the ocean.
Not a street car was in sight,
Someone raised a cloud of dust.
And it rained all night.

And there are endless tales like this:

Said the boy octopus to the girl octopus, "Let's walk hand in hand in hand in hand in hand in hand. . . ."

And there are jump rope rhymes like this:

> There was an old lady who sat on a pin.
> How many inches did it go in?
> 1, 2, 3, 4, 5, 6, 7, 8, 9, 10, 11, 12. . . .

And there are other rhymes like this:

> I am a little chestnut brown
> Lying on the cold, cold ground.
> Somebody came and stepped on me.
> I'm as cracked as I can be.
> I'm a nut — (make a clicking sound with
>   your tongue, then another)
> I'm a nut (click, click)
> I'm a nut (click), a nut (click), a nut (click, click).

And there are songs like this, which Alexander Franklin Sherwin, aged six, of Princeton, New Jersey, contributed:

> Sitting on a playground on a summer's day.
> Chatting with my classmates, passing time away.
> Underneath the shadows, underneath the trees,
> Goodness how delicious, eating goober peas.
> Peas, peas, peas, peas, eating goober peas.
> Goodness how delicious, eating goober peas.

Alex sings "Goober Peas" much of the time these days. My nineteen-year-old son Peter sang that song when he was six. Alex doesn't know "Goober Peas" is a mutation of a Civil War song. Neither did Peter. Where did Alex learn that song? Where did Peter? From other kids. Where did *they* learn it? From still others. It is a good example of folklore at work.

If one explores written literature, one will find lovely nonsense — Lewis Carroll's *Through the Looking-Glass*, for example.

"Which reminds me — " the White Queen said, looking down and nervously clasping and unclasping her hands, "we had *such* a thunderstorm last Tuesday — I mean one of the last set of Tuesdays, you know."

Alice was puzzled. "In *our* country," she remarked, "there's only one day at a time."

The Red Queen said "That's a poor thin way of doing things. Now *here*, we mostly have days and nights two and three at a time, and sometimes in the winter we take as many as five nights together — for warmth, you know."

The work of the nineteenth-century humorist, Artemus Ward (Charles Farrar Browne) of Waterford, Maine, offers other examples of nonsense. In a talk he gave on foolishness, he asked, " 'Why is this thus? What is the cause of this thusness?' " Which is something to ponder.

Like almost everyone, children respond to hyperbole in humor. This device has been one of the principal characteristics of American humor since the nation began to emerge as a cultural entity in the 1830s. Two intriguing forms are the tall tale, which is essentially a joke in slow motion, and the lie, a related mode. When one thinks of the tall tale, one thinks of mythic heroes like the river boatman Mike Fink, whose real life exploits served as the nucleus for a body of overstatement. Or of John Henry, who did not live except as the embodiment of the experience of a particular group. Or of Paul Bunyan, whose existence is largely the creation of an advertising campaign for a Minnesota lumber company in 1911. Curiously, when I tell children about Bunyan's origins, many refuse to accept them, so firm is their belief in him.

But beyond the mythic hero there is a rich body of humor which deals with ordinary people and the extraordinary experiences they never had. I should underscore that here we are dealing with artifacts, not living material, for it is unusually difficult nowadays to collect tall tales and folkloristic lies. The only lying tale I can remember collecting from children in recent years is this one.

Two boys are boasting. One says, "My father dug out the Mississippi River and with the dirt made the Rocky Mountains." The other says, "That's nothing. You've heard of the Dead Sea? My father killed it."

One Saturday as part of a book talk at the Donnell Branch of The New York Public Library, I ran a lie-telling contest. But it was hard going. The librarian later observed, correctly I believe, that few children of school age are told enough tales any more to know how to create them or tell them. Yet they are intrigued by such material. That Saturday they liked these hoary lies about the weather.

In Kansas, where the wind is strong, a storm blew the hair off a man's head, the whiskers off his face, the shoes off his socks, and the socks off his feet. People foolish enough to venture out were blown up against walls, flattened thin as wafers by the wind, then peeled off by a businessman and sold as circus posters.

In Missouri one day it got so hot the corn in a field popped, and a mule who saw it thought it was snowing and lay down and froze to death. The heat was so bad that day the farmer who owned the mule fed his hens cracked ice to keep them from laying hard-boiled eggs.

They also liked this tale about a man named Babcock.

One night Babcock was jumped by a war party of fifty Sioux who chased him into a canyon, where he finally left them behind. But after a while he discovered the canyon was only a box gulch, a dead end with straight walls a thousand feet high. His only choice was to turn back and face his pursuers. At that point Babcock stopped his tale, leaned back in his chair, closed his eyes and fondled his whiskers. "What happened?" one of his listeners asked impatiently. "What happened?" "What happened?" Babcock replied in a hoarse whisper. "Why they killed me, b'God, they killed me."

There is a major body of children's humor that includes horseplay at one end of the scale and hostility and verbal abuse at the other. "Do you collect stamps?" somebody asks. "Yes," his companion replies. "Well, then," he responds, "here is one for your collection." And he stamps on his friend's foot as hard as he can. Or "Do you know Tony Chestnut?" he may ask. "No," his companion replies. Then, according to ritual, the joker stamps on his friend's toe, raps him on the knee, taps him on the chest, and thumps him on the head, or nut. Thus, toe-knee-chest-nut. Then he shouts, "NOW you know him!"

And there are other such jokes, scores of them. Not too long ago a librarian accused me of encouraging hostility in children by including these things in my books. My only defense was that children had taught them to me and would learn them and use them no matter what I did, folklore being what it is and children being what they are. But why smacking somebody or tramping on his foot is funny is something to consider. Research suggests that when we are feeling playful, a peculiar shift of values takes place. What ordinarily is pleasant continues to be regarded as pleasant. However, what ordinarily would be regarded as disagreeable is now more acceptable and more likely to provoke a laugh. The scholar Max Eastman stated it this way: To a child who is feeling playful, "every untoward, . . . inauspicious, ugly, . . . puzzling, startling, deceiving, shaking, . . . jolting, deafening, banging, bumping . . . thing is funny." And the child adjusts his values accordingly.

But often the joking that children — and adults — do is not rooted in a playful shift of values but in anxiety and hostility. Much of this kind of humor does not involve horseplay but verbal abuse and cruelty. In part, I am referring to the ethnic joke and the racial joke. To place this kind of humor in a context, however, it is useful first to consider a far more gentle form, the noodle or fool tale, which for thousands of years has served to poke fun at absurd behavior. One finds such tales in ancient Chinese material, in ancient Greek material, and in the reports of events in places like Gotham in England, which had more boobies per square inch than any place on earth. Thus,

> Three wise men of Gotham went to sea in a bowl.
> And if the bowl had been stronger, my tale would be longer.

Since the 1940's the Little Moron has functioned off and on as our Number One National Noodle. At one point, you may recall, he threw his shoes away because they were sticking their tongues out at him. At another, he moved to the city because the country was at war. At still another, he sat in the living room because he thought he was dying.

It is intriguing that through some warped mutation such gentle material has become parent to ethnic and racial jokes, which do not poke fun at foolish behavior but attack those we fear. These jokes are the most prevalent forms of humor in this country, not only among children but among adults. They are examples of how we use humor not for fun but as a weapon against people who threaten us because they are different. They are also examples of humor which produces laughter not necessarily good for the soul. Blacks and people of Polish, Italian, and Puerto Rican extraction are the principal targets. A twelve-year-old-boy in Rhinebeck, New York, provides this example:

> What is yellow on the outside, black on the inside, and screams?
> A school bus full of niggers going over a cliff.

Poor whites who have migrated from Kentucky and West Virginia to Ohio and Indiana have also received such treatment. Around Dayton, Ohio, for example, a series of Briar jokes has grown up about these people and their home states. A Briar is a nickname for a Kentuckian. One of these jokes goes this way:

> I hear Cincinnati is expanding its zoo. They are building a fence around Kentucky.

In considering the universality of such material, it is of interest that five hundred miles away my wife encountered the same comment in the upper-middle-class school where she was teaching. In that case the reference was to another city with another population that was different.

There is a related form of humor young people use which should also be mentioned. It is the so-called *cruel joke* or *sick joke*. Versions of this genre, which Mark Twain called "puerile and decadent," circulated in England at the turn of the century. In fact, a book called *Ruthless Rimes for Heartless Homes* was published during that period. Its hero was a boy named Billy. Here is one of the episodes in which he was involved.

> Billy in one of his nice new sashes
> Fell into the fire and was burned to ashes.
> Now although the room grows chilly
> I have not the heart to poke poor Billy.

Not much later Billy crossed the Atlantic as Little Willy, and after that, through some mysterious transformation, he emerged as Little Audrey. But all of this material was relatively innocuous In its modern garb the cruel or sick joke dates from the 1950's and continues to circulate. It deals freely with the murder and mutilation of parents and children, with cannibalism, with indifference to human affliction, and with other subjects that in the past were ordinarily not regarded as amusing, at least not in public. Here are two examples.

Mommy, why do I keep walking in circles?
Shut up, or I'll nail your other foot to the floor.

Mommy, is Daddy still sleeping?
Shut up and keep digging.

It may be that such jokes reflect the increased freedom of young people, but it is difficult not to see in this material expressions of anxiety over the unusually disoriented period in which we live. One finds a startling range in the kinds of humor which appeal to children, from the use of word play and nonsense to the use of horseplay and anger. To place all this in perspective, it is necessary to remember that we are dealing with part of our folklore, the result of a process at once simple and complex, which ordinary people have developed over thousands of years to meet many of their psychic and their practical needs.

Just what is folklore? A Canadian anthropologist, Marius

Barbeau, offers this definition: "Whenever a lullaby is sung to a child; whenever . . . a riddle, a tongue-twister, or a counting-out rime is used . . .; whenever sayings, proverbs, fables, noodle-stories, folktales . . . are retold; whenever, out of habit or incli-nation, the folk indulge in songs and dances, in ancient games, in merry-making, to mark the passing of the year or the usual festivities; whenever a mother shows her daughter how to sew, knit, spin, weave, embroider, make a coverlet . . . bake . . . [a] pie; whenever a . . . craftsman . . . trains his apprentice in the use of tools, shows him how to cut a mortise and peg in a tenon, how to raise a frame house or a barn, how to string a snowshoe . . . then we have folklore in its own perennial domain . . . always apt to grasp and assimilate new elements. . . . it is the born opponent of the serial number, the stamped product, and the patented standard."*

I first became interested in folklore when most of us do, in childhood. But at that time I had no idea that the games, sayings, songs, rhymes, taunts, and jokes I knew; the things I wrote on walls; the superstitions I relied on; the tales I heard and learned; the customs we practiced at home; or the ways we had of doing things were all folklore. I also did not realize that much of this lore gave my life structure and continuity, that these games, songs, jokes, tales, and customs were often very old, that or-dinary people like me had created them, and that all this had survived simply and remarkably because one person had told another. With each retelling the result — be it a tale or a taunt — often changed slightly to reflect the circumstances of the individual involved. In fact, when one considers the countless variants of any joke, saying, tale, ballad, or song, it is almost as if one were encountering the assembled impressions of a series of prints pulled from a stone — all are the same, yet each is different.

It also did not occur to me as a child that the folklore we create, pass on, and change says a good deal about us, about the times in which we live, and about the needs we have. Our jests provide pleasure, but they also provide emotional release. When they deal with racial and ethnic groups and with parents and siblings, they provide weaponry. The tall tales which so amuse us spring from the vastness of a frontier wilderness where life

*As quoted in Tristram Potter Coffin, ed., *Our Living Traditions* (New York, Basic, 1968), p. 13.

was brutal and the people diminished and fearful. They created incredible lies in which individuals were larger and taller than life and could not fail, no matter what. Our superstitions provide answers to things we do not understand and cannot explain. Even today, when we know so much, we turn for answers to astrology and to the occult; and like our ancestors, we continue to cross our fingers, wish on stars, and knock on wood.

I am frequently asked where I obtain the folklore I include in my books for young people. Whenever it is feasible, I collect material from the folk — particularly from children, our strongest, most cohesive folk group, and from the elderly, who in many respects are as important. I do my collecting in schoolyards, in classrooms, in summer camps, on street corners, at church picnics, in city homes, in country stores, on farms, in shopping centers. Some days I find little or nothing, for this search is very much like prospecting. But other days I strike gold. I also rely on regular contacts with a half dozen schools, each in a different kind of community, which I visit at intervals or with whose pupils I correspond. And clearly I rely on archives and libraries.

My collections include folklore ranging in age from a few weeks to thousands of years. The "Peter Piper" twister recently observed its three hundredth anniversary in print, but it seems far older. The ethnic joke has its roots in ancient days. The hoary tale "The Man With the Golden Arm" — which Mark Twain called a lovely scare story — was old when it arrived here two centuries ago from England. And over the years countless variations have developed as one person has told it to another. During a recent summer at a children's camp in New England, my young daughter learned a version of the Golden Arm tale I had not earlier encountered. When she got home, she told it to a friend. In her retelling she added her imprint, which is one of the traditional functions of any member of a folk group. And in doing so, she performed another traditional function: She transmitted the lore.

We tend to think of folklore as old-fashioned. But whenever people interact and share problems, possibilities, solutions, and pain, they continue to create and use the stuff of folklore to deal with their needs. This process is at work on farms, in city neighborhoods, in hospitals, in jails, in factories and stores, in the armed forces, on playgrounds, in schools, and in many other

215

places. Yet, for several reasons, we have come to depend less on folklore. As our technology has advanced we have come to rely increasingly on other people for goods, services, and entertainment and less on ourselves and on those we know. The extended family and the traditions it preserved have disappeared. We move about the country to an extraordinary extent; each year one family out of four moves from one place to another. As a result of such changes, we have to a serious extent become alienated from our traditions and have lost a sense of place and a sense of self. If this perception is correct, we have altered the fabric of our society, and we are changing from something we were to something we have not yet become.

In light of all this, what am I trying to say to a child who reads my books of folklore? Laugh when you can. As Josh Billings suggested, "[O]pen your mouth wide enough for the noise to get out without squealing, throw your head back as though you was going to be shaved, hold on to your false hair with both hands and then laugh till your soul gets thoroughly rested."

Understand that you are not very different from people who lived before you, despite the trappings of modern life. You experience the same joys, the same fears, the same anger, the same love, the same need for dignity, the same need for security.

Understand that you are part of a living tradition to which you contribute and from which you draw. You are deeply rooted in the experience of the human race and are part of something remarkable and continuous — the folk. At a time when everyone and everything seem in transit, it is good to know this.

This article was prepared for the June 1977 and August 1977 *Horn Book*.

VIII

MAKING THE PAST
UNDERSTANDABLE

The development of freer and bolder forms of realism in children's literature has led, almost compelled, writers of fantasy to come to their own defense. Authors like Ursula Le Guin and Lloyd Alexander are impelled to find a philosophical justification for the kind of fiction they write, appealing to what they conceive of as a higher kind of realism. Similarly, during an era when interest in historical fiction seems to be at a low ebb, writers of historical novels need to come to terms with their guiding principles and to justify their art.

Jill Paton Walsh distinguishes between what she calls the costume novel and the historical novel, which "is wholly or partly about . . . public events and social conditions . . . regardless of the time at which it is written," and she reminds us that "history itself is a construct of the mind. The evidence has been selected, and patterned, and arranged." Coincidentally suggesting Janet McNeill's insights into the literary transition from childhood to youth, Penelope Lively stresses "the part continuity plays in imaginative development" and propounds a humanistic doctrine of a child's relationship to history. "To have a sense of history is, above all, to have a sense of one's humanity. . . . For the child, it is a step forward in awareness of other people, which is the most vital step toward being not just an adult, but a mature adult."

Published during the reminiscent period of our nation's Bicentennial, Christopher Collier's essay on the various historiographic approaches to the study of the American Revolution came as a refreshing reminder of the many ways of seeing the same event. Olivia Coolidge's justification for a young adult book on Lincoln echoes Sylvia Engdahl's vote of confidence to young people. Mrs. Coolidge writes, "I want to give them adult ideas and conceptions, and I hope they like to think as well as to be told."

HISTORY IS FICTION

By JILL PATON WALSH

HISTORICAL NOVELS have come down in the world
since Walter Scott set Europe by the ears with them.
They struggle for a readership in an atmosphere of
amused dismissiveness — the very same atmosphere that so often
meets children's books. Indeed, an impression has got about that
they *are* children's books; merely by being historical, they are
unfit for adults. At the same time, most of the increasing band of
raiders — adults sneaking secret reading off the children's bookshelf — are after the historical treasure store they find there. For,
in historical novels for children, the adult usually finds a book
worth full adult attention; just as in the historical novel for adults,
the child is likely to find a book accessible to him. At one time nobody asked whom a novel in the genre was for; everybody read
Rob Roy and *Kidnapped* and enjoyed them; but times have
changed.

Well, why are historical novels under a cloud? It cannot be
because many of them are bad. Many of them are, of course,
really dreadful; but the existence of bad books cannot be the only
reason why historical writing is suspect, otherwise there would
surely be enough bad books to disgrace every other literary mode.
There must be some more integral cause. Surely it has something
to do with the fact that historical fiction is a mixed form, and open
— as mixed forms tend to be — to devastating objections based
on principle, very much like those of the man at the opera who
objected, "But people in danger of death don't sing!"

The objections to historical fiction come from two opposed directions: From the believers in fiction, who adopt a high aesthetic
tone and think that the fiction should not be adulterated with a
dross of history; and from the historians, who put on the armor
of truth and object strenuously to the mingling of anything com-
pounded with the pure ore of historical fact. Let us challenge first
the high aesthetic objection.

From a proponent of the high aesthetic standard we shall easily
get agreement about the high status of fiction. Fiction is a mode of
perception, a positive method of thinking things out, feeling
things through. Why then can it not be a method of thinking and

feeling about the past? We are likely to be offered two reasons. The Philistine reason is that history itself does not matter and that important fiction will offer, therefore, insights into the world only as it is now (a reason closely related to the demand of contemporary students for relevant studies). The answer would have to be a well-constructed defense of the importance of history for an understanding of the present, a defense for which I have no space here.

But the second reason we might be offered is a more theoretical one: Direct observation, the writer's direct experience, is intrinsically more valuable than secondhand experience. In treating what is contemporary, the writer is giving us his immediate experience, whereas the historical writer makes his books out of other books — the insights shop-soiled, the observation secondhand. Is there truth in this? What kind of life, for example, are we projecting onto Mr. Gore Vidal, if we think that *Myra Breckinridge* is a more direct report on his experience of life than *Julian*? Merely making the inquiry reveals that we are being asked to believe that contemporary novels are "direct" merely because they are contemporary. The truth of the matter is that they involve quite as much imagination as any other sort, and any writer interpreting the past uses nearly the whole of his knowledge of the present. Questions like "What would it have felt like to be Nero?" or "What sort of man would fiddle while Rome burned?" are answers as much out of the writer's experience of contemporary humanity as are any contemporary questions. For, however historical the perspective in which one looks back, however carefully one reconstructs different beliefs and feelings from past epochs, to think that one's knowledge of the present does not apply at all — with no matter how many qualifications — to the past is to think that we do not share a common humanity with the dead. Surely I am right to call that a Philistine belief, since it would dismantle civilization.

I have one more rejoinder to launch against the cult of contemporaneity: It is a totally nonliterary concern. It is occupied not with the validity of the words on the page, but with the dates of the author, and with his supposed relationship to his material. Suppose, for example, that someone asks whether *War and Peace* is a historical novel. Shall we say, "I'm not sure. Hang on while I look up Tolstoy's dates"? *War and Peace* would be a historical novel if Tolstoy had written it in a prophetic trance a hundred years before the birth of Napoleon; *War and Peace* is a historical novel because of what it is *about*. With that perception I offer a definition of historical novel which by-passes the contemporaneity stuff altogether. A novel is a historical novel when it is wholly or partly about the public events and social conditions which are the material of history, regardless of the time at which it is written.

In offering this definition I am very well aware that it leads to odd results. A certain kind of contemporary novel may be historical while many novels set in the past will not be. For example, merely choosing a Cavalier and Roundhead setting for a romance does not, in itself, make that a romance *about* the time of the English Civil War. We shall need a new name for the nonhistorical books with a setting in the past; I suggest we call them costume novels. To distinguish the historical from the costume novel we need only apply a simple test: Can we imagine the plot and characters set in any other period? If we can, then the book is not in any organic way *about* its historical period. It may be a very good book, but it is not a historical novel.

I have now reached a conclusion contrary to common sense, for surely the common sense understanding of the words historical novel is, precisely, "a novel set in the past," and I had better explain and defend myself. A historical setting does not suffice to make a novel historical because the setting of fiction is not fundamentally of the first importance. A novel is not quintessentially descriptive or evocative. A novel is quintessentially a prose narrative. However good the description and incidentals which make up the setting, however deeply they enrich the novel, the heart of the matter is always the story — complex interactions of character and event. If the novel as a form of art can have anything to say about history, it must say it through the story, through character and event, not merely through setting. Thus I have reached a statement of what I — and I daresay other historical writers — am trying to do: to enshrine in the heart of the novel, in the very center of its being, a truly historical insight.

From this lofty position I shall at last find courage to tackle the other objector, the historian robed in the armor of truth. His objection to historical fiction is an objection on principle — that historical fiction is not true. This is a very ancient objection. It is much older than the historical novel. It is as old as Plato, who called poets liars, crowned them at the gates, and banished them from his Republic. Aristotle disagreed. "The distinction between historian and poet . . . consists really in this, that the one describes the thing that has been, and the other a kind of thing that might be. Hence poetry is something more philosophic and of graver import than history, since its statements are of the nature rather of universals, whereas those of history are singulars. By a universal statement I mean one as to what such or such a kind of man will probably or necessarily say or do — which is the aim of poetry, though it affixes proper names to the characters; by a singular statement, one as to what, say, Alcibiades did or had done to him."* There are two ways, then, to write of Alcibiades; and Aristotle prefers the poetic — that is, the fictional — way as being of graver import. It is comforting to have Aristotle on our side as we proceed.

We should proceed, I think, with an important distinction. That is the distinction between "not true" meaning "not known to be true" and "not true" meaning "known not to be true." Now, I do not think any intellectually honest person should have anything to do with the "known not to be true." I do not think that the "known not to be true" should appear in literature, and I do not think that calling the book fiction provides the slightest excuse. The "not known to be true" is quite another matter. The "not known to be true" is the whole point of writing historical novels. If we were content with what can be certainly known, we would stick with history; but the art of fiction constantly demands that we go beyond the safe, solid footing of the "known to be true" onto the thrilling quagmire of the "might have been." Yet, this dangerous departure is subject to the most exacting restraints. It is not the orgy of self-indulgent, wish-fulfillment writing that it might seem from the historian's point of view. Let me give an example of how it works out.

The historian writing of the Battle of Marathon is at liberty to say that the Athenian army marched out on their famous "dash to the rescue" by either the coast road or the hill road (it is not known which). Colonel Hammond, he can tell you in a footnote, believes in the hill road, and his opinion is worth something, for he has served as a soldier in Greece. Other scholars, however, may disagree for various reasons. But the novelist describing Marathon must either omit all mention of the march, or choose which route the army took. Perhaps he could give a sensible reason for his choice, a very responsible reason — that he is con-

*Aristotle, *Poetics*, 1451, lines 1-11

222

vinced by Colonel Hammond; or an irresponsible reason — that he prefers writing about hill scenery. Perhaps he could give no reason at all. But the choice must be made, and his account will therefore go beyond the known, into the "not known to be true." And that's all right, isn't it? To object to that really is to say that people in danger of death don't sing! But it would not be all right to have them all take ship, or staying at home. I am making the point that because some invention, and speculation, and certainty beyond the evidence is all right in fiction, it does not in the least follow that anything goes.

Last year I visited Knossos in Crete and went to look at the famous frescoes depicting bulls and fantastically nubile girls. And actually seeing these frescoes was a great shock. For astonishingly little of those great pictures has survived. They consist of tiny fragments of painted plaster, mounted in arrangement; and the rest was drawn in and painted in suitable colors by Arthur Evans' workmen. Look carefully at the color reproductions in an art book, and you will see. Now, I am not saying there is anything wrong in this, but I do want to say two things about it. First, the frescoes go miles beyond the "known to be true": There is even one large scene of a blue monkey eating nuts, which scholars now rather shamefacedly say is not really about a blue monkey at all, but about something quite different. Secondly, that if Arthur Evans had been a purist and had simply put the little pieces higgledy-piggledy in cabinets, there would be nothing of interest for the untrained eye to see. Luckily, he produced instead the visual equivalent of the historical novel — and aren't those frescoes marvelous?

Think about the job of assembling the plaster fragments, and you will see at once some of the restraints which govern the apparently free-hand bits. It is clear the reconstructor can extend and complete the lines in all of his fragments without going far beyond the evidence. He may have to guess the arrangement. Perhaps we will not mind too much if, having lost the left-hand bottom corner and observing that the ancient artist filled all available spaces, he puts imaginary flowers in the grass. But if, just suppose, his flowers leave him with no space for the dull, little, brown, plain bit that he has left over. If he knows it belongs somewhere there in that area but it spoils his own drawing, how tempting to throw just that little bit away surreptitiously! But *that* just will not do. It is not honest. However small, minute, plain, and dull the awkward fragment, it is evidence. The moment you depart from the evidence you are no longer reconstructing the Palace of Minos, or writing a *historical* novel, you are painting or writing for yourself, in the ordinary way. No reason exists why you should not have set out to do that in the first place, but there is an element of dishonesty in presenting your work as Minoan, when all the time that tiny tell-tale fragment lies in the dustbin, giving the lie to you. And the fragment cannot be too small or too trivial to matter, for to ignore it would betray an attitude not sufficiently scrupulous, not interested disinterestedly enough in the truth. And that attitude might have let all sorts of false emphases slip by.

What I am saying amounts, in effect, to saying that to be a historical novelist you have to be as good at history as any historian. You have to do the work; you have to have the right attitude; you have to have a historian's allegiance to history. You have to want to write what did happen and what it felt like, and not what would have been romantic had it happened, or what you wish it had been like, or what would make a much better story if only it had been true. You have to believe, I think, that what really happened is bound to make the best story of all.

And now, at last, I am going to turn from the defensive to the form of attack called *tu quoque,* and complain that the historian is simply the pot calling the kettle black. For what does the historical novelist do that is not also done by historians? History is indeed *fact* — the Latin word for something that was done — but it is also *fict* — the Latin word for something made. For where and what is history, anyway? You cannot take a bus and go round it, as you can go round the Tower of London. Vast stretches of it are totally unverifiable, having left no monuments at all. Even when physical evidence exists, it needs interpretation. Have you ever tried going round the Tower of London without a guide book, or understanding a dig without the archeologist at your side? Nine-tenths or more of what is known about the past rests only upon the evidence of the written word. And written words have a lot in common, whether they are drafted by novelists or by historians.

And that is not really surprising. For in both sorts of writing a very similar process is going on. History does not exist somewhere; it is not really something indisputable. The evidence for it — a vast jumbled assortment of many kinds of data — exists;

but history itself is a construct of the mind. The evidence has been selected, and patterned, and arranged; it has been master-minded into significance by the writer of the history book. How very like the writing of a novel I make it sound. For the novelist, too, confronts the inchoate material of the past and brings out of it an imposed narrative coherence — a story, or a history.

And although plot in literature is often treated as the undis-cussable, simple element, in fact — as any writer knows — it is not simple. For narrative relates fundamentally to a view of the world, to an understanding of events. A belief in luck, for ex-ample, produces an episodic narrative like *Tom Jones*. A belief in predestination underlies and shapes a story like *Jude the Ob-scure*. In our century existentialism dissolved the structure of causality, and people write novels without plots. Similarly, the world view of a historian influences where he begins and ends, and how he connects one event with another. Gibbon wrote *The Decline and Fall of the Roman Empire* as a story of moral deca-dence. Nowadays, it would more likely be written as the story of how and why Diocletian's price and income controls failed to work. Both novelist and historian — merely in recounting a se-quence of events — reveal the orientation of their most profound beliefs. There is no such thing as a simple story.

The writing of a historical novel, then, is a task of great com-plexity, an exacting exercise of mind and heart. The fruits of the writer's self-imposed ordeal are as likely to be worth serious atten-tion from the reader as is writing of any other kind. The historical novel does not deserve the poor esteem in which it is often held. Moreover, as a literary genre it is "suitable for children," but not in any condescending sense; it is suitable for children neither more nor less than for adults. It was, after all, a historical tale — the ballad of Percy — of which Sir Philip Sidney said that it drew the children from play, and the old men from the chimney corner: Surely the best tribute ever given to a good story.

From *The Horn Book* for February 1972

225

CHILDREN AND MEMORY

By PENELOPE LIVELY

WHAT IS THE RELATIONSHIP between history and children's books? I hope you'll forgive me if I expand upon this question, or distort it — I'm not sure which it is — and discuss the importance of something that I would call continuity rather than history. It could also be called memory, but the word *history* is imprecise, because I want to talk about the past in a personal as well as in a collective sense and about the part continuity plays in imaginative development. I am simply interested in that step toward maturity a child takes when it ceases to see people as static, frozen at a moment in time, but sees them instead as changing and developing creatures. Such a perception is concerned with realizations about time and about aging, but also, I think, with realizations about history. It is the perception, often startling, that places have a past, that they are now but also were then, and that if peopled now, they were peopled then. It is a step aside from self, a step out of the child's self-preoccupation, and, therefore, a step toward maturity. And it is a step that might come as often from reading as from observation.

To read Hardy, for example, is to get satisfaction as much from the sense of human lives set in a timeless and ancient landscape as from the power of the narrative. I'm sure that for children, too, the use of place — as a way of evoking historical memory — can be particularly important. Landscape can be used, not because it is important in itself, but because what has happened there is important. In the same way, a house is a preservative, a record of the lives it has sheltered. No one has used place more effectively than Lucy Boston: The house and the garden in the Green Knowe books are her medium for talking about continuity. And, of course, *Tom's Midnight Garden* (Lippincott) is a book that perfectly uses the device of memory enshrined not only in a house, but in people.

To write for children about continuity is to try to share a commitment to the past, to history, if you like. The difficulty is that you are not trying to transmit a vague mystical experience but a perfectly definite one, which depends on a breadth of historical knowledge that children obviously cannot have.

Now, certain places are possessed of a historical charge that sets the imagination flaring with an immediacy that nothing else can. In particular, I am thinking of places where private and public experiences collide — battlefields, the sites of deserted villages, places where people's lives have been disrupted by the force of historical change. But awareness of these events comes from an acquired experience of the past: To feel the impact of a place like the battlefield at Edgehill, you must know something of the tormented history of seventeenth-century England, or it is nothing but an attractive piece of Warwickshire landscape.

How do you transmit this feeling to a child? How do you make a child aware that other people have been here before us and that the totality of their experience is still found in the world we inhabit? Obviously, you can demonstrate this best by being a historian, by transmitting the facts. Facts by themselves may be awkward, but fiction can lure a child toward them. For any of us to reach the point at which we perceive that the past is true, there has first to be an imaginative experience; before the books, must come some kind of awakening about history as fact. And this kind of awakening is often brought about by the power of place.

Place is a medium, a channel for the transmission of memory. Without it, we would be in real danger of forgetting or ignoring our own past. We need it, and the need, though rarely defined, seems to me to be expressed in England by a deep-seated preference for old things and old houses and by the uneasiness that people feel in places entirely without a visible past — new towns, new housing estates, high-rise flats. The objections may be differently phrased, but I suspect that they may often be linked with loss of memory. Loss of memory and removal from the kind of idealized, rural past that most people regard as natural to them, even if they have never known it.

In any case, why should the development of a child's perception about the past matter? To have a sense of history is, above all, to have a sense of one's own humanity, and without that we are nothing. For the child, it is a step toward an awareness of other people, which is the most vital step toward being not just an adult, but a mature adult. When a small child takes his first disinterested action, he learns that he is not the only one, but that there are other people. When an older child is able to feel an involvement with the past, he learns that there were other societies before his own. He may be shocked by social injustice in the nineteenth century, or stirred by past causes, or able to appreciate the stresses that produce civil war or revolution. There has to be an appreciation of the past as fact, and not just as a complicated mythology quite possibly invented by a conspiracy of teachers. History can seem like that, and all too often does. And this is why the power of place is important. We have to set the child down in a tangible landscape and say, "You are here . . . now . . . today, but here also have been other people. Just think about that." And children will, being — on the whole — obliging creatures.

The historical novel, or the novel that is in some way concerned with the past, is not simply a stepping stone to the reading of history proper. Obviously not, because if the book is any good, it has to stand on its own as a story. The best historical novels are, in one sense, timeless. They can be detached from their period and looked at simply as an account of human experience. But they should also say something about human experience within a historic framework, about the collision between private and public affairs. We lead private lives, but private lives susceptible to events beyond our control. A child growing up in this century of galloping social changes may find analogies in Rosemary Sutcliff's examination of uneasy eras in early English history — times when people were unsure of themselves, uncertain of their status and their function. Children aware of present-day racial problems will recognize the same kind of tensions in other societies removed in time, and see themselves as part of the whole pattern of human experience. To help a child see himself as part of a whole historical perspective is to extend his imagination. Without such awareness he is blinkered, confined by self, and dangerous.

The historical novel, at its best, can bring this kind of awareness. At its worst, of course, it diminishes the subject and offers a cheap excursion ticket to the past — a quick trip to look at high life in the eighteenth century and back in time for tea. When I was young, most historical novels seemed to present the past as a place peopled entirely by sex-mad aristocrats, whose activities bore no relation whatsoever to what goes on in any viable society. They were fantasies in the pejorative sense of the word. By the time I had grown up, I had total contempt for the historical novel as a literary form. However, during the last ten years, my opinion has been completely reversed by my reading of Henry Treece and Rosemary Sutcliff and other writers who have added a new dimension to the historical novel.

One way of expressing a commitment to the past is to write historical novels. Another way is to write about memory. Now, if a novel for adults concerns itself with memory, it will probably consider it in the context of a lifetime rather than in the context of history. If you are writing for children, you cannot deal with memory in quite the same way: A child's life has been too short for him to appreciate the part that memory plays as one grows older. With a child, you can talk about historical memory as found in stories and places. Or you can try to present people as accumulations of experience — functioning, like places, in layers so that an old woman is both an old woman and the child she once was. I suspect that this concept is one of the most difficult for children to grasp. Time in childhood is a continuous present. The idea of time as progression only comes much later, so that against all evidence, no child entirely believes either that he will grow up, or that his parents were once children. You can write of individual memory through the medium of a character; and, for that reason, I particularly admire those children's writers who successfully present the old as central characters in a book.

We are all, collectively or individually, sustained by memory. In an individual, the disintegration of personality comes when memory goes: We are what we have been. Societies collapse when their cultural roots are destroyed. This is obvious to us as adults, but not at all so to the child. To be unaware of a sense of continuity is to be affected by a kind of paralysis of the imagination. We've all come across, at one time or another, the eighteen-year-olds with whom communication is impossible, because they are fossilized in the conception of themselves as "the young." This present-day phenomenon is fostered by the tendency to see society as chopped up into strata of "the young," the "middle-aged," and "the old." The conception is an artificial one, created for the convenience of the producers in a consumer society. The outcome is a generation that thinks of itself as neatly fenced-off from other people by date of birth.

One of the oddest things we do to children is to confront them with someone else who is also eight, or ten, or seven, and insist that they be friends. Why should we assume that they have any more in common than I have with Mrs. Jones, simply because she is also thirty-nine? A friend, a contemporary, said to me plaintively the other day that we were never young. She meant, I think, that we never had a strong consciousness of ourselves as being so. Maybe we missed something, but I'm not particularly concerned about that. What concerns me is the misconception that people are fossilized at any particular point in a lifetime. We are none of us "the young," or "the middle-aged," or "the old." We are all of these things. To allow children to think otherwise is to encourage a disability — a disability both of awareness and of communication.

The right books, at the right moment, might be valuable. Such books, written with children in mind, were not around when I was a child; or if they were, I missed them. But the need was there, because I remember a strong dissatisfaction with the adventure genre of the time, which seemed the wildest kind of fantasy because it postulated a situation where people were either children — and therefore heroic and at the center of things — or adult — and therefore evil or else conveniently negative. The real world was demonstrably different, and I remember turning to Dickens for comfort and the assurance that people come in all ages and sizes and temperaments. Nowadays, children are better provided for. They've got plenty of writers giving them adult characters who are vulnerable, have pasts, and are not just put together temporarily for the purposes of the plot. They've got William Mayne attending to the power of the place, half-a-dozen good historical novelists, and a lot of hard-to-categorize writers, whose books often get lumped together in that convenient bracket — fantasy.

In my own books, I have been concerned with the themes of continuity and memory. *Astercote* (Dutton), my first attempt at writing for children, reflected an obsession I had at the time with the sites of deserted medieval villages. In *The Whispering Knights* and *The Wild Hunt of the Ghost Hounds* (Dutton), I tried to make something of two recurrent themes in English folklore which have fascinated me for years: in the first case, the strange mystique attached to standing stones; and in the second, the widespread, ancient, and powerful legend of the ghostly hunt. I think that the compelling quality of both of these themes, for anyone concerned about continuity, is that they are clearly the legacy of unbelievably ancient involvements with place and are so strong that there still lingers an echo of what they were. Writing *The Wild Hunt* gave me a taste for ghosts which I've indulged in in *The Ghost of Thomas Kempe*, a light-hearted affair on the whole, but concerned with the serious matter of a child's awaking to the concept of memory. And finally *The Driftway* (Dutton) was an attempt to write about the jolt given to a child's self-absorption by an imaginative involvement with other people's lives; in this instance, lives removed in time rather than in space. I wanted to use landscape as a channel for historical memory — a road, in fact, a perfectly ordinary road, B4525 from Banbury to Northampton, but a road that is very ancient and seemed to lend itself perfectly to a double symbolism. All of these books are — on one level — about continuity. My way of trying to tackle the subject has been by fusing past and present to make a point about memory rather than by writing directly of the past.

Children need both kinds of memory — both historical and personal. They need them because they've lost two things in this century that I'm sure are vital to childhood. One is oral tradition. We no longer know how to tell children stories; we don't even know the stories to tell them. The stories survive, because people like Katherine Briggs see that they do. But they don't survive as a living force; they are dead and interred in books. An African friend told me recently of his childhood in Uganda. His upbringing would be regarded by most people as extremely underprivileged, but he had one experience that few children in England have had — a rich, spoken, narrative tradition, taught by grandparents to children as a vital and essential part of their upbringing and as a precise and established store of knowledge in which each child must be word perfect. In his mid-twenties, this man, a university graduate, could still repeat a vast range of stories, myths, and fables learned before he could read or write.

Our children have no oral tradition. Of course, I must concede the Opies; but what I'm talking about is narrative tradition, which is almost dead. The oral tradition is doomed as soon as literacy becomes universal; its death-blow has been dealt by television; and the process is inevitable and irreversible. We have other things to give our children now, but perhaps we should pay attention to what we have lost on the way. I have a very uncomfortable feeling — listening to old people talk and comparing their conversation with that of my own generation — that a kind of articulacy is vanishing, too. Not the articulacy of saying exactly what you mean, but of being able to say it with distinction. Old country people, people who are older than the century, retain a beauty of speech and an individuality of expression that you rarely hear nowadays.

I was talking recently to an elderly neighbor, a man of eighty-six, who only once in his life left the Oxfordshire village where we both live — to be pitched into the trenches in 1918. We were discussing the destruction of the wood near the village by a local landowner, and my neighbor was telling me of how he used to go there as a boy and of the variety of trees in the wood. He didn't say, "There were lots of different kinds of trees," but said, "There was oak, and there was ash, and there was sycamore, and there was beech, and then there was spruce and birch and elm and hazel; and you'd find spurge growing, and wood anemones, and primroses, and ramsons, and yellow archangel." The list went on and on: It was like Homer's catalogue of the ships. It took time, but a proper use had been made of language; and, by the end, I knew with accuracy what the wood must have been like many years ago.

Children are also in danger of losing the personal memory that comes from contact with the old. Most children know their grandparents, but they don't live with them; the children probably live in the artificial social segregation of a housing estate or a block of flats where young families keep company with other young families, and the old are somewhere else. Children need old people; they need people with a slower pace and people released from pressures of work and responsibility; and, above all, they need people with memories. Children are listeners; they are unencumbered with preconceptions and opinions and prejudices. The old have stories to tell, and are often the last people left with the ability to tell them. The two age groups should not be separated as they too often are. We can't do much about the situation; this is how we live now. I'm sure childhood must have been richer when the source of entertainment was not the faceless telly in the corner, but the grandmother at the fireside.

Books can't be a substitute for reality. They can't be a substitute for the grandmother by the fireside, nor should they be.

Since our children's lives may be starved of memory and of a sense of continuity because of the loss of oral tradition and because of the shrinking and isolation of families, it may be that books attending to memory, both historical and personal, are more important to children than ever before. Life is very immediate now for children. The pop songs, the catch phrases from the latest television series, the folk heroes — all change within a matter of months. They are ephemeral — shadows passing over the consciousness — and leave no permanent flavor. Five years ago my children's games were dominated by the Batman craze. I reminded them of it recently; they were completely blank and could remember nothing of it. So much for the imaginative stimulus. My husband, on the other hand, who grew up in the age of Flash Gordon in the local Odeon on Saturday mornings, says I am too stern about an alternative narrative tradition which gave him a vast amount of pleasure and suspense.

Whatever the function of Batman or Flash Gordon, and I wouldn't deny that they have a function, I still feel certain that children need something that goes deeper than the newest craze; and I'm not merely talking about particular books, or good or literary books. Children need to sense that we live in a permanent world that reaches away, behind and ahead of us, and that the span of a lifetime is something to be wondered at, and thought about, and that — above all — people evolve during their own lives. People are never complete, as it were, but knowledge expands and contracts, opinions harden and soften, and people end up as a curious, irrational blend of experience and memory. Children have to be told about these things because they haven't had time to see how time works on them, or to see how it works on other people. They haven't yet seen the process, as we have seen it on the faces of friends and relatives. They can't yet place themselves in a wider framework of time and space than *today* and *here*. But they have to, if they are not to grow up enclosed in their own personalities. Perhaps books can help, just a little.

From *The Horn Book* for August 1973

JOHNNY AND SAM:
OLD AND NEW APPROACHES TO
THE AMERICAN REVOLUTION

By CHRISTOPHER COLLIER

FOR perhaps the tenth time in as many weeks I listened with embarrassment as my host introduced me — on this occasion to about a hundred Connecticut reading specialists — as someone who had at last found something new to say about the American Revolution. Surely, I thought, there are some people in my audience who will think me pretentious and recognize the preposterousness of the statement. If, among the thousands of teachers and librarians I have addressed in the year and a half since the publication of *My Brother Sam Is Dead*, there were those who thought the statement absurd, none have been so rude as to say so. They have left that welcome job to me.

The embarrassment I have felt on these occasions stems from the fact that what is seen as new in the book my brother and I wrote has behind it at least two generations of scholarship among academic historians. The interpretation of the American Revolution that informs *Brother Sam* was thoroughly developed and precisely stated during the first quarter of the twentieth century. Though the historiographic approach is not new, its popularization in juvenile literature apparently is. Indeed, it was largely to fill an historiographic gap that I was moved to persuade my brother, James Lincoln Collier, to collaborate on the work. Historiography — the methodology of historical research and the study of varying historical interpretations — is the great mass of work that lies beneath the tip of the historical iceberg. The method, buried in scholarly apparatus, is concealed from the lay public; and the interpretation is normally so well integrated with description and narration that nonprofessionals are unaware of it. But all written history is interpretation, and novelists present their own historical interpretation whether they are conscious of it or not. Thus, a particular historiographic view is frequently brought unconsciously to readers who are bound to absorb it equally unconsciously.

To state it simply, the historiography of the American Revolution breaks down into three schools of thought — the Whig, the

Imperialist, and the Progressive. The range of interpretation is vast, of course, and includes eighteenth-century Patriot and Loyalist presentations as well as Marxist, Stalinist, Freudian, and other off-beat modes. But the main body of secondary literature about the Revolution written over the past century and a half falls into one or the other of these three dominant groups, though some historians combine elements of two of them, and no two interpretations are identical.

The Whig interpretation, which takes its name from the Parliamentary faction opposed to George III's colonial policies, dominated the nineteenth century during the era before the professionalization of the practice of history. Its principal popularizer was George Bancroft (1800-1891), and thus it is frequently referred to as the Bancroftian view. Nineteenth-century Whig historians saw the Revolution as a spontaneous and universal uprising of the colonial yeomanry. Americans, they claimed, had taken up the cause of traditional English liberty in a struggle against the regressive policies of a tyrannical king who was supported by a venal ministry that had, in turn, bought off and corrupted the larger part of Commons. The Whig picture was moralistic and pedantic, depicting simple, freedom-loving farmers marching in a crusade to fulfill God's plan for a rationally ordered society based on principles of liberty and equality. The Whig effort wanted to teach a national patriotism based upon a respectful adoration of the principles of natural rights and social contract and of the men who died to protect them. A much more sophisticated version of the Whig interpretation — the twentieth-century one — shows a great middle-class America fighting to preserve the right to practice self-government under a universally-accepted concept of the British Constitution constructed on Lockean social contract. This viewpoint has dominated professional historiography since World War II, but its nineteenth-century ancestor has never lost its hold over popular and juvenile literature.

The Bancroftian view of the Revolution came under severe attack by the newly-risen class of professional historians during the late nineteenth and early twentieth centuries. The entrance of the United States upon her own imperialist adventures in the 1890's, together with a developing Anglophilia and a host of other changes in the American political and intellectual climate, drew attention to the English side of the conflict. The Imperialist historians sought a much more objective approach to the conflict and looked for research materials in London as well as in the archives of the former colonies. For them, a true view of the war could only be obtained from the center of the empire looking out. They pointed to the fact that there were twenty-four British American colonies, and the reasons for the loyalty of nearly half of them were certainly as worthy of study as the revolt of the others. The Imperialist historians tend to see the American Patriot position as small-minded, short-sighted, and selfish. They served as a much-needed counterbalance to the flamboyant chauvinism of the filiopietistic Christian gentlemen who wrote history in the Victorian era. The Imperialist historians, however, have had no effect on the writing of popular history or children's literature. But what an intriguing idea: to see the American Revolution through the eyes of a white teenager in Nova Scotia or Quebec or of a black boy in Bermuda or Jamaica — to say nothing of the point of view of a ten-year-old cotton mill worker thrown out on the streets of Manchester as a result of the American embargo!

Though the Imperialists sharply undermined the nationalism of the old Whigs, there is nothing about their interpretation that necessarily requires a British or a world view. One could approach the study of the Revolution from English sources and still conclude that the Americans had been right in their sense of repression and in their understanding of the rights of man. The same cannot be said about the Progressive interpretation.

Arising contemporaneously with the Imperial view, but developing out of domestic rather than world events, the Progressive concept of the Anglo-American conflict of 1763-1783 was set against a background of internal political strife, economic motivations, and rapid social changes. As young historians looked about them in the 1890's and the years before World War I, they saw an America wracked by a too-rapid industrialization and urbanization with the accompanying tortures of class conflict, the corruption of the political system, and the dominance of economics over ideology. And they read the past through spectacles tinted by the social conditioning of the late ninteenth- and early twentieth-century reform movements known as Progressivism.

The Progressive historians elevated economic impetus — both in its individual and in its collective or class manifestations — above ideological or religious motivations. To them reality was found only in concrete economic fact. They also took the social conflict that engulfed their America — geographically based, class motivated, politically inspired but not, however, generational, sexual, or racial as it might be seen today — to be the normal state of events. They turned to sources that would reveal this reality as it existed in the English colonies of the late eighteenth century. The picture they painted enraged, confused, and ultimately confounded both the old Whigs and the young Imperialists.

The Progressive historians — the most sensational and prolific of whom was Charles A. Beard — developed sufficient evidence to indict the Revolutionary leaders for being interested in throwing off the imperial yoke in order to liberate their own economic and political opportunities; or, at least, to serve the economic interests of a large, though minority, commercial class. The question, in the most famous of all our historiographic phrases, was not only one of home rule, but of *who* should rule at home. As a result of the insights thrown out by the Progressives (and of the needs of thousands of eager dissertation writers), the history of America has been studied and displayed in monograph after monograph of minute investigation of countless local political squabbles, economic biographies of influential figures, and interpretations which assume fundamental conflicts in American society. During the heyday of Progressive historiography—roughly the period marked by the two World Wars inclusively — the old middle-class consensus on eighteenth-century liberalism was pictured as a myth of the romantic early nineteenth century. Really, the Anglo-American conflict was seen as but a by-product of the local economic and political ambitions of a dynamic colonial leadership no longer able to tolerate the restraints of a second-class imperial citizenship. The American War for Independence was only part of a civil war that pitted brother against brother as aristocratic and popular interests struggled to control the policy-making machinery of their respective colonies.

Progressive historiography has, then, a hoary if feisty heritage. However, despite its crude popularization — a caricature really — in the form of the debunking biographies so prevalent in the 1920's, the Progressive concept never really permeated popular literature. Furthermore, the solidifying events of the 1940's and the 1950's — decades so dominated by ideological shadows of hot and cold wars — dealt a severe blow to its chances for general, popular acceptance. For the new Whigs of the postwar generation have revived principle as a motivating force, and consensus, on certain attitudes at least if not on a fullblown ideology, as informing the reasons for war in 1775.

The reason, I suspect, that *My Brother Sam Is Dead* appears

237

to say something new is that it stands alone among Revolutionary juvenile literature as an effort to present a view of the war that incorporates elements of both the Whig and Progressive interpretations, with a strong emphasis on the latter. Few children's books on the subject make any attempt to deal with issues at all. For the most part they are merely stories laid in the period and given verisimilitude by incorporating authentic detail.

Consider one of the best of these, Elsie Singmaster's *Rifles for Washington*, written in 1938 when the Great Depression had given the Progressive interpretation its most dramatic claim to the public attention. One reads through this marvelously detailed and carefully researched work without gaining any idea at all of why Americans were fighting the British army in the first place. " '[T]he people want freedom,' " says Peter at one point; and Uncle Proudfoot quotes Thomas Paine, saying " 'the voice of weeping nachure cries it is time to part' "; and fragments of the Declaration of Independence are thrown out as background to a martial scene later on. Once the author seems to notice some political divisions in American society. An anonymous man stands opposite a graveyard and declares angrily, " 'I have rope to hang all the members of Congress. . . . We have no grounds for war.' " But the approach is shallow and simplistic, and ultimately the politics are wholly irrelevant to the story that Elsie Singmaster tells so dramatically. *Rifles for Washington* is not actually about the American Revolution; it is just a wonderful story set in the time and place.

Johnny Tremain, of course, is the work that must be dealt with. The year before its publication in 1943 Esther Forbes had written *Paul Revere and the World He Lived In*. Though she was not a trained historian, her *Paul Revere* is listed in the prestigious *Harvard Guide to American History*, a selective work which also puts *Johnny Tremain* in a list of historical novels useful for delineating their eras. Miss Forbes, I venture to say, knew what she was talking about.

Diligently as one may search through *Johnny Tremain*, however, one finds no deviation from the standard Whig treatment. Perhaps Johnny's thought as he watches a British officer slap a wounded enlisted man — " 'We are fighting, partly, for just that. Because a man is a private is no reason he should be treated like cordwood' " — is a conscious effort on the author's part to note the equalitarianism that the Progressives tended to emphasize as opposed to the Whig's libertarianism. Or again, she shows her awareness of the Imperial school when she has an English doctor say, " 'You remember that *we* don't like being here in Boston any better than you like having us. . . . We're both in a tight spot. But if we keep our tempers and you keep your tempers, why, we can fix up things between us somehow. We're all one people, you know.' "

Esther Forbes does deal with issues; her story is intrinsically about the American Revolution; a different time and place would make it a different story. She tips her hand early while explaining that the new tea tax would actually reduce the price of tea in the colonies. "Weren't the Americans, after all, human beings?" she has a cynical Parliament ask. "Wouldn't they care more for their pocketbooks than their principles?" The rest of her book demonstrates the reverse. Her treatment is pure nineteenth-century Bancroft. Her spokesman is James Otis — in real life scorned by 1775 by the radical revolutionaries as too conservative and untrustworthy in his divided loyalties. Miss Forbes depicts him as fallen from leadership not because of political events but because of his increasingly frequent periods of insanity — also historically accurate. She brings Otis back to give, in a crowded, smoky, attic meeting place of the Sons of Liberty, a spirited statement of old-fashioned American Lockeanism.

" 'For what will we fight?' " demands Otis.

" 'We will fight for the rights of Americans. England cannot take our money away by taxes,' " is the reply of Sam Adams.

" 'No, no. For something more important than the pocketbooks of our American citizens. . . . For men and women and children all over the world. . . . There shall be no more tyranny. A handful of men cannot seize power over thousands. A man shall choose who it is shall rule over him.' "

Otis then proceeds to demonstrate that John Hancock will give up his property, Joseph Warren sacrifice his family, Paul Revere his business, and John Adams his career — all to make the world safe for democracy. Sam Adams with his talk of taxes is dismissed: " 'what it is really about . . . you'll never know,' " says Otis. " 'It is all so much simpler than you think,' " the old firebrand announces after downing a second tankard of punch. " 'We give all we have, lives, property, safety, skills . . . we fight, we die, for a simple thing. Only that a man can stand up.' " Esther Forbes leaves no doubt about her meaning, for the final

chapter is entitled "A Man Can Stand Up," and at the close of
the profoundly touching description of the events after Lexing-
ton and Concord and the death of Johnny's closest friend Rab,
Johnny thinks again, "True, Rab had died. Hundreds would die,
but not the thing they died for.

" 'A man can stand up. . . .' "

Johnny Tremain, with its message of ideologically motivated
war, is so much the product of World War II that one who
grew up in the 1940's must honor its clear one-sidedness.
Younger historians, products of the 1960's who are currently
busy reviving the Progressive interpretation of a generation ago,
would be less tolerant. But without denying its outstanding
literary merit, Miss Forbes' presentation of the American Revolution does not pass muster as serious, professional history. Not
so much because it is so sharply biased, but because it is so
simplistic. Life is not like that — and we may be sure it was not
like that two hundred years ago. Such an event as a war involving the three major European nations, with implications for the
western power structure for centuries to come, is bound to be a
complex matter. To present history in simple, one-sided — almost moralistic — terms, is to teach nothing worth learning and
to falsify the past in a way that provides worse than no help in
understanding the present or in meeting the future.

Perhaps *Brother Sam* benefits from the revolution of our own
times in that publishers are ready now to present teenagers
with some complex issues and some raw reality to chew on. If
there is a ring of novelty in our book about the conflict Americans celebrate this year, the sound is not in the ears of historians,
but only in the ears of children. And that is revolution enough.

From *The Horn Book* for April 1976

WRITING ABOUT
ABRAHAM LINCOLN*

By Olivia Coolidge

WHEN I WAS ASKED some nine months ago to do an article for the *Wilson Library Bulletin* on the writing of young adult biographies, I did not realize that I should be honored by an invitation to speak at the luncheon of the Washington, D. C. Children's Book Guild. And when the invitation did arrive, I did not calculate on the article appearing some three weeks before I would be delivering this talk. To compare great things with small, I find myself in the position of Abraham Lincoln, who came to New York in 1860 to make an important speech and went on to New Hampshire to visit his son Robert at school. Inevitably he was asked to speak again, and he wrote to his wife that if he had foreseen this toil he would not have come East at all. "The speech in New York," he told her, "being within my calculation before I started, went off passably well and gave me no trouble whatever. The difficulty was to make nine others before reading audiences who had already seen all my ideas in print." For my part, I could wish that you were not a reading audience, but I have a sad suspicion that possibly some of you are. This being so, I decided to speak on writing a pair of books about Abraham Lincoln, rather than on my biographies in general — hoping in this fashion to defraud you all by passing out the same ideas in a different setting.

Miss Lee Anna Deadrick of Scribner's brought to my attention the fact that no young adult book on Lincoln existed, and she provoked a hearty laugh at what I assumed must be her folly. But Miss Deadrick isn't foolish, and when I looked into the matter, I perceived not only a vacancy, but a challenge. Briefly, what I have set out to do is to write two separate books on Abraham Lincoln's career for anyone between the ages of fifteen and ninety who may not have time to read long books, may not read fluently enough to get through them, or is interested in the subject only in passing. Such people are not necessarily unintelligent. Indeed, the more intelligent they are, the more I am pleased. I want to give them adult ideas and conceptions, and I hope they like to think as well as to be told.

*Given at the Children's Book Fair Luncheon, November 9, 1974, in Washington, D.C.

Part of the challenge of work like mine is that the education of my readers is generally unfinished. One person knows one thing and one another, so that I find it safest to assume that my readers know practically nothing. Being intelligent, however, they do not want to be lectured; besides, I am writing about Abraham Lincoln — not about economics, slavery, or the American political system of the period. A great deal of thought and skill is required to produce a book which explains itself as it goes along, keeps its eye firmly on Lincoln, and yet develops the national issues important in his life. If you say Lincoln is too big a subject to write about in a couple of two-hundred-page books, I admit you are probably correct, but I wanted to try.

One dear friend of mine, long a children's editor, wrote in honest astonishment, "But oughtn't children of that age to be reading Sandburg?" Now *The Prairie Years* alone is nine hundred pages long; and with all its literary merits — indeed to some extent because of them — it gives an idealized picture of Lincoln. But evidently my friend felt that I could not compete with it, particularly for the high-school reader. My husband has a good Civil War library — and what is in the house I tend to read — but, as she knew, nobody would call me a Lincoln scholar. Perhaps my best excuse for attempting the task was that I could not immediately think of anybody who would take more trouble for the sake of producing a couple of young adult books. I don't pretend to greatness, but I take my work seriously.

One of the chief difficulties with any young adult biography is particularly present in a short book on Lincoln. Since it is impossible in the compass of such a volume to discuss every controversy that has been raised in connection with Lincoln's acts, political or military judgment, thoughts, health, and family, I am frequently in the position of having to make up my mind about Lincoln's motives, or even his mistakes, without arguing details. Heaven help me if some greater scholar feels that he has proved a point which I don't agree with, but have no space to discuss. It is true that when I have to consider opposing points of view, I try to analyze the basic problem, which is often not whether Lincoln was right or wrong, but what were his options. In some situations there is no right decision, or even no best one — merely two or three possible ones all unsatisfactory in different ways. By keeping such considerations in mind, I am at least able to avoid long arguments about whether we ought to approve or disapprove of what he did. Even more emphatically do I eschew the admittedly fascinating subject of what would have happened if he had done something else — a subject which, in the hands of certain writers, is good for several pages of penetrating analysis without any basis in reality. By dogging Lincoln's footsteps obstinately, I can try to avoid imposing too many of my own opinions. But still the mass of material breaks my bounds and makes it difficult to keep from overemphasizing my views for brevity's sake. In writing other books, I have had practice in suggesting — here by a word and there by a phrase — some contrary opinion; but I have never had greater trouble in compressing without becoming arbitrary.

My task is particularly delicate when I deal with Lincoln, not only because of the complexity of Lincoln scholarship but because the whole period engenders passions which are still strongly felt. What, for instance, am I to think of the judgment of one of Lincoln's most famous twentieth-century biographers when I find that he (since he admires Stonewall Jackson) respects, even if he does not share, Jackson's private conviction that God thought precisely as Jackson did? Yet, New England abolitionists and their friends, also religious men but distasteful to the author, appear in his pages as "oily hypocrites." I am ashamed to encounter such stuff in a biography with so many merits. These lapses tend to undermine my faith in his conclusions about Lincoln, which are in many ways fresh and interesting. They also give me a forecast of what I may possibly suffer at the hands of this excellent author's fervid admirers when I publish, as I plan to do, a book on the Lincoln presidency. It is, I believe, the most difficult book I have ever undertaken. Indeed, I may say that the strain of keeping an eye on two presidents at once (or rather, now, two ex-presidents) has driven me in the past year very nearly to distraction.

The intense interest aroused by Lincoln's era has produced not only a flood of contemporary memoirs and multi-volume biographies with copious footnotes, but also what, for the sake of definition, I call Ph.D. theses, which examine a small period under a microscope and, turning up records not previously consulted, sometimes correct the great biographers on matters of detail. A number of these works are excellent; some are only fair; and some mere froth. It is not hard to separate the sheep from the goats but extremely difficult to be sure that any list of worthwhile publications is complete. I have actually seen a small error occurring in one of the great biographies, corrected by a thesis ten years later, but repeated by a reputable Lincoln scholar ten years after that. Now, a conclusion I come to about Lincoln may infuriate one critic; all the same, it may actually please another. But an error in factual detail, though made by better scholars before me, will be thought inexcusable for one who has the temerity to tackle Lincoln without spending half a lifetime on the job. I suppose I shall make some small mistakes, and I assure you that the dread of doing so is a constant nightmare.

As you can see from what I say, there are bound to be limits on the scope of my research. I am not, for instance, trying to consult unpublished records in the hope of finding something to contradict or some new fact to convey. How awful if I should come across any such thing! How on earth would I squeeze it into my books? Although a young adult biography may sometimes introduce new material, that is not — in my view — its primary duty. A young adult book essentially provides background which may serve as a magnet to attract and hold other knowledge. It would be enough for me if someone were to say, "I got interested in Lincoln through a book I once read by somebody called *College*." It would be even better if a man who had read something else on Lincoln were to say, "You know, I'm suspicious about that Ann Rutledge story. There was a rather good book I once read by someone or other which said there was not much in it. I wonder . . ." Wondering is the beginning of understanding.

My research is limited to what appears in print, and, obviously, I cannot read everything about Lincoln. I try to concentrate on the first-class material — the contemporary memoirs, the speculations of really good minds, the big biographies, the work of those who know how to handle documents and records, the eight closely-printed volumes of Lincoln's speeches and letters, the books that are impeccable in detail. My problem is to find them all amid the mass of worthless stuff.

You must be concluding that I am very foolish. Why did I plunge into a task for which I admit I am ill-prepared and which sounds impossible in any case? I did it because in a certain sense I am prepared. I've been writing young adult biographies (interspersed with fiction) for twenty years. I've been improving my clarity of thought and expression, polishing my ability to say much in little space, enlarging my repertoire of tricks to ensure that information flows from me to my readers without obscuring the personality I want to present. I've been balancing the expression of my own opinions against the need to let my audience make decisions. I've been increasingly conscious that every phrase should give my readers the pleasures of visualizing, of forming an opinion, of absorbing an idea which will linger in the mind. I've even been going through the mental processes of a biographer who has as much space as he needs to develop his theme — and then reducing the result to miniature. I've been developing a natural liking for historical research and a desire to do it very well within the limits that I set myself.

What tempted me to write about Abraham Lincoln was the hope that I had learned enough to tackle a subject which would challenge all my powers and might possibly find them insufficient. I wouldn't do it for everyone — but Lincoln is such a fascinating man and was caught up in events of such importance that I believe he is worth the effort. I don't want to come out with a "Father Abraham" biography, or a revisionist one which tries to treat Lincoln as a man by emphasizing his weaknesses and mistakes. I don't want to belong to any school, but to do my own thinking — and a long, slow process it is on such a subject. This is only a young adult work, which Lincoln scholars will, at best, pat on the head as they pass it by. Librarians may perhaps do the same. But maybe, just maybe, I'll bring off something that not everyone could do. It won't give me fame and presumably won't make my fortune. But what a triumph to feel satisfied.

From *The Horn Book* for February 1975

IX

THE INTERNATIONAL WORLD OF CHILDREN'S BOOKS

Even during the eighteenth century, children's books were disregarding national boundaries. Perrault's fairy tales were translated into English in 1729, and after the American Revolution *A Little Pretty Pocket-Book* was offered for sale by Isaiah Thomas of Worcester, Massachusetts. As the nineteenth century progressed, the give-and-take increased. Peter Parley was as familiar in England as in the United States, *Little Women* was soon translated into Swedish and Russian, and young people of English-speaking countries had at their disposal Grimm's tales from Germany and Andersen's stories from Denmark. Before the century was over, *Heidi* and *Pinocchio* had joined the international world of children's books. In this century, the internationalization of children's literature has been deliberately fostered since the end of World War II by the founding of the International Youth Library in Munich and by the creation of the International Board on Books for Young People.

In the two following essays by Mary Ørvig, the reader is made aware of the existence of conditions and problems that face the authors and critics of children's literature in other parts of the world. At the same time, it is obvious that points of contact between them and us are not lacking. For example, Astrid Lindgren, Tove Jansson, and Maria Gripe are certainly widely cherished for their originality and their sensitivity to the dilemmas of the modern world; and Kornei Chukovsky touches the Anglo-American world of children's books not only because of his adaptation of *The Story of Dr. Dolittle* but because of his famous discussion of a perennial conflict: "The Battle of the Fairy Tale."

247

A COLLAGE:
Eight Women Who Write Books in Swedish for Children

By Mary Ørvig

BEFORE WORLD WAR I, the staple Swedish exports in the field of children's books were Selma Lagerlöf's *The Wonderful Adventures of Nils* [Pantheon]* and some of Elsa Beskow's picture books. Zacharias Topelius from Finland and Jeanna Oterdahl were also translated — but that was about all. Since World War II, the Swedish children's book has doubtless increased its hold on the export market since a number of authors have surmounted the language barriers of both East and West. Pride of place goes to ASTRID LINDGREN, whose *Pippi Longstocking* [Viking] has been translated into Bulgarian, Danish, English, Estonian, Finnish, French, Hebrew, Dutch, Icelandic, Italian, Japanese, Norwegian, Polish, Portuguese, Russian, Serbo-Croatian, Slovakian, Slovenian, Spanish, Swahili, German, and other languages, while Persian and Singhalese editions are now in preparation. Thus, Pippi speaks in a language which the majority of children can understand, regardless of where they live and how they are brought up.

Pippi Longstocking is a prime example of the anti-authoritarian book, of which there is much talk in Europe. Pippi stands for every child's dream of doing exactly what he or she wants to (regardless of any prohibitions), of feeling his or her strength and ability, and of enjoying himself or herself every minute. The book can be described as a children's safety valve against the pressure of authority and daily life: This is the secret of its incredible success.

There are still many adults — both parents and the experts in children's books — who do not understand its success. Actually, children's literature is well-endowed with independent and disobedient children, and books with characters of this kind can be regarded as children's protest literature written by authors who are on their side. Moreover, *Pippi Longstocking* is marked by a

*When a book has not been translated into English, the Swedish title will be given. When a translation has been made, the American or English publisher will be listed in brackets. The publication dates in the article indicate when the book was first published in Sweden.

curious kind of emancipation: Adults are completely superfluous. The main difference between Pippi and the libertarian characters of, say, James Barrie, Antoine de Saint-Exupéry, Maurice Druon, and Penelope Farmer — to mention only a few authors — is that Pippi is strong, cheerful, and generally happy, while the other children are delicate and mournful and bear all the trouble of the world on their small shoulders.

Many translations have succeeded in making Astrid Lindgren's writing well-known, but what is surprising is that her fairy tales have not aroused interest abroad. She has published three volumes in this genre: *Nils Karlsson-Pyssling* (1949), which won her the Nils Holgersson plaque in 1950; *Kajsa Kavat och andra barn* (1950); and *Sunnanäng* (1959). These stories have a melodious quality of their own which has not been equaled in Swedish storytelling since Selma Lagerlöf. The combination of an amazing plausibility in depicting the labyrinths of fantasy, a tenderness untrammeled by any vestige of sentimentality, and the wisdom by which the mental world of children is re-created makes these stories quite unforgettable. Most of them describe how lonely and sick children create a world of their own, which transcends the dreariness of their surroundings and enriches their lives. Astrid Lindgren frequently oscillates between black and pink. The gloomier aspect is particularly apparent in *Sunnanäng*, four fairy tales about Swedish poverty in the nineteenth century — full of poetry and compassionate melancholy.

Apart from Astrid Lindgren, the seven women authors to be presented in this collage are Tove Jansson, Irmelin Sandman Lilius, Edith Unnerstad, Britt C. Hallqvist, Anna Lisa Wärnlöf, Maria Gripe, and Gunnel Linde. Different as they are, they share the virtue of being able to write at the child's own level. Tove Jansson and Irmelin Sandman Lilius write in Swedish but live in Finland.

Finland is a bilingual country and has developed an interesting production of books in the Finnish language. This is a comparatively new departure, for it was only during the nineteenth century — when Finland was a Grand Duchy under Russian suzerainty — that the necessity and importance of children's literature in the native language began to be accepted — the motive, as usual, being nationalism and thoughts of independence. Before then — when Sweden and Finland were politically united — culture, literature, and education had been completely in the hands of the Swedes, who constituted the upper classes of Finland. During the 1860's the cultural elite began to forsake their native Swedish in favor of Finnish, so that material was needed to teach children their new language. In Finland, as in many other European countries at this time, children's books became a weapon in the struggle for a national culture, and many outstanding personalities made decisive contributions to this end.

The axiom that literature for children and young people does not move with the general tide of literary development and that it seldom reflects the period to which it belongs was valid in both Sweden and Finland. In Sweden, the years after 1812 were marked by unbroken peace. It has been our good fortune to have kept out of international conflicts, but Finland has been through a succession of agonizing wars. First came the Great War of 1914 and the final achievement of independence in 1917, which brought a bitter civil war in its wake. This was followed by a brief period of peace before the winter war of 1939-1940 and the vicissitudes of World War II. It was a long time before writers felt able to write about things nearer home; it was as if the turbulence and suffering of their times forced them to take sanctuary in the tranquility of nature, the idyll of childhood, or the carefreeness of school life. But presaged by developments in Sweden since 1945, the 1950's were a watershed in Finland, which resulted in the elimination of many well-worn clichés of children's literature.

TOVE JANSSON (born 1914) has illustrated her books herself, and the reader soon gets to know her Moomin world. The Moomins, although they walk on two legs, are not altogether unlike small hippopotami. They live in a family in their idyllic valley close to the sea or, as in one of the more recent books, in a lighthouse on a remote island. There is the adventurous Moominpappa, the Moomintroll, and the Snork maiden; the carefree, daydreaming Snufkin; Sniff, who is mean and edgy; My, an irascible little realist; conforming middle-class Hemulen; and a host of other creatures. All the books in this series so far have had a continuous plot, except for *Det osynliga barnet* (1962), a collection of short stories. *Moominpappa at Sea* [Walck], published in 1965, is a single novel with the depth and seriousness of the short stories.

In most of the Moomin books, the mainspring of events is some kind of disaster. The Moomin world is afflicted by floods, falling rockets, volcanic eruptions, and hurricanes. But these adversities serve only to heighten what is most important of all: liberty, friendship, and love. Tove Jansson writes about relationships to possessions and to a traditional way-of-life, about loneliness, fear, and security. The Moomin books depict the insecurity of contemporary man; at the same time, they show a genuine way to live. The most important thing is to cut loose from acquisitiveness and to love one's neighbor without expecting anything in return. Tove Jansson's writing is very much concerned with social relations and the importance of people coming to terms with each other. Although she had a predilection for idyllic family relations in her writing, the idyll is not hermetically sealed off from the outside world; for there is always lurking an unidentified menace which can obliterate everything in the twinkling of an eye. Nothing on this earth can endure, and inward calm is attainable if one does not clutch at transient things. Tootick, one of the key figures in *Moominland Midwinter* (1957) [Walck], says: "Everything is so uncertain and that is what I find so reassuring."

The debut of IRMELIN SANDMAN LILIUS (born 1936) as a realistic children's writer came in 1958 with *Historien om oss*, an unsentimental description of four motherless cousins living with their grandmother. Soon, however, she found her element in the fantastic tale. In 1962 she published *The Unicorn* [London: Lutterworth Press], the first of a series of books about Muddle, a girl whose happy homelife is accompanied by an intense world of fantasy. In the sequel, *The Maharajah Adventure* (1964) [London: Lutterworth Press], Muddle falls out with her parents and leaves home to encounter a host of adventures. The main character in the fourth book, *Morgonlandet* (1968), is Rufa, who wishes to leave this vale of tears because her father is going to remarry. Rufa and Muddle run away to an unknown country, Morgonlandet, where they meet with people from another planet. Eventually, they return home to encounter the new and unknown elements of everyday life with more assurance. This is the outward plot of the four books. In fact, the plot exists at many levels, and all of the many fantastic elements are apposite allusions to reality.

Like Tove Jansson, Irmelin Sandman Lilius raises many questions concerning the nature of life, such as relationship to possessions, reverence for life, or the rootlessness of mankind. She has also published a trilogy about Mrs. Sola, set in the small town

251

of Tulavall, with an orphan girl called Bonadea as the main character. Bonadea is the free and independent child who can shape her own life and can experience the world around her more intensely than anybody else. Irmelin Sandman Lilius has a poet's command of imagery. Her books depict the human situation, the hopes and beliefs of mankind. Many of her children's books have been translated into other languages, and it is good to know that children in other parts of the world have been given the chance to encounter her world of fantasy.

EDITH UNNERSTAD (born 1900) was also born and bred in Finland but moved to Sweden with her family in 1910. Her debut as a children's author came in 1932. A prolific writer, she is equally at home in the past and in the present. Her strength lies in presenting family relations and vivid personal portraits, and she has a formidable background knowledge. She stands with both feet firmly on the ground and describes exactly what she sees, accurately and dispassionately, but her view of reality is colored by the buoyancy of her narrative technique and by her positive attitude to life. She is also a writer of serious, melancholy, and ambiguous stories. There are probably few who know that she also has a large number of adult works to her credit.

The many books about that happy family of children, the Larssons, are too well-known to need mentioning. Instead, a few words may be said about *The Journey with Grandmother* (1960) [Macmillan] and *A Journey to England* (1960) [Macmillan, O.P.]. One is impressed by the profound, detailed knowledge to which these books bear witness. At the same time, the stories develop fluently, and the events are well-arranged. The two books about the haircraft workers have endowed children's literature with cultural history of the highest quality, thanks to the author's ability to bring her material to life and make it intelligible to children. Edith Unnerstad does not romanticize poverty; on the contrary, she gives us an authentic picture of the misery it entails. Thus, a reviewer in the *New Statesman* remarked that *A Journey to England* could equally well have been written in England — which is praise indeed.

Edith Unnerstad is one of the few Swedish children's writers to have dealt with the problems of the alien. In *Ensam hemma med Johnny* (1951), she portrayed a well-intentioned Swedish family, who consider it their duty to take care of the daughter of a Czech friend of theirs. The story is set during the years immediately following World War II; the main character is Tina, a Czech refugee longing for love and for proximity to those around her. She is in the middle of the puberty crisis and is finding it hard to come to terms with herself. The people around her are helpless when confronted by her demand for love and affection, and their predominant reaction is one of irritation. The fact that Tina has fallen in love with Johnny is only a side issue; for Johnny, like the idyllic summer island of the story, merely forms the backdrop to Tina's incurable alienation.

Edith Unnerstad does not believe that Tina will have an easy time of it: She is just as much on her own at the end of the book as in the beginning.

No, she doesn't remember much. But one thing she does know. In Prague she had everything which nobody can give her here. There she was at the center of everything. The whole world revolved about her and her alone. She knows this for sure, even though she cannot prove it. She needs no proof of it, except for other people. They do not understand. They do not believe.

Britt G. Hallqvist (born 1914) first made her mark as a writer in 1950 with *Rappens pa Blasopp*, which in verse and prose told the story of an ordinary Swedish family in its everyday tasks and flights of fancy. Earlier she had studied at the University of Lund, where she had displayed a capacity for writing verse to suit the most varied occasions. A funeral oration in verse, which she gave in Lund, caused Ragnar Josephson, at that time director of the Swedish National Theater, to commission her to translate Christopher Fry's *The Lady's Not for Burning*.

Britt Hallqvist married a clergyman, had four children, and moved from one parsonage to another until she finally returned to Lund. She feels that the many years she spent in different parts of Sweden did a great deal for her personal development: Intermittent changes of surroundings enable one to learn more about other people. She likes to frequent playgrounds and other places where children come together, studying their attitudes and listening to their talk.

Her debut in 1950 was followed by her *ABC* (1951), illustrated by Stig Lindberg, one of the loveliest and funniest picture books in Sweden. Then came a succession of books, one every year or so, some of them about everyday things and others pitched at a more fantastic level. There can be no doubt that she is one of

Sweden's most outstanding nonsense poets. She also writes straightforward and vigorous religious poetry for children, with no sobstuff or sentimentality. In *Jag skall fraga Gud* (1968), she portrays the relationship of a child to God in a way which is both self-evident and sincere. This anthology includes specimens of the kind of free verse which has interested her recently. One of the poems is called "Questions."

> When I see God
> I've got lots of things to ask Him about.
> Why there are snakes.
> Why there are wars.
> Why I can't do handstands
> Even though I practice.
> Why they let them shoot rabbits.
> Why everybody everywhere in the world
> can't get enough to eat.
> God won't be like grownups and say
> "I don't know"
> or "You wouldn't understand anyway."

Britt G. Hallqvist has a unique capacity for expressing herself in simple terms and putting herself in other people's places. Perhaps this is what makes her such an outstanding translator. Among other things, she has translated works by Edward Lear, Goethe's *Faust*, T. S. Eliot's *Old Possum's Book of Practical Cats* [Harcourt], and A. A. Milne's *When We Were Very Young* [Dutton] and *Now We Are Six* [Dutton]. In an anthology entitled *En vers i fickan* (1967), she has provided a cross section of German, English, and American children's poetry, including selections by Carl Sandburg, Hilda Conklin, Walter de la Mare, Beatrice Schenk de Regniers, Christian Morgenstern, and James Krüss. From the German, she has also translated Czech nursery rhymes and the poetry of Frantisek Hrubín. In Sweden, children's literature would have been a great deal poorer had it not been for Britt Hallqvist.

ANNA LISA WÄRNLÖF (born 1911) is a celebrated columnist, who has contributed under the pen name of Claque to some of Sweden's largest newspapers since 1942. *Pellas bok*, published in 1958, was commissioned by the editor of the Saga Publishing House, Harriet Alfons, who had read a childhood portrait written by Claque in 1956. It made such an impression on Mrs. Alfons — she felt as though it were a revelation of her own childhood — that she wrote and asked whether Claque would undertake to write a book. Eventually the answer came: "The only thing that worries me is that there won't be enough of a plot. . . . And it will be as old-fashioned as anything. Does it matter?"

Claque soon realized that she could dispense with plot. On the other hand, wittingly or unwittingly, she fell into a pattern of her own. On reading all of her books at one go, one is struck by the way in which the characters develop in a parallel manner. Claque is quite meticulous in following them up, even her newspaper characters who never find their way into a book.*

Two of the girl characters in her books are called Pella and Fredrika, both of whom mature consistently from their different starting points. Pella is a thoroughly positive, vivacious, and easily approachable personality, whose infectious humor never flags even when she is describing her more dismal moods. When Fredrika grows desperate, she is not easily distracted; her despair is so profound that the reader fears for her life. She has good reason to be gloomy: Everything she does goes wrong. If she extends her confidence — the dearest thing she possesses — to some miserable outcast, he turns out to be the most brutal robber and murderer that ever drew breath. If she lights a fire, the house burns down. If she falls in love, the object of her affections, the father in *The Boy Upstairs* (1961) [Harcourt, O.P.], is totally inaccessible. In her eagerness to please him, she almost cuts off her thumb. Worst of all are the ghastly cruelties that force their way over her lips when she is determined to be friendly to Susanne, her infinitely patient mother. One consistent theme in Claque's writing is that nothing is more harmful than mothers — at least where children and, above all, girls are concerned. There seem to be about three innocuous mothers in all her books, and they are all the mothers of boys.

Thus, Pella and Fredrika are as different as chalk and cheese, as night and day, but they do have one thing in common — they are sticklers for their integrity. In *Pellas andra bok* (1959), we read: "I don't want to feel sorry for people. I don't want them to feel sorry for me. It's not right to feel sorry for people. Sympathy, real sympathy, is different." In both cases, of course, barriers are broken down by love. Claque has not spent many words on love, and she is more interested in subtle erotic tension than in sexuality. But this only makes what she has written all the more effec-

*Based in part on an article about Claque by Harriet Alfons in the journal *Barn och kultur* (1970/5).

tive. Not only does she know how love arises; she can also show how it ceases: Witness what is perhaps her most remarkable book, *Boken om Agnes* (1963), which is mainly concerned with the integrity and friendship of two girls.

"Great artists are like the sea. They have room for everything, even the smallest things."* These statements are very true of Claque herself. Her books are packed tight with concrete details; she remembers everything. But one also has the impression that she has led a very mobile life in the center of her time. She must have sat in cafés listening to young people talking; she must have been in Paris and watched the deft fingers of the women knitting on the Métro. She knows exactly what line a seventeen-year-old girl will take in a particular emotional state. She displays a livelv and knowledgeable interest in clothes, food, and — above all — home design. And she can draw on an inexhaustible range of characters. It all seems so incredible when one learns that Claque is constantly on the move from one small Swedish town to another, carrying a minimum of luggage. She lives in almost complete seclusion, only communicating with the outside world through her husband, the artist Gustaf Adolf Wärnlöf. What is the secret of her incredible insight? Is it that her unique sensibility has enabled her to lay up an everlasting store of experiences with things and people?

MARIA GRIPE (born 1923) made her debut in 1954 with *I var lilla stad*, which told the story of a small town inhabited by humanized animals. During the next few years, this book was followed by two more books in the same style. In 1956 she published *Kvarteret Labyrinten*, which depicts the budding friendship of a boy and a girl living in the same block. We also meet an unknown, almost mystical boy, who appears from nowhere and foreshadows similar characters in later books. Many of these books have an atmosphere or an attitude which she was later to develop more deliberately. Her changes in literary style have been analyzed by Carin Mannheimer in an article in *Barn och kultur* (1971/2). *Pappa Pellerin's Daughter* [John Day], which appeared in 1963, is definitely something new in her development as a writer. The main character is Loella, a gaunt, patient figure continually battling with inward weaknesses and outward adversities. She is the odd child out, a school-girl village character. When her mother leaves for America, Loella is separated from her brothers and

*From *Pella i praktiken* (1960).

256

sisters and put into a children's home. She is forced to leave the forest and start life in the city. Loella is a child of impeccable integrity but devoid of humor or of any sense of security.

The book about Josephine, *Josephine* [Delacorte], which came out in 1961, is also about a lonely, insecure child. This was the book which made Maria Gripe's reputation. It is a restrained portrait of childhood in the realistic vein; the author tries to penetrate the mentality of the child to a greater depth than is commonly undertaken in children's books. Accordingly, *Josephine* is not so much about adventures and funny incidents as it is about the threads joining the comprehensible and the remote. Josephine knows that she is quite a different person from what her parents imagine, but she is mistaken concerning their expectations of her. She is a child who listens to adults and lets her own imagination and limited experience get to work on what she hears; and the result is a dangerous misunderstanding. But the misunderstanding is cleared up, and the world is put right again for Josephine.

In *Hugo and Josephine* (1962) [Delacorte], Josephine launches out into a much larger and more difficult world — school. She guesses what she is expected to do, namely to make herself the same as the others, in order to win acceptance. The scene is transformed by the arrival of Hugo. In him Josephine finds a friend who is different from everybody else. He does not need to know what other people think of him in order to feel that he exists. Josephine herself discovers the difference between them: "Either you must be exactly like all the others. Or you must be completely different from them — as Hugo is. You musn't ever be *nearly* like everyone else. As Josephine is." Hugo questions the rules laid down by school and society and is prepared to cut loose from everything without hurting anybody. This he does, knowing that rules and regulations are stupid and unnecessary and that he personally can manage best without them.

Hugo has a history of his own, and in the book called *Hugo* [Delacorte], published in 1966, we get to know him at close quarters and not merely through the effect he has on his surroundings. His mother is dead, and his father is serving a prison sentence — two events which arouse tremendous curiosity among his classmates but which he himself regards with superb equanimity. His norms are not those of the village. His world is not bounded by death or the prison gateway. Hugo breeds spiders, which give him ideas about human behavior patterns. He takes his leave of the village school because he has to find out "what happens when two rivers join up and flow together."

Apart from her realistic books, Maria Gripe has also written a series of others, including *Glasblasarns barn* (1964). The whole of this fairy tale is interwoven with a pattern of poetry, magic, mysticism, and shifts in time. At the bottom of it all is a fight between good and evil, life and death. *Glastunneln* (1969) combines both realism and fantasy. The book is about an ordinary Swedish boy who runs away from his family to Stockholm and makes friends with a blind girl, but the actual story is written in an elusive, almost surrealistic fairy-tale manner.

The basic theme of Maria Gripe's books — at least those written since 1960 — is the relationship between people and their role in life. In all her books she seeks opportunities of self-realization and liberation for her characters; she is constantly probing the boundaries constricting our lives. She is highly critical of the way in which adults treat children.

GUNNEL LINDE (born 1924) started with a book which appealed to practically no adults and practically all children. *Osynliga klubben och hönshusbaten* (1958) began as a radio program by Gunnel Linde, who is a producer at the Swedish Broadcasting Corporation and who now works on television. The book was written with a complete disregard for the interests of adult readers, and Gunnel Linde has consistently adhered to the same principle ever since.

The following year came *Chimney-Top Lane* (1959) [Harcourt], which — among other things — tells the story of nine-year-old Lena Maria Johansson. The house where she lives is old and gray and dreary, although the stones of which it is built have a golden glitter when the sun shines. *Chimney-Top Lane* is a reassuring idyll, but it does have its darker moments and is well-rooted in reality. Loneliness, unhappiness, and malice are also found in it. In 1962 came a sequel entitled *Till äventyrs i Skorstensgränd.*

Chimney-Top Lane was accompanied to the press by *Lurituri* (1959), a reassuring, humorous, and very exciting book for the young child. In this book Gunnel Linde gives free rein to her imagination and works in songs which are easy to read and sing. *Fröken Ensam Hemma aker gungstol* (1963) describes seven wonderful journeys made by a little girl in her rocking chair while her mother is out. She is accompanied on her travels by her teddy bears and a collection of imaginary animals. The writer has drawn an amusing landscape to illustrate the journeys. The girl in the stories conquers the horrors of life by facing up to them, and within her own world she can even overcome death. The text is punctuated at judicious intervals by verses which either summarize, explain, or anticipate. When the girl's mother returns home, the old room is almost exactly the same as when she left it.

The White Stone [Harcourt], which is unquestionably the richest and most mature of Gunnel Linde's works, came out in 1964. The story takes place about forty years ago and deals with the love of two children. It also deals with changes of identity and with the importance of creating an imaginary world when the everyday one becomes insufferably dreary. In this imaginary world the oppressed can gather strength and protection for their integrity, and human dignity can be repaired. None of Gunnel Linde's books can rival the way in which this one expresses that kind of human affection and understanding of which social involvement is but a small component. It is a wide-awake, sensible book — many-sided, with adventure and mysticism, fear and baseness, love and a wonderful happiness. It is impregnated with the author's joyful laughter and superb sense of humor. In her more recent books, such as *Eva-sjams land* (1967), one observes a change of style and method and an approach to a multitude of complex problems of human relations. Whenever we choose the person who is right, or the person we ought to feel sorry for, somebody is always left out, left in solitude.

Swedish children's literature during the sixties was marked by a broad social and even geographical frame of reference. New authors introduced new themes: the destruction of environment, the problems of the developing countries, the equality or inequality of the sexes, the pollution of the air, political violence, the class struggle, wars of aggression — the entire reality of our times. The authors tried to help children to see the nightmarish reality as it was and to encounter it in a new way. It will be interesting to see how these authors develop, for we should be grateful for provocative literature — provided it is well-written and to the point.

SOURCES REFERRED TO IN THE TEXT

Gripe, Maria. *Glasblasarns barn.* Stockholm: Bonnier, 1964.
Gripe, Maria. *Glastunneln.* Stockholm: Bonnier, 1969.
Gripe, Maria. *Hugo.* New York: Delacorte, 1970.
Gripe, Maria. *Hugo and Josephine.* New York: Delacorte, 1969.
Gripe, Maria. *I var lilla stad.* Stockholm: Bonnier, 1954.

Gripe, Maria. *Josephine*. New York: Delacorte, 1970.
Gripe, Maria. *Kvarteret Labyrinten*. Stockholm: Bonnier, 1956.
Gripe, Maria. *Pappa Pellerin's Daughter*. New York: John Day, 1966.
Hallqvist, Britt G. *Jag skall fraga Gud*. Stockholm: Bonnier, 1968.
Hallqvist, Britt G. *Rappens pa Blasopp*. Stockholm: Bonnier, 1950.
Hallqvist, Britt G. and Stig Lindberg. *ABC*. Stockholm: Natur och Kultur, 1951.
Jansson, Tove. *Det osynliga barnet och andra berättelser*. Stockholm: Gebers, 1962.
Jansson, Tove. *Moominland Midwinter*. New York: Walck, 1962.
Jansson, Tove. *Moominpappa at Sea*. New York: Walck, 1967.
Linde, Gunnel. *Chimney-Top Lane*. New York: Harcourt, Brace and World, 1965.
Linde, Gunnel. *Eva-sjams land*. Stockholm: Bonnier, 1967.
Linde, Gunnel. *Fröken Ensam Hemma aker gungstol*. Stockholm: Bonnier, 1963.
Linde, Gunnel. *Lurituri*. Stockholm: Bonnier, 1959.
Linde, Gunnel. *Osynliga klubben och hönshusbaten*. Stockholm: Bonnier, 1958.
Linde, Gunnel. *Till äventyrs i Skorstensgränd*. Stockholm: Bonnier, 1962.
Linde, Gunnel. *The White Stone*. New York: Harcourt, Brace and World, 1966.
Lindgren, Astrid. *Kajsa Kavat och andra barn*. Stockholm: Rabén & Sjögren, 1950.
  Brenda Brave Helps Grandmother. Adapted from the original by Kay Ware and Lucille Sutherland. St. Louis: Webster Publishing Company, 1961, O.P.
  Brenda Helps Grandmother. London: Burke, 1966.
  (Translations of one of the stories in the Swedish original.)
Lindgren, Astrid. *Nils Karlsson-Pyssling*. Stockholm: Rabén & Sjögren, 1949.
Lindgren, Astrid. *Pippi Longstocking*. New York: Viking, 1950.
Lindgren, Astrid. *Sunnanäng*. Stockholm: Rabén & Sjögren, 1959.
Sandman Lilius, Irmelin. *Historien om oss*. Stockholm: Bonnier, 1958.
Sandman Lilius, Irmelin. *The Maharajah Adventure*. London: Lutterworth Press, 1966.
Sandman Lilius, Irmelin. *Morgonlandet*. Stockholm: Bonnier, 1968.
Sandman Lilius, Irmelin. *The Unicorn*. London: Lutterworth Press, 1964.
Unnerstad, Edith. *Ensam hemma med Johnny*. Stockholm: Norstedt, 1951.
Unnerstad, Edith. *A Journey to England*. New York: Macmillan, 1961, O.P.
Unnerstad, Edith. *The Journey with Grandmother*. New York: Macmillan, 1960.
Wärnlöf, Anna Lisa. *Boken om Agnes*. Stockholm: Svensk läraretidnings förlag, 1963.
Wärnlöf, Anna Lisa. *The Boy Upstairs*. New York: Harcourt, Brace and World, 1963, O.P.
Wärnlöf, Anna Lisa. *Pella i praktiken*. Stockholm: Svensk läraretidnings förlag, 1960,
Wärnlöf, Anna Lisa. *Pellas andra bok*. Stockholm: Svensk läraretidnings förlag, 1959.
Wärnlöf, Anna Lisa. *Pellas bok*. Stockholm: Svensk läraretidnings förlag, 1958.

From *The Horn Book* for February 1973 and April 1973

A RUSSIAN VIEW OF CHILDHOOD: THE CONTRIBUTION OF KORNEI I. CHUKOVSKY (1882-1969)*

By MARY ØRVIG

ORNEI CHUKOVSKY'S death on October 28, 1969, in the writers' village of Peredelkino near Moscow, deprived Soviet Russian children's literature, literary criticism, and journalism of a key figure. Talented, knowledgeable, and incessantly active, he lived to the great age of eighty-seven, retaining his vitality and *joie de vivre* almost to the very end; few could rival his command of Soviet Russian children's literature produced after the October Revolution of 1917. He witnessed the troubled birth and the protracted growing pains of that literature, but he had been interested in children's literature even before the Revolution when — as literary critic for various periodicals — he strongly attacked children's writers and editors of children's magazines for their ignorance of the interests of children. As one of the leading Soviet critics and — at the height of his extraordinarily productive career — as a translator of the classics of the Western world, he also played an important role as a great children's poet, adored by his readers.

Chukovsky took an active part in the debate concerning children's literature; his criticism and commentaries were uncompromising and undeviating — but there was always a twinkle in his eye. Even in the somber climate of Soviet literature, he had the courage to maintain that ideologically inspired children's books were worthless unless they were also endowed with artistic merit and unless their authors were adept at writing specifically for children. After 1917, during a period in which more and more pressure was put on children's literature as an instrument of socialist education, Chukovsky's poems and stories for children showed a deliberate drift towards humorous tales and nonsense verses. Before his time, exuberant play on words had hardly existed in Russian literary verse, al-

Translated by Roger G. Tanner

*Given on July 10, 1974, in New York City at the Children's Book Council/ALA Joint Committee Meeting honoring the *Horn Book Magazine*.

though centuries of Czarist oppression had made Russian authors past masters at allegory and allusion, expecting the public to read between the lines. In a succession of polemic articles, Chukovsky was to defend nonsense and fantasy as important components in children's books, questioning at the same time the didactic and the platitudinous. He refused to accept that children's literature should be stamped by the bitterness of the times, by party consciousness, and by the demand for unconditional ideological involvement. Although Chukovsky was a member of the Communist party, he saw through the ideological frauds of the Stalin era and still managed to survive. He bequeathed the proceeds of several of his works to Alexander Solzhenitsyn in order to alleviate the difficult conditions under which Solzhenitsyn had to work. Chukovsky was a man of courage and integrity.

On a variety of occasions, Chukovsky sketched the contours of his life. He was born in St. Petersburg on April 1, 1882, the son of a student and a peasant girl from the Ukraine. His mother's name was Jekaterina Osipovna Kornejtjuk; the name of his father is unknown. The couple went their separate ways when Chukovsky was about three, and his mother took him to Odessa, where she settled and obtained work as a cook. They lived in great poverty, but the boy was able to go to school for a while, though later he was expelled; eventually, he matriculated as a private candidate. The reason for his expulsion is to be found in a memorandum issued in 1887 by the Imperial Office of Education, proclaiming that children of coachmen, footmen, and cooks — among others — had no need of higher education. Chukovsky was trained as a bookbinder, earned his living at a variety of occupations, and read everything he could lay his hands on.

He tells the interesting story of a turning point in his life. One day in 1898 he went to the town's flea market to buy a Russian edition of *Astronomie populaire* by the French astronomer Camille Flammarion. It was not to be found, even though Chukovsky made a very thorough search; but to mollify the bookseller, he bought a book called *Teach Yourself English*. It was a dirty, dog-eared, old volume; and there were many pages missing. But even before he got home to his attic, he had learned several words of English. This book was to entrance him for an entire year.

Chukovsky — the future translator and translation theorist — considered the penetration of a new language as one of the major experiences of his life; and he came to regard private study as an important method which should be tried by as many people as possible. As we know, Maxim Gorky was of the same opinion. Chukovsky attached primary importance to what the individual discovered for himself: By this method, children found their way in the world; and he felt that everybody else should do likewise. In addition, Chukovsky became acquainted with the poetry of Walt Whitman. Whitman's free verse and his proclamation of democratic brotherhood made an indelible impression on the young Russian and caused him to see everything in a new light: the stars, plants and animals, the whole of human life. At the age of seventeen, Chukovsky began translating Whitman into Russian. Later on, of course, he was not satisfied with this first version, and he revised it — as, indeed, he was constantly doing with most of his translations. His Whitman translations went through several editions in the Soviet Union, number eleven having appeared in 1969.

Of course, the important Russian writers meant a great deal to him during these early years, especially Anton Chekhov. He lived with the works of Chekhov, and later said that he was never to experience again such a degree of identification between literature and life. He knew nothing about life as yet, but Chekhov supplied him with insights through the power of his human portraits and the skill of his imagery.

In 1898 Chukovsky also embarked on his first attempt at writing — which he characterized as a profound philosophical work. One chapter dealt with contemporary art, and a good friend who heard it read aloud took the section with him to the periodical *Odesskije Novosti* (*The Odessa News*). The chapter was published, and Chukovsky was offered employment. He received more and more commissions — he wrote about authors, exhibitions of art, and foreign literature — until eventually he was able to live on his writing. In 1903 the editors decided to make him their London correspondent with a monthly salary of one hundred rubles. But, in the meantime, the journal — or at least its foreign coverage — was banned, and Chukovsky suddenly found himself marooned in London with nothing to live on. He stayed there for a year and a half, living on or below the bread line; but during this period he nevertheless contrived to study the works of the great English and American writers, as well as nonsense and nursery rhymes. Fifty-eight years later he returned to England to receive an honorary doctorate from the University of Oxford in recognition of his great services as a translator. He had translated works by Walt Whitman, Mark Twain, Oscar Wilde, Rudyard Kipling, G. K. Chesterton, and O. Henry. He also retold *Robinson Crusoe* and *The Story of Dr. Dolittle*.

Chukovsky managed to get a free passage on board the ship *Gisela Gredle*, bound for Constantinople. From there he made his way back to Odessa. It was now 1905, and the Russian Revolution had broken out. In the Black Sea, the crew of the battleship *Potemkin* had mutinied. This made a profound impression on Chukovsky, and by the time he joined the editorial staff of the periodical *Signal* in St. Petersburg, he had sided with the Revolution. His openness of speech, naturally enough, got him into trouble, including an indictment for *lèse majesté*. As usual, the trial took place *in camera*, but Chukovsky was fortunate enough to be defended by the famous Oscar Grusenberg, who had previously defended Maxim Gorky and Vladimir Korolenko against similar charges. Chukovsky was acquitted but went in for less politically controversial journalism. By 1909 he had made a name for himself as a literary critic, and he had become a highly prolific writer. Also, at this time, he began to take an interest in children's literature; and in a pamphlet "*K materjam o detskich zjurnalach*" ("To Mothers Concerning Magazines for Children") published in 1911, he attacked the inferior quality and artificiality of contemporary children's literature in Russia. Even before World War I, he had published his first paper on the language of children.

In 1915 Maxim Gorky decided to add a children's book department to his publishing house Parus (The Snail). Gorky and Chukovsky had not met, but Gorky had been aware of Chukovsky's criticism since 1911. Together they decided to visit the Russian painter Ilya Repin, who had devoted his art to the life and history of the oppressed Russian people. Repin lived in the authors' and artists' village Kuokkola in Finland, a gathering place for the St. Petersburg intelligentsia. Gorky and Chukovsky hoped to find drawings which they could use for their children's books. The two first met on the train, and the story goes they had trouble conversing. Suddenly, Gorky proposed, "Let's talk about children," whereupon they began to discuss the policy of their children's publishing venture, the anthologies that might be considered, and the commissioned works that should be planned. Before the end of the journey, they managed to outline the whole of their program. Chukovsky undertook an anthology, which was later published under the title *Jolka* (*The Fir Tree*). Gorky and Chukovsky met again several times; one day Gorky said that the anthology should also include poetry for children and suggested that Chukovsky try his hand at this genre. Chukovsky demurred, for he had never written anything in the way of children's poetry.

By now, Chukovsky was married to Maria Borisovna Goldfield and had a family. In 1916 his little son had fallen ill in Helsinki, and he traveled there to fetch him. The boy was running a high temperature and was uneasy, so to calm him and give him something else to think about, his father began telling him a story in verse to the rhythm of the train about a crocodile who used to saunter round the streets puffing out smoke. His name was, of course, Krokodil Krokodilovitch. The following year, the story was published in twelve installments in the children's book supplement of the journal *Niva* (*The Field*). Chukovsky was the editor of this supplement.

In 1917 came the October Revolution and a harsher reality. As early as 1905, in his work *Party Organization and Party Literature*, Lenin had introduced the concept of "party literature," which should join forces with the political movement within the truly progressive and revolutionary class. In 1924, the Thirteenth Communist Party Congress passed a resolution calling for the creation of a children's literature under the close supervision and direction of the Party, with a view to initiating children into the idea of the class struggle and thus promoting proletarian internationalism and collective work. Many authors and artists became aware of strong political pressure; at the same time, they also understood the needs and demands of the times regarding literature and art. A number of writers and poets with a sense of artistic responsibility tried their hand at stories and tales for children, not only because they expected to find political security in the sphere of children's books — which soon enough turned out to be a mistake — but because fantastic tales and the nonsense genre were the ideal vehicles for what they had to say. C. S. Lewis makes exactly this point in his essay "On Three Ways of Writing for Children":

The third way, which is the only one I could ever use myself, consists in writing a children's story because a children's story is the best art form for something you have to say: just as a composer might write a Dead March not because there was a public funeral in view but because certain musical ideas that had occurred to him went best into that form. This method could apply to other kinds of children's literature besides stories.*

The truth of this statement is particularly borne out by authors and poets belonging to the Oberiutists. The Russian Oberiutists (the name is an abbreviation of the Russian expression *Association for True Art*) and the Western Dadaists had a great deal in common, but it was impossible in the new Soviet society for the Oberiutists to devote themselves exclusively to the apparently meaningless. Political realities were too obtrusive and many of the exponents of the genre were too outspoken: Daniel Charms (pseudonym for Daniel Yuvatchov), Nikolai Oleynikov, Alexandr Vvedensky, and Constantine Vaginov, all of whom were born in about 1900. They came from nonliterary environments and were interested in rhymes, doggerels, word games, and tales, which they reshaped and recited during many literary happenings. They delighted in presenting their surroundings in childlike terms — blowing it up, scaling it down, standing to one side of it; in short, they used all the various stylistic devices of fantasy. Together these four comprised the brain trust of the children's magazines *Jozj* (*Hedgehog*) and *Tjizj* (*Siskin*). An outstanding sample of the work of the group is the verse tale "Ivan Ivanovitch Samovar," published by Daniel Charms in 1929, based to a large extent on the treasury of Russian proverbs. But unlike the Dadaists of the West, the Oberiutists were not allowed to grow old in peace; many of them died in the prisons and concentration camps of the Stalin era or during the hardships of World War II.

After "Crocodile," Chukovsky wrote a long succession of narrative poems. The twenties and thirties were a very productive period for him, but his children's poetry was often rejected until the farsighted editor Lev Kliatchko ventured to publish Chukovsky's rhyming tales, full of linguistic fun and games, and im-

*C. S. Lewis. "On Three Ways of Writing for Children." *Horn Book Magazine* XXXIX (October 1963), p. 460.

bued with a profound understanding of the child's urge to laugh. One example of the critical attitude taken to Chukovsky's poetry for children is to be found in the *Smaller Soviet Encyclopaedia* (10 volumes, 1931) where we read, in an article signed G. Lelevitch, that Chukovsky's small books for children reflect the atmosphere in the nursery of a bourgeois family of the prerevolutionary intelligentsia. The *Greater Soviet Encyclopaedia* (40 volumes, 1934) condemns Chukovsky's poetry for children on account of certain elements of bourgeois ideology.

Chukovsky fought for the child's right to optimism and fantasy; and concern for the child's integrity is a consistent feature of his authorship. He defended children's need for fairy tales and their right to develop their imagination and strengthen their grasp of reality by this means. Unlike many, he refused to see the child merely as a participant in the contemporary ideological drama, even though he also dreamed of the ultimate objective of the free, happy socialist individual. Many courageous and visionary poets sympathized with him, but he came in for a great deal of vehement criticism, especially from the educationalists. By 1925 Chukovsky thought that a rejoinder was called for, and in that year he published the first edition of his book *Ot dvuch do pjati* (*From Two to Five*), which first appeared under the title *Malenkije deti* (*Small Children*). In this book — apart from his important studies of children's own poetic composition, their linguistic development, their attitude to life, their urge to conquest, and their powers of observation — he also presented his views of the principles governing children's literature and its position and function in a socialist society. It should be borne in mind that in Czarist Russia hardly any debate on children's literature had existed in the true sense of the term — the literary climate was too austere for that. One of the few persons to have taken an interest in such matters was the well-known literary critic Vissarion Belinsky (1811-1848).

A completely new generation of children's writers emerged during the twenties and thirties. Some writers for adults also became interested in children's books, encouraged above all by Maxim Gorky, who became the leader, theoretician, and critic of this literature. Like Chukovsky, Gorky defended the place of the fairy tale in children's reading, though he accorded the ideological importance of children's books a much more prominent position in the development of the socialist society than did

Chukovsky. Vladimir Mayakovsky (1894-1930), one of the great names in early Soviet Russian poetry, published a succession of children's poems. Often specially commissioned, they were suitable for recitation — for example, *"Tjto takoje chorosjo i tjto takoje plocho"* ("What Is Good and What Is Bad," 1925). Mayakovsky is known as an exquisite stylist and is not considered to have compromised his style in his didactic poems. Anton Makarenko (1888-1939), a friend of Gorky's, played an important part. Between 1933 and 1935, he published *"Pedagogitjeskaja poema"* ("A Pedagogical Poem"), a well-known work in Eastern Europe, whose main character is not an individual child but an entire colony of children. Makarenko had worked during the twenties together with orphans, or "wild children" as they were called, and had evolved his own methods of child education by practical experimentation. Despite heavy resistance at first from the professional pedagogues, he eventually became something of an authority in this sphere. He is also known by his *Lektsii dlja roditelej* (*Lectures to Parents*, 1940).* Another prominent name is that of Lionka Panteleyev (1908-), pseudonym for Alexey Ivanovitch Yeremeyev. Panteleyev had been one of the "wild children" and in his book *Tjasy* (1929), about Petka and the watch, he tells the story of a boy whose life takes a new direction in an orphanage.

As mentioned earlier, Chukovsky's *From Two to Five* was first published in 1925. By 1970 it had gone through twenty-one Russian editions (none were allowed to appear between 1939 and 1955). The book is bibliographically troublesome, and one has great difficulty following the revisions and expansions of the various Russian editions. A Slovakian edition appeared in 1959, a Czech in 1960, a Polish in 1962, an American in 1963, and an East German in 1968. It is interesting to note how different emphases are effected in the American and East German editions by the disposition of the chapters and by means of abridgments and adaptations. In the American edition one misses, regretfully, Chukovsky's own account of his years of silence when his children's books were officially banned.

The Swedish edition, to be published during 1974 and translated by Staffan Skott, a Slavonic linguist, is based on the nineteenth Russian edition printed in 1966. In a postscript, Skott has

*A. S. Makarenko, *Collective Family: A Handbook for Russian Parents* (Gloucester, Massachusetts: Peter Smith, 1973).

given a detailed account of the work of translation, of the procedure he has adopted with quotations and anecdotes and untranslatable Russian concepts. From a linguistic point of view he stresses that the Russian language is often more easily accessible to children than, for example, the Swedish: Russian has a large number of prefixes and suffixes, while Swedish forms words by amalgamation — which can be perplexing for children.

In the first chapter of his book, Chukovsky establishes that no adult works as hard as the child during the first phase of language learning. He refutes the theorists who maintain that the child merely passively imitates adult speech, quoting clear examples of how children constantly oppose adult ways of talking. He stresses the importance of knowledgeable and sensible language training; for unless care is taken, one is liable to inhibit the child's immense joy of discovery in the course of its linguistic development, and its language may become as insipid as that of adults. In the second chapter, entitled "The Tireless Explorer," Chukovsky draws our attention to the problems and dilemmas which the child can encounter during its daily exploration of reality. The whole of the child's effort is aimed at endowing the chaos around it with at least a semblance of order. It is up to adults to answer and try to resolve the child's interminable questions, but we should do so with moderation and discrimination.

Sensitivity and tact play major parts in connection with children's questions about the origin of life and death. In the section on the concept of death, Chukovsky refers to the child's need for optimism. All children between the ages of two and five believe or want to believe that the aim of life is pleasure and happiness, and this belief is crucial to their mental growth. Chukovsky regards their inherent *joie de vivre* as a great source of strength on which children can draw during long periods of illness or in adversity of other kinds. He applies this need for happiness to children's reading preferences and sees the happy ending as something important to them. He illustrates this by giving samples of children's own versions of well-known folk tales — for example, "Little Red Riding Hood." Immediately after hearing this story, one little girl drew something resembling a large toadstool and told the family: "This is a rock — the Grandmother hid herself behind it. The wolf couldn't find her and didn't eat her up." Chukovsky also gives examples of the new attitudes of

269

Soviet children concerning God, equality, and nationalized means of production. Where sex education is concerned, Chukovsky believes that children are capable of defending themselves against impatient adults who try to inform them prematurely. On this point, he quotes A. S. Makarenko, whose attitude to sexual issues was surely unusually prudish even then and is by now completely passé.

In later editions of his book, Chukovsky defines the problems more closely in the chapter "The Battle for the Fairy Tale" by recalling events which he had experienced since 1929. For instance, in 1929 he was in a children's hospital in the Crimea. To cheer up the sick, unhappy children, he read a Munchausen story. He was interrupted by one of the nurses, who was appalled by his choice of literature. An educationalist also rushed to the scene, protesting that fairy tales and untruthful stories were not the thing for Soviet children. What they needed first and foremost was facts and reality. Chukovsky retorted that it was this very confrontation with fantasy that enabled children to try out their sense of reality — but to no avail. All his efforts at using other books were vetoed; the staff insisted on books about diesel engines and radio. After this cautionary tale, Chukovsky embarks on his brilliant defense of the child's right to fantasy, nonsense, and fairy tales. He makes short shrift of those writers who have conformed to a narrow-minded type of realism, and he demands a sense of proportion.

Chukovsky refutes those who claim that the fairy tale is hostile to Leninism. By 1956 he imagined that the so-called Battle for the Fairy Tale was over and that the role of the fairy tale in developing children and stimulating their imagination had been established once and for all. But to his chagrin he found that the advance of preschool pedagogics had not put an end to narrow-mindedness and arbitrary criticism. He also takes exception to certain attitudes towards fairy stories and tales of fantasy in books for small children expressed in many resolutions adopted by the children's literature section of the Soviet Federation of Authors. Although basic points of view within the Federation had changed, Chukovsky was perturbed by the meddling disposition of the dogmatists and called for renewed and unceasing vigilance.

Using Russian children's rhymes and doggerel as a basis, Chukovsky proceeds to analyze what he terms "plausible absurdities" — children's love of the absurd, the upside down, whatever breaks up the established order of things. He shows how children learn via nonsense to understand the mechanics of humor. As the child's apprehension of nonsense increases, so does its knowledge of the proper order of things. Every deviation in stories, rhymes, and doggerels from what is correct and conventional reinforces the child's knowledge of reality. Accordingly, nonsense is an important means of intellectual training.

Chukovsky also discusses the opposition to nonsense put up by the educationalists during periods when facts and realism were regarded as the only reading matter fit for children. He recalls earlier British and American writers whose books were solely designed to establish religion and good habits. The English philosopher John Locke gets a broadside in Chukovsky's own inimitable way. Chukovsky brings his criticism up to the present age and waxes satirical over what he terms the "English provincial mentality," which he discerns in both adaptations and illustrations of English nursery rhymes. Personally, I think Chukovsky is being unfair on this point since — most unusually for him — he bases a cast-iron contention on far too little material. In this particular respect, the prolonged cultural isolation of the U. S. S. R. affected the prominent translator and linguistic theorist. It is interesting to note that the East German edition of *From Two to Five* devotes a great deal of space to Chukovsky's criticism of English attitudes.

In the chapter entitled "Children and Their Poetry," Chukovsky claims that, in their efforts to master language, children always try to range words in pairs, in a pattern. This soon leads them to attempt rhyming, usually in connection with their own rhythmical games. Rhyming often comes to an end when the time of childish running and skipping is over. Up to the age of four, children are spontaneous poets, singers, and dancers. Beyond that age their poetry becomes deliberate, and they imitate adults a great deal. Here Chukovsky sharply criticizes school anthologies of poetry and teachers' red pens; he regrets that so many poets and writers have been lost through incompetence and misguided opinions. However, he claims, the situation is changing in the Soviet Union, and he quotes Russian literature on the subject to prove his point. The chapter concludes with an incisive analysis of language and form in the poetry of children and states again and again its important function — to put thoughts and feelings in order, to familiarize the child with, and to enrich a child's use of, language.

The final chapter contains Chukovsky's thirteen commandments to children's poets, or, as he prefers to call them, thirteen modest rules. First, he dwells on a number of Russian poets who have successfully drawn on popular poetry — Piotr Ershov and Vladimir Mayakovsky — and also on the writer of fables, Ivan Krylov. In these thirteen commandments Chukovsky stresses, among other things, the importance of children's verses being made clear, rhythmical, and musical. They should also be suitable for use in games. The rhymes should bring out the meaning and significance of the words; every line must have an independent meaning. It is essential to avoid using too many adjectives. On this point he quotes the German specialist on the child's language, William Stern (1881-1938), who claimed that when children accumulate their vocabularies, nouns come first, then verbs, and adjectives last. Chukovsky also believes that the best meter is the trochee.

Finally, Chukovsky is at pains to point out that, even while taking all these factors into consideration, children's poets are not entitled to disregard the basic demands of adult poetry. A badly constructed poem cannot be either pleasurable or useful to the child who reads it. The poet should not only work at the child's level but should also help the child to acquire new thoughts and insights; and he should do so slowly and gently. Chukovsky considers it unfortunate in the extreme that many educationalists and critics still judge children's poetry on the basis of its content without realizing that the finest content is of no avail when presented in the form of bad poetry. Still, as Chukovsky sees it, Soviet poets and writers have the advantage of working closer to the children who constitute their reading public and of enjoying more intimate communication with many different kinds of children than is the case with Western writers. In *From Two to Five*, the message is one of urgency. It is time, Chukovsky says, for the adult world to change its approach to children, to try to live with them and not to one side of them.

Despite Chukovsky's unique vitality, there is, nevertheless, no doubt that he was unacquainted with many features of modern Western research in children's linguistic development. Besides, Chukovsky was a linguistic nationalist obsessed by the beautiful, expressive Russian language, so full of linguistic possibilities. Linguistic poverty in our sense of the word did not exist for him, and it would have been interesting to know how he would have interpreted the reluctance to read that exists today in so many Western countries where illiteracy is considered a thing of the past.

In one of his last works, written during the autumn of 1969,* Chukovsky describes the origins of many of his narrative poems, including his famous "Dr. Aybolit" ("Dr. Oùch-It-Hurts"). Dr. Aybolit, a Russian Dr. Dolittle, helps animals with their aches, pains, and problems. Later on, Chukovsky also made an adaptation of Hugh Lofting's *The Story of Dr. Dolittle*, combining it with various additions from "Dr. Aybolit." In the autobiographical article, Chukovsky gives interesting working descriptions and humorous closeups, and we are also made to understand restrictions on his writing during various periods. He had difficulties especially with children's poetry, whereas his literary criticism and his portraits of authors went unscathed. Chukovsky declares that writing poetry for children demanded that he adopt an optimistic standpoint and that good must be made to triumph over evil. This optimism frequently eluded him during the long years of dogmatic stagnation in the intellectual life of the Soviet Union, and he was prey to a despair which one does not normally associate with him. In the article, he tries to give an indication of the paralysis and silence which have afflicted so many Soviet writers.

During the last decade or so of his life, Chukovsky came to be greatly appreciated by Soviet officialdom. He received the Order of Lenin in 1957 and became an honorary Ph.D. of Moscow University the same year. He was awarded the Lenin Prize — the finest distinction attainable by a Russian author — in 1962, the same year as he received an honorary doctorate from the University of Oxford. But one wishes that, despite all this recognition, he had enjoyed complete liberty of the spoken and written word, so that he could have told us even more about the thoughts and feelings of children.

NOTES AND COMMENTS

Chukovsky dealt with the theory of translation in *Vysokoje iskusstvo, o printsipach chudozjestvennogo perevoda*, first pub-

*Published in *Literaturnaya Rossiya*, No. 4, January 23, 1970; No. 5, January 30, 1970; also in English in *The Horn Book Magazine*, December 1970 and February 1971.

lished in 1941; later edition, 1964. His autobiography is called *Iz vospominanij* (1958). The year of the publication of his pamphlet *"K materjam o detskich zjurnalach"* ("To Mothers Concerning Magazines for Children") has already been given in the article as 1911. (In an autobiographical note in *"Sovetskije pisateli, avtobiografiji,"** however, he himself is not quite certain of the date.) Also, other early articles about children's books were included in this pamphlet.

Biographical material about Chukovsky is fairly abundant outside the Soviet Union, although there are differences concerning facts and dates. In searching for such material, however, it should be borne in mind that because of differences in transcription of the Cyrillic alphabet, his name has many spellings — in English, Chukovsky; in German, Tschukowski; in Polish, Czech, Slovak, Cukovskij; and in Swedish, Tjukovskij. In Eastern Europe one finds several articles about Chukovsky in journals and newspapers, but also quite a few in the West. In Sweden, for instance, Hans Björkegren (a journalist and the translator of Alexander Solzhenitsyn) wrote a lengthy article about Chukovsky on the occasion of his honorary degree at Oxford (*Stockholms-Tidningen*, August 2, 1962). Worth noting is Lauren G. Leighton's translation of Chukovsky's "Confessions of an Old Story-Teller," published in *The Horn Book Magazine* in December 1970 and February 1971.

Finally, generous help with facts and bibliographic details given in Stockholm by the Slavonic literary historian Lars Erik Blomqvist and of the Slavonic linguist Staffan Skott should be gratefully acknowledged.

*Part 2 (Moscow 1959), p. 636.

From *The Horn Book* for October 1974

X

TRANSLATION

The concept of an international children's literature is liberating, for it ignores national boundaries and accepts the idea that an outstanding children's book can appeal to any citizen of "the republic of childhood." Considered more carefully, the concept needs occasionally to be approached pragmatically and seen in relationship to the difficult and delicate task of translation. It is at this point that both children's literature and adult literature can be conceived as going in absolutely the same direction, since the standards for translating a children's book can be no different from those for translating an adult book.

Some of the problems of translation are technical; for example, both Elizabeth Shub and Maria Polushkin tell of their struggles — some of them humorous — in conveying the connotation of particular words. Erik Haugaard's reflections are more general in nature, and he tells of the insights he gained from his work as a translator of Andersen. Edward Fenton considers the possibilities of language and the complexities of words, working toward the proposition that a translation should be a work of literature in its own right. He says, "A literary translation is only truly successful if it has the qualities of credibility, of inevitability, of authority. It has to give the impression of having been written originally in the language of the reader." In other words, even in the translation of a children's book, one is trying to convey the sense and direction of a culture as well as of a language.

RANDOM THOUGHTS BY
A TRANSLATOR OF ANDERSEN

By Erik Christian Haugaard

TIME SEEMS TO HAVE CHANGED ITS PACE; and though our life is longer than our forefathers' was, the minutes, hours, and days of which it consists, seem to pass with such rapidity that we have no time to reflect upon our fate. Tomorrow becomes yesterday without ever having had the chance of being today. We change our philosophers and heroes with more ease than we change our breakfast food. The great, unchanging nature which, like a giant clock, kept time for generations of men, we have destroyed in the cities and suburbs. Soon — maybe even in a generation — we shall have wrecked our earth for those who, either by choice or circumstance, may be living a different kind of life from ours. Truly, our time is difficult, and I do not envy the children who are growing up in it.

Now, if I had a solution, if I were like the medicine peddlers of another age who with simple ointment could cure anything from a rattlesnake bite to tuberculosis, then I should use my own books as a drum to beat upon in order to attract your attention. I would scream: "Read Haugaard and be cured!" But I have no solution: no slogan, nor prescription, nor pill that can be swallowed painlessly to bring you happiness and contentment. Indeed, if I had such a cure or were such a prophet, I might even remain mute for the sake of the "salvation market," which — it seems to me — is in a sad state of overproduction since so many of its wares are being sold as bargains.

Because I have not found, nor even searched for, the magic word which opens the door to the mountain cave where all the treasures of the world are hidden, it does not mean that I have neither values nor philosophy to guide me. To me, being human is infinitely difficult, for we are the jest of the universe: the mortal Gods. I do believe that there is something called truth; and like Orwell, I think it goes on existing regardless of how many lies we tell. I know, too, that the pleasures and pains of loving are unchanged and uninfluenced by such things as rocket flights to the moon. Even when I was very young, I felt that I was alone, and to bear that loneliness I needed friends. This search for truth, love, and friendship made me read; and in literature I found an echo of my own aspirations. The suffering of those who had lived before me took some of the sting out of my own suffering, whereas their joy and happiness enhanced mine and made it even more intense. The world became very large because it was not curtailed by time, and graves and tombs did not contain corpses but people who were wonderfully alive. Only those ages before art or literature existed were, indeed, truly dark; all the rest belonged to me—a treasure given to everyone who cares to claim it. Each generation has been enriched by the artists, philosophers, musicians of its time; and the wealth of the world is ever increasing. It has always seemed to me a sad lot to have lived before Mozart or Shakespeare, and never to have known them.

Folk tales and fairy tales were the first literature that I came into contact with, and I still have a taste for them. Their world — of good and evil, of magic, of spells cast by nasty stepmothers, of brooks and trees that speak — is too pleasant a place to be reserved only for children. The fairy tale is, in a way, our most constant friend, for it stays with us through all the phases of our life, unlike other forms of art and literature.

Hans Christian Andersen's fairy tales differ greatly from the traditional fairy tales and folk tales: They have the stamp of his personal views and of his particular genius. He borrowed the structure and the simplicity of the folk tale; but unlike certain other writers who have tried to write in the same form, he never became a prisoner of it. I think his ease with the form stems from familiarity, a feeling that these stories belonged to him and his class. Whatever you really own, you are free to dispose of, to change, and to treat in whatever manner you care to. I think Andersen felt this sense of freedom towards the fairy tale, a sense he did not feel towards the other literary forms he tried.

Andersen says in his little sketch *The Thorny Path*, "The fairy tale and reality are not far apart, but the fairy tale is in harmony: earthly, and time-bound. Reality has harmony, too; but it can only be found in the boundless time of eternity." I think it is exactly this harmony which makes the fairy tales so irresistible and so comforting to read. For though our age denies it, there is within most human beings a longing for harmony.

The second part of the statement is interesting, too; for Hans

Christian Andersen takes for granted that in the unknown, in the boundless time of eternity, man's life will achieve a harmony denied to it in its short space of years on earth. This idea is based on faith, but so is the idea that only disharmony exists; and of the two beliefs, the first is by far the easier to live by and, I think, the better for producing art. If the absurd is time-bound, it becomes possible to smile at it or laugh about it; but if the absurd is eternal and disharmony endless, then both laughter and tears are out of place; and only the scream of the madman seems fitting for this world of ours.

In order to understand Andersen, it is not enough to notice what he ridiculed and what he questioned. It is well to understand, too, what he deemed above questioning and beyond ridicule. In a very nonsectarian way, he was a Christian. He did believe in the existence of a just God and a life after this one. Such a belief was necessary in order to make life bearable for him. The injustices he had seen in his childhood were so great that unless there was a just afterlife, God was nothing but a cruel tyrant. That possibility was far more than he could face; the suffering he had seen must have had meaning.

The second thing beyond questioning was the worthwhileness of art and literature. "First one goes through such terrible suffering and then one becomes famous," he once wrote, and because of this particular sentence he has been much ridiculed. Yet, I think it shows good sense, and it would be a fitting — if a brief — biography of most great poets. In an age in which it is the height of fashion to declare that you create only for your own time, for the moment, and that you do not care if your works live, Andersen's point of view must seem terribly dated and presumptuous. He wanted fame passionately; he desired immortality. He wanted to create something worthy of being compared to the works of those great writers who had lived before him. He felt such an ambition was not dishonorable; on the contrary, I am sure he took for granted that it was virtuous. I am afraid that in the eyes of our modest poets and artists of today, who carefully stay away from fame in order to seek notoriety, poor Andersen's ambition may indeed seem very childish. But the wish for fame and immortality is a great spur; it makes the artist try to expand his talent. For only through what he creates can immortality be won — politics stop at the grave, even in art.

Andersen's first few fairy tales were written specifically for children, though grownups should be able to bear listening as well. The tales were meant to be read aloud, just as the fairy tales and folk tales of the people always have been. I have tried to keep this spoken quality in my translation, and I hope that I have succeeded.

As I plowed through such a tremendous undertaking as this translation has been, thoughts and ideas about Andersen's fairy tales came to me. For Andersen — though he appears so simple and direct — is not so easy to dissect, and every statement that one makes about his style can also be easily refuted. Still, there is one observation which might be of value. That animals, or even plants, have a soul is not so surprising — they do in many fables and fairy tales. But that inanimate objects — such as darning needles, collars, or chairs — also possess a soul is, I believe, Andersen's own discovery.

What Andersen does is to make the darning needle into a human being, which is something quite different from making a human being into a darning needle. The darning needle speaks and reasons as a needle: Its past, all its memories and desires are a needle's, *not a human being's*. This is why his inanimate objects are so terribly real. They speak with human voices about their experiences as objects. He deals in a similar manner with animals: A duck does not question that fatness is beauty, any more than a rat would question that a larder is paradise. They have desires and are frustrated when they cannot fulfill them; but their desires are reasonable for their kind. Therefore, they are sometimes tragic, sometimes funny, but never cute.

To Andersen the new world of science and technology was both attractive and frightening. He concerned himself with it again and again; in 1850 he foresaw that travel by air would eventually surpass other forms of transportation. In a little sketch called *The Millennium*, which is about the future citizens of America who would come to visit the old country, he has the tourists carry a little book which is a best seller in the Western Hemisphere — *Europe Seen in Eight Days*.

As I translated, I became exceedingly aware of Andersen's amazing ability to read the future. But still, it came as a surprise to me when I found out that he had an opinion about children looking at television. In a story called *The Philosopher's Stone*, a magician, the wisest of all men, lives in a castle built in the center of the enormous Tree of the Sun. In one of the lower chambers of the castle he has a room with walls of glass, which mirror the whole world and enable him to see what is happening everywhere. "The pictures on the walls were alive and moving; they showed everything that was taking place, no matter where it was happening; all one had to have were the time and the desire to look. But too much is too much, even for the wisest of men." But the wisest of men had children, and they were fond of this particular room in the castle, and they did not feel that too much was too much. "Many times his young sons expressed a wish to take part in the struggles, they were seeing on the walls, and perform great deeds of valour. Then their father would sigh and say: 'The ways of the world are bitter and filled with grief, what you see is not reality, for you watch it from the safe world of childhood and that makes all the difference.' " I think the difference between reality and what is shown on the screen could hardly be better expressed.

Few writers have written so much and so realistically about the poet and his relationship to his patrons and to his public. *The Nightingale, In the Duckyard,* and *The Gardener and His Master,* and many others all have this relationship as their theme. In order for one to understand fully and appreciate the sharpness and bitterness running through these stories, I should explain something about the Danish character. We Danes are very fond of sarcasm; and whereas satire is a sharp knife, sarcasm is a rusty, blunted one which leaves an ugly gash and often leads to blood poisoning. From childhood, a Dane gets used to being called a sweet child when he is naughty, and clever when he is stupid. He learns that words have only the meaning implied by the tone in which they are said. He is taught to defend himself against ridicule by making others ridiculous. This Danish vice can at times become a virtue: It partly accounts for a person like Hitler being regarded as absurd. But before one rejoices too much, one has to remember that a true Dane will laugh as heartily and as viciously at a Kierkegaard or a Hans Christian Andersen. The worst crime that any Dane can commit is to think that he is "something," that he may be a swan instead of an ugly duckling. From the very beginning of his literary career Andersen wanted to become a great writer; his ambitions were enormous. For this he was punished again and again, and he could not really understand why; for what harm was there in wanting to become great, in wishing for eternal fame? None in reality, but the Danes are a friendly people: They like to feel at home, like to be cozy, and have mistaken comfort for happiness. And one cannot be cozy except with one's own kind: The hen yard with a couple of swans running about is just not cozy; one must either make them into ducks or hens, or get rid of them altogether.

If there had been only bitterness in Hans Christian Andersen, he would not have survived. His greatness lies in the fact that he did understand the ducks and the hens, even though he was a swan. Besides talent and intelligence, he had what I believe is terribly important for any writer to possess — a deep feeling of pity. This feeling of pity came from his ability to identify with and understand the basic tragicomedy of being human. It is the ability to see beyond your own intelligence to your own foolishness, and beyond your own sensitivity to your own brutality, which makes the whole process of creation possible.

What I have written are random thoughts on Andersen. I had hoped when I began my translation, that I would ultimately be able to make some valuable remarks about translating. But Andersen's style is unique, and what I might say about translating Andersen would hardly be applicable to anyone else. Besides, if I have discovered anything at all, it is that there are no rules: Translation is a matter of constant compromise; and whenever a sacrifice had to be made, the alternatives were different in nature. Only the feeling of regret and frustration was the same.

I am a poet, not a scholar. I wanted to make a new translation because I felt that one was needed and that I could do it, since I write in both Danish and English. (Though I prefer the latter language, the former was my only tongue until my seventeenth year.) The work was far more difficult than I dreamt it would be, but I hope most fervently that my readers will deem my translation worthwhile.

From *The Horn Book* for December 1972

A FEW WORDS ON TRANSLATION

By Maria Polushkin

I HAVE NEVER REALLY THOUGHT of myself as a translator; and when I was asked to speak about translation, my feeling was one of surprise. For most of my adult life, I have been an editor of children's books. Circumstances have drawn me away from the publishing world, at least physically; and I confess that I am very much pleased to find myself in the role of a translator instead of that of an editor. How did it happen?

I sometimes feel as though I have come to translating the easy way, having been born in Russia, always speaking Russian at home, yet growing up in America. I have never gone through the ordeal of slowly, bit by bit, acquiring a second language through scholarship. My two languages have always been there, a legacy from my *émigré* parents, who have crossed many borders in their lifetime. My image of a translator as a person of vast academic learning — well, it just doesn't apply to me.

When I was an editor, I read a great deal of work, some of it quite dreadful; but every once in a while I came across something that was terrific. It made me feel good, and I wanted to do what I could to help make it available to a larger public. Now, when it comes to translation, it is very much the same kind of process. Because of my Russian background, I naturally read a great deal of Russian writing; much of it also quite dreadful. But, once in a great while, I discover something that is truly exciting. So, my impulse to translate is not very different from my longstanding professional inclinations.

At a translation seminar at Columbia University, Jorge Luis Borges stated that he thought there were two legitimate ways of translating. "One way," he said, "is to attempt a literal translation; the other, is to try a *re-creation*." Although I hope I have never wandered so far afield as to be accused of taking unwarranted liberties with another writer's work, I must say that I favor re-creation to literal translation. I think Borges made the point most tellingly when he reminded the audience of the Latin sentence *"Ars longa, vita brevis."* "When Chaucer," he said, "chose to put that into English, he did not write 'Art long, life short,' which would have been rather cut and dried, but he

283

translated it in this fashion: 'The lyf so short, the craft so longe to lerne.' "

My own view is that, first of all, a translator must be a reader — a sympathetic, analytic reader — and, secondly, that she ought to be a writer herself. I am beginning to suspect that my old image of a translator as a person bent over a huge array of dictionaries and obscure volumes on syntactical usage is not really what translation is all about. For me, translation is more like a creative art than a science. I immerse myself in another writer's art, probing and analyzing every nuance; and, then, I set about trying to re-create that work in what amounts to a different medium — in this case, the English language.

When I read Anatolii Aleksin's *A Late-born Child* (World), which turned out to be my first translation, I was genuinely entertained. I laughed out loud in several places and was moved to sadness in others. I had found a good book. What next? If I had read this in English, I would certainly have wanted to publish it. But, better yet, I thought, why not translate it myself? I wrote a reader's report, sent it to a publisher, and waited for the decision. "Yes. It sounds good; go ahead," they said. And then the work began. I read the book again. I made notes and jotted down obvious problems. What would I do about the names? It seems only a Russian can keep the names in a Russian novel straight. Ivan is never just Ivan; he can also be Ivan Petrovitch, Vanya, Vanyushka, Ivan Petrovitch Popov. In my translation, the protagonist Leonid, Lenya in the familiar form, became Anglicized to Lenny.

How would I find words in English that would convey to an American reader what I had experienced when I read the Russian? I had been reading just for the pleasure of it, not aware of language at all, taking my two languages for granted. Now, the parts that had been funny suddenly made me sad. How could I have failed to notice that they had only been funny because of a twist in a familiar Russian word, a pun that defied translation?

Once I was past my initial interest and excitement, the process of translation was one of intense anxiety and disorientation. For long periods of time, I felt like a person suffering from aphasia in two languages at once. But, a commitment had been made; there were promises to keep; and sometimes only the prospect of having to face my editor kept me going.

After some of the initial problems were solved — such as what to do about the names — and a certain pace of work had been established, other problems began to arise. I began to see defects in the original story that were not apparent to me in my first enthusiastic reading. The going was slow. My translation, if accurate, seemed clumsy; if elegant, then perhaps faithless to the original. By that time, I was genuinely sorry that I had ever conceived of the entire project. I was sure that what I had in hand was pure drivel.

Somehow, the problems were worked out one by one. I wish I could tell you how. The first draft became the second; and the second, the third; and finally, because the publisher was pushing me, there came a final version. And I returned to a normal existence. The reviews were pleasing; and, perhaps not so strangely, the problems faded quickly from my memory.

About two and one half years later, I found myself reading another Russian book that held me spellbound, A. Linevski's *An Old Tale Carved Out of Stone* (Crown). It couldn't have been more different from the first, and I forgot my resolve never to do another translation. It was a story set in Neolithic Siberia. The protagonist was a young boy who was forced to become shaman for his tribe. It was a great story, full of adventure and action and problems that for all their antiquity could not have been more relevant for today's young people. A tiny voice crept into my consciousness, frantically trying to remind me of the agonies I had gone through in the past. As I considered undertaking this new translation, I said to myself, "But, listen; this is really different. You won't have to worry about translating all those patronymics that no one understands. You won't have to deal with the familiar and polite usages of *you* and *thou*. This story is set in the past. This is all different." Well, I bit. And no sooner had the actual work of translating begun than there I was, struggling with totally new problems that were just as difficult to solve. I could *not* find a word for the female equivalent of shaman. There were *witches, priestesses, sorceresses*; but none of those words had the flavor or feeling that I needed to convey. The word would have to denote an entire class of female makers of magic as well as their leader. My solution, for better or worse, was a plural ending for the Russian word *koldunya*. Thus, the High Koldunya was the leader of all the *koldunyii*. A similar problem with the title

285

for the leader of the warrior class led to an unintentional pun that went unnoticed until my somewhat overly amused husband pointed it out. For three chapters I had been referring to the Head Hunter. Though an evil man in the story, the Glavni, as I later decided to call him, was far from a head-hunting cannibal.

Though they may seem petty, I think these problems illustrate the most central difficulty in translation. What do you do when there is simply no equivalent word in English? It's hard to overestimate my despair. I combed dictionaries, encyclopedias, and archaeological texts. I telephoned my anthropology professor at Hunter College. (Her specialty was Siberia, and she knew Russian well.) I even wrote desperate letters to my father, who works at the Library of Congress. No one had an answer that didn't entail a footnote as long as your arm. The solution, as I've said, was simple but illuminating. The Russian words would have to stay. Some words are not translatable, and that's how the Head Hunter became the Glavni.

It would seem that I've learned my lesson twice over. Surely, the art of translation demands too high a price. It couldn't possibly be worth the anxiety and the aggravation. Friends and relatives who have seen me in the throes of a translation say that it couldn't, and I might have agreed with them — if I hadn't stumbled on a book of Russian fairy tales the other day. They've never been translated quite right, I thought . . .

From *The Horn Book* for June 1974

AN ADVENTURE IN TRANSLATION

By Elizabeth Shub

I ONCE KNEW A PHILOLOGIST who traveled to India in search of a verb, or rather, in search of a verb root. He found it and had a very pleasant journey besides.

I was reminded of my friend recently in connection with a small linguistic adventure of my own. Mine took place at home base, mainly at my desk, and my search was for a noun — in fact, for the definition of the German word *Raspelbrot*, which appeared in a story by the Brothers Grimm that I was translating. I was being forced to conclude that the word was "untranslatable." But no translator comes to such a humiliating decision lightly. If he cannot use what he finds, he knows he must find something he can use.

This is the story of *Raspelbrot*.

Raspelbrot? Obviously some kind of bread.

I pick up my trusty *Cassell's*. It isn't in it.

I pick up the telephone and call a friend whose mother tongue is German.

"Never heard of it. Must be something local. Probably obsolete. Call so-and-so. She will surely know."

So-and-so is a lovely elderly lady, very cultured and scholarly. Her mother tongue, too, is German.

"Have you tried the dictionary?"

"Yes."

"Of course you know that *Brot* means bread?"

"Yes, of course."

"Therefore, it was a kind of bread. . . ."

"Yes."

"And *Raspel* . . ." she said. "We have an expression *Süssholz raspeln*. It means to say sweet things if you are flirting. I do not see how this can be bread . . . unless . . . maybe sweet bread? Wait one moment. I will look in *my* dictionary."

"But. . . ."

A long pause. I had just about decided that shortcuts never work and that the time had come to pay a visit to the New York Public Library's foreign-language section and do some honest-to-goodness research. . . .

A triumphant voice returned to the phone.

"I have found it in *my* dictionary. It means 'rasped bread.' "

"Rasped bread! What is that?"

"I do not know. It is English!"

"What dictionary do you have?"

"*Cassell's.*"

"So do I. It's not in mine. Is yours an old edition?"

"Not very. It is 1912."

I thanked her and hung up, feeling quite confident that since I had a definition I would be able to find exactly what *Raspelbrot* was. I got a bright idea. If anyone could tell me about rasped bread it would be Craig Claiborne. I called *The New York Times*. Craig Claiborne was in Europe. No one on the Desk had ever heard of rasped bread. When I found out, would I please let them know?

I decided to call the foreign-language library before I went there. The German-language librarian did not know what *Raspelbrot* was, but most obligingly suggested that she would look it up in her "large" dictionary.

"Here it is!" she said. "It means 'grated bread.' It is clear," she continued, "*Raspel* means file or grate, *Brot* means bread — grated bread!"

"Do you mean bread crumbs?" I asked.

"I think you are right," she replied admiringly. "But I suggest you call Goethe House. Someone there may know exactly."

For a fleeting moment I was quite happy with bread crumbs. But when I translated the sentence in question it read: "I have just eaten an ovenful of bread crumbs. . . ."

I knew there was something wrong. An ovenful of *bread crumbs!*

The Grimms had lived in both Kassel and Berlin, and many of the folk tales had originated in the Kassel area.

I wrote a letter to a friend in Berlin.

I wrote a letter to a friend in Kassel.

Within a week both replied. *Raspelbrot* means bread crumbs.

I began to rationalize. Perhaps it was intended to be funny. And, after all, the character involved was one of those little old gray men in disguise. He *might* have eaten bread crumbs. Nevertheless, it wasn't convincing.

Why not just use the word bread?

It's not bread; it's *Raspelbrot*.

I called Goethe House. The very nice young lady to whom I spoke did not know what *Raspelbrot* was. It did sound familiar though. It reminded her of something in her childhood. Something with raisins in it. She wasn't sure. She would ask around. Would I call her tomorrow?

When I called the following day, she explained that the raisin bread of her childhood had been something quite different. A colleague of hers, however, had a very plausible theory. There was an old prison in Kassel called Raspelhaus; *Raspelbrot* was probably the prison bread. It also sounded plausible to me. But, alas, it didn't work. Why would a character as free as a bird eat an ovenful of prison bread?

The young lady had also mentioned to me that there was a Grimm museum in Kassel. Conscience dictated that I write to it. In due course, I received a reply from the director of the Grimm museum himself.

"*Raspelbrot*," he wrote, "is a white bread baked at intense heat. The high-temperature baking results in a crust so hard that it must be rasped or filed off with a rasp (a very coarse file) before the inner eatable bread can be consumed. *Raspelbrot*, a food of inferior quality, was eaten by the poor and usually baked in a community oven. Because of its low nutritional value it was not very filling. In the context of the story, it follows that a hunger as great as the starving man's could not be stilled even though he ate the whole ovenful of such bread. As far as I know, there is no English expression for this word. I'm afraid you will have to write around it."

I must admit that I was briefly tempted to intrude a parenthetical explanatory sentence or two in deference to the Grimms' ethnological orientation. Luckily the temptation was brief. Surely I could find one or two brilliant words that would do it. But try finding one or two words for "a poor man's white bread of inferior nutritional value, baked at intense heat so that the resulting crust is stone hard and must be rasped off before the inner eatable bread can be consumed."

Besides, today the common meaning of *Raspelbrot* is "bread crumbs." For purposes of this story I said firmly to myself, *Raspelbrot* is untranslatable. I took the museum director's advice and wrote "around it."

With some satisfaction I called my scholarly friend and told her my solution. "After all," I said, "every translation has its own limitations." There was a pause.

"Of course, you have read the Schlegel and Tieck translations of Shakespeare," she replied. "*They* are better than the original."

BLIND IDIOT: THE PROBLEMS OF TRANSLATION*

By EDWARD FENTON

THE FOREIGNER who lives in Greece, which happens to be my home now both by adoption and by marriage, has to confront a great many problems. One of the most serious of these is going to the movies. For one thing, Greek is not dubbed into films from abroad. This lack could be a distinct advantage; but since most Greeks cannot follow the dialogue in American, English, French, or Italian they chatter all through the film and rely on subtitles printed in Greek. For the foreigner, however, in whose native language the film was originally made, it is not always easy to understand what is being said on the screen. First of all, the Greeks all around him, acting as though in church, invariably have a great deal of pressing gossip to exchange and consider being shushed as an intolerable rudeness on the part of others. Secondly, in most cases the projectionist, ignorant of the film's original tongue, is apt to have the sound track slightly off-register so that even if the dialogue were being attended to by the audience with the respect usually reserved for dire political news, it would be utterly incomprehensible, like the announcements of flights at airports. As a result, one learns in sheer self-defense to read the Greek subtitles. Eventually one even develops considerable fluency and can laugh at the right places.

Not long ago, I was rewarded in an Athenian cinema by being able simultaneously to catch both the spoken dialogue and the Greek translation. The actor on the screen was quoting a familiar line from Shakespeare. "Friends, Romans, countrymen!" he said. And the Greek subtitler, having omitted the word *Romans* as making no sense in that particular context — there being no Italians evident on the screen — conveyed the line as "Friends, farmers!" I feel that there is no more appropriate way to launch into a discussion of the problems of translation than by greeting the reader in the same way. "Friends, farmers. . . ."

*Based on a speech given on May 4, 1976, for the Children's Books International II at the Boston Public Library.

In post-Renaissance Western thought, everything turns out to be, eventually, an echo from the Italian. We might as well begin with a well-known Italian saying and go on from there. "*Traduttore, traditore.*" Italians have said it since Petrarch's time, if not before. "Translator, traitor." The problem seems to have started in a place which has since given its name to confusion. According to Genesis, it happened some time after Noah's flood.

And the whole earth was of one language, and of one speech. And it came to pass, as they journeyed from the east, that they found a plain in the land of Shinar; and they dwelt there. And they said, one to another, Go to, let us make brick, and burn them thoroughly. . . . And they said, Go to, let us build us a city and a tower, whose top may reach unto heaven; and let us make us a name, lest we be scattered abroad upon the face of the whole earth. And the Lord came down to see the city and the tower, which the children of men builded. And the Lord said, Behold, the people is one, and they have all one language . . . and now nothing will be restrained from them, which they have imagined to do. Go to, let us go down, and there confound their language, that they may not understand one another's speech. So the Lord scattered them abroad from thence upon the face of all the earth: and they left off to build the city. Therefore is the name of it called Babel; because the Lord did there confound the language of all the earth: and from thence did the Lord scatter them abroad upon the face of all the earth.

This account can be said to be the first recorded instance of culture shock.

Two points strike me as being especially significant. First, the importance of a name. "Let us make us a *name* lest we be scattered abroad upon the face of the whole earth." And secondly, the jealousy of the Lord that men, having one language, would be so powerful that "nothing will be restrained from them" and would, therefore, be a threat to Him.

Ever since the crumbling of Babel's tower, human beings have been divided by speech. It is still, as it was then, a source of profound confusion for men to be confronted with other men who possess all the same organs and functions, presumably experience the same feelings, and certainly belong to the same species — and have as their only difference the fundamental difference of speech. What is even more astonishing is the fact that within the same language men are further divided, cut off by divisions of geography, class, occupation and, a fairly recent phenomenon, generation.

Before we can tackle the problems of translation from one language to another, it might be appropriate to define what we actually mean by language. According to the nearest dictionary, language is a combination of vocal sounds to which meaning is attributed: the expression or communication of thoughts and feelings. On that basis, we could declare language to be concrete, or organized, thought. Language is also the way of thought of a people. It contains a collective past, a way of life, a code of social manners, sexual mores, and even a pattern of worship. It is a culture. Significantly, in this context the only requirements which the Byzantines set down for membership in the Eastern Roman Empire were not those of race or color, but religion and language. To be a citizen you had to be Christian and Greek-speaking.

To demonstrate how language can reflect a specific way of life, I would like to tell of a situation once pointed out to me by an Arabic scholar. A Moslem patriarch, being polygamous, is entitled to take on young wives. His wealth and power are judged, after all, by his progeny. At the same time he must not forget his obligation to his first wife, who possesses seniority and the position of honor in his household. In a part of the world where women blossom early and lose their bloom comparatively quickly, this obligation is not always easy to carry out. Therefore, it is not uncustomary for the patriarch to take to his bed, along with the senior spouse, one of the more recent wives who will provide the stimulus to enable him to fulfill his duties toward the first wife. This complicated social situation, which has required an extended paragraph to explain in English, is covered in the Arabic language by a single word of one syllable.

"It is only upon contact with a foreign language," wrote André Gide, "that one becomes aware of the deficiencies of one's own. A Frenchman who only knows French can never perceive its shortcomings."

In today's liberal circles it is unfashionable to generalize about other national groups, much less to indulge in laughter at them. The truth, however, is that nations do differ insofar as their languages cause them to think differently. Anyone who is bilingual or multilingual will reveal that moving from one language into another is not a matter merely of the substitution of one word for another but a complete shifting of mental gears. One simply does not think in Italian as one does in German. The very placing of the verb at the end of the sentence, which occurs in German, alters the mental process. It is safe to say that the

French language, which is so balanced and logical, reflects the French turn of mind if, indeed, it does not actually shape it. Italian is an open, emotional language, direct and personal. At the same time it is so formal as to have three forms of the second person. One could go on infinitely, discussing the national character of any country as mirrored in its language. We even speak, for instance, of the Englishman's special humor. Which brings us, briefly, to English.

Without being in the least chauvinistic, I can say that few of us fully realize our tremendous good fortune in having what is called English as our mother tongue. It is a language of extraordinary flexibility and richness. English has constantly been fed and replenished by other languages. The old Anglo-Saxon foundation has had blood transfusions from the Norse, the Teutonic, Latin, and Greek; 1066 meant not only the Norman Conquest but also the vein of French speech which crossed the English Channel with William the Conqueror. More recently, American speech with its varied and fascinating forms — some of them reflecting waves of post-Plymouth Rock immigration, such as Yiddish, Italian, the Slavic tongues — has also become an integral part of English. And while other languages remained frozen in a dichotomy between the written tongue and the demotic (a problem which some languages such as Greek face even today), English possesses its historical richness and suppleness because the writers who have used it have always written in the language spoken by the people.

This consideration brings us to another important aspect of language: the historical. Speech reflects the moral, sexual, social, and even religious climate of a period. People in Chaucer's time spoke differently from those in Shakespeare's and from those in the Augustan Age of Pope. Nowadays the gallop of language is even faster. The language of each decade possesses a different coloration from that of the preceding one. The Victorians could not use a more explicit word for a woman's legs than *limbs*. Imagine them confronted with the anatomical and pathological explicitness of today's journals and daily newspapers. Even morality in language is a matter of time and geography. One is reminded of those well-meaning missionaries who went to Polynesia and provided their would-be converts with bright cotton Mother Hubbards to cover up their nakedness, only to find that the garments had been quite logically and sensibly translated into gay turbans and headcloths, leaving the heathen areas completely unconverted.

Aside from the historical shifts in a language, there is the fact — as we have already mentioned — that languages exist within a language. To begin with, there are the divisions caused by geography. I can remember sitting in a square in Ravenna with a Florentine friend. When I asked him what the people at the next table were saying, he said that he hadn't the faintest notion. The local dialect was incomprehensible to him. Yet Ravenna is only a few hours drive from Florence. One has only to think of the extraordinary variations in English to be found in the British Isles, not only among the Scotch, the Welsh, and the Irish but among the English alone. There are differences of class — the subject of George Bernard Shaw's play *Pygmalion*, in which his cockney drab of a heroine is transformed, via speech, into my fair lady. In almost all countries social class is strongly marked by speech. I remember a South African girl during the war complaining about the American troops she met at dances in Capetown. In talking to them, she said in distress, you could never be sure whether they were gentlemen or not. The French, if you make an error in their language, seldom attribute it to your being a foreigner but assume at once that you are *mal élevé* — ill-bred.

Even more fascinating than the social differences affecting a language are the differences of occupation. Cant, or jargon, was — to begin with — the secret slang of thieves or beggars. Words from thieves' rhyming slang are now part of normal English usage, such as, *use your loaf. Loaf* in this case derives from *loaf of bread*, to rhyme with *head*. A great many other such languages keep coming to light, surfacing from many subcultures and minorities — sexual, criminal, and professional as well as ethnic.

Finally, there is the language within a language created by the gap between generations. Teenagers are a comparatively recent division of society. Many of us can recall a time when, as a class, they did not exist. Now they comprise a formidable force with their own economic and social clout and, furthermore, with their own constantly shifting language. In passing, I would like to mention that in some languages, such as Italian, there is an entirely special vocabulary of tenderness which is used in addressing small children. By this I do not mean baby talk, which is detestable and degrading in any language.

Another aspect of a language which must be considered is the effect of its own literature upon it. A living language is like a palimpsest, layer upon layer, with meanings shining through it with curious iridescence. What would English be without, for instance, such all-pervading influences as the King James version of the Bible, Mother Goose, Shakespeare, Lewis Carroll, and Hemingway — to take a few names at random? In Italy the language was marked forever by Dante, and it is only since World War II that Italian writers have been able to emerge from the shadow of his *dolce stil nuovo* which, when it first appeared, acted as a crystallizing agent. Like all molds, however, when adhered to too long, it ended up as a paralyzer.

We must also consider the musical quality of a language: its sound, its rhythm. A Danish friend who has lived in America for many years reports that whenever she returns to Copenhagen to see her family she has a sore throat for weeks as a result of repitching her voice. African bushmen have a peculiar kind of speech composed of clicking sounds, which are almost impossible for anyone not born to them to master. John Millington Synge wrote of Irish that there was no language like it "for soothing and quieting." When spoken properly, French employs an entirely different set of muscles from those which produce English or German.

I often think that one of the reasons the Greeks and the Turks find it so difficult to resolve their acute differences is the fact that their respective languages contrast so radically and are so differently produced. The Greeks are generally small and quick. They are not quiet people by nature. They revel in sound. Out of them come explosive syllables which originate deep in the belly and emerge from full throats. The Greek word for *no* is *ochi*, with a deeply gutteral *ch*. The Turks on the other hand are dignified and quiet. They are large, solid, sedentary, and stately people from whom, to one's astonishment, come a series of high head tones. Their word for *no* is, characteristically, *yok* or merely a silent jerking backward of the head, frequently accompanied by a lordly lowering of the eyelids.

Perhaps one of the most revealing clues to the special qualities of different languages was given to me by a friend from Italy who was reading an American comic strip one day. He looked up and asked what was meant by the words *arf-arf* which he had just encountered. I explained that it was an alternate for *woof-woof* or *bow-wow* and that it indicated canine speech. He regarded me indignantly. He was sure I was concealing something. "How can you say such a thing," he said, "when everyone knows that what a dog says is *boo-boo*?" The Babel-like confusion prevails even in a case like this, which one would consider comparatively simple. Do dogs change their barking accents when they cross human language boundaries? Evidently they do. German dogs say *wau-wau*. French dogs, presumably more refined, express themselves with *oua-oua*. In Greek it is *gav-gav* and in Arabic, *gau-gau*. A Japanese dog, however, says *wan-wan*. Eventually some learned agency will doubtless make a fascinating intercultural or cross-cultural survey of animal sounds around the world.

I have already tried to explain why we are so fortunate in possessing English as our mother tongue. I was discussing it then purely from the point of view of its qualities as an instrument of thought, as a language per se. There is also a practical aspect to consider.

English is today's universal lingua franca. We learn that the people of India, divided by their own languages, communicate with each other in the language of the defunct and deposed Empire. We travel all over the world confident that wherever we end up, we will encounter someone who knows a little English. The airlines all use English. It is possible for a person who knows only English to keep thoroughly up-to-date in any professional field, however scientifically recondite. In fact, a monolingual person whose only language is English can actually be what we call a cultivated person or at least pass for such. Everything exists in English. We are, in fact, apt to be rather smug about it.

Let us, with a thrust of the imagination, consider the reverse of the medal. We might start with the most elementary of cultural exchanges, foreign travel. Does a Finn, a Pole, or a Moslem Indian expect to be understood in Finnish, Polish, or Urdu wherever he goes? Furthermore, in a country with only a few million speakers of the language, no one can even pretend to be educated or even practice one of the learned professions without being fluent in one or two of the so-called world languages. In Greece I am constantly being reminded of this. Almost every street corner in Athens has its foreign-language institute where, according to the signboards, one can learn German and French and, more importantly, English or American. Even for the lower middle classes in small countries, a knowledge of English or French is today a matter of economic life or death.

Consider the problem of a writer in Dutch, Hungarian, or Greek. His audience is limited by the fact that he writes in a language understood at best by only a small percentage of the world's population. I remember the astonishment expressed by a group of Greek writers when they learned that I could make a living, modest enough to be sure, solely by writing, even though I was neither a Hemingway, a Faulkner, nor a Jacqueline Susann. I think rather sadly of such writers as Xenopoulos and Papadiamandis in Greece — and there must be many others like them in other countries — who, had they been born into a world language like English, French, or German, would have enjoyed a wide celebrity and the material comforts which accompany it. Because they wrote in Greek, however, and were never adequately translated (if at all), they never found a public beyond the frontiers of Greek and, despite their genius, remain known to a relatively small circle of readers.

For those languages which, for lack of a better word, we must call minority tongues, translation is the lifeline — not merely on a technological but also on a bread-and-butter level. It is a matter of economic survival. As for us, in our secure fortress of English, it does not behoove us to remain complacent. The problem of translation is fully as important for us as it is for the users of less privileged languages. We, too, require to be nourished by other cultures and by other ages. Without our bridges to them we would become isolated, insular, falsely arrogant — not to say inbred. Without this exchange we would suffer a kind of cultural anemia.

Take the field of children's books alone. Where would we be without the art of the translator? To begin with, we would not have those profound wells of the Bible, Greek mythology, the Trojan War, and Ovid's *Metamorphoses*. We would have no fables, neither Aesop nor Jataka nor La Fontaine. We would have no *Arabian Nights*, no Grimm, no Hans Christian Andersen, no *Don Quixote*, no *Reynard the Fox*, no *Pinocchio*, no *Nils*, no *Pippi Longstocking* (Viking), no *Emil and the Detectives* (Doubleday), no *Babar* (Random), no *Little Prince* (Harcourt). Without Perrault there would be no "Cinderella," no "Sleeping Beauty."

297

In short, without translation, there would be no Hell and no Heaven for any of us in the English-speaking world, since it was Dante who created our concepts of them both, drawing up the architectural and philosophical plans of both the "Inferno" and the "Paradiso" in his native Tuscan.

The need for translation does not apply only to the immediate present, to the need for understanding the dialogue in a Bergman film or to be *au courant* with the postwar French philosophical movements. It works through time as well. Cyril Connolly, remarking on the fact that there has been no translation of Balzac's *Comédie Humaine* in this century, observed: "Every generation requires its own rendering of the great books of the past." In one of his essays in *The Sacred Wood*, T. S. Eliot quite justifiably attacked the sacrosanct Gilbert Murray translations of the ancient Greek dramatists as being not ancient Greek in feeling so much as watered-down Swinburne.

"Translator, traitor," as the Italian proverb has it. But on the other hand the translator can also provide a bridge between nations, between us and other minds, as well as across centuries. He can fire the passion which compels people in wartime to risk their lives for another country because they had read and loved Dickens and Lewis Carroll. The translator can, as the Italians claim, sink us all. But at best he can link us all.

What are the elements involved in the process? How do we, as translators, avoid betraying the writers who lie like patients etherized upon a library table awaiting our surgery, which can mean transcultural survival or oblivion?

As we noted earlier, the act of transference from one language to another is a shifting of mental gears. The problem is to keep the vehicle moving along as it should, going to its destination without any audible grinding of the machinery. It could be argued in this age of highly advanced technological accomplishment that surely a translator's job could be done by a competent computing machine. Feed two dictionaries into it, input the required text, press the proper buttons, and await the output.

It doesn't work, however. Why not? Because the words get in the way. Which brings us to the word itself.

In one of her short stories Doris Lessing, describing an inarticulate character, explains that he came from a family which had never enjoyed words. A serious limitation, obviously.

I can recall W. H. Auden saying that when he spoke at universities and students came up to tell him that they, too, wanted to become poets, he would ask them, "Why?" The most frequent answer was that they felt that they had something to say to the world. His reply to this would be noncommittal. But when the reply came that they wanted to be poets because they loved words, his face would light up. There was hope. For a poet, words are the only true beginning.

"In the beginning was the Word," St. John trumpeted, starting off his good news, his good spell, his gospel, "and the Word was with God, and the Word was God." In the Greek testament, St. John's word for *word* is *logos*, which means speech, reason (as in logic) as well as word. "In the beginning was speech?" "In the beginning was reason?" Or did St. John actually mean that in the beginning was the word itself? We say, "I give my word" or "upon my word" or "so-and-so's word is law." I could go on into infinity on the importance, the divinity of the word, as St. John would have it, since the word is God.

Let us try to examine this elusive, divine thing — the word. The more we consider it, we find that it is a complex, disembodied entity, almost with a life of its own. Primitive people know that words are magic. They are on guard against the incantatory abracadabran power of words. Sometime when you are alone (because if you do it in the presence of others it may lead to considerable embarrassment), try taking some utterly familiar word which you use a hundred times a day: *toothpaste* or *drugstore*. Repeat it aloud for a full minute and see what happens. It *will* become strange and independent, like a flying missile — an utterly unfamiliar entity with a nightmare ability to drive you mad.

Concretely, a word is a sound caused by a number of muscular reflexes which occur in the mouth and throat, involving the tongue, the lips, the palate, the esophagus — as well as the entire breathing apparatus. It consists of so many syllables and is indicated by so many written letters.

Now as to its meaning. Most words possess an exact, hard, objective significance. They are the names of objects, places, actions. They describe qualities. In primitive languages they are very concrete, indeed. As thought becomes more complex and pushes toward more exact definition, however, words which are no longer concrete creep into language to express abstractions and approximations. Then we find that a word often shifts its

299

meaning according to context or even according to inflection. Take a word like *cool*. Specifically, it refers to a relative lowness of temperature. When we are talking about soup, "cool it" has an unequivocal meaning. "Cool it," when heard under other circumstances, however, has several entirely different meanings. Even as an adjective it varies, depending on context.

Words have historical identity as well. As we know, words change their meaning from generation to generation. In Blake's time, for instance, *silly* still meant innocent or blessed. His silly sheep were neither stupid nor idiotic. Some words die, or merely survive as indications of another period in time. *Zounds, gadzooks:* Who uses them now? But the very sound or sight of them sweeps one back into a long-past era.

Words also have their emotional resonance. André Gide, in his preface to his translation of Shakespeare into French, refers to this quality of suggestion, of special nuance, when he writes of the "halo of evocation and reminiscences, certain kinds of harmonics which could not be the same in another language and which a translation cannot hope to keep."

Words have their musical value as well, a quality of sound for sound's sake. Why are small children so hypnotized by Edward Lear and by Lewis Carroll, especially by "Jabberwocky"? Why do certain syllables or combinations of syllables move us to pleasure, even to tears? Or why, in some cases, do they grate as strongly as a rasp? It was Aldous Huxley who said that to his ears the most beautifully moving word in the English language was "cellar-door."

Finally, we must add that words also have gender, although not in English grammar. In most of the other European tongues, however, every noun is male, female, or neuter. This attribution of sex, or lack of it, cannot help affecting the identity of a word.

Having established the complexity of words, how does one go about the business of shifting a text, a poem, a book, a whole system of thought and emotions from one language to another without acting as a traitor?

First of all, there are two levels of translation to consider. The first is the factual one, the rendering of a text which is commercial, scientific, or technical. The translator's job here is relatively simple. His aim is perfect clarity, the transmission of facts. Businessmen and scientists, however — to one's unending astonishment, since they are supposed to exist in a more practical world than that of the poet — are not always clear in their thinking, or, let us say, in the writing which presumably reflects their thinking. A Greek friend of mine wrote a learned paper on a recondite musical subject which was to appear in an international scholarly journal published in Hungary and which had to be rendered into English. "It won't take you long," I was assured. "It's all facts, very straightforward. Nothing literary." After several readings of the straightforward, nonliterary text, I was compelled to decorate the manuscript with a lavish sprinkling of interrogation points. In order to translate specific facts I had to know exactly what the writer was trying to say. In this instance, the writer was compelled to confess that she was not precisely sure. She had to rewrite the entire article.

Any writer who is anxious to achieve clarity should, perhaps, stop to reflect occasionally whether his manuscript would offer difficulties to a translator. When faced with ambiguity, however, a translator cannot always go back and ask the writer what he was trying to say. As a result, so many so-called translators simply plug ahead, hacklike, word for word, like the old Latin trots. Result: total incomprehension on the part of the reader. To this day, I am sure that most of us who managed to pony up a passing mark in Caesar still haven't the faintest notion as to what those Gallic Wars were all about.

What all this has been leading up to is the matter of literary translation, the sea change which occurs when a work of the imagination is metamorphosed into another language.

Poetry is the crown of all literature, the very pulse beat of a language. Why is it so difficult, almost impossible, to translate? Why, for instance, despite so many valiant tries, do we have no translation of Goethe, Pushkin, Racine, or Dante which can give the English-speaking reader more than the faintest glimmer of the greatness of these poets?

To begin to understand the problem of translating poetry we have to consider its source. Synge wrote that "a translation is no translation unless it will give you the music of a poem, along with the words of it." Even then, something is likely to be missing.

Poetry is not so much meaning, as Auden would remind us, as a kind of word music, a reverberation. Take Poe's "Annabel Lee." The gist of it, reported in prose, is that some time ago the poet fell in love with a girl who inhabited some unspecified seaside resort and that his feelings were not unrequited: a bit of information hardly sufficient to justify our remembering the source for more than five minutes. And yet Poe's poem has haunted our collective memory for well over a century and shows no sign of dropping out of the language. Likewise, it looks as though his raven will be with us forevermore. What is the curious quality which makes a poem or a stanza not only memorable and significant but which also gives it what we might call a verbal felicity, an inevitability? And, which is more to our purpose here, how does one go about translating it?

Let us take a few random examples of well-known poems in English: Blake's "Tiger, tiger, burning bright/ In the forests of the night" or Byron's

> There be none of Beauty's daughters
> With a magic like thee,
> And like music on the waters
> Is thy sweet voice to me.

Or even a modern lyric, like e. e. cummings'

> in Just-
> spring   when the world is mud-
> luscious the little
> lame balloonman
>
> whistles   far   and wee

One suspects that all three of them are utterly untranslatable into any other language. The words can be rendered; a skillful craftsman might even manage to indicate some of the music. But what about the meaning beyond meaning, the reverberation, the spell-casting magic, the *inevitability* which makes each of these poems seem so much a part of the English language that one can only with difficulty imagine a time when they did not exist?

The same, of course, is also true of most folk ballads and even of many popular songs. Like most wines and opera libretti, they don't travel. Or if they do, they lose a lot of their bouquet on the way. One is reminded of the famous German song of the 1920's of which the original words, so wanton and provocative, are "Ich bin von Kopf bis Fuss auf Liebe eingestellt." For all these years it has been known to us flatfootedly as "Falling in Love Again." George Borrow wrote in *Lavengro*, "Translation is at best an echo."

In Gide's preface to his translation into French of Shakespeare's complete theatrical works, he wrote with perception about the matter of the interpretation of variant meanings, especially in poetry. How can the translator make the decision as to which is the correct interpretation to choose? And what about the benefit of the indecision which exists in the original and is lost in translation, once a definite interpretation has been decided upon?

This brings us to the more general problems of a translator. James Howell, in the seventeenth century, wrote:

> Some hold translations not unlike to be
> The wrong side of a Turkey tapestry.

How does one go about creating another good side for a Turkish carpet? It is, curiously enough, a creative process as much as an interpretive one.

The first and foremost aspect of translation is, of course, that of meaning. The translator must know both languages well enough to know what is meant in the original language and then to dredge from the depths of his experience and judgment in the second language the most effectve, most suitable, and most evocative equivalent word or phrase. In addition to this, translation is not merely a matter of shifting linguistic gears. It is also a shift from one culture to another, from one way of thought into another, from one way of life into another. What may be strange and exotic must be made to seem, if not familiar, at least rational and acceptable.

This shift is especially important in books for children, where one simply cannot assume the wide knowledge on the part of the young reader which an adult presumably possesses. When confronted with these cultural differences, with references to widely unfamiliar ways of thought and life, what does the translator do? Should he stop and explain, using some parallel expression or a rough approximation in the cultural pattern of the reader and move on? Or should he translate directly and employ footnotes which, at best, are unsuitable and unpleasant in a narrative work, jerking the reader out of the world the writer has so carefully attempted to create?

What about dialogue? How do we keep its sparkle? Hemingway, in his books about Spain, managed to convey the sonority and the special dignity of Spanish speech by almost literal translation. But it is a device which, while often startling and effective, can also come perilously close to parody. We have all come across translations in which a low-class dialect in another language was approximated by British cockney. Does that sound right, or is it forced? Does it come as a shock? In any case, the translator has to manage to render the flavor of speech, which is often richly regional. Without making it sound quaint or patronizing, he must be sure that it is as fresh and natural-sounding as the original. Then, how does one go about translating humor and wit, sometimes so delicate that it hangs upon the hairsbreadth turning of a phrase?

Another element to be considered in translation is that of time, of historical period. A novel less than a century old is apt to contain turns of speech and references to forgotten personalities and events no longer clear even to those who read it today in its original language. The reader can skim carelessly over these passages, relying on context. The translator, however, cannot. He has to be a detective as well, discovering exactly what the author meant and exactly what contemporary events were referred to.

What about the emotional mood of a work? This, too, must be conveyed in the translation, even though that all-important aura is often as elusive as the Gioconda's smile. Which brings us, finally, to the translation of that curious quality called style. Consider Matthew Arnold's remarks in "On Translating Homer."

[T]he translator of Homer should above all be penetrated by a sense of four qualities of his author; — that he is eminently rapid; that he is eminently plain and direct, both in the evolution of his thought and in the expression of it, that is, both in his syntax and in his words; that he is eminently plain and direct in the substance of his thought, that is, in his matter and ideas; and, finally, that he is eminently noble.

In other words, one is translating not only a work but its creator's personality.

How does one go about conveying that personality without violating it with too strong an injection of the translator's own? When breathing your own life into another man's work, how do you keep from going too far and making it your own?

Finally, there is the problem of rendition versus translation. How closely must the translator hew to the original text? As you progress, you learn that often only by departing from the word itself can you cleave to the spirit. The question is how much liberty is a translator entitled to take?

Perhaps many scholars, especially writers of Ph.D. theses, will differ with me. But it seems that the art of translating actually involves three books. In the beginning is the work. Secondly, there is its literal rendition into another language. And, finally, we have its re-creation into a third work which will stand on its own.

A literary translation is only truly successful if it has the qualities of credibility, of inevitability, of authority. It has to give the impression of having been written originally in the language of the reader. Of course, there are books which defy any translator to destroy them, just as there are works of art which manage somehow to survive any debasement in reproduction. However, if what we are reading reads like a translation, it is safe to say that what we have got hold of is the wrong side of James Howell's Turkish tapestry. We have the facts, perhaps, but not the phosphorescence.

"*Traduttore, traditore.*" Nothing proves more vividly how the translator can turn into a traitor than the example which comes to mind of an old English saying which was translated into Japanese and then, from the Japanese, back into English again. In its final transmutation it emerged as "blind idiot." What was the original saying, before it crossed the Pacific to suffer its sea change? One must remember that the Japanese are a highly logical people. "Blind idiot" is a perfectly correct and justifiable translation of "out of sight, out of mind."

Let us go back to the dictionary. "Translate: to change from one language into another; hence, to change into another medium or form: as, translate ideas into action; to put into different words, interpret; to repeat or retransmit (a telegraphic message) by means of an automatic relay; [Archaic or Rare], to enrapture; entrance." I would passionately hope that the last-given meaning of translate is not so archaic, or rare, as *Webster's New World Dictionary* would have it.

As Virginia Woolf characterized writing as bringing order out of chaos, so I would like to describe all art as being an act of translation: of action into ideas; of word into image and image back into word; of thought and feeling into words. The most important aspect of this process, whether from life to art or from one language to another, is to remember that our function as translators is not to be blind idiots, but to enrapture, to entrance.

This article was prepared for the October 1977 and December 1977 *Horn Book*.

XI

BOOKS AND AUTHORS

In the long run, the most important task that criticism sets itself is to consider the meaning and literary significance of individual books and authors. Most of the previous sections of this volume have concentrated upon general elements and topics essentially valuable for recognizing the patterns and the cross-currents which may appear in various ways in individual works of literature. Although a given book may suggest different meanings to different readers, the purpose of the critic is always the same — to make the book comprehensible. It is encouraging to know that Georg Brandes, the famous Danish critic, once wrote to Hans Christian Andersen, "A literary critic is someone WHO KNOWS HOW TO READ, and who teaches the art of reading."[1]

The essays that follow contain evaluations and reevaluations of a number of books. Those on *Watership Down*, *Red Shift*, and *A Wizard of Earthsea* were — significantly — written soon after the publication of the books. The articles on *Tom Sawyer* and *The Mouse and His Child* represent "second looks," the kind of examination that is always necessary when time has gone by, even if a book has achieved the status of a classic. The juxtaposition of different points of view may indicate that critics are frequently at cross-purposes; but, then, critics can scarcely be accused of being indifferent. To quote Brandes again: "To me literary criticism is a branch of learning and a passion, and of course, . . . I imagine that everybody else must be able to see the excellence of my profession."[2]

1. Elias Bredsdorff, *Hans Christian Andersen: The Story of His Life and Work 1805-1875* (New York: Scribner, 1975), p. 255.
2. *Ibid.*, p. 254.

LETTER FROM ENGLAND:
Great Leaping Lapins!

By AIDAN CHAMBERS

ATERSHIP DOWN is presently a name to conjure with. An extraordinary feat of sustained
narrative, the novel appeared in England towards
the end of 1972. The coterie critics got excited before it was
even published, the reviewers duly raved, and everyone who
bothers at all about children's books (and some who don't) have
now formed extreme opinions — this being one of those books
about which it is not easy, if at all possible, to be neutral. I've
no doubt that, as with Alice, the hobbits, and Batman, there'll
be cultishness to cope with before long.

I gather Macmillan is bringing it out in the States, and I
shall be fascinated to discover the kind of response this quintessentially English book stirs in American commentators. As I
wouldn't want to steal one rumble of their thunder, my instinctive impulse to launch into a detailed revelation of all that
makes this epic novel so unusual is as instinctively frustrated.
Nevertheless, I cannot possibly report on children's books in
this country without saying something about it, however tantalizing, however premature it might be.

Watership Down was written by Richard Adams, who, it turns
out, is an official in the Department of the Environment — a
biographical nicety not without ironic overtones, as may become
clear in a moment. He is new to the ranks of published authors;
has, I fancy, spent years on his novel; and hawked the bulky
manuscript round numerous reputable houses — all of which
turned it down and must now be suffering agonies of belated
regret — before finding his way to the desk of Rex Collings.

Mr. Collings is one of a new breed. Until recently an editor
with a monolith firm, he decided to opt out from literary factory-
production dominated by accountants and to set up on his own
in faith and hope, if not on — or even in — charity. There are
a number of people trying the same optimistic gambit just
now, and one cannot but applaud their efforts to revivify literary
publishing.

According to his own somewhat sugary publicity, Mr. Collings was forced at bowler point to read the daunting manuscript by its desperate author, found himself hooked by the end of the first chapter, and thereafter took the undoubtedly courageous step (for such a young firm) of publishing the fat volume. Unfortunately, his courage was not matched by his production skills: He designed an ugly edition, with cramped typography and dressed in an appallingly inept dust-jacket. The outward and visible appearance doubtless turned off more readers than were turned on.

The hardback edition is, in fact, four hundred and thirteen pages thick, fifty chapters and one map long, and is all about rabbits. Now, lapine fantasy is not my literary cup of tea — be it for children or not, and I question whether *Watership Down* was ever really intended for children until the question of publication arose. Rabbits, to my mind, are best left to their own rodent activities. And had I not had to review the tome, I would certainly have given it the go-by. (Will one ever learn to judge books, like people, only after listening a while! For sure, first impressions were utterly deceptive in this case, and ugliness only jacket deep.)

What next took me aback was that a quotation from Aeschylus's *Agamemnon* stood sentinel at the head of Chapter One, a lost Victorian device made the more startling because it was quoted in the original Greek. I flipped the pages. Quotations sprouted like thorny, protective hedges at the beginning of every chapter, taken from sources as disparate as the aforementioned classic to bits from R. M. Lockley's erudite treatise on your true and living bunny.

Disconsolate, a reviewer in professional straits, I set to work. But work it remained for only a page or two. Thereafter, I was an addict. I could have stayed on Watership Down (which, incidentally, is a real and visitable part of chalky Hampshire, as are all the places named in the book) as long as Mr. Adams wished to keep me there. Four hundred and thirteen pages seemed, when they were finished, a less than generous amount. Absorbing, sensational, staggeringly unexpected, flawed to the point of critical disaster, brilliant, exciting, evocative (the sense of place and atmosphere, climate and season is beautifully achieved), English to the last full-stop, tough, gentle, bloodshot, violent, satisfying, humorous. The list of epithets, superlatives, qualifiers, paradoxes, and blazoned blooming nouns could cover the rest of the space allotted me.

In sum, *Watership Down*, though not a comfortable nor even a lovely book, is deeply moving and vividly memorable in the way that all "good" books, all works of true art, are: They implant themselves — some by main force, others by subtle injection — into the living tissues of your being, to remain there, illuminating your view of life ever after. Most obviously and least importantly, rabbits will never be the same again for me, a warren never again be simply a collection of messy holes in the ground. But to say that is to say little. There are some who speak of allegory and hint at many hidden and profound meanings burrowed beneath the surface of the narrative. They may well be right. But I suspect there are as many different tunnels of meaning as one cares to dig. So, to return for now to the pleasantly simple and obvious: I shall never again watch a bobbed and white-lined tail stub its way across a field in pursuit of a hedge without believing it belongs to a lapine guerrilla from the warren Mr. Adams biographs in such rich and intimate detail.

The story is what one might expect had *Wind in the Willows* been written after two World Wars, various marks of nuclear bomb, the Korean and Vietnam obscenities, and half-a-dozen other hells created by the inexhaustibly evil powers of Man. In fact, the tale begins with a deliberate act of demolition, when human beings destroy an ancient warren in order to clear a building site, inadvertently leaving alive a handful of ill-assorted rabbits to wander the countryside as refugees. Despite all the calamities that befall luckless Toad, no one ever dreamt Toad Hall would be bulldozed. And putting the pick into the medieval rooms inhabited by Badger would have been unthinkable. But that was 1908. And 1908 is gone, *Wind in the Willows* with it. *Watership Down*, if none the wiser than that wise and lovely book, is a great deal better informed.

But I must stop. To go on would be to spoil things for your own reviewers. Let me finish by mentioning that Puffin paperbacks will soon be publishing the book in better and more attractive clothes. Then we shall very soon discover how much it is a children's book children will read, and how much it is enjoyed by adults only.

Watership Down has received the Seventh Annual Guardian Award.

From *The Horn Book* for June 1973

OLD WORLDS AND NEW:
Anti-Feminism in "Watership Down"

By Jane Resh Thomas

WRITERS OF FANTASY enjoy the incomparable opportunity to create the world anew, but they suffer from the same problem as Archimedes, who said he could move the world with a system of levers if only he were given a place to stand apart. In creating the new world of *Watership Down* (Macmillan), Richard Adams stands squarely in the old one. His novel draws upon not only epic and picaresque literary traditions but also an anti-feminist social tradition which, removed from the usual human context and imposed upon rabbits, is eerie in its clarity.

Watership Down well deserves the Carnegie Medal and the praise it has won from critics and reviewers, for Adams has created a splendid story, admirable for its originality as much as for its craft. Since the stereotype to which the female characters conform dictates their colorlessness and limits their social range, they are so peripheral they are scarcely noticeable. Its anti-feminist bias, therefore, damages the novel in only a minor way.

A literary work may survive such flaws as peripheral prejudice or cruelty or racism. It is important that the soldier in Andersen's "The Tinderbox" gratuitously murders the old woman and does so with impunity; it is important that the elephants in the Babar books sometimes seem more human than the "savages." But despite what may be viewed as ethical lapses, these stories still merit qualified praise. Just so, it is important that in *Watership Down*, Richard Adams has grafted exalted human spirits to the rabbit bodies of his male characters and has made the females mere rabbits. The males are superhuman and the females subhuman, creatures who occupy only a utilitarian place in the novel's world. That fact is important, notwithstanding the artistic merit of the work as a whole.

Adams' band of rabbit refugees who escape the poison gas and bulldozers of a housing project are not the sweet bunny rabbits that have accompanied the treacle into the nursery ever since imitators first bowdlerized Beatrix Potter's miniature hair-raisers. No. The refugees are literal rabbits, subject to the dictates of biology, to the compulsions of their reproductive impulses, their hunger, and their need for shelter. So they recognize and name every plant they encounter, or they feel inborn terror when they smell a dog approaching.

The refugees owe their survival and the establishment of a new warren to the variety of their talents. They exhibit admirable human traits — bravery to support their daring; the common-sense kind of wisdom; originality; reverence for history tempered by flexibility; compassion. The group includes a bard, a politician, a seer, a soldier, and even an intellectual. As they travel together, they improvise a new community which not only accommodates but values their great differences. Thus, it seems an enormously civilized and humane society, an association of equals whose personal gifts are recognized. But the members of this civilized society are all males.

To my mind, a just community is a cooperative venture which enriches individual lives instead of restricting them for the supposed good of the group. Even when membership is exclusive, one can admire fictitious community where one finds it — in a rathole with Mole and Ratty in *The Wind in the Willows* (Scribner) or on a journey through Mirkwood in *The Hobbit* (Houghton) — if one ignores any deprived class. So Kenneth Grahame and J. R. R. Tolkien wisely avoid the intrusion of females into the fraternity, just as cultivated gentlemen lock the massive doors of their oak-and-leather clubs. The illusion of civilization, of equalitarian warmth and respect, could hardly be maintained in the presence of a declassed group.

Richard Adams himself avoids that problem throughout the first half of *Watership Down*, which describes the itinerants' perilous journey. Like Grahame and Tolkien, he simply omits females from consciousness. However, when the rabbit troupe settle down, they begin to long for female companionship, a longing based on afterthought.

For one thing, they'd like to have some females around to do the work: In established warrens, nubile females do all of the serious digging. Adams has so skillfully bridged the distance between rabbits and people that, whoever digs the burrows in rabbit reality, one easily draws conclusions from Adams' rabbit fiction about the appropriate roles of men and women. The girl who rescues chief Hazel from a barnyard cat's jaws receives her orders from men with a lapine docility that reinforces this rabbit/human connection.

Additional considerations also bring females to the refugees' minds. As Hazel observes, "We have no does — not one — and no does means no kittens and in a few years no warren." The narrator further explains the need for females after Hazel kidnaps two does from Nuthanger Farm:

The kind of ideas that have become natural to many male human beings in thinking of females — ideas of protection, fidelity, romantic love and so on — are, of course, unknown to rabbits, although rabbits certainly do form exclusive attachments. . . . However, they are not romantic and it came naturally to Hazel and Holly to consider the two Nuthanger does simply as breeding stock for the warren.*

Although the males are rarely called *bucks* but are individually designated by name and collectively referred to as *rabbits*, the females are usually called *does*, a distinction analogous to the classifications *people* and *women* with reference to human males and females. For all its subtlety, that is a psychologically charged distinction, as Simone de Beauvoir suggested when she wrote that there are two classes of people, human beings and women. When women try to be human beings, she said, they are accused of acting like men.

Furthermore, the narrator makes it clear that only two alternatives exist in relations between sexes, the human way of romantic idolatry or the rabbit way of animal husbandry. In either case, the female is deprived of anything like the participation granted male members of the brotherhood by virtue of their maleness. Consorting with females seems to be an onerous necessity.

Eventually the refugees act on their longing and raid Efrafa, a neighboring rabbit police state. Of the ten does who willingly escape the totalitarian rule of General Woundwort, only two are even superficially characterized. One is a scatter-brained youngster who reveals the escape plan by chattering uncontrollably to Efrafan officers. All of the others, except Hyzenthlay, are powerless to act on their own initiative — paralyzed by fear at every critical turn.

*Richard Adams. *Watership Down* (New York: Macmillan, 1972), p. 222.

Only Hyzenthlay possesses courage or dignity. She is a seer, gifted like the male Fiver, with prophetic vision. And like Dandelion, the refugees' bard, she is an artist, a poet whose lament resembles primitive poetry. But her artistic energies, like her determination to escape, are biologically directed, for what she laments is lost opportunities for reproduction. Although the males' sex makes demands upon them, as do their needs for food and shelter, sex does not dictate every form and detail of their lives. But Hyzenthlay is first and only a female, with her poetry seeming merely an aspect of her femaleness. Indeed, since her talents are neither admired nor even noticed, the rabbits of Hazel's warren consult her only as mate, not as prophet or bard. With motherhood, her poetry apparently ends.

A male victim of Efrafan violence says without correction when a fox kills one of the females, "What's a doe more or less?" He accepts the leader's decisions automatically, even forgetting his own opinions if they differ from those of the chief. Asked if her thought processes are like those of the Efrafan male, Hyzenthlay cryptically replies, "I'm a doe." After her brief heroism in the run for freedom, Hyzenthlay turns, in accordance with her sexual definition, to the roles of mate and mother. Her presence on stage is so brief, though, it hardly matters.

Watership Down survives the flawed characterization and the discrepancy between the richness of the male rabbits' lives and the spiritual penury of the females'. Although it seems odd that Adams counters an ugly totalitarian society with a system where females are merely interchangeable ciphers, one easily ignores that discrepancy too, because the females are unessential baggage, present only to motivate the male characters, not necessary to the story for their own individual sakes.

All of this is important, like the murder of Andersen's expendable old woman and like the beastiality of Babar's black neighbors. Within the framework of an otherwise delightful story, Richard Adams has embodied an anti-feminism which deprives his female characters of the spiritual fruit of community.

From *The Horn Book* for August 1974

LETTER FROM ENGLAND:
Literary Crossword Puzzle . . .
or Masterpiece?

By AIDAN CHAMBERS

R ED SHIFT, says the *World Book Encyclopedia* with characteristic clarity, "is a shift in the *spectrum* (color pattern) of a galaxy or another astronomical object toward the longer (red) wave lengths." Among other things, apparently, it shows that "every galaxy is moving away from every other galaxy, and therefore that the universe is expanding." Knowing this, you might be forgiven for supposing that a novel entitled *Red Shift* dealt with a science-fiction plot. When you found it didn't, you might also be forgiven for guessing that the choice of title was intentionally symbolic and reach the not very profound conclusion that the story ponders the way people — individual human galaxies — are forever moving away from each other so that real contact, understanding, and close relationships become less possible every day.

Alan Garner's new book is called *Red Shift*, and I'm writing this comment to you before its publication in England for one very good reason. Garner is attended to much more in England than in the United States — a writer frequently discussed and gossiped about, often in deeply respectful, even tribute-paying tones. His last novel, *The Owl Service* (Walck), published six years ago, has suffered the deadly fate of achieving classic status and has been set as a text for compulsory study in many high schools, after winning the Carnegie Medal from the librarians, the *Guardian* newspaper annual children's book award, and the populist honor of serialization on television. When a writer produces as little as Garner and as slowly, has generated the kind of applause he has, and is astutely publicized, a full head of critical steam builds up before each new book appears. So, if I'm to give you an uninfluenced response to *Red Shift*, I must do so now before the reviewing boiler bursts.

The book's top tune — the main plot and the easiest to follow — tells of an intelligent, oversensitive teenager, Tom (his wit saves him from being an emotionally spotty bore), who lives in a trailer with his disagreeably possessive mother and weak-willed army pa (overworked stock characters in teenage fiction, but given some vitality and individuality here). Tom is in love with a better-balanced, equally intelligent girl, Jan, whose own parents enter the story only as absentee landlords, because they are busybody social workers always out helping other people. Jan leaves messages for them on the house ansaphone. The plot begins with Jan preparing to move to London, and Tom toiling in an emotional panic that reaches a volcanic climax when his parents ask if he and Jan have "had any occasion to do anything to make us ashamed of you."

In order to solve their separation the young lovers arrange to meet regularly on Crewe station, a rail junction which for years has been the butt of vaudeville gags. For a while all is sunshine and flowers — romance among the railway engines — until happiness is curdled by Tom's prying mum and finally turned sour when Tom thinks Jan is playing him false. The book ends with the breakup of the relationship. Betrayal, you might say, is what it's all about. "It doesn't matter. Not really now not any more," says the last line on the last page. But, of course, it does matter (to Garner if to no one else), or why bother to write such a difficult thing as a novel about it?

Orchestrated with the top tune are two subplots, one set in an immediately post-Roman time, the other in the seventeenth-century civil war period. Both involve the places lived in and visited by the twentieth-century protagonists. I call them subplots, but I fancy Garner means them to be co-plots, the function of which is not simply to support the top tune but to add variations to the main theme. In other words, and changing the image, the book is a decorated prism which turns to show — incident by incident — first one face, then another. In the last section, the prism spins so fast that the three faces merge into one color, one time, one place, one set of people, one meaning.

I cannot dwell here on the fascinating details of the novel. The way, for example, Garner suggests his historical periods, and especially the way he uses the brutal gutter talk of American commandos in Vietnam to suggest the post-Roman incidents. Or the grueling description of the massacre of a village in the civil war scenes. Nor have I space to say anything about the transitions between plots, made by using painful moments in the characters' experiences to break through the time barrier, as though pain were a kind of telepathic switching gear. If I could expand on anything, I'd choose what for me is Garner's most admirable achievement in *Red Shift*: the terrible accuracy of his dialogue, not only as lingua verita, but in the way he uses it to reveal his characters, powering the words with meanings beyond the obvious.

Your own reviewers must speak of these things when eventually Macmillan brings the book out in the States. I can do no more now than prepare you for the central dilemma of this complex and difficult work. Is it a technically brilliant literary crossword puzzle, or is it masterpiece? Is the red shift symbol all-inclusive of the book or to be interpreted more cautiously?

There are plenty of clues to work on. Indeed, as I read, I was acutely aware of being tested. Can you or can't you find the hidden references? How many did you score? Hit the hundred, and join the author's elect (for he, schoolmasterly, can't lose because he set the traps and knows the answers). Consider, for example, some of the evidence laid rather too obviously on the surface. Jan tells Tom, "You're always so tolerant with strangers. . . . You savage the people near you." "We're," says Tom pompously, "bits of other futures." And he "sees everything at once," makes witticisms about the M6 (a road route) and M35 (a galaxy near our own), telling Jan meanwhile, "We were born grown up." "We've both betrayed," says one of the historical characters. "There'll be a price." Tom could almost be replying when he says, "It's a pretty mean galaxy."

Put this sort of thing together, and you feel convinced the book has as its larger theme the red shift of parting worlds, of the impossibility of reconciliatory contact. If, however, you apply the symbol only partially and reinterpret the clues, you come out with a very much less metaphysical solution supported by another speech of Tom's: "I see and can't understand. I need to adjust my spectrum, pull myself away from the blue end. I could do with a red shift. Galaxies and Rectors have them. Why not me?" Follow that hint, and you must decide the book is really saying nothing more startling than this: Everyone needs a little distance from the deepest pains of living before the pain is understood and can be coped with, before experience can be given perspective, and be made bearable. And I suppose you could add that adolescence is a time when emotional pain is raw and intensely felt, is often exaggerated and too closely inspected.

317

Literary code-cracking aside, what I find critically worrying is not the novel's complexity but its failure to work on the plane on which it asks to be accepted. We are intended, I'm sure, to feel very deeply, to empathize with Tom and his predicament. *The Owl Service* worked memorably in this manner despite its technical faults and constructional weaknesses. It didn't matter whether you understood completely and intellectually the below-surface meanings. You felt them strongly. *Red Shift* — brilliantly organized though it is, inventive, so tautly written it nearly snaps, honed, scrubbed, made concentratedly dense — is yet too clever by half. It doesn't touch the nerves of feeling that it reaches out, somewhat coldly, to finger.

In *The Owl Service* mythical history repeated itself in the lives of two boys and a girl and was, for me, utterly convincing in the telling. In *Red Shift* a boy and a girl are once again swept along with historic inevitability, trapped in the red shift effect; and though the idea is attractive, though I admire the technical achievements, I am neither convinced nor much moved except by isolated scenes.

Maybe the fault is mine; perhaps I need to give the book more time. After all, Garner has spent six years making it. Why should I expect to plumb its depths in a couple of readings? But of one thing I'm sure. Garner has given up any pretense of writing for children and is now writing entirely to please himself and those mature, sophisticated, literate readers who care to study his work. I'm not moaning about this; it is a fact of the writer's life. But because Garner is one of our most talented and exciting authors, I hope he won't forget where his career began and will occasionally let down his literary hair and again tell a story to children.

From *The Horn Book* for October. 1973

OFF THE BEATEN PATH

By Paul Heins

A S THINGS STAND NOW, it is not necessary to discuss at length in *The Horn Book Magazine* the content, the technique, or the style of Alan Garner's latest novel, *Red Shift*. Aidan Chamber's analysis in his October "Letter from England" dealt lucidly and skillfully with the novel's subject matter and treatment and hit the nail on the head in the subtitle of the article: "Literary Crossword Puzzle . . . or Masterpiece?"

For what is disturbing is not the book, but the evaluation of the book. It may well be a masterpiece. It is certainly of a piece with Garner's earlier books in its feeling for his native Cheshire; it contains his explorations of the uncanny, of the irruptions of the past into the present; it creates powerful situations that end with an emotional smash. Yet, the conflicting opinions regarding *Red Shift* leave one uneasy, since some critics — like Margery Fisher and Brian Alderson — have greeted it with superlatives, while Aidan Chambers hopes that Garner "will . . . let down his literary hair and again tell a story to children"; the reviewer in the *Times Literary Supplement* says of the book "it may prove impenetrable to most readers."

With the publication of *Red Shift*, we come to the logical conclusion of an era: The dividing lines between children's books and adult books have grown more and more faint. Should one any longer speak of children's books, or should they be regarded as a somewhat late Victorian invention that is fast becoming superannuated? Of course, there are readers for all kinds of books, no matter how published or by what department of a publishing firm. But one must posit a reader of *Red Shift* at the youngest as an exceptional high school student who has already dipped into James Joyce's *Ulysses* and joined the class of very specialized adult readers for whom literature is a passionate sport as well as a pastime. Such a youthful enthusiast will not be fazed by the fact that there are at least three characters named Tom in *Red Shift* and that the terse dialogue which dominates the narrative requires great concentration as well as patient ingenuity on the part of the reader.

From *The Horn Book* for December 1973

A SECOND LOOK:
A Centennial for Tom

By Clifton Fadiman

CHILDREN'S CLASSICS may be dead, comatose, or alive. Charlotte Yonge's *The Little Duke* is probably dead. *Toby Tyler* may be comatose. *The Adventures of Tom Sawyer*, with eleven American editions in print, seems alive and well. *Tom Sawyer* is doing rather better after one century than that other work of art, the Republic itself, after two.

Alive and well? An interesting question. I have just reread the book for perhaps the sixth time, experiencing fresh pleasures — but also feeling certain doubts. To what extent has time turned it into an historical novel? After all, Mark Twain's Missouri hamlet of the 1830's or 1840's reflects a parochial preindustrial culture. Its economy is primitive and partly slave-based; racism (not Joe, but *Injun* Joe) and a naïve gentility mark its social outlook. Its ethics are rooted in an antiquated puritanism; its theology is a simple pietism. Is *Tom Sawyer*, for the adult reader, a mere curio, a charming memento of the Age of Innocence? And what about today's young reader? Here is a book built on a series of alternating humorous vignettes, Norman Rockwell chromos of pre-adolescent love, and episodes of Gothic melodrama. But the contemporary young reader's familiar world is one in which wholesale violence, torture, murder, vulgarity, sexual obsession, and corruption rewarded by pardon are virtually advertised as the norm. What bridge links Jackson's Island and Manhattan Island? Is *Tom Sawyer* still a pleasurable reading experience for the young? Or just another *Silas Marner*?

With the passage of years the novel of childhood and early youth has absorbed certain salutary lessons. Today it tries to present life from the inside, to bar the author from the page. And so even the child may squirm when Mark Twain, getting into the act, says that Tom "began to 'show off' in all sorts of absurd boyish ways"; or, again, "boylike, he determined to yield to the stronger inclination." An inept Thackeray (and Thackeray was not so ept himself), Mark Twain cheerfully kills his effect with "Let us draw the curtain of charity over the rest of the scene." However loving and understanding, he is a poor judge of distance, too often concerned with showing us how amused he is by his own boyhood. It is a false note our slicker, if lesser, writers have learned not to strike.

There are other flaws. "TOM!" and "Call me Ishmael" may be the two most arresting first lines in American fiction. Yet the beginning at once starts to creak, and, though the story gathers confidence and ends strongly enough, the progression is irregular. Flat stretches intervene, sensed even by the naïve reader. How laborious, like a humorous schoolboy composition, is the examination day episode in chapter twenty-one. Compare the clumsy, pat introduction of the treasure theme, the fortuitous finding of the Murrel gang's gold hoard with the cunning and elaborate persuasiveness of *Treasure Island*. The genius in Mark Twain, never steady, kept up an unremitting struggle with the hack journalist — and often lost. That is why the adult reader, using hindsight, tends to sum up *Tom Sawyer* as finger exercises for developing the technique required for the sweeping tone poem, *The Adventures of Huckleberry Finn*.

Think but an instant, however, and we realize the unfairness of the comparison. Take Huck himself. The real Huck lies in the future; here he is hardly an embryo. True, he is detectable. When Huck obeys the same moral imperative that was to save Jim in the sequel and saves the Widow Douglas from impending torture, he steps clearly out of his subordinate role. The dim spiritual confusion that in *Huckleberry Finn* generates a profound psychological study is foreshadowed in the touching, broken phrases he uses about an old Negro: "Sometimes I've set right down and eat *with* him. But you needn't tell that. A body's got to do things when he's awful hungry he wouldn't want to do as a steady thing." At the very end the easy-going humor suddenly deepens as Huck (a tiny mirror of the Gilded Age to come) gravely accepts the fact that he can join the robber gang only if he becomes respectable. But throughout most of the book Huck plays a rather pale Watson to Tom's Sherlock Holmes. He is dominated, overborne by Tom's aggressive, romantic imagination. Huck does not yet know, Mark Twain did not yet know, that he is the true poet, the epic tale-teller, the one with the real vision of his society. The two books should not be set side by side. *Tom Sawyer* belongs to the secondary art of memory, *Huckleberry Finn* to the primary one of creation.

But within the bounds of that secondary art, and for all its embarrassing weaknesses, *Tom Sawyer* is still, I think, alive and well. Alive and well even for the youthful reader who has been conditioned by network sadism, by advanced pornography, by the trivialization of human life to which his culture seems to be avidly devoted. The proof is simple: even when it is forced upon them by teachers, children read *Tom Sawyer*. They read it when other books of its kind, however excellent — Henry Shute's *The Real Diary of a Real Boy*, George W. Peck's *Peck's Bad Boy*, Thomas B. Aldrich's *The Story of a Bad Boy* — are forgotten or revived only in a spirit of nostalgic piety.

Tom Sawyer still works. Our Nixonian culture instructs the young that conscience is a dictionary word, *obs*. But, countering that culture and peer-group pressure and the normal impulse of bravado, something deeper lives in the boy or the girl, a passion for wanting the good guys to lick the bad guys. The child doesn't really want to accept the bribe held out to his conscience; so he responds, however dimly, to the underlying truth in human character. Something happens as he works out the complex meaning of Aunt Polly's words: "Every time I let him off, my conscience does hurt me so, and every time I hit him my old heart most breaks." The statement is true to the demands of human experience, just as the blood-drenched TV drama is true to the demands of the sponsor. Part of the young reader, part of the time, appreciates the first truth as opposed to the second.

Technology and the current world nightmare that is technology's hyperkinetic offspring are doing their level best to throttle the Tom Sawyer in boys and girls. The child may be replaced with a new mechanical model — dreamless, conditionable, finding in the imitation of media-violence and media-vulgarity the illusion of freedom. If so, *Tom Sawyer* will die, and childhood, except as a phase of biological growth, will die with it. Meanwhile, the book lives not only as a hymn to Mark Twain's own boyhood, but as a hymn to boyhood itself, boyhood viewed both seriously and humorously as a conflict between freedom and civilization. The theme may sound more plangently in *Huckleberry Finn*, but the average young reader will respond more eagerly to *Tom Sawyer* just because the story is simpler, less demanding, and because it moves more quickly.

The conflict in Tom results from his realizing how he should behave and knowing how he'd like to behave. The narrow puritanism of St. Petersburg tells him how he should behave, just as the brutal anarchy of our own culture tells today's Tom how he should behave. Tom Sawyer is neither good nor bad. He is just natural — that is to say, something tells him that if he is to grow up into a real human being, unlike such petrified models as the schoolmaster, the judge, or the minister, he must follow certain impulses that will enlarge rather than diminish him.

These gestures toward freedom — Aunt Polly would call them naughtiness, Sid would call them showing off — are not large or magnificent. Chafing under civilization embodied in church-going, Tom arranges an enlivening contest between a poodle and a pinch-bug. To lighten the repressive gloom of the classroom he creates a diversion by playing with a tick. By conning his friends into whitewashing a fence, he carves out for himself a tiny freedom-space. To expand his identity he tries on extra personalities drawn from books, legend, or superstition. Writing an oath in blood is a gesture that at once sets him apart from the bloodless conformity of the adult world. His friendship with Huck is even more profoundly *soul-making*, to use Keats' term.

Falling in love with Becky, too, is soul-making: It yields that boyish version of introspection, pleasurable suffering. For a time he transports himself to an alternative world, Jackson's Island. True enough, it is a play-world; for by playing at being someone else, children learn who they are. But McDougal's cave is no play-world — it is real enough, the book's true emotional center and climax. Apparently it is mere childish carelessness that draws Tom and Becky into the cave. But they are really led there, one feels, by the pressure of the unconscious. It is a symbolic testing-place. In it the freedom-seeking Tom can measure his courage, his enter-prise, most of all his power to love — the most liberating of all emotions. He triumphs — that is, the free Tom, rather than the good Tom, triumphs. Civilization not only forgives him — it makes a hero of him. And in his triumph the young reader also triumphs.

What gives this hymn to freedom its lyrical tone is something all of us, but especially young people, respond to, because we are losing it. It is Time. Tom and Huck — and Mark Twain — had plenty of time, like the Mississippi. Technology cannot give us time; it can give us only leisure. With this leisure we can, as we say, kill time. Kill it by aimless mobility (the Miracle of Transportation); by the endless manufacture of useless or lethal articles (the Miracle of Production); by the passive intake of vicarious experience (the Miracle of Communication). But Tom's time is real Time. It cannot be killed; it can only be lived. True, there are interruptions — chores, church, school, civilization — but these irritants serve only to make more beautiful the Heaven of Time about him. Time to contemplate a dead cat or attend one's own funeral, time to be Robin Hood or the Black Avenger or to be sick from pipe-smoking.

A grown-up relaxes: merely another dutiful exercise of the will. But a child can be creatively idle — something quite different from relaxation — if he lives in a culture, however narrow, that makes this possible. For all its murders and melodrama, *Tom Sawyer* is a kind of dream of Free Time, a boy's dream. Withhold that dream, as our culture prefers to do, and the child shrinks into a different and a lesser being.

Why is Huck — the Huck of the sequel — a great, perhaps *the* great American hero, our Roland, our Beowulf, our Siegfried? I think it is because he is the archetype of a paradise we have lost — Free Time, and the adjective is as important as the noun. It is as though we, the foremost creators of technoculture, were almost from our beginnings prescient of our destiny. Into our whole literature is infused an anti-civilization tradition. More than sentimental Rousseauism, more than a response to our country's original and unspoiled primal beauty, it is a reflection of the conflict between the mandate that bids us love our fate — technoculture — and the impulse that makes us fear it.

In its simple, awkward, "boy's book" way, *Tom Sawyer* embodies this conflict. Thus I venture to suggest that the young reader, committing himself to a book about a peculiar society that died out almost a century ago, may react in three different ways. First, because the mores of that society and the mores of his technoculture are not tangential, he may view some of the book with bafflement or, more probably, with patronizing superiority. In that respect he will get little from *The Adventures of Tom Sawyer*. The book has become an historical novel. Second, the child will still respond, simply because at his best Mark Twain is a cunning teller of tales, to whatever else remains fresh — the book's humor, its clear, unsubtle characterizations, the suspense narrative of Injun Joe and the treasure.

But most essentially — and this is why we are celebrating the centennial of a live classic — he will feel, however cloudily, the energy of the subtext, the poem hidden between the lines of prose, the lyric *yes* that affirms the right of the boy to seek the identity that takes its shape out of idleness, out of dream, out of fantasy, out of freedom.

From *The Horn Book* for April 1976

LETTER FROM ENGLAND:
A Tale of Two Toms

By AIDAN CHAMBERS

THE ADVENTURES OF TOM SAWYER was one of the few books read to me in my grade school days. My pals and I chortled at the fence-painting and Tom's cunning, and shivered at the scary adventure in the churchyard as Tom and Huck meet at midnight to banish warts with spells and, instead, conjure nothing less than a brutal murder. We felt outwardly embarrassed and inwardly moved by the comic-tender scenes between Tom and Becky, and we were thrilled at their experiences in the caves. Most of all we envied Tom his cavalier command and Huck his abandoned freedom: just as Mark Twain knew we would, we boys, whether American or British — or Afghan come to that.

What we found so much to admire and clutch to ourselves so that the impression remains powerful still was *Tom Sawyer's* richness, its humor, its unrestrained, optimistic vigor. Mark Twain liked sparky boys; boys, sparky or not, responded. And still do. During the last two years the book has been adapted in Britain into a musical film, revived at least twice on TV (the old film version I remember from my childhood and a new TV version); it has been published in play form for children to act and has remained, despite the cutbacks, in print in Puffin paperback as well as in a number of other editions.

A hundred years after its birth, *Tom Sawyer* is still going strong. By any standard it is a great children's book. And no doubt because of those early impressions formed by schoolroom readings listened to with pleasure in the late afternoon just before class got out, Tom stands in my mind for the old America just as his cousin, in *Tom Brown's Schooldays*, stands for the old England of the same period.

Tom-America is a roamer, frisky, rebellious against authority, brimming with self-confidence, always trying to live out some adventurous fantasy — a man of action who feels more at home in the open air than in the ordered domestic confines of a house. Tom and Huck are nobody's fools, nobody's men but their own. They are naïve and suspicious, loyal but not subservient, so cussedly uncivilized they strain the belt.

Tom-England shares some of the same qualities — as cousins often do: native intelligence, robust courage, independence of mind. But there are profound differences between the two. Tom Sawyer's adventures occur away from home and school in untamed country. Tom Brown's are entirely contained inside his school and the cultivated country around it. Tom Sawyer lives by rules he and his friends make up as they go along; Tom Brown is keen to become part of a tradition whose rituals go back many years, whose rules are strict and hierarchically imposed. (It is because Dr. Arnold is trying to reform the more barbarous of these rules that he is opposed by some of his staff and by boys like the bully, Flashman.) Nothing pleases Tom Brown more than to please Dr. Arnold; nothing would make Tom Sawyer feel more abashed.

Two nations, two cultures, two histories find expression in those two boys. You can even see it all operating in the authors' styles: Twain's direct, idiosyncratic, forged from his own speech and the demotic, colloquial language around him; Hughes's measured, trained by a careful study of a received and approved tradition.

Tom Brown, in the book published in 1857, is the child of an old society, an old order, living in and loving a school which reflects and perpetuates the society. He's a reformer in the end, but a conservative gradualist, not a rebel. Tom Sawyer is the child of a society still finding its identity, looking for new myths to live by, determined to be itself, loving freedom and uninhibited informality. And each character, each book appeals to young readers because each offers something of one side or the other of a boy's nature: the wild-and-free adventurer who is only happy while there's a frontier to explore, and the member of a closed community of the elite-and-elect who is the latest in a long line of chiefs and kings.

Both Toms love heroes and are themselves heroes in others' eyes. But each looks to different gods for his energy and inspiration, and the gods they choose are themselves significant. Tom Brown looks to Dr. Arnold, Old Brooke, and the corporate body of Rugby School (just as the old England looked to the Monarchy, Great Statesmen, and the corporate body of England). Tom Sawyer's models are far less stable or tangible: They shift according to his mood, but are always drawn from mythical fantasy — Robin Hood, romantic pirates, rebel adventurers. It wasn't till Mark Twain reached *The Adventures of Huckleberry Finn* in 1884 that we see him sorting out through Huck more solid images to live by, images closer to the truth of life. It wasn't just an accident that he dropped Tom Sawyer so abruptly from the story. That happened because the heroes Tom had to offer were no longer good enough. Huck decides "all that stuff was only just one of Tom Sawyer's lies." And he sets off alone to find something better. On the way he picks up black Jim, and Huck-America is never the same again.

Meanwhile in England at roughly the same time as Huck is breaking free from Tom Sawyer, Tom Brown is being shed too. Not this time by his creator, but by another born of the same line. Kipling published *Stalky and Co.* in 1899 and in it the old England was sloughed off as the old America was left behind by *Huckleberry Finn*.

And where are we now? Is there any parallel to be found in Robert Cormier's *The Chocolate War* (Pantheon) — which is *Tom Brown's Schooldays* so far subverted that Flashman/Archie is in charge with Dr. Arnold's/Brother Leon's (both clerics!) connivance and in which Tom/Jerry is carried off stage all but dead? And Tom Sawyer? Is it he who roams the streets of the urban twilight in S. E. Hinton's *Rumble Fish* (Delacorte)? The blurb in the British publisher's catalog, announcing the book's publication here soon, reads:

the story of Rusty-James, a boy with a reputation for toughness: he runs his own gang, and attends school only when he has nothing better to do.

So far, so Tom Sawyer. But:

Rusty-James's blind ambition to be just like his glamorous older brother, the Motorcycle Boy (so called for his habit of stealing motorbikes), leads to an explosive and tragic climax.

Put like that, is it fanciful to wonder whether *Rumble Fish* isn't the two Toms in one, a symbiosis in disillusion? There's Tom Sawyer, tough, with his gang, and going to school only now and then; and there's Tom Brown wanting to be like his glamorous brother-hero who embodies the approved myths of a closed elite. But this time, the end is — apparently — violent tragedy.

Does the centenary of Tom Sawyer and the Bicentennial of America the Brave mark a moment when we — old society and new — have come full circle, and, Ouroboros-like, find ourselves eating own own tails?

A gloomy thought. But there are signs that the gloom is lightening. And about that I'll have more to say in another letter. For the moment, it's a pleasure to go back to *Tom Sawyer* and be a sparky boy again.

From *The Horn Book* for April 1976

A SECOND LOOK:
"The Mouse and His Child"

By JOHN ROWE TOWNSEND

RUSSELL HOBAN'S *The Mouse and His Child* (Harper) was published in the United States in 1967 and in England two years later. In England it is widely seen as a modern classic, one of the three or four outstanding children's books of the thirty years since World War II. In the United States it had a lukewarm reception, and opinion about it has remained lukewarm ever since. In the 1969 revision of the *Critical History of Children's Literature* by Cornelia Meigs et al., it is not mentioned; in the 1972 edition of *Children and Books*, by May Hill Arbuthnot and Zena Sutherland, it gets a brief paragraph under the heading: "Other Stories about Toys." I have seldom met an American who was enthusiastic about it. For once, minds failed to meet in mid-Atlantic.

The book tells of the pilgrimage of a clockwork mouse father and son — through a cruel though comic world in which real and toy animals mix — toward the fulfillment of the mouse child's vision of a family life and a permanent home in a doll's house. Their enemy is villainous Manny Rat, ruler of a garbage-dump kingdom, who deals with uncooperative or worn-out toys by consigning their innards to the spare-parts can. The mouse and his child long to become self-winding. And in the end their quest is achieved; they find their home, and a reformed Manny Rat adjusts their mechanism so that it will run for a long time — though not forever.

I share the British view that this is a splendid book. It operates on several levels; it can be read as a simple adventure story, packed with incident, and with a fair amount of BONK! SPLASH! KERPLONK! The mouse and his child are captured by Manny Rat, made to take part in a bank robbery, involved in a war between rival armies of shrews, drawn into an experimental theater performance, and carried off through the air in the claws of a parrot — and this is only a part of the first half of the book. On this level it is accessible to any child who reads willingly, and to my knowledge it has been enjoyed by many ten-to-twelves who are not special readers.

There is a good deal of not-too-difficult verbal humor; and

there is much satire, some of which again is of a fairly obvious kind: the armies of shrews that almost wipe each other out, leaving the survivors to be eaten by weasels; the bluejay reporter who screams the news in headlines to the world. And the allegory of the toys' longing to be self-winding is well within children's comprehension.

But there is also a wry, dry wit for those who are ready for it. And beneath the book's bright, busy surface lie philosophical and psychological depths. There is, for instance, the matter of the dogmeat cans that keep cropping up. On their labels is a picture of a dog carrying a can that has a picture of a dog carrying a can that has a picture of a dog carrying a can . . . and so on until the dogs are too small to be seen. A phrase that echoes through the story is "beyond the last visible dog." For a long time the mouse and his child are stuck in the mud at the bottom of a pond, contemplating infinity in the form of one of these cans. This, I think, is the deepest point of the book, illuminated by Hoban's remark elsewhere that

> In all of us, I think, there remains some awareness, rudimentary and inchoate, far down, dim in green light through the ancient reeds and tasting of the primal salt, in which there is no "I", no person, no identity, but only the passage, moment by moment, of time through being undisturbed by birth or death. . . . I think we have to . . . dive for it and touch it before returning to the sunlight and the present.*

The mouse child sees that beyond the last visible dog is nothing; but the nothing is "nothing but us." And he finds a way to the surface.

It's an extremely rich and crowded book. Though there are no human characters except the tramp who sets the toys in motion near the beginning and who tells them to "be happy" at the end (and you may well wonder who *he* is), it is, in fact, a deeply human story. The mouse and his child clearly are loving *people*, totally interdependent. The author's sense of the pathos of a toy's life — the sadness of rusted metal and rotting plush, the decline from freshness and efficiency toward the rubbish dump — is, of course, a sense of the pathos of human life. But there's hope as well as pain in this pilgrimage; and, significantly, it's the child who hopes, the child who perseveres when

*Russell Hoban, "Thoughts on Being and Writing," in *The Thorny Paradise: Writers on Writing for Children*, edited by Edward Blishen (London, Kestrel Books, 1975).

the father would give up. This is a book that can be returned to many times at many ages, and there will always be something new to be found in it.

From *The Horn Book* for October 1975

HIGH FANTASY:
A WIZARD OF EARTHSEA*
By ELEANOR CAMERON

IT IS NEVER IMPORTANT TO PIGEONHOLE works of fiction nor to insist that a certain book should belong, in a child's estimation, in this category or that (which is why I regret that in many libraries fantasy and fairy tales are separated from the realistic fiction so that a child's initial predilection often remains entrenched for years, possibly for life). What matters is what the child loves and what each book does for him. Though what it does we may never learn, for the child usually cannot tell us what lies down deep — if he himself knows.

I am thinking here, specifically, of the words "high fantasy," the subject for the 1969 New England Round Table of Children's Librarians.† It is not in the least surprising that Ursula Le Guin should have written, in *A Wizard of Earthsea*, a work which is a noble example of the term. Of it she has said, "I think 'High Fantasy' a beautiful phrase. It summarizes, for me, what I value most in an imaginative work: the fact that the author takes absolutely seriously the world and the people which he has created, as seriously as Homer took the Trojan War, and Odysseus; that he plays his game with all his skill, and all his art, and all his heart. When he does that, the fantasy game becomes one of the High Games men play. Otherwise, you might as well play Monopoly."

If, as I believe, the tests of high fantasy (and certainly of any outstanding piece of fiction) lie in strength and cleanness of structure, the overwhelming sense of reality, the pervading sense of place, the communication of the visual perceptiveness of the writer, exactness of detail, the originality and discipline with which materials are handled, excellence of style, richness of character portrayal and depth of vision, then I can say with assurance that *A Wizard of Earthsea* is indeed high fantasy.

Ursula Le Guin has been writing since she was nine and almost all of what she wrote before publication was fantasy in the style

A Wizard of Earthsea (Parnassus) by Ursula K. Le Guin received the 1969 Boston Globe—Horn Book Award.
†Given at the New England Round Table of Children's Librarians, October, 1969.

of Isak Dinesen's tales or Austin Tappan Wright's *Islandia* (tales happening in the world we know rather than in the realm of fairy tale): some, traditional and folkloristic in the vein of Dunsany; some, as science fiction. It was not until she was thirty and becoming concerned that she might grow introverted, self-indulgent and, finally, stale should she continue unpublished, that she found a helpful editor and made a first sale to *Fantastic Stories* when they took a short piece of conventional pulp fantasy. Her reading since childhood had found its chief pleasure in fantasy and science fiction, so that upon acceptance of that story she continued to write both, though mainly a certain kind of science fiction for adults.

On the whole I do not care for the genre as I have known it; but I have read her works — *Rocannon's World, Planet of Exile, City of Illusions*, and *The Left Hand of Darkness* — with interest and pleasure, though not the deep pleasure, I shall have to admit, with which I read *A Wizard of Earthsea*. Particularly in *The Left Hand of Darkness*, Mrs. Le Guin has come into her own as a writer and as a stylist, who is exploring, not the development of technology as the triumphant flowering of civilization, but a future in which man will be struggling even more desperately than now to discover his way out of the tyrannies which technology's misuses have imposed upon him. She is dealing, therefore, with the possibilities inherent in ideas rather than in inventions. And concerning her use of ideas, formed in the minds of many-faceted protagonists rather than in puppets pasted against plot, we see clearly the emphasis in current science fiction. It is upon the implications for the future as divined by the writer when he extrapolates through sociology and anthropology rather than through technology alone.

And it is precisely this knowledge of anthropology that is everywhere apparent in *A Wizard of Earthsea*, making itself felt not as a science but aesthetically as a mood of the writer. Mrs. Le Guin confesses to having only an interested layman's knowledge of the subject, plus an attitude given her by her anthropologist father, A. L. Kroeber,* and strengthened by her historian husband. She is aware that this attitude has colored her work, but she cannot define it; she feels that certain elements of it must

*Her mother, Theodora Kroeber, wrote *Ishi, Last of His Tribe* (Parnassus) for children and *Ishi in Two Worlds: A Biography of the Last Wild Indian in North America* for adults.

be "a curiosity about people different from one's own kind; interest in artifacts; interest in languages; delight in the idiosyncracies of various cultures; a sense that time is long yet that human history is very short — and therefore a sense of kinship across seas and centuries; a love of strangeness; a love of exactness." It is these very loves and interests which enrich the quality, the texture, and the spirit of *A Wizard of Earthsea*.

A Wizard of Earthsea is, above all, a book of magic and of learning; its theme is the misuse of the power magic bestows, and its protagonists are the great magi and the lesser magicians and their pupils. In fact one is moved to believe, as one turns the pages of the book, that surely this is one of the most complete pictures of a world immersed in magic ever written for youth, with its detailing of the daily lives of its great magicians and their prentices as well as of its little ordinary people, who have no desire to understand magic but who live in daily awareness of it. But in *A Wizard of Earthsea*, magic, though it is a pervading presence, is never the main interest, never an end in itself. Always the implications go beyond the practices of magic to what, humanly and spiritually, lies behind each discipline the prentice must undergo. The great magi are not simply great magicians. They are wise men: wise in the ways of their Art, but beyond this kind of wisdom, wise in the ways of mankind and wise as to how mankind must learn from life. As they have penetrated ever more deeply into their craft, they have come to comprehend the relationship of each one of our acts to every other, and the urgent necessity we are all under to remember this relationship.

Ged, in a single, tragic moment early in his apprenticeship, fails to remember. Out of his treacherous pride, his touchiness, his hunger for recognition, for domination, he calls upon the long-dead in shameless answer to a challenge cynically given. In that instant, when the pale figure with the terrified face appears out of the past at Ged's call, the shadow-beast — "a clot of black shadow, quick and hideous," that "leaped straight out at Ged's face" — breaks from unlife and is released upon the world. Its power is this: that if it can overtake and conquer Ged, it can core him out, possess him, and use his knowledge to its own mindless ends. To Ged, the Archmage Gensher says, " 'The power you had to call it gives it power over you: you are connected. It is the shadow of your arrogance, the shadow of your ignorance, the shadow you cast. Has a shadow a name?' "

It is a question Ged is long in answering. He flees from the shadow-beast, for if it conquers him, the innocent will suffer. He runs until at last the word is spoken that makes him turn and face his shadow, and grapple with it, and name it.

Two things Ged learns of Ogion, his first teacher, that he recalls later in the extremity of despair. The first: that naming sets limits to power, and that he who knows a man's true name (i. e., his true being) holds that man's life in his keeping. The second: that danger must surround power as shadow does light, and that sorcery is not a game played for pleasure or for praise. Ogion had said, " 'Think of this: that every word, every act of our Art is said and is done either for good, or for evil. Before you speak or do, you must know the price that is to pay.' " And at the School in Roke, the Master Hand spoke to Ged in the same vein, words which transcend the context of Ged's struggle and tower behind our own struggles with those forces we ourselves have released but have not yet the power, the knowledge, or the insight to control, and may not learn to control until it is too late:

To change this rock into a jewel, you must change its true name. And to do that, my son, even to so small a scrap of the world, is to change the world. It can be done. Indeed it can be done. It is the art of the Master Changer, and you will learn it, when you are ready to learn it. But you must not change one thing, one pebble, one grain of sand, until you know what good and evil will follow on that act. The world is in balance, in Equilibrium. A wizard's power of Changing and of Summoning can shake the balance of the world. It is dangerous, that power. It is most perilous. It must follow knowledge, and serve need. To light a candle is to cast a shadow. . . .

With what ominous meaning do these words ring upon our ears today! In the end Ged realizes that his task has never been to undo what he had done, but *to finish what he had begun.* The deep subject of the book is the necessity for the individual's return to self, the necessity for seeing one's self, one's acts, and the motives for those acts in a clear, searching light. And this is not done, in Ged's case, through the *escape* power of magic, but through the use of an intense discipline gained through the practice of magic. Ged knew, having recognized at last what was fundamental to himself, that as his power grew and his knowledge widened, the way he could go narrowed, until in the end he could choose nothing, but could do only what he must do. And he realized as well that:

[he] had neither lost nor won but, naming the shadow of his death with his own name, had made himself whole: a man: who, knowing his whole true self, cannot be used or possessed by any power other than himself, and whose life is therefore lived for life's sake and never in the service of ruin, or pain, or hatred, or the dark. In the *Creation of Ea*, which is the oldest song, it is said, "Only in silence the word, only in dark the light, only in dying life: bright the hawk's flight on the empty sky."

As the reader has perceived, what Ged was dealing with throughout his long journey toward a final understanding of himself and his struggles were names and shadows. They haunt the book, they are woven through all its patterns, they lie at the heart of every scene. Recalling Ursula Le Guin's knowledge of anthropology, it is not surprising that she has used these two ancient and potent subjects to underlie and illumine her meanings. In Frazer's *The Golden Bough* we learn how far back in time the preoccupation with names and shadows goes, how widespread is and has been the belief in their powers among the primitive tribes of Africa, among North and South American Indians, and the various island peoples of the world.

Jung, in discussing archetypes and the collective unconscious, calls the inferior side of ourselves, which is to be found in the personal unconscious, the *shadow*. And the shadow represents, for him, all that we do not allow ourselves to do, all that we do not want to be. If we commit some regrettable act in a rage, we say, "I was not myself." That inferior, primitive person we encounter in dreams, that person whose qualities we fear and dislike, is the shadow. It possesses passions we are ashamed of; it cannot be educated; it is instinctive man: greedy, cruel, selfish, amoral. It is useless to repress it. Man must recognize it and either wrestle with it or try to change those situations which provoke it. So Ged's shadow-beast, which he himself had released, must be sought out, recognized, and wrestled with. Concerning Ged's final struggle, we are reminded of Jung's individuation process, neither a neurotic nor a pathological phenomenon, but a struggle which all who are becoming self-aware will gradually engage in. It is an effort to become whole, to recognize and to give wise expression to both sides of one's being. "The shadow," Jung* says, "is a moral problem that challenges the whole ego personality. . . ."
It is possible to give here only scattered examples of Ged's in-

*Carl Jung, *The Collected Works*, translated by R. F. C. Hull, Bollingen Series XX, Vol. 9, II, "Aion," copyright © 1959 by Princeton University Press, p. 8.

volvements with all those names and shadows lying within the richness of *A Wizard of Earthsea*. " 'What is its use, Master?' " he asks Ogion, the Wizard of Gont, concerning the flower fourfoil. " 'None I know of,' " replies Ogion. " 'When you know the fourfoil in all its seasons root and leaf and flower, by sight and scent and seed, then you may learn its true name, knowing its being: which is more than its use.' " When Ged leaves Gont, his home island, for Roke, the island of the School of Wizards, he goes in the craft *Shadow*. When he is challenged to that fatal act which releases the shadow-beast, he cries, " 'By my name, I will do it!' " And he means, terribly, his true name, which none can know save the magus who gave it him, or that person to whom Ged chooses to tell it, thus putting his life, his very being, into the hands of his confidant with the utmost trust and love and devotion. And when Ged comes near the end of his final journey, he cries aloud in anguish that he is bound to the foul cruel thing, the shadow-beast, and will be forever, " 'unless I can learn the word that masters it: its name.' "

As for the little names of *A Wizard of Earthsea*, the names of plants and birds and fish and places and people, it would seem that Ursula Le Guin must herself be a wizard at naming. In Tolkien's books, when it comes to birds and animals and plants, we do not find strange names. In Walter de la Mare's *The Three Royal Monkeys*, we find, on the contrary, all names to be strange. As I have said in *The Green and Burning Tree*,† "Tolkien speaks of cream and honey and clover and cocks-comb and pines and bracken. But de la Mare puts before us a flora of evening-blooming Immamoosa, of Gelica, Exxwixxia, Samarak, Manga, Nano and Ukka trees. Little Nod stores Ukka nuts against the Witzaweelwūlla, the White Winter, and makes Sudd loaves, Manaka cake, Manga cheese, and Subbub, a kind of drink." Ursula Le Guin does something different again. She combines known names with strange ones. Perriot leaves are used with cobwebs to stanch the flow of blood from wounds. On Low Torning in the Ninety Isles where lies Pendor, the "dragon-spoiled isle," housewives row across from isle to isle to have a cup of rushwash tea with a neighbor, and nets are strung across the straits to catch small silver fish called turbies, the oil of which is the wealth of the Ninety Isles. Witch women make a smoke of corly-root to heal

†Eleanor Cameron, *The Green and Burning Tree: On the Writing and Enjoyment of Children's Books* (Boston, Atlantic-Little, Brown and Company, 1969), p. 198.

the sick while they sing the Nagian Chant. On Roke there is a plant called sparkweed, which grows " 'where the wind dropped the ashes of burning Ilien, when Erreth-Akbe defended the Inward Isle from the Firelord.' " When the wind blows the withered flowerheads, the loosened seeds fly up "like sparks of fire in the sun." The master of *Shadow* was an Andradean from an island above Gont, and he wore "a red cloak trimmed with pellawi-fur such as Andradean merchants wear." As well as the small fish called turbies, there are pannies. And there are pendick-trees, and a certain little lizard called a harrekki, and Ged's treasured pet is an otak, a rare strange beast found on only four of the southernmost isles of the Archipelago. It is small, sleek, with a broad face, fur dark or brindled; it has great bright eyes, cruel teeth, a sharp temper, no voice, and a little brown tongue like a dried leaf.

As for the names of people, why the name of Serret, the Lady of Terranon, or of little Yarrow, whose true name was Kest, which means minnow, should seem airy and feminine and utterly right to me, I do not know. There is a boatman named Pechvarry. The three great wizards who teach Ged are Ogion, Nemmerle, and Gensher. Yarrow's brother is Vetch, whose true name is Estarriol. The dragon whom Ged defeats with a single stroke of knowledge is called Yevaud.* *Yevaud!* Do you feel what I feel in those syllables? The sound of these names falls upon my ear with ease and a sense of complete appropriateness, given the nature and atmosphere of Earthsea, but I cannot explain my satisfaction as, ideally perhaps, I should not be able to. However, the rightness of the name Skiorh I think I can explain: to me it calls up "scour," "skewer," and "core," and the man who had once owned it was hollowed out by the shadow-beast and possessed in order that it could lead Ged to a certain desolate place and turn upon him. Whether Mrs. Le Guin heard those words as overtones for Skiorh, I do not know.

I have not spoken of the names of the islands of Earthsea, picked out on the maps drawn for *A Wizard of Earthsea* (as were the small decorative pictures, which evoke to perfection in treatment and style the subject, the place, and the timelessness of the book). But any child, youth, or adult delighting in maps will want every now and then to orient himself — on Havnor, perhaps, to find Havnor Great Port or Eskel. He may want to swing quickly

*He appears in Mrs. Le Guin's short story "The Rule of Names," where, for the first time, the Archipelago is introduced and we discover a foreshadowing of *A Wizard of Earthsea*.

across to the Kargad Lands composed of Karego-At, Atuan, Hur-at-Hur, and Atnini, names which call up tones of ancient Assyria, or is it Tibet? Or he may want to speed across Gont, lying in the Gontish Sea and surrounded by Andrad, Perregal, Spevy, Torheven, Barnisk, and Oranéa. When Ged asks Vetch where he hails from, Vetch speaks warmly of his home islands with the funny names, Korp, Kopp, and Holp, Venway and Vemish, Iffish, Koppish, and Sneg.

To me, it is as if Ursula Le Guin herself has lived on the Archipelago, minutely observing and noting down the habits and idiosyncracies of the culture from island to island, variations in dress and food and ways of living, in climate, languages, attitudes of the inhabitants and atmospheres of cities and towns. Nothing has escaped the notice of her imagination's seeking eye, but always she has chosen her details with the discrimination of an artist for whom economy of style is the ideal. We know that the essence of any novel is its human situation, but essence without a superbly convincing context is nothing. It is only the beginning, only an idea. Henry James* spoke of the necessity for precision, exactness. "The supreme virtue of a novel," he said, "the merit on which all its other merits . . . helplessly and submissively depend," is its truth of detail, its air of reality, its "solidity of specification . . . . If [that] be not there, all other merits are as nothing, and if these be there, they owe their effect to the success with which the author has produced the illusion of life."

Like all the great fantasies, A Wizard of Earthsea leaves an echoing in our minds, that sense of having experienced something we can never quite put into words — a divine discontent, more to be desired, C. S. Lewis believed, than any possible satisfaction. The great fantasies leave with child readers a scarcely realized sense of something beyond their reach, which gives another dimension to the world of reality. They help children to orient themselves, help them to distinguish good from evil, and to learn how the forces of good and evil work. Great fantasies prepare them for the fact that just as good is a power, so is evil, and enables them, through identification with heroes, as Kornei Chukovsky has said, to regard themeselves as fearless participants in imaginary struggles for justice and goodness and freedom. Very often danger and horror are made harshly vivid, but because

*Henry James, The Art of the Novel (New York, Charles Scribner's Sons, 1934).

these dangers and horrors occur in timelessness and in the world of magic, children learn to face without shock what otherwise might be unendurable: the force of that dark message which both dreams and fantasy so often bring. Finally, it is not only facts about the world that children need to know, Joanna Field says in *A Life of One's Own*, but facts about themselves, and only through the imaginative symbols of fantasy and fairy tales and legends can they at first express themselves and understand something of their own deeper natures.

Gore Vidal* has something to say about fiction which reminds me of *A Wizard of Earthsea*. "[N]ovel writing goes, at its best, beyond cleverness to that point where one's whole mind and experience and vision *are* the novel and the effort to translate this wholeness into prose *is* the life: a circle of creation." This kind of wholeness is, I believe, what Mrs. Le Guin has accomplished: She has created a world, a country of the mind, its people and ways and languages and character, translating this wholeness into prose in such a way that, through an experience private to her country of the mind because of its intimacy with magic, she takes us beyond magic to an understanding of truths which illuminate our difficulties in the world of reality. For *A Wizard of Earthsea* is a work which, though it is fantasy, continually returns us to the world about us, its forces and powers; returns us to ourselves, to our own struggles and aspirations, to the very core of human responsibility.

*Gore Vidal, *Rocking the Boat* (Boston, Little, Brown and Company, 1962), p. 262.

From *The Horn Book* for April 1971

THE NARRATIVE ART OF
PENELOPE LIVELY

By David Rees

"I T IS THE PERCEPTION, often startling, that places have a past, that they are now but also then, and that if peopled now, they were peopled then." This quotation, from a *Horn Book* article entitled "Children and Memory"* — based on a lecture which Penelope Lively gave at the Exeter, England, conference on Children's Literature in Education, 1972 — well-illustrates the major preoccupation of her novels; it is a theme that occurs and recurs, almost obsessively, in all her books from *Astercote* to *The House in Norham Gardens* (both Dutton). It is a perception, she states in the same lecture, that is "a step out of the child's self-preoccupation"; it is "a step towards maturity." And all her novels have, as their main characters, children who are making that step toward maturity.

Penelope Lively would have to write only slightly differently to find herself labeled by those people who need to pigeonhole books into categories as an historical novelist for children and to find herself compared with Rosemary Sutcliff, Henry Treece, or other writers of that genre. After all, her interests seem to be historical — the Black Death, Morgan le Fay, seventeenth-century ghosts, ancient ritual dances of the Exmoor area. None of her books, of course, is set in the period of any of these; they are set firmly in the mid-twentieth century; and the reader is constantly made aware of this fact by references to supermarkets, plans for building motorways, rows of council houses. "Places . . . are now but also then." In her concern for what is happening now and how the past helps to shape the present, Penelope Lively differs from the historical novelist who is more interested, perhaps exclusively interested, in what happened "then." She is nearer to the writer of fantasy, the writer who uses parallel stories of past and present — such as Lucy Boston in *The Children of Green Knowe* (Harcourt) or, less obviously perhaps, John Christopher, who uses a real past and a fantasy future to meditate on the problems of the present.

But these comparisons are inexact; though there is a similar

*August 1973.

342

feeling, as in Lucy Boston, of the influence of place and history in shaping the lives of those who people her books, there is not the sense of displacement, of disorientation, that so interests Lucy Boston — Ping, the Chinese boy, and Guy, the gorilla, set in utterly alien environments. Much luckier, much more capable of enrichment, are the children in Penelope Lively's novels. Even if those children come originally from other places and their middle-class backgrounds mean some loss of roots, their own lives are firmly involved in the community: the large sprawling Midlands villages with their sense of the past — ancient field-patterns and parish registers — and with their thriving present — new housing estates and traffic problems. And unlike John Christopher, Penelope Lively is not asking what kind of society we wish to live in, how we wish to develop; society to her evolves from a slow, natural growth and is not capable of violent change, nor does it need such change. The past is never made to seem worse than the present, nor better — Chipping Ledbury must cope with the problems caused by motorway planners that threaten to destroy it, and Astercote had to cope with the Black Death. The Harrison family has all the advantages of the comforts of modern living combined with a rewarding sense of the past; but not so for Betsy Tranter, who has all the disadvantages of such a combination.

Comparisons with other authors lead nowhere when writing about Penelope Lively. There may be a hint of Virginia Woolf, even of Philippa Pearce, in *The House in Norham Gardens*, only because of a slight similarity in language; there may be a hint of Penelope Farmer in *The Wild Hunt of the Ghost Hounds* (Dutton), but only because of a likeness in landscape. What Penelope Lively has achieved in her six novels is something unique, a kind of book that is neither history nor fantasy but has something of both, and that cannot be labeled conveniently — a book where the power of place is a stronger force than most of the characters, where "history is now."

How has she managed to achieve such an individual niche in the very cluttered world of children's books, where works of fantasy and history come ten a penny? It is obvious from her first novel *Astercote* that, despite its faults, here is a writer who is capable of putting together an exciting narrative, one in which the pace is exactly right and which, if nothing else, will keep the reader turning the pages to see what happens. This is no achievement to be scorned; unfolding a story bit by bit is to most writers a much more difficult task than composing a poetic piece about a sunset. *Astercote* seems immediately different from most other books. Goacher, one feels, is a character who could have been conceived by no other writer; and who else would posit a suggestion — one that the reader is made to take seriously — that the theft of Astercote's chalice could actually lead to a possibility of an outbreak of bubonic plague? There are faults in the writing: Some of the characterization, particularly that of the district nurse, is thin and unconvincing; and there seems to be a curious infirmity of purpose at one important point in the novel, as if the author had not really made up her mind which way the book was going to develop — will the plague *really* return? The reader is a little disappointed that it does not: He is left with a feeling that the author has avoided that possibility because it was, at that point, beyond her power to deal with.

Most of these awkwardnesses are ironed out in the next two books, *The Whispering Knights* and *The Wild Hunt of the Ghost Hounds*. Both deal with similar themes and are structurally similar to *Astercote*. The children, however, are much more sharply individualized in *The Whispering Knights* than in *Astercote*; and the minor characters in *The Wild Hunt of the Ghost Hounds* are treated ironically — a very successful excursion into satirical social observation and a way of looking at character that Penelope Lively does not use elsewhere. Irony would have improved *Astercote*.

In *The Whispering Knights* Morgan le Fay affects the lives of Susie, Martha, and William; and in *The Wild Hunt* the revival of the horn dance affects Lucy and Kester more than the stolen chalice affects Mair and Peter in *Astercote*. The difference between these two books and *Astercote* is that the evil caused by a silly meddling with the past is a real evil, not an imaginary one. As a result, there is no slackening of the narrative tension in the last stages of *The Wild Hunt* or *The Whispering Knights;* on the contrary, the concluding chapters contain the most exciting writing of the books — where the struggle between good and evil reaches its climax. In *The Whispering Knights*, there are hints in the character of Martha that Penelope Lively is beginning to be interested in children who are not wholly uncomplicated and nice. And in *The Wild Hunt* there is a very odd and unusual, but sympathetic character, Kester: a child who deliberately invites persecution; in Kester there is something more complex than what she has achieved before — a convincing mixture of contradictions.

If the first three novels are similar in theme and structure, the last three are not only very different, but different from each other in these respects, though the preoccupations with "places . . . are now but also then" and with how it was for the people "then" remain. *The Driftway* (Dutton), Penelope Lively says in "Children and Memory," "was an attempt to write about the jolt given to a child's self-absorption by an imaginative involvement with other people's lives. . . . I wanted to use landscape as a channel for historical memory — a road, in fact, a perfectly ordinary road, B4525 from Banbury to Northampton, but a road that is very ancient and seemed to lend itself perfectly to a double symbolism." The road actually becomes the central character of the book rather than the boy, Paul, who is traveling on it, and it is used to hang somewhat loosely together various self-contained stories set in the past: the adventures, for example, of an eighteenth-century highwayman and a soldier escaping from a battle in the Civil War. It is probably the least successful of Penelope Lively's books, the only one which readers consistently say is dull. There is no loss in the quality of her writing ability; indeed there are passages, notably of landscape description, that are finer than anything she had previously done. But the book is shapeless. It seems to be the length it is because that is the standard length required by publishers. It could have been longer (a few more historical episodes inserted would not seem out of place), or shorter (a few of these episodes less and the reader would not notice anything missing). Old Bill, the cart-driver, is a totally unconvincing rustic, made of sentimental clichés about rural characters. The predicament of the central figure, Paul — who is running away from home because he cannot face up to the implications of his father's second marriage — remains curiously unfelt. The reader is never allowed to come fully to terms with the situation: Paul's father and stepmother remain outside the narrative and are only present in Paul's thoughts. So the reader is asked to share a vague emotive identification with Paul without enough information to go on.

Why does *The Driftway* fail so badly? Largely because the author has abandoned the technique she has mastered so ably — telling in a tight, exciting manner a highly readable narrative that has a beginning, a middle, and an end — and has substituted an experimental, impressionistic framework she does not know how to handle. In *The Ghost of Thomas Kempe* (Dutton), which deservedly won the Carnegie Medal in 1974, and in *The House in Norham Gardens*, she returns, fortunately, to the business of telling a story — in both books with triumphant success. *Thomas Kempe* is about a poltergeist, an unsuccessful ghost who begs to be allowed to return to his own time and place. *The Wild Hunt of the Ghost Hounds* had shown how well Penelope Lively could write, if only fleetingly, in a comic vein; *Thomas Kempe* is a comedy from beginning to end and has a lightness of touch that never fails. Not only is the poor poltergeist a figure of fun, but Aunt Fanny's journal is a magnificent pastiche of a Victorian diary-writer. (One grumble: Would such a masterpiece have ever been thrown out onto a bonfire?) And James, the central character — a sound, solid, boy-like boy — is just a bit larger than life, not exaggerated enough to be a caricature, but a little like Tom Sawyer. He fits perfectly into the world of this novel. Parents play a larger part in this book than in the previous three; quite correctly, for the absence of parents in many children's books is often a self-indulgence on the writer's part. Who, if not parents, play the largest role in a child's life? So here are Mr. and Mrs. Harrison, amusing and uncomprehending, so busily engaged in the tasks of earning a living or doing the housework that they cannot possibly begin to understand the fantastic or the supernatural, cannot even allow that they may exist. Poor James has to battle with Thomas Kempe alone.

The Ghost of Thomas Kempe is perhaps the first of Penelope Lively's novels in which the reader feels that the author is completely sure of her own abilities, and the prose has a positiveness that derives from the author's pleasure in her awareness of these abilities. Certainly it was her finest book so far, and armed with this new-found authority, she went on to deal with her most profound exploration, in *The House in Norham Gardens*, of the same themes that have always preoccupied her. She has written, as a result, one of the best of all modern children's books, one that stands up with *Tom's Midnight Garden*

(Lippincott) and *The Owl Service* (Walck), or with any other yardstick of quality. The prose has a poetic, luminous quality that is a sheer delight; like *The Children of the House* (Lippincott), it is a prose poem from beginning to end.

And the snow fell. Indiscriminately, blotting out grass and pavements and road alike so that by evening the houses stood in a strange, undefined landscape neither town nor country. Cars were silenced and slowed, creeping past with diffidence, as though perhaps they had no business here. With darkness came a deep silence. Clare, lying in bed, awake in dark reaches of the night, strained for sounds and heard nothing. She could have been deaf, enclosed within her own mind and body. She had to get up and open the window to reassure herself. Somewhere, a car banged and people shouted to one another. She went back to bed again.

This is a far cry from the prose of *Astercote*, which was competent but flat, unmemorable.

Adults become even more important in *Norham Gardens* than in *Thomas Kempe*. Aunt Anne and Aunt Susan are observed by both Clare and the author: difficult, eccentric, very old, wrapped in a way of life that has long since ceased to exist, only vaguely aware of the hardships they cause Clare, yet credible and sympathetic. Penelope Lively writes in "Children and Memory": "I think that for children an important moment of perception is when they see other people as not necessarily frozen at a moment in time — now — but as extended backwards. Parents as once children, grandparents as once young men and women. Themselves as potentially someone different."* The emphasis in *Norham Gardens* lies not so much on "places . . . are now but also then" but on people who are now but also then. Not that place is neglected. The decaying Victorian suburbs of Oxford — with their grandiose houses that are symbols of an age of greater certainties than ours, crumbling or split up into flats, their gardens filled with weeds and students' bicycles — are created with great lovingness and care. But Aunt Anne and Aunt Susan are *people* from history and also of now, and this theme beguiles both the reader and Clare into an awareness that the hardships of her existence are mitigated by imaginative rewards denied to most modern children. "We are none of us 'the young,' or 'the middle-aged,' or 'the old.' We are all of these things. To allow children to think otherwise is to en-

*Delivered in the lecture but not included in the *Horn Book* article.

courage a disability — a disability both of awareness and of communication."

The house is now and then; so are the aunts; and so, as a result, the element of fantasy in this novel is less strong than in any other of Penelope Lively's books, except perhaps for *Astercote*. Indeed it might have been dispensed with altogether; not that one wishes it were not there — for the fusion of the theme with the quest of the brown men of New Guinea for their lost shield is highly successful. In fact, the fantasy element shows another perspective of history and memory and their relationship to the present — not only are people and places of now and then, but also objects, even when they are torn out of their environment and taken into other, incongruous situations where they apparently have no meaning.

Children "can't yet place themselves in a wider framework of time and space than *today* and *here*. But they have to, if they are not to grow up enclosed in their own personalities. Perhaps books can help, just a little." With such a moral preoccupation about what she hopes are the functions and uses of her novels, it can be expected that Penelope Lively will continue to write about the themes she has already chosen and made her own. It is interesting to speculate about how these can be treated. There is little danger of her repeating herself; the area is so enormous, so important. Perhaps the element of fantasy will disappear altogether, and history and memory of people, places, and things will be dealt with in a totally realistic manner. Already Penelope Lively's achievement is considerable, and her two most recent novels place her among the most interesting and important writers of children's books. The area she has made peculiarly her own is open to much more exploration; one hopes that there will be at least half a dozen more books from her of equally fine quality.

From *The Horn Book* for April 1971

58831